THE WALLFLOWER

YAMATONADESHIKO SHICHIHENGE

♥ 8 ♥

Tomoko Hayakawa

TRANSLATED AND ADAPTED BY
David Ury

LETTERED BY
Dana Hayward

DEL REY

BALLANTINE BOOKS • NEW YORK

A Del Rey Trade Paperback Original

Published in the United States by Del Rey Books, an imprint of The Random House Publishing Group, a division of Random House Inc., New York.

DEL REY is a registered trademark and the Del Rey colophon is a trademark of Random House, Inc.

Publication rights arranged through Kodansha, Ltd.

First published in Japan in 2003 by Kodansha Ltd., Tokyo, as *Yamatonadeshiko Shichihenge*.

ISBN 0-345-48526-2

Printed in the United States of America

www.delreymanga.com

9 8 7 6 5 4 3

Translator and adaptor—David Ury

Lettering—Dana Hayward

Cover Design—David Stevenson

Contents

Honorifics

Throughout the Del Rey Manga books, you will find Japanese honorifics left intact in the translations. For those not familiar with how the Japanese use honorifics, and more important, how they differ from American honorifics, we present this brief overview.

Politeness has always been a critical facet of Japanese culture. Ever since the feudal era, when Japan was a highly stratified society, use of honorifics—which can be defined as polite speech that indicates relationship or status—has played an essential role in the Japanese language. When addressing someone in Japanese, an honorific usually takes the form of a suffix attached to one's name (example: "Asuna-san"), or as a title at the end of one's name or in place of the name itself (example: "Negi-sensei," or simply "Sensei!").

Honorifics can be expressions of respect or endearment. In the context of manga and anime, honorifics give insight into the nature of the relationship between characters. Many English translations leave out these important honorifics, and therefore distort the "feel" of the original Japanese. Because Japanese honorifics contain nuances that English honorifics lack, it is our policy at Del Rey not to translate them. Here, instead, is a guide to some of the honorifics you may encounter in Del Rey Manga.

-san: This is the most common honorific, and is equivalent to Mr., Miss, Ms., Mrs. It is the all-purpose honorific and can be used in any situation where politeness is required.

-sama: This is one level higher than "-san" and is used to confer great respect.

-dono: This comes from the word "tono," which means "lord." It is even a higher level than "-sama" and confers utmost respect.

-kun: This suffix is used at the end of boys' names to express familiarity or endearment. It is also sometimes used by men amongst friends, or when addressing someone younger or of a lower station.

-chan: This is used to express endearment, mostly toward girls. It is also used for little boys, pets, and even among lovers. It gives a sense of childish cuteness.

Bozu: This is an informal way to refer to a boy, similar to the English term "kid" or "squirt."

Sempai/senpai: This title suggests that the addressee is one's "senior" in a group or organization. It is most often used in a school setting, where underclassmen refer to their upperclassmen as "sempai." It can also be used in the workplace, such as when a newer employee addresses an employee who has seniority in the company.

Kohai: This is the opposite of "sempai," and is used toward underclassmen in school or newcomers in the workplace. It connotes that the addressee is of lower station.

Sensei: Literally meaning "one who has come before," this title is used for teachers, doctors, or masters of any profession or art.

[blank]: This is usually forgotten in these lists, but perhaps the most significant difference between Japanese and English. The lack of honorific means that the speaker has permission to address the person in a very intimate way. Usually, only family, spouses, or very close friends have this kind of permission. Known as *yobisute,* it can be gratifying when someone who has earned the intimacy starts to call one by one's name without an honorific. But when that intimacy hasn't been earned, it can be very insulting.

A Note from the Author

♥ I'm picking up from where I left off in Book 7. This is another section of my living room. I hope you can make it out okay. I have a lot more skulls in my bedroom. I've got tons of *Nightmare Before Christmas* stuff too, but they won't let me show pictures of it. I'm also using lots of the stuff that readers have sent in. ♥

—Tomoko Hayakawa

THE wallflower

YAMATONADESHIKO SHICHIHENGE

ヤマトナデシコ七変化♡

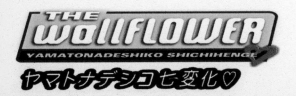

CONTENTS

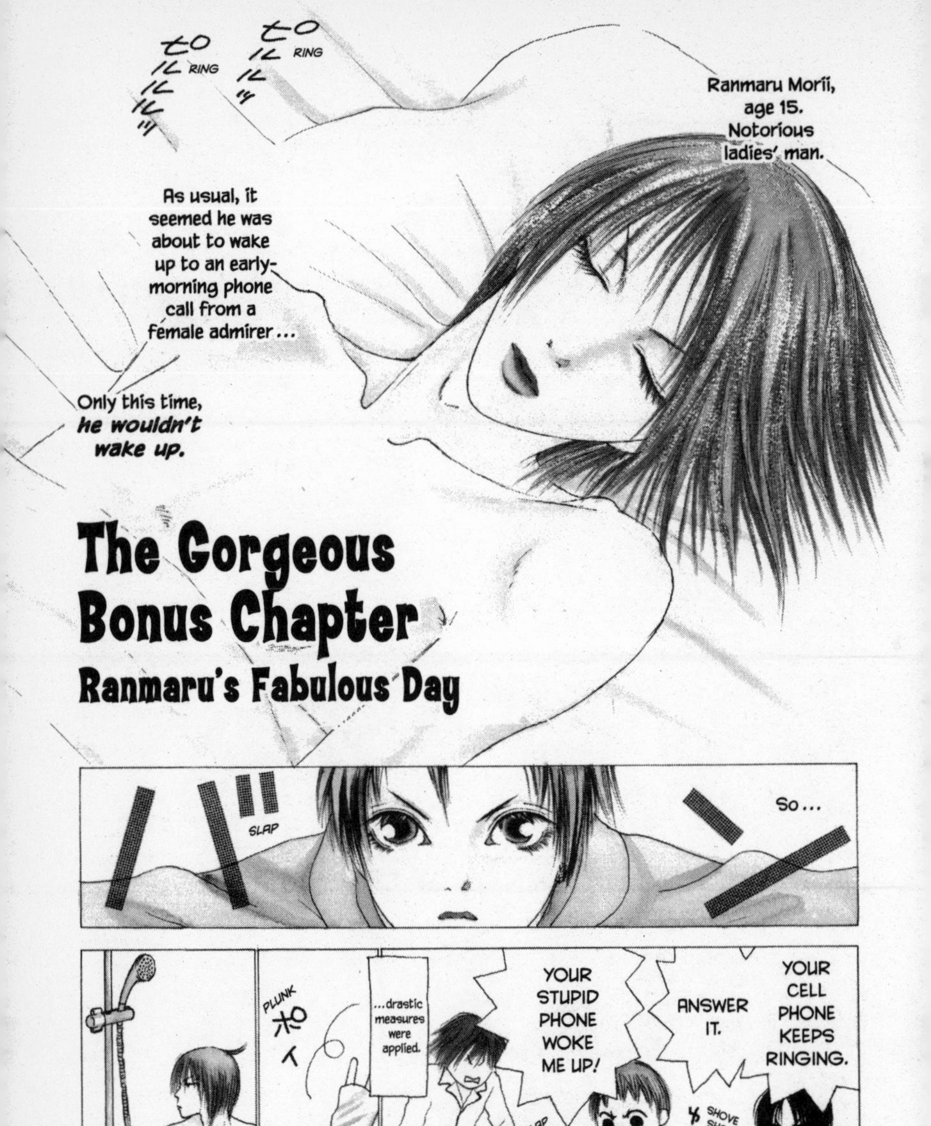
Ranmaru Morii, age 15. Notorious ladies' man.
RING
RING
As usual, it seemed he was about to wake up to an early-morning phone call from a female admirer...
Only this time, *he wouldn't wake up.*
The Gorgeous Bonus Chapter
Ranmaru's Fabulous Day
So...
SLAP
YOUR CELL PHONE KEEPS RINGING.
ANSWER IT.
YOUR STUPID PHONE WOKE ME UP!
SHOVE SHOVE
SLAP
TICKLE TICKLE
SLAP
SLAP
SLAP
...drastic measures were applied.
PLUNK

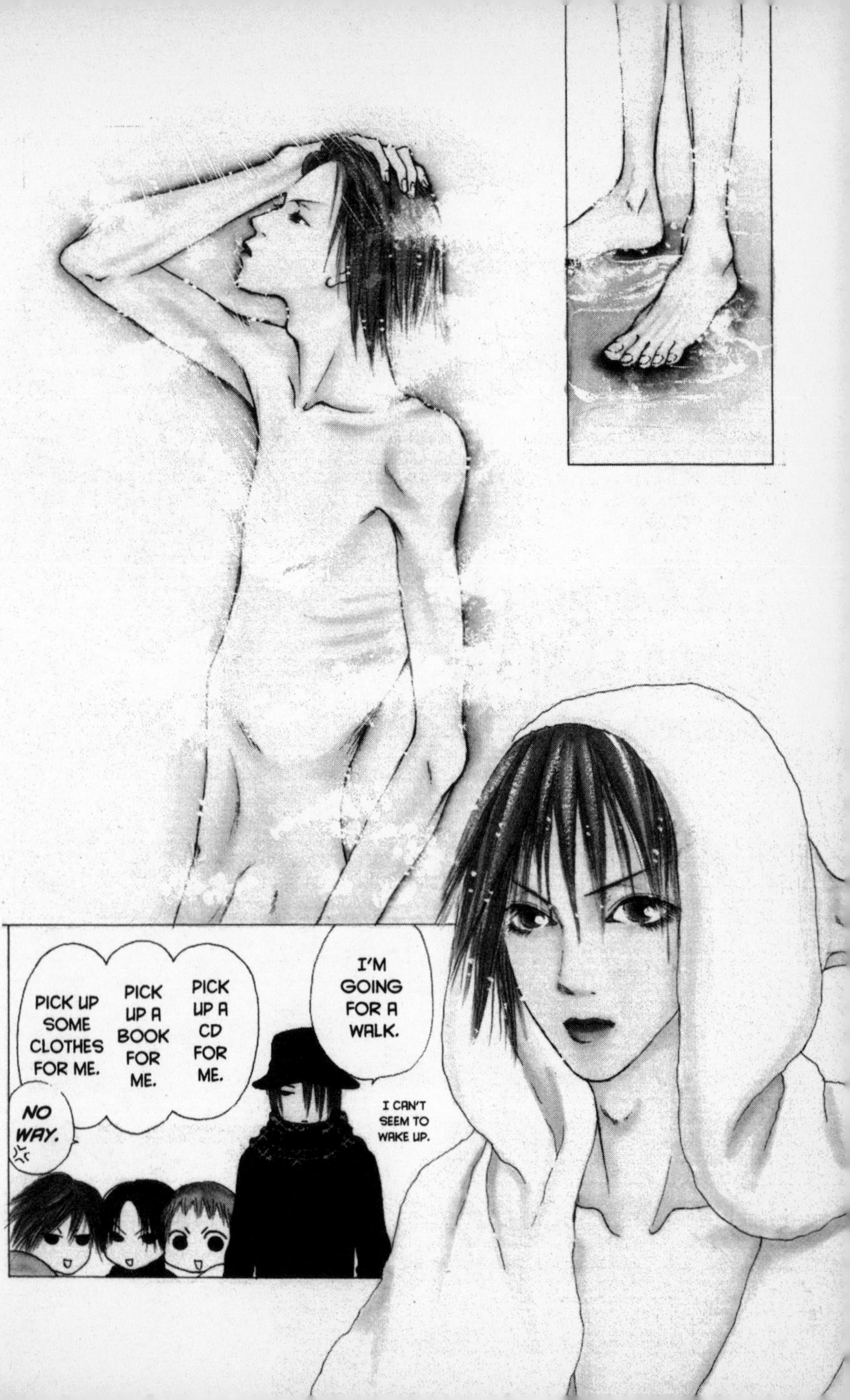
I'M GOING FOR A WALK.
I CAN'T SEEM TO WAKE UP.
PICK UP A CD FOR ME.
PICK UP A BOOK FOR ME.
PICK UP SOME CLOTHES FOR ME.
NO WAY.

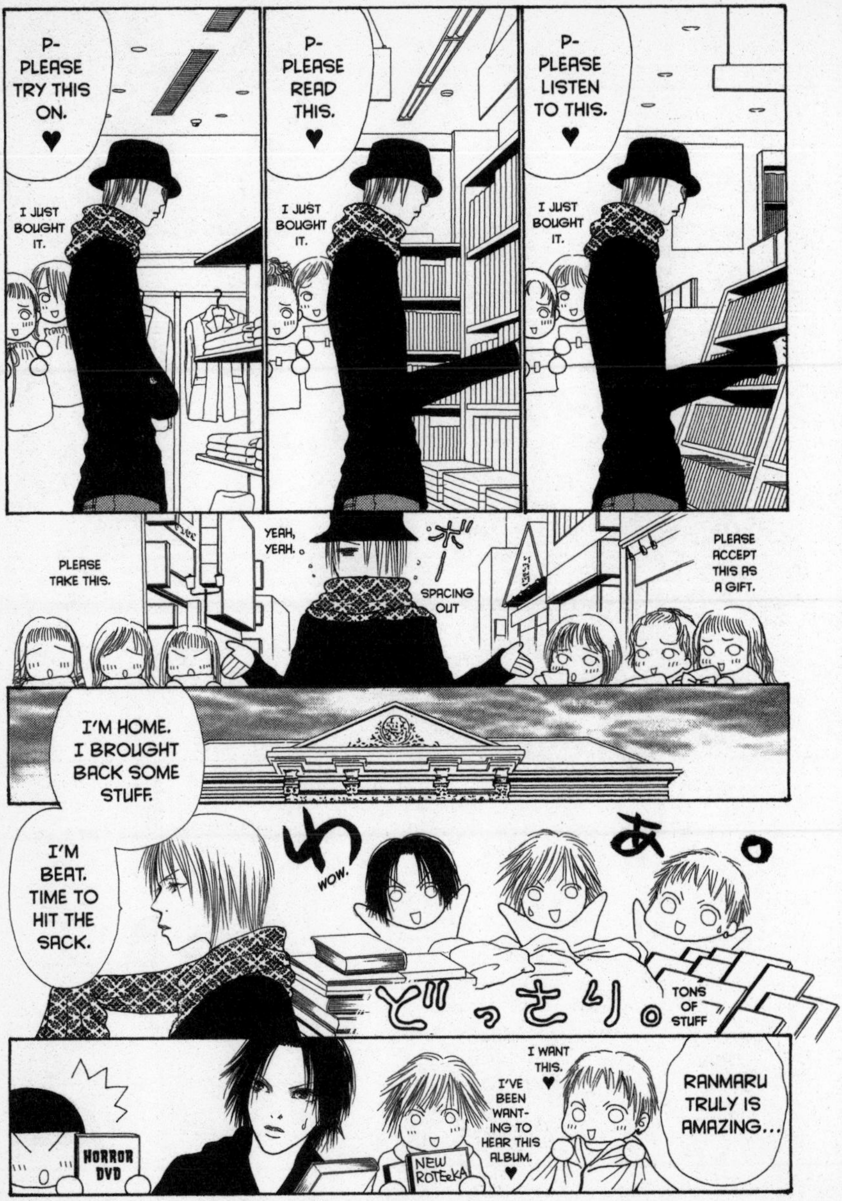
P- PLEASE LISTEN TO THIS. ♥
I JUST BOUGHT IT.
P- PLEASE READ THIS. ♥
I JUST BOUGHT IT.
P- PLEASE TRY THIS ON. ♥
I JUST BOUGHT IT.
PLEASE ACCEPT THIS AS A GIFT.
ボー
SPACING OUT
YEAH, YEAH.
PLEASE TAKE THIS.
I'M HOME. I BROUGHT BACK SOME STUFF.
わあ。
WOW.
どっさり。
TONS OF STUFF
I'M BEAT. TIME TO HIT THE SACK.
RANMARU TRULY IS AMAZING...
I WANT THIS. ♥
I'VE BEEN WANTING TO HEAR THIS ALBUM. ♥
NEW ROTEeKA
HORROR DVD

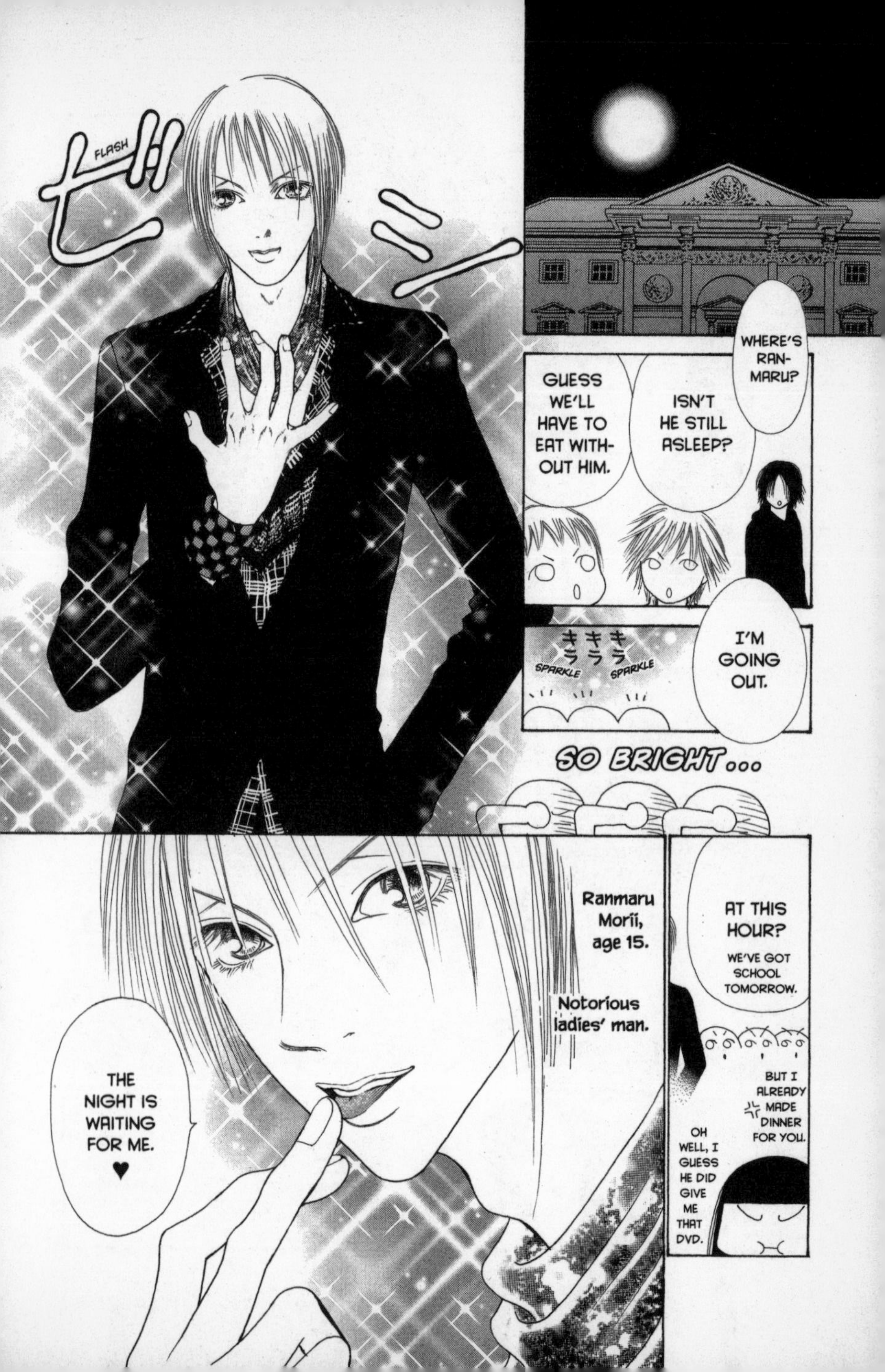
WHERE'S RAN-MARU?
ISN'T HE STILL ASLEEP?
GUESS WE'LL HAVE TO EAT WITH-OUT HIM.
I'M GOING OUT.
キキキ ラララ
SPARKLE SPARKLE
SO BRIGHT...
FLASH
AT THIS HOUR?
WE'VE GOT SCHOOL TOMORROW.
BUT I ALREADY MADE DINNER FOR YOU.
OH WELL, I GUESS HE DID GIVE ME THAT DVD.
Ranmaru Morii, age 15.
Notorious ladies' man.
THE NIGHT IS WAITING FOR ME. ♥

Chapter 31
His True Feelings

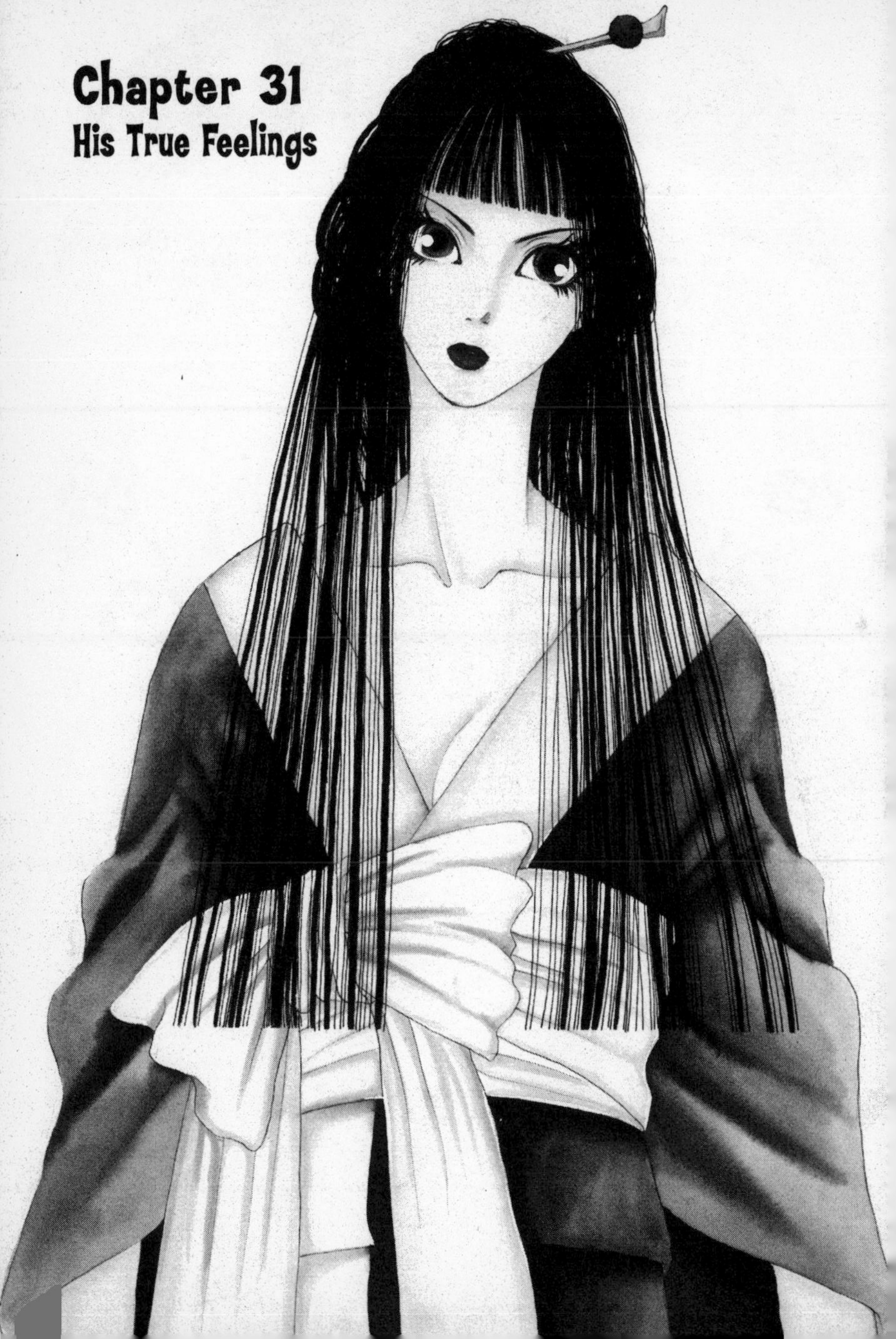

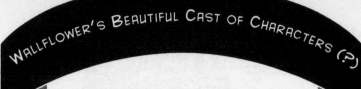

Wallflower's Beautiful Cast of Characters (?)

SUNAKO IS A DARK LONER WHO LOVES HORROR MOVIES. WHEN HER AUNT, THE LANDLADY OF A BOARDINGHOUSE, LEAVES TOWN WITH HER BOYFRIEND, SUNAKO IS FORCED TO LIVE WITH FOUR HANDSOME GUYS. SUNAKO'S AUNT MAKES A DEAL WITH THE BOYS, WHICH CAUSES NOTHING BUT HEADACHES FOR SUNAKO. "MAKE SUNAKO INTO A LADY, AND YOU CAN LIVE RENT FREE."

NOI-CHAN, TAKENAGA'S SUPER-HOT LOVE INTEREST, HAS BECOME A HUGE SUNAKO FAN, BUT THAT HASN'T BROUGHT SUNAKO ANY CLOSER TO BECOMING A LADY.

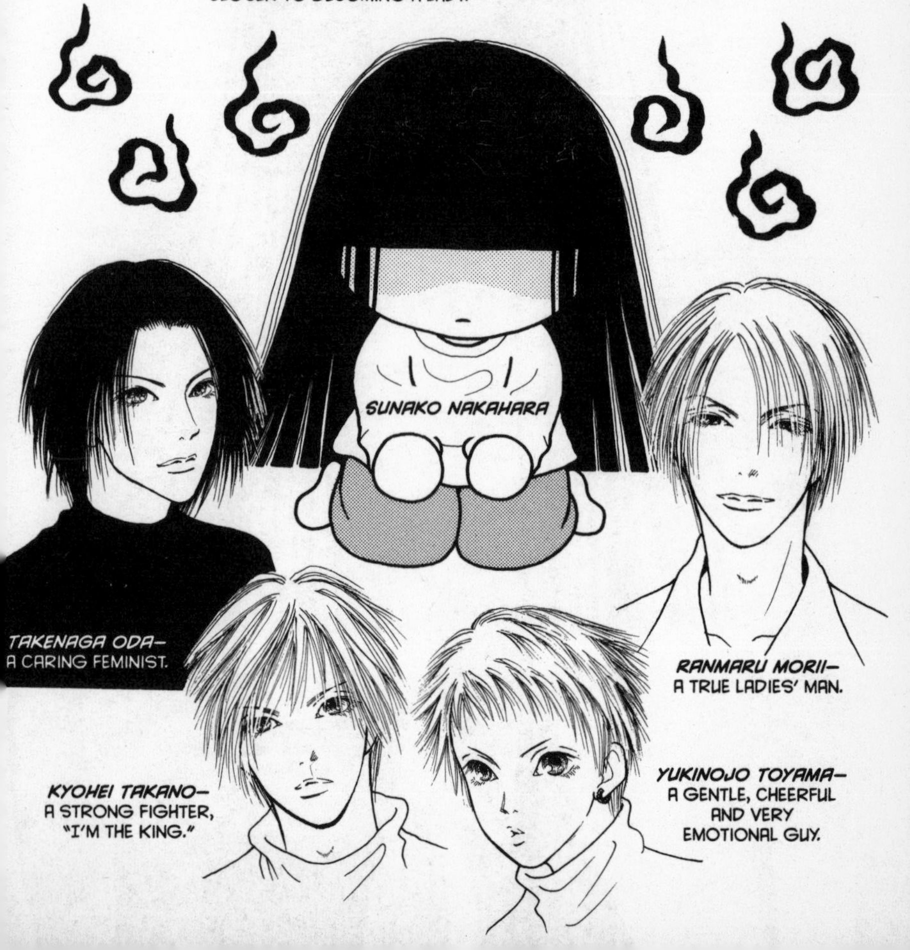
SUNAKO NAKAHARA
TAKENAGA ODA– A CARING FEMINIST.
RANMARU MORII– A TRUE LADIES' MAN.
KYOHEI TAKANO– A STRONG FIGHTER, "I'M THE KING."
YUKINOJO TOYAMA– A GENTLE, CHEERFUL AND VERY EMOTIONAL GUY.

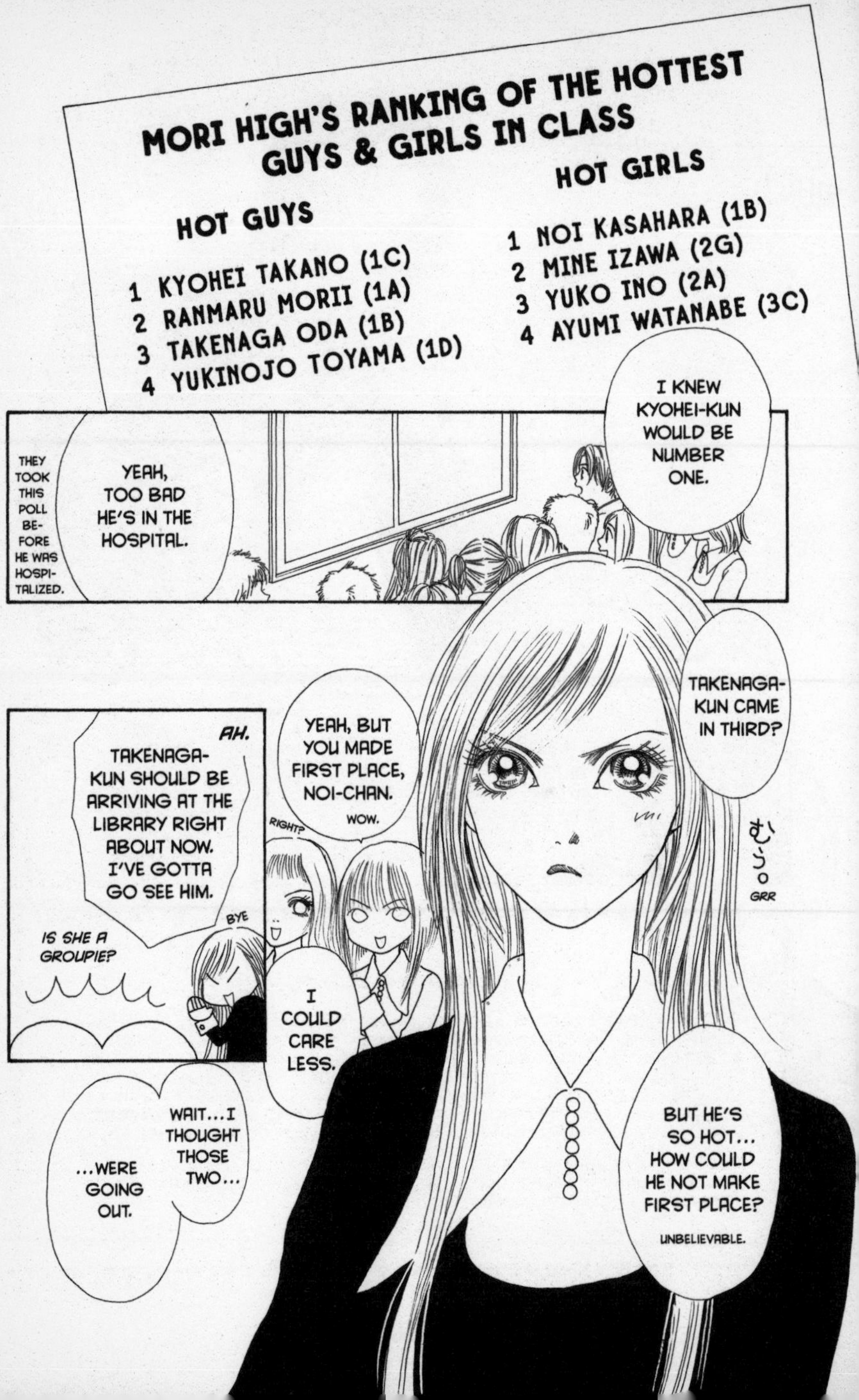
MORI HIGH'S RANKING OF THE HOTTEST GUYS & GIRLS IN CLASS
HOT GUYS
1 KYOHEI TAKANO (1C)
2 RANMARU MORII (1A)
3 TAKENAGA ODA (1B)
4 YUKINOJO TOYAMA (1D)
HOT GIRLS
1 NOI KASAHARA (1B)
2 MINE IZAWA (2G)
3 YUKO INO (2A)
4 AYUMI WATANABE (3C)
I KNEW KYOHEI-KUN WOULD BE NUMBER ONE.
YEAH, TOO BAD HE'S IN THE HOSPITAL.
THEY TOOK THIS POLL BEFORE HE WAS HOSPITALIZED.
TAKENAGA-KUN CAME IN THIRD?
むぅ。
GRR
YEAH, BUT YOU MADE FIRST PLACE, NOI-CHAN.
WOW.
RIGHT?
AH.
TAKENAGA-KUN SHOULD BE ARRIVING AT THE LIBRARY RIGHT ABOUT NOW. I'VE GOTTA GO SEE HIM.
BYE
IS SHE A GROUPIE?
I COULD CARE LESS.
BUT HE'S SO HOT... HOW COULD HE NOT MAKE FIRST PLACE?
UNBELIEVABLE.
WAIT...I THOUGHT THOSE TWO...
...WERE GOING OUT.

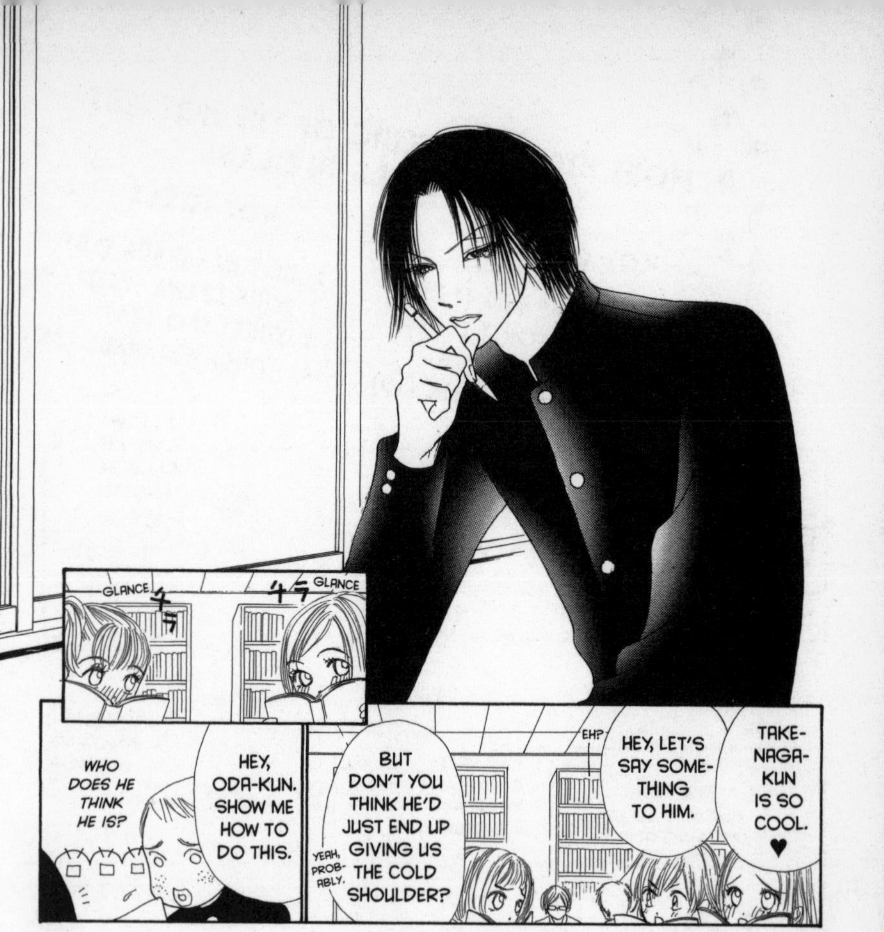
GLANCE
GLANCE
TAKE-NAGA-KUN IS SO COOL. ♥
HEY, LET'S SAY SOME-THING TO HIM.
EH?
BUT DON'T YOU THINK HE'D JUST END UP GIVING US THE COLD SHOULDER?
YEAH, PROB-ABLY.
HEY, ODA-KUN. SHOW ME HOW TO DO THIS.
WHO DOES HE THINK HE IS?

BEHIND THE SCENES

WHILE WORKING ON THIS BOOK, I ENDED UP HAVING TO MOVE. I THOUGHT I COULD SOMEHOW MANAGE THE MOVE WITHOUT ALTERING MY SUPER-HARD SCHEDULE. BAD IDEA. I STARTED OUT BY JUST UNPACKING MY WORK STUFF, AND TRYING TO WORK OUT OF MY MESSY NEW PLACE. BUT THERE ARE NO RESTAURANTS NEARBY. THEY'RE ALL REALLY FAR AWAY. NO SUPERMARKETS EITHER. BEFORE I MOVED, I LIVED WITHIN WALKING DISTANCE OF ALL KINDS OF PLACES. I MISS KOMAZAWA. MY ASSISTANTS CAME TO HELP OUT, AND ALL I COULD GIVE THEM WERE BENTO LUNCHES FROM A CONVENIENCE STORE. SORRY, GUYS. NOW I COOK FOR THEM. HEH, HEH.

TAKENAGA AND NOI-CHAN'S LOVE HAS FINALLY STARTED TO DEVELOP INTO SOMETHING… THANK GOD. MAYBE IT'S ABOUT TIME I COME UP WITH A GIRLFRIEND FOR RANMARU TOO… NOT THAT I'VE REALLY BEEN THINKING ABOUT IT OR ANYTHING.

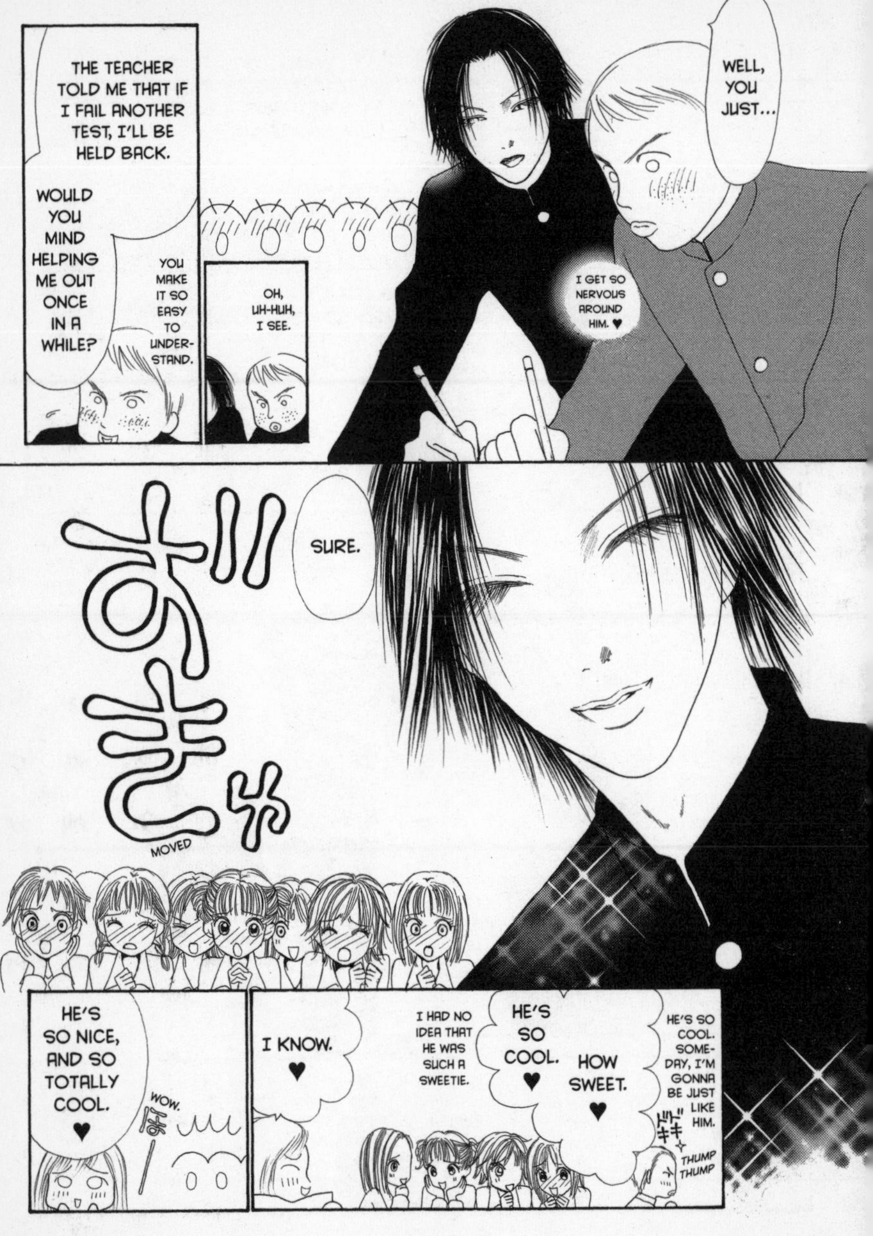
WELL, YOU JUST...
I GET SO NERVOUS AROUND HIM. ♥
YOU MAKE IT SO EASY TO UNDER-STAND.
OH, UH-HUH, I SEE.
THE TEACHER TOLD ME THAT IF I FAIL ANOTHER TEST, I'LL BE HELD BACK.
WOULD YOU MIND HELPING ME OUT ONCE IN A WHILE?
SURE.
MOVED
HE'S SO COOL. SOME-DAY, I'M GONNA BE JUST LIKE HIM.
THUMP THUMP
HOW SWEET. ♥
HE'S SO COOL. ♥
I HAD NO IDEA THAT HE WAS SUCH A SWEETIE.
I KNOW. ♥
HE'S SO NICE, AND SO TOTALLY COOL. ♥
WOW.

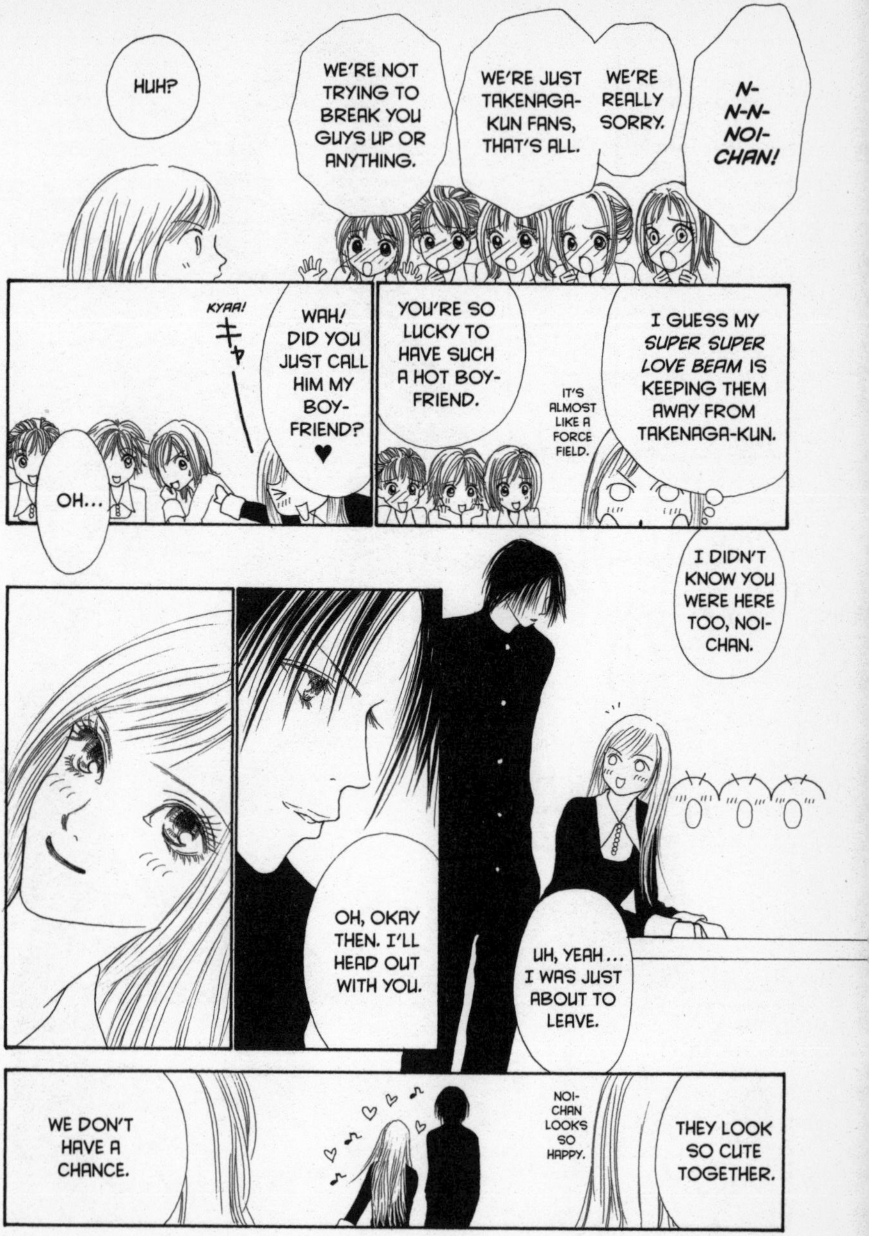
N-N-N-NOI-CHAN!
WE'RE REALLY SORRY.
WE'RE JUST TAKENAGA-KUN FANS, THAT'S ALL.
WE'RE NOT TRYING TO BREAK YOU GUYS UP OR ANYTHING.
HUH?
I GUESS MY *SUPER SUPER LOVE BEAM* IS KEEPING THEM AWAY FROM TAKENAGA-KUN.
IT'S ALMOST LIKE A FORCE FIELD.
YOU'RE SO LUCKY TO HAVE SUCH A HOT BOY-FRIEND.
WAH! DID YOU JUST CALL HIM MY BOY-FRIEND? ♥
KYAA!
OH...
I DIDN'T KNOW YOU WERE HERE TOO, NOI-CHAN.
UH, YEAH... I WAS JUST ABOUT TO LEAVE.
OH, OKAY THEN. I'LL HEAD OUT WITH YOU.
THEY LOOK SO CUTE TOGETHER.
NOI-CHAN LOOKS SO HAPPY.
WE DON'T HAVE A CHANCE.

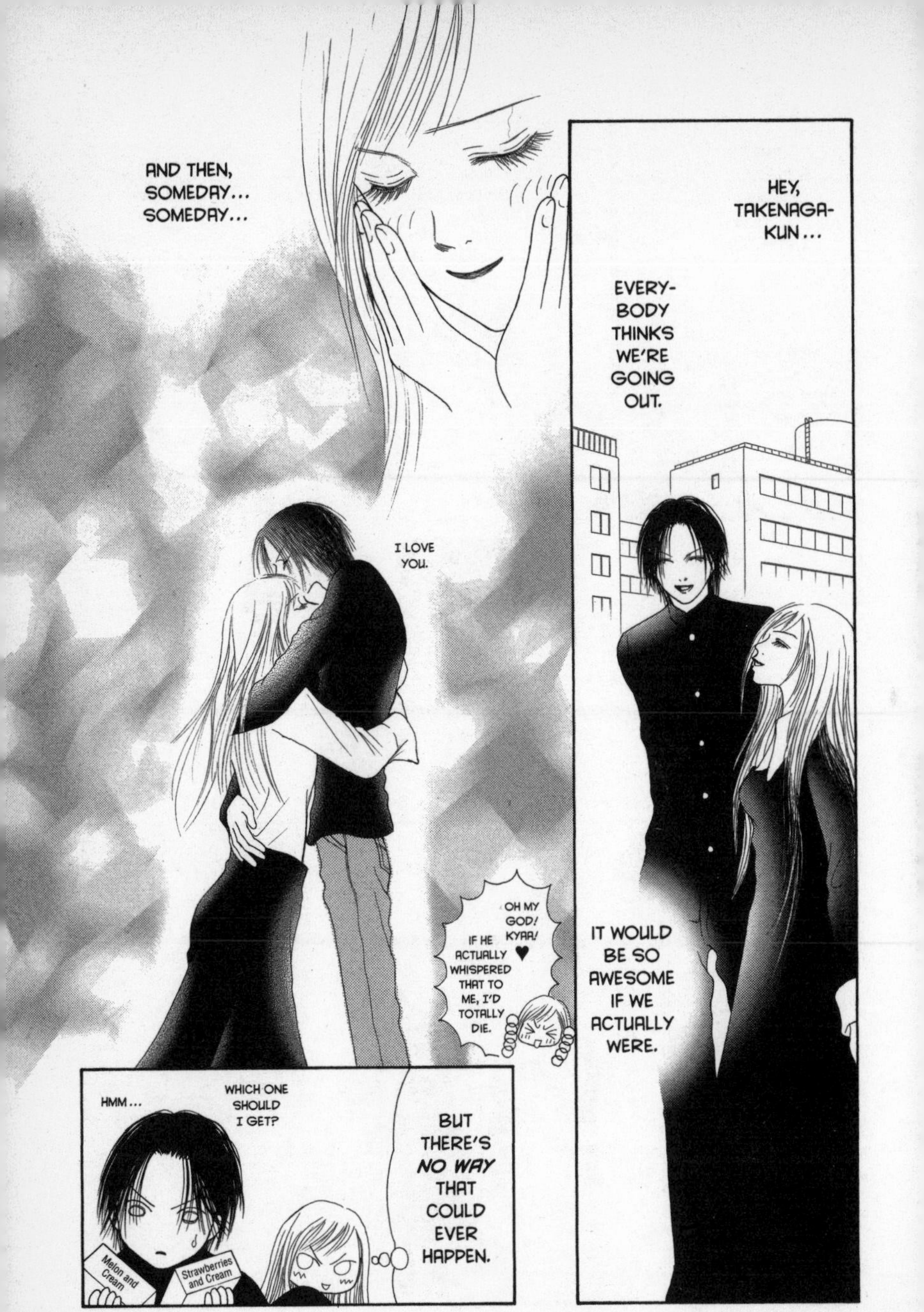
HEY, TAKENAGA-KUN...
EVERYBODY THINKS WE'RE GOING OUT.
IT WOULD BE SO AWESOME IF WE ACTUALLY WERE.
AND THEN, SOMEDAY... SOMEDAY...
I LOVE YOU.
OH MY GOD! KYAA!
IF HE ACTUALLY WHISPERED THAT TO ME, I'D TOTALLY DIE.
BUT THERE'S *NO WAY* THAT COULD EVER HAPPEN.
WHICH ONE SHOULD I GET?
HMM...
Strawberries and Cream
Melon and Cream

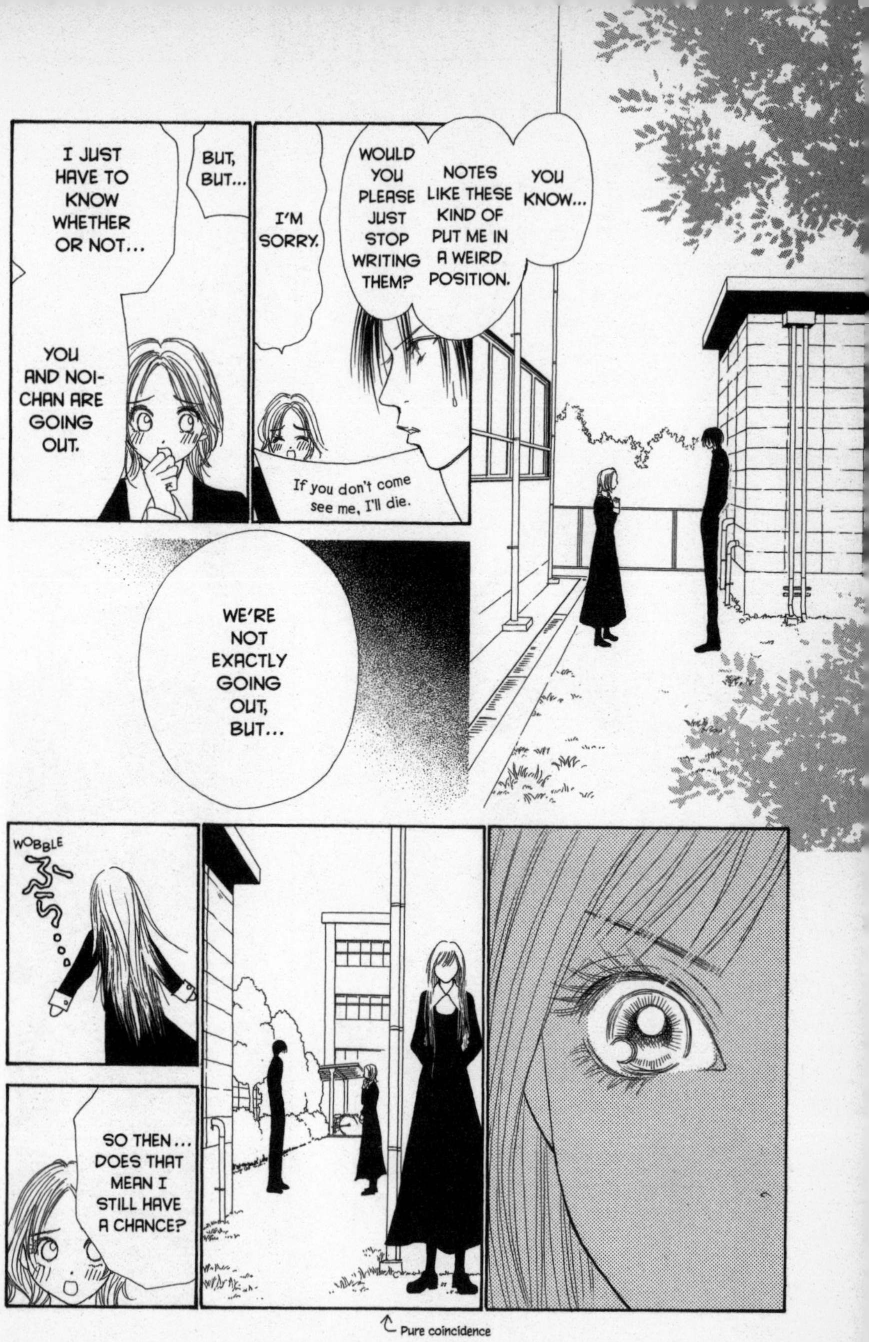
YOU KNOW...
NOTES LIKE THESE KIND OF PUT ME IN A WEIRD POSITION.
WOULD YOU PLEASE JUST STOP WRITING THEM?
I'M SORRY.
If you don't come see me, I'll die.
BUT, BUT...
I JUST HAVE TO KNOW WHETHER OR NOT...
YOU AND NOI-CHAN ARE GOING OUT.
WE'RE NOT EXACTLY GOING OUT, BUT...
WOBBLE
SO THEN... DOES THAT MEAN I STILL HAVE A CHANCE?
↖ Pure coincidence

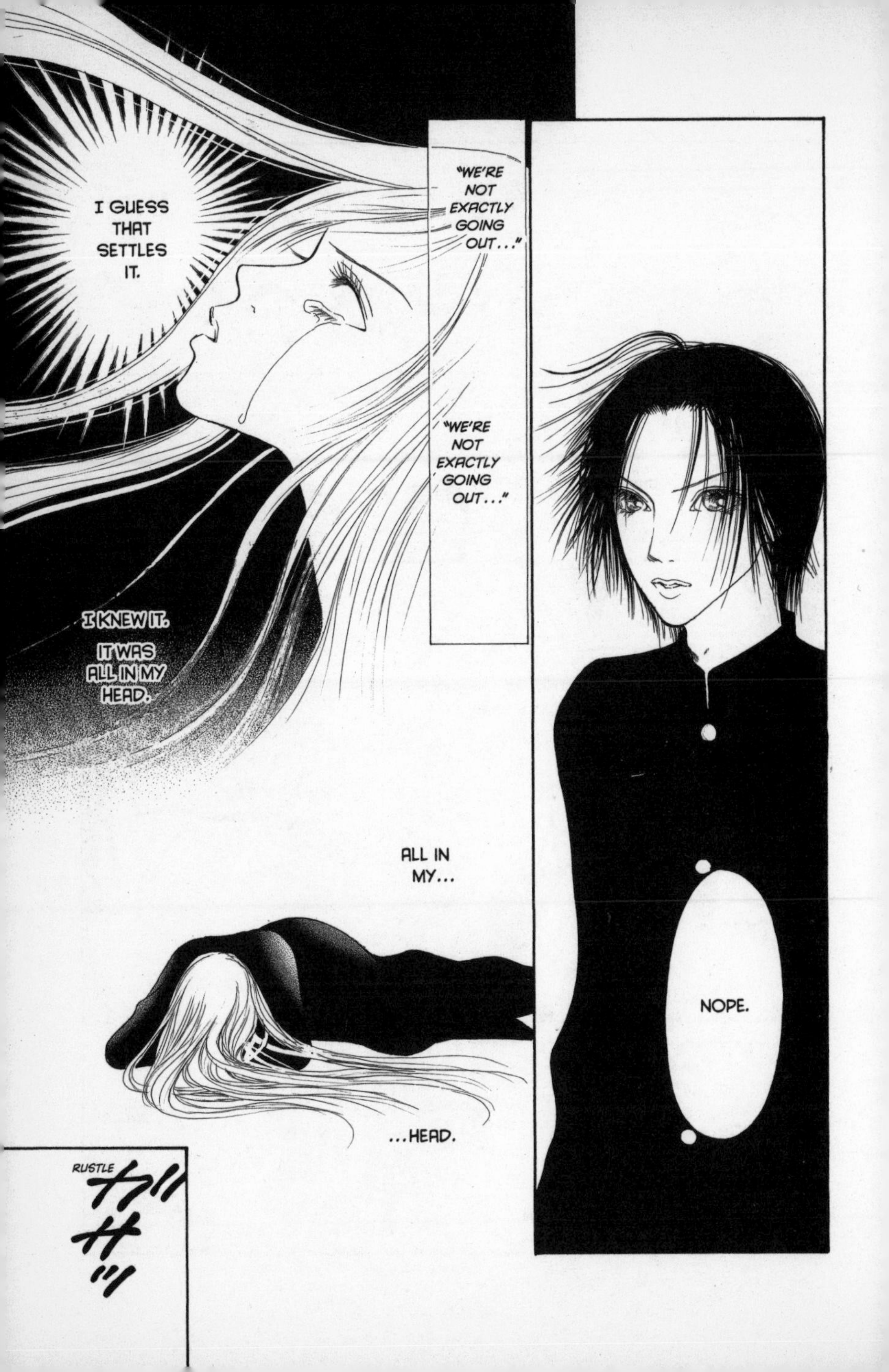
"WE'RE NOT EXACTLY GOING OUT..."
"WE'RE NOT EXACTLY GOING OUT..."
I GUESS THAT SETTLES IT.
I KNEW IT.
IT WAS ALL IN MY HEAD.
ALL IN MY...
...HEAD.
NOPE.
RUSTLE

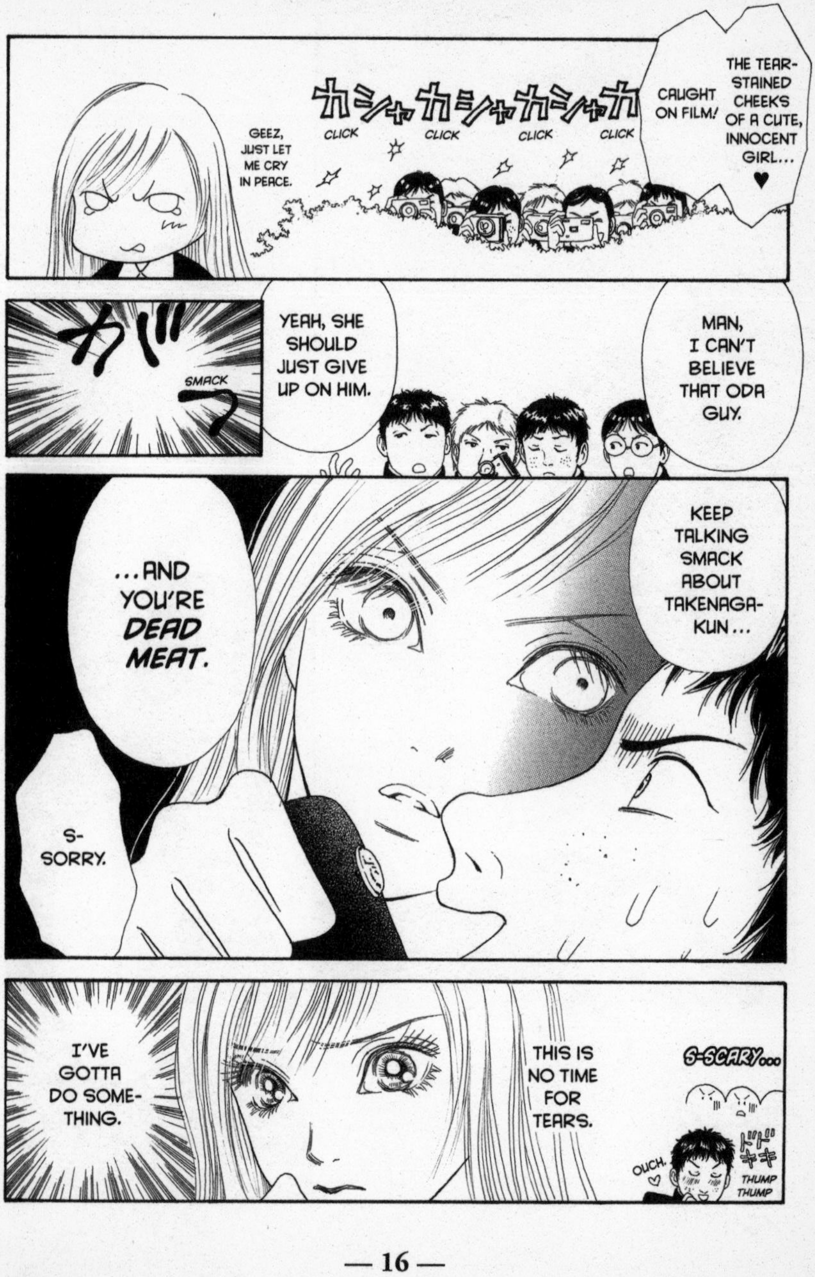
THE TEAR-STAINED CHEEKS OF A CUTE, INNOCENT GIRL... ♥
CAUGHT ON FILM!
カシャカシャカシャカ
CLICK CLICK CLICK CLICK
GEEZ, JUST LET ME CRY IN PEACE.
MAN, I CAN'T BELIEVE THAT ODA GUY.
YEAH, SHE SHOULD JUST GIVE UP ON HIM.
ガツ
SMACK
KEEP TALKING SMACK ABOUT TAKENAGA-KUN...
...AND YOU'RE *DEAD MEAT*.
S-SORRY.
S-SCARY...
ドキドキ
THUMP THUMP
OUCH. ♡
THIS IS NO TIME FOR TEARS.
I'VE GOTTA DO SOMETHING.

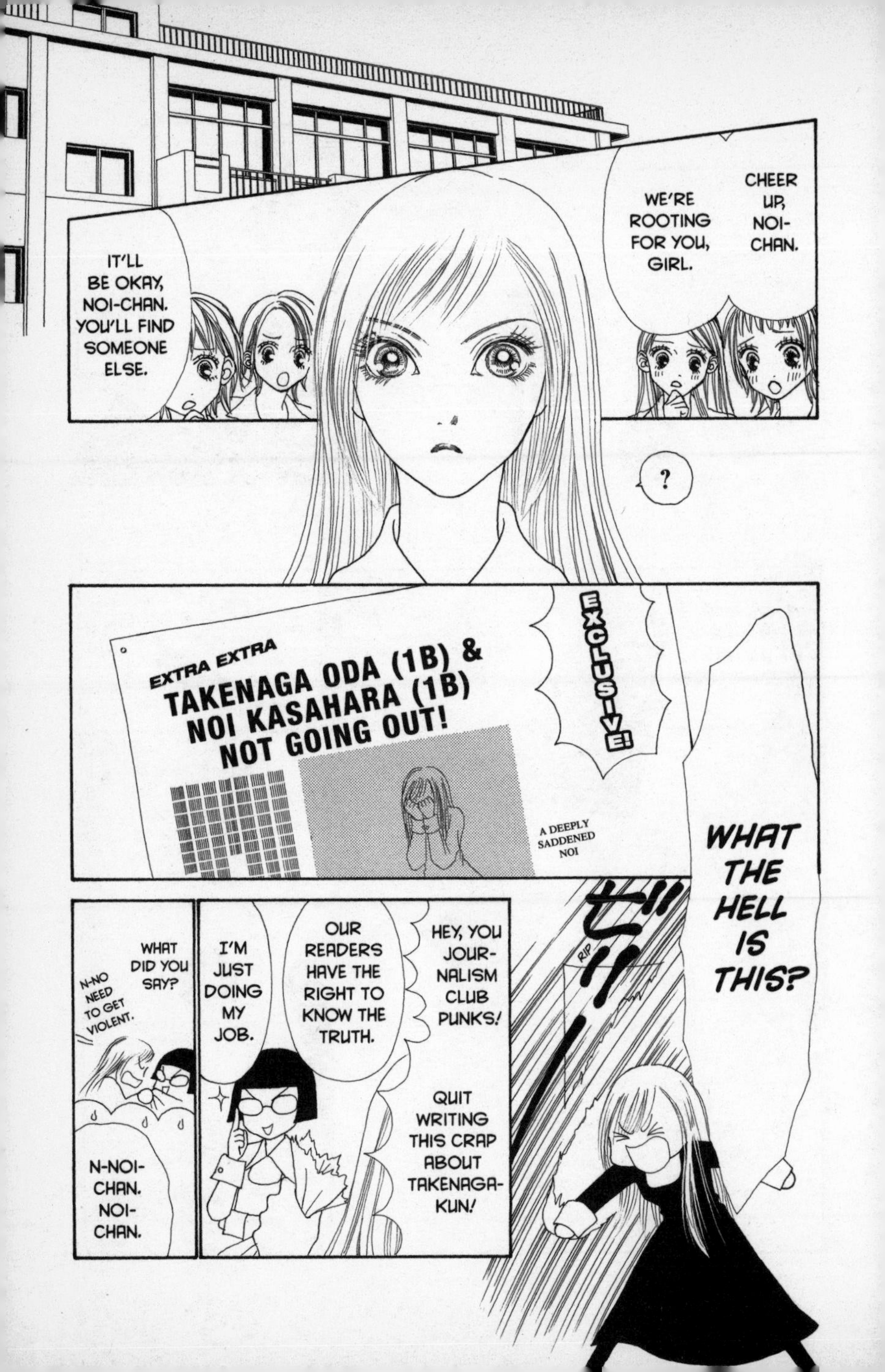

CHEER UP, NOI-CHAN.
WE'RE ROOTING FOR YOU, GIRL.
IT'LL BE OKAY, NOI-CHAN. YOU'LL FIND SOMEONE ELSE.
?
EXCLUSIVE!
EXTRA EXTRA
TAKENAGA ODA (1B) & NOI KASAHARA (1B) NOT GOING OUT!
A DEEPLY SADDENED NOI
WHAT THE HELL IS THIS?
RIP
HEY, YOU JOURNALISM CLUB PUNKS!
QUIT WRITING THIS CRAP ABOUT TAKENAGA-KUN!
OUR READERS HAVE THE RIGHT TO KNOW THE TRUTH.
I'M JUST DOING MY JOB.
WHAT DID YOU SAY?
N-NO NEED TO GET VIOLENT.
N-NOI-CHAN. NOI-CHAN.

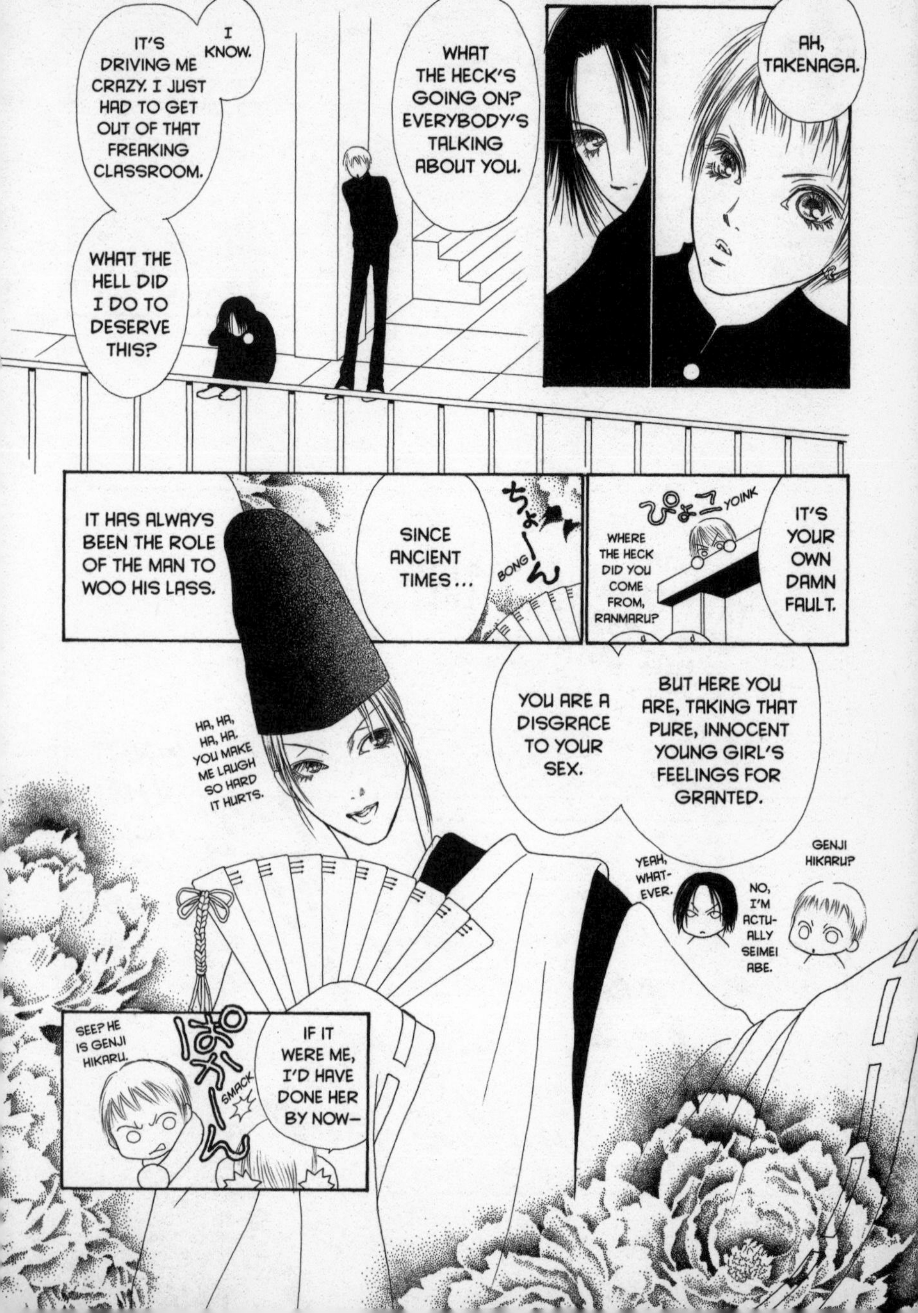
AH, TAKENAGA.
WHAT THE HECK'S GOING ON? EVERYBODY'S TALKING ABOUT YOU.
I KNOW.
IT'S DRIVING ME CRAZY. I JUST HAD TO GET OUT OF THAT FREAKING CLASSROOM.
WHAT THE HELL DID I DO TO DESERVE THIS?
IT'S YOUR OWN DAMN FAULT.
ぴょこ YOINK
WHERE THE HECK DID YOU COME FROM, RANMARU?
ちょーん BONG
SINCE ANCIENT TIMES...
IT HAS ALWAYS BEEN THE ROLE OF THE MAN TO WOO HIS LASS.
BUT HERE YOU ARE, TAKING THAT PURE, INNOCENT YOUNG GIRL'S FEELINGS FOR GRANTED.
YOU ARE A DISGRACE TO YOUR SEX.
HA, HA, HA, HA. YOU MAKE ME LAUGH SO HARD IT HURTS.
GENJI HIKARU?
NO, I'M ACTUALLY SEIMEI ABE.
YEAH, WHAT-EVER.
IF IT WERE ME, I'D HAVE DONE HER BY NOW–
ぱかーん SMACK
SEE? HE IS GENJI HIKARU.

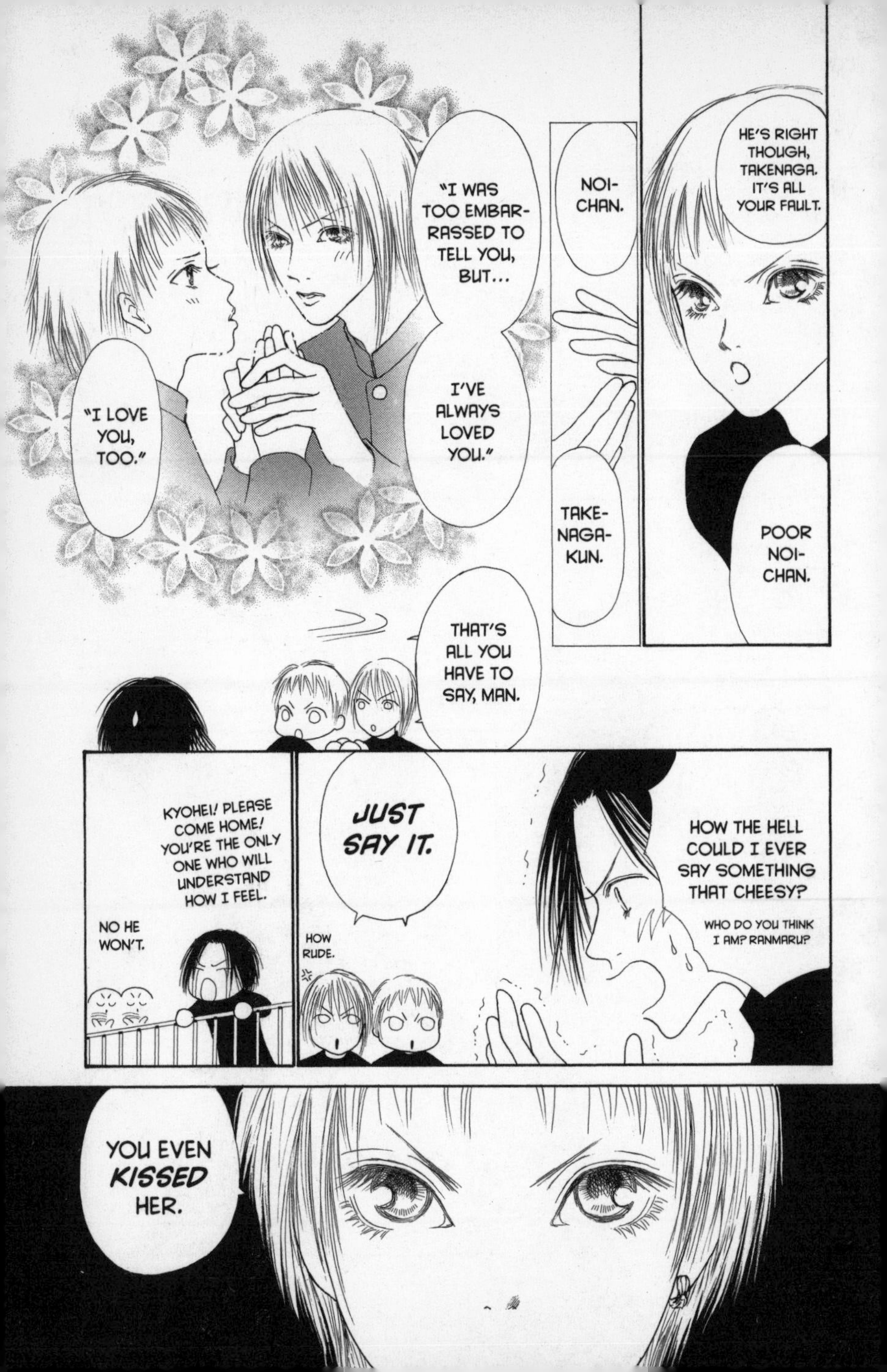
HE'S RIGHT THOUGH, TAKENAGA. IT'S ALL YOUR FAULT.
POOR NOI-CHAN.
NOI-CHAN.
TAKE-NAGA-KUN.
"I WAS TOO EMBAR-RASSED TO TELL YOU, BUT...
I'VE ALWAYS LOVED YOU."
"I LOVE YOU, TOO."
THAT'S ALL YOU HAVE TO SAY, MAN.
HOW THE HELL COULD I EVER SAY SOMETHING THAT CHEESY?
WHO DO YOU THINK I AM? RANMARU?
JUST SAY IT.
HOW RUDE.
KYOHEI! PLEASE COME HOME! YOU'RE THE ONLY ONE WHO WILL UNDERSTAND HOW I FEEL.
NO HE WON'T.
YOU EVEN KISSED HER.

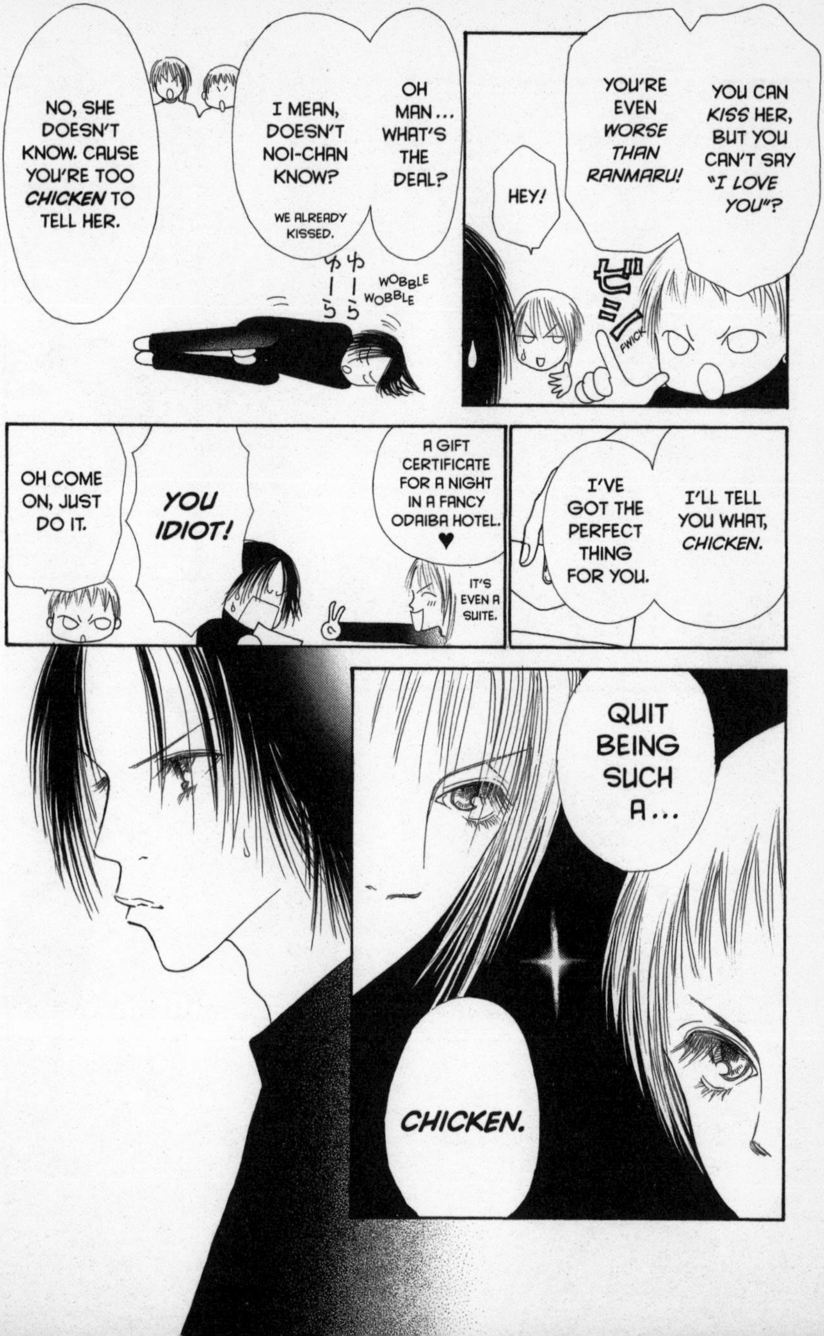
YOU CAN KISS HER, BUT YOU CAN'T SAY "I LOVE YOU"?
YOU'RE EVEN WORSE THAN RANMARU!
HEY!
FWICK
OH MAN... WHAT'S THE DEAL?
I MEAN, DOESN'T NOI-CHAN KNOW?
WE ALREADY KISSED.
ゆーら ゆーら
WOBBLE WOBBLE
NO, SHE DOESN'T KNOW. CAUSE YOU'RE TOO CHICKEN TO TELL HER.
I'LL TELL YOU WHAT, CHICKEN.
I'VE GOT THE PERFECT THING FOR YOU.
A GIFT CERTIFICATE FOR A NIGHT IN A FANCY ODAIBA HOTEL. ♥
IT'S EVEN A SUITE.
YOU IDIOT!
OH COME ON, JUST DO IT.
QUIT BEING SUCH A...
CHICKEN.

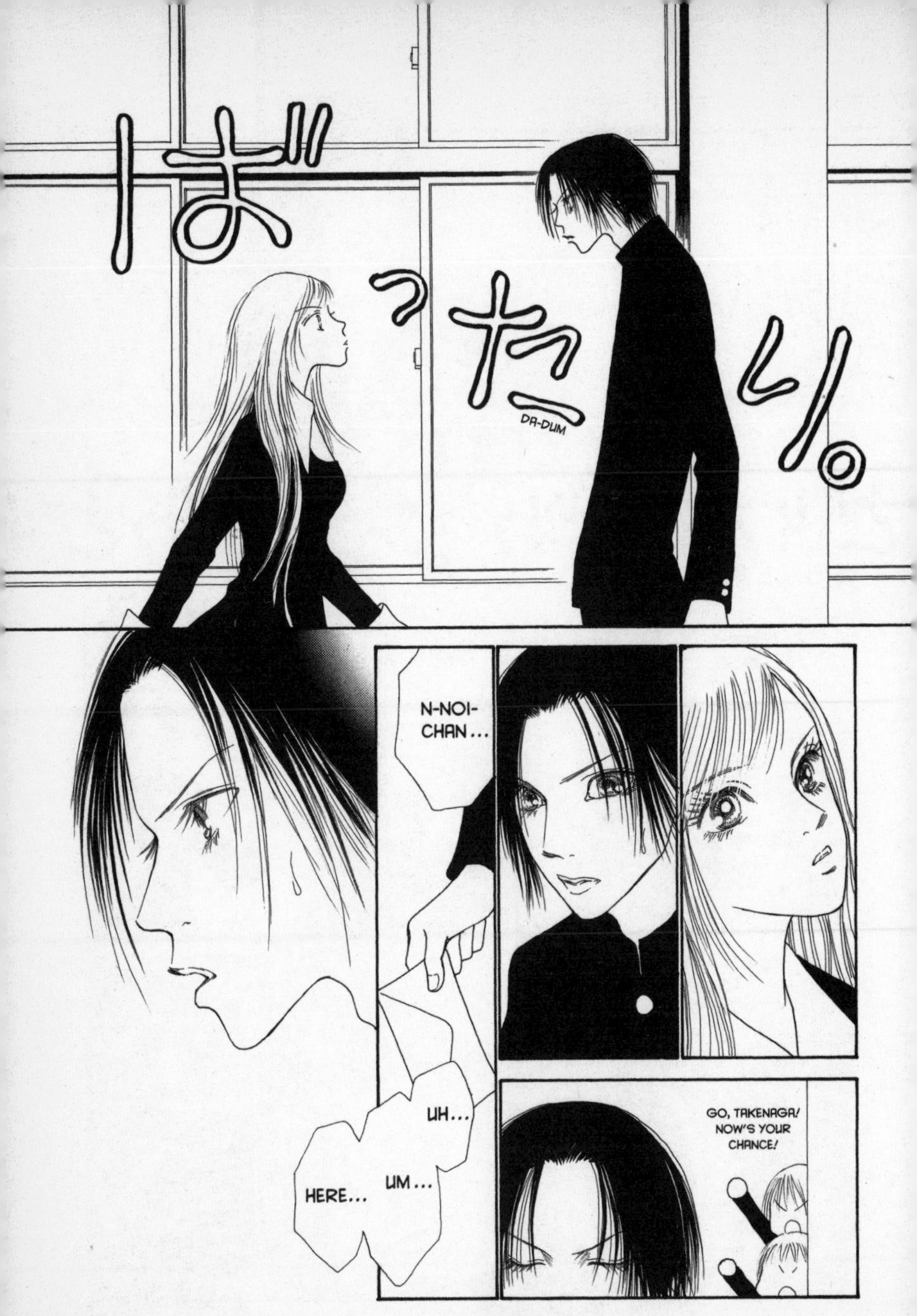
ばったん。
DA-DUM
N-NOI-CHAN...
GO, TAKENAGA! NOW'S YOUR CHANCE!
UH...
UM...
HERE...

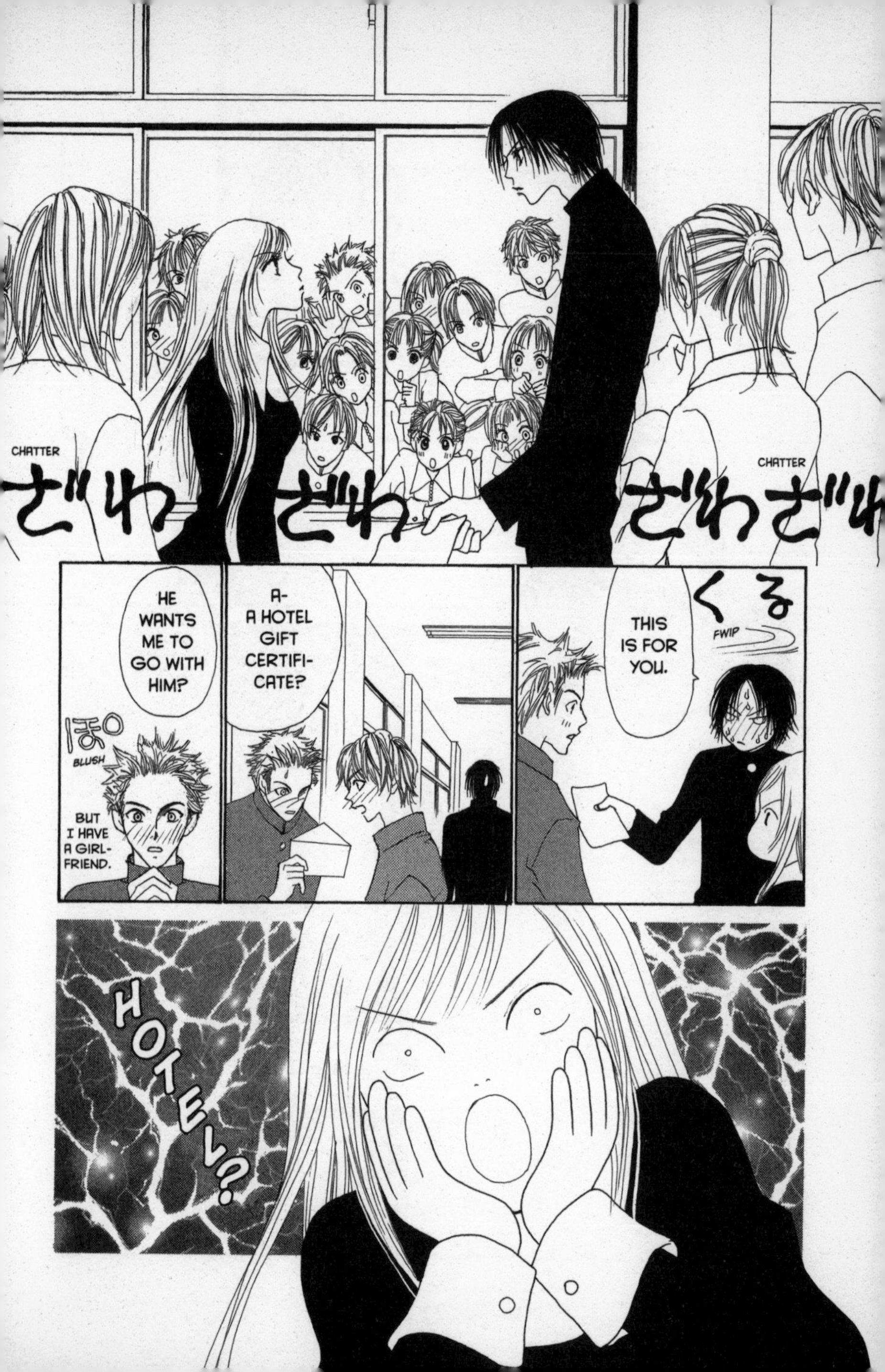
CHATTER
ざわざわ
CHATTER
ざわ ざわ
くる
FWIP
THIS IS FOR YOU.
A- A HOTEL GIFT CERTIFI-CATE?
HE WANTS ME TO GO WITH HIM?
ぽっ
BLUSH
BUT I HAVE A GIRL-FRIEND.
HOTEL?

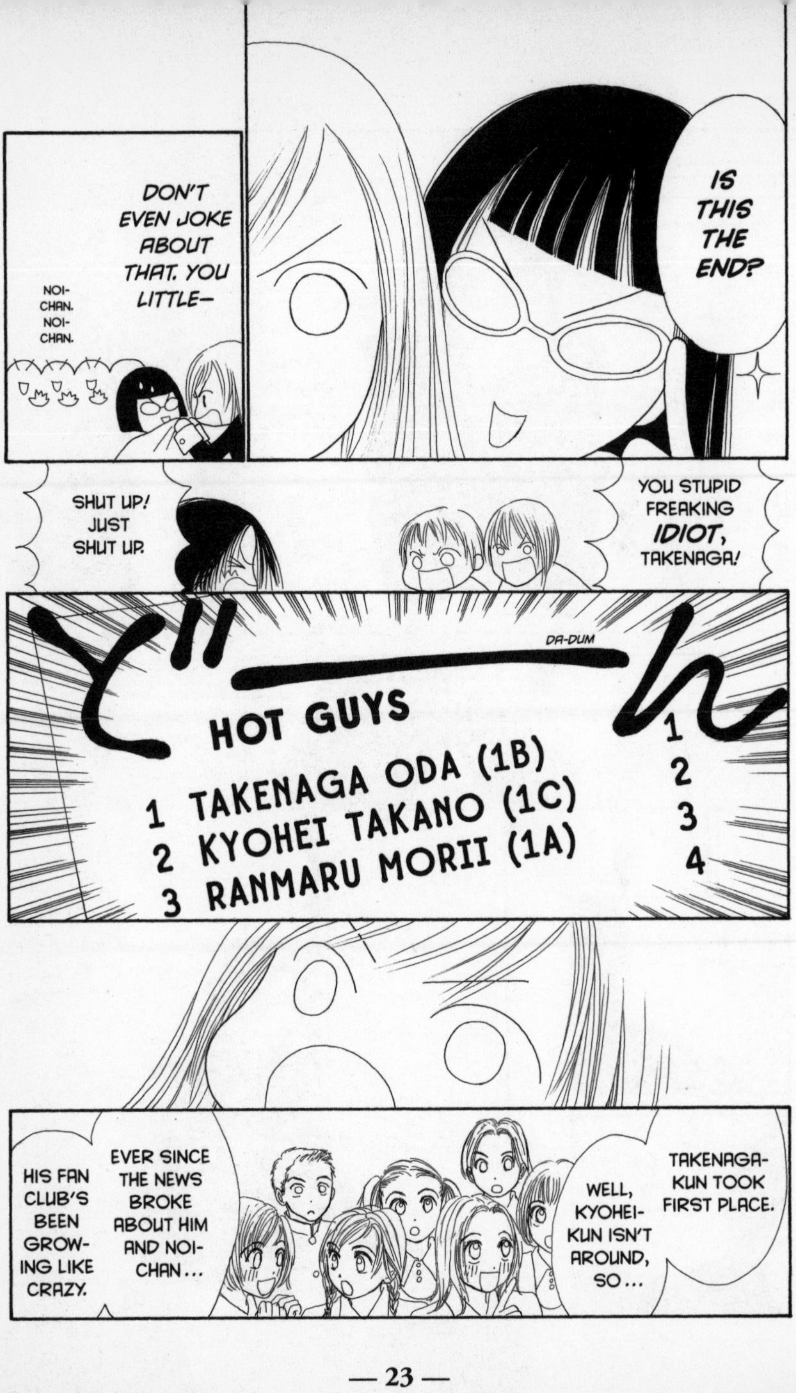
IS THIS THE END?
DON'T EVEN JOKE ABOUT THAT. YOU LITTLE—
NOI-CHAN. NOI-CHAN.
YOU STUPID FREAKING *IDIOT*, TAKENAGA!
SHUT UP! JUST SHUT UP.
どーん
DA-DUM
HOT GUYS
1 TAKENAGA ODA (1B)
2 KYOHEI TAKANO (1C)
3 RANMARU MORII (1A)
1
2
3
4
TAKENAGA-KUN TOOK FIRST PLACE.
WELL, KYOHEI-KUN ISN'T AROUND, SO…
EVER SINCE THE NEWS BROKE ABOUT HIM AND NOI-CHAN…
HIS FAN CLUB'S BEEN GROW-ING LIKE CRAZY.

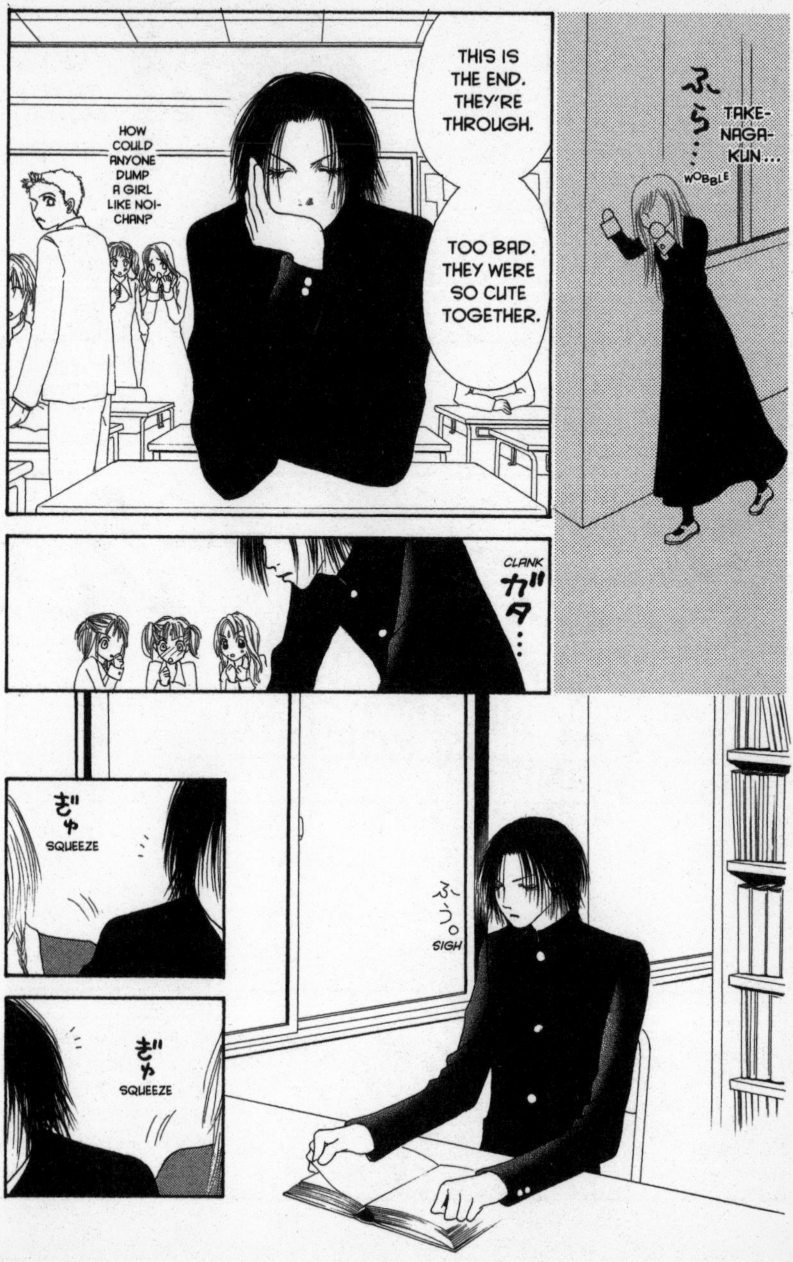

ふら…
TAKE-NAGA-KUN…
WOBBLE
THIS IS THE END. THEY'RE THROUGH.
TOO BAD. THEY WERE SO CUTE TOGETHER.
HOW COULD ANYONE DUMP A GIRL LIKE NOI-CHAN?
CLANK
ガタ…
ふう。
SIGH
ぎゅ
SQUEEZE
ぎゅ
SQUEEZE

JAM PACKED

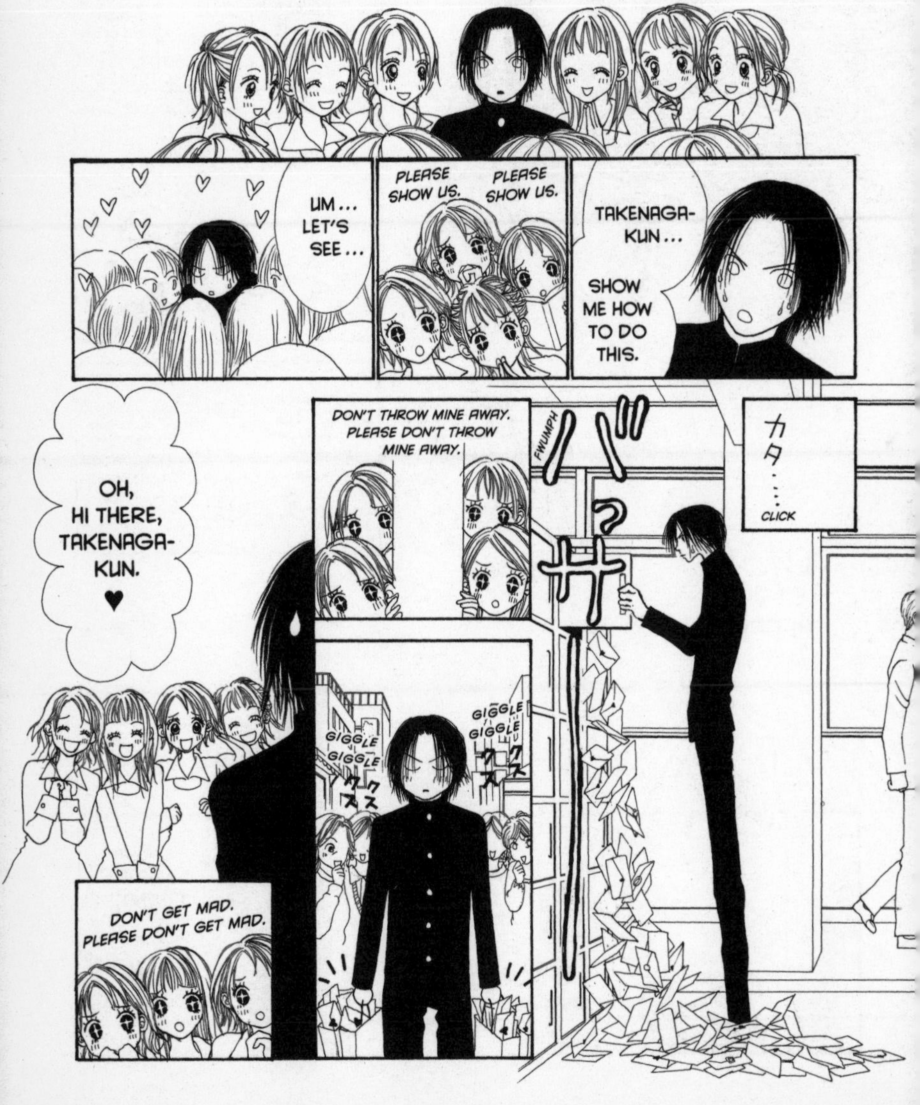
TAKENAGA-KUN...
SHOW ME HOW TO DO THIS.
PLEASE SHOW US.
PLEASE SHOW US.
UM... LET'S SEE...
カタ...
CLICK
バッサ
FWUMPH
DON'T THROW MINE AWAY. PLEASE DON'T THROW MINE AWAY.
GIGGLE GIGGLE
クスクス
GIGGLE GIGGLE
クスクス
OH, HI THERE, TAKENAGA-KUN. ♥
DON'T GET MAD. PLEASE DON'T GET MAD.

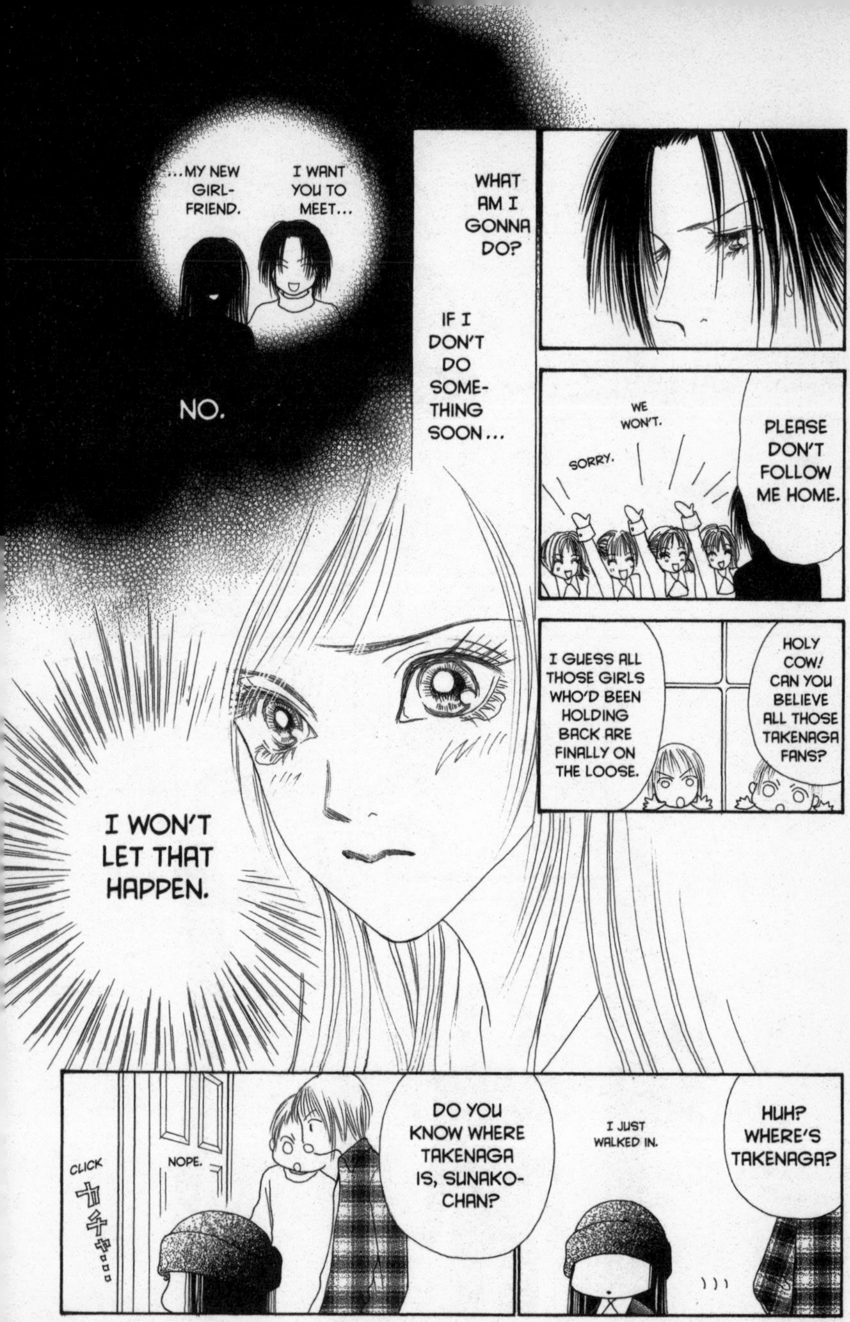
PLEASE DON'T FOLLOW ME HOME.
WE WON'T.
SORRY.
HOLY COW! CAN YOU BELIEVE ALL THOSE TAKENAGA FANS?
I GUESS ALL THOSE GIRLS WHO'D BEEN HOLDING BACK ARE FINALLY ON THE LOOSE.
WHAT AM I GONNA DO?
IF I DON'T DO SOMETHING SOON...
I WANT YOU TO MEET...
...MY NEW GIRLFRIEND.
NO.
I WON'T LET THAT HAPPEN.
HUH? WHERE'S TAKENAGA?
I JUST WALKED IN.
DO YOU KNOW WHERE TAKENAGA IS, SUNAKO-CHAN?
NOPE.
CLICK
カチャ

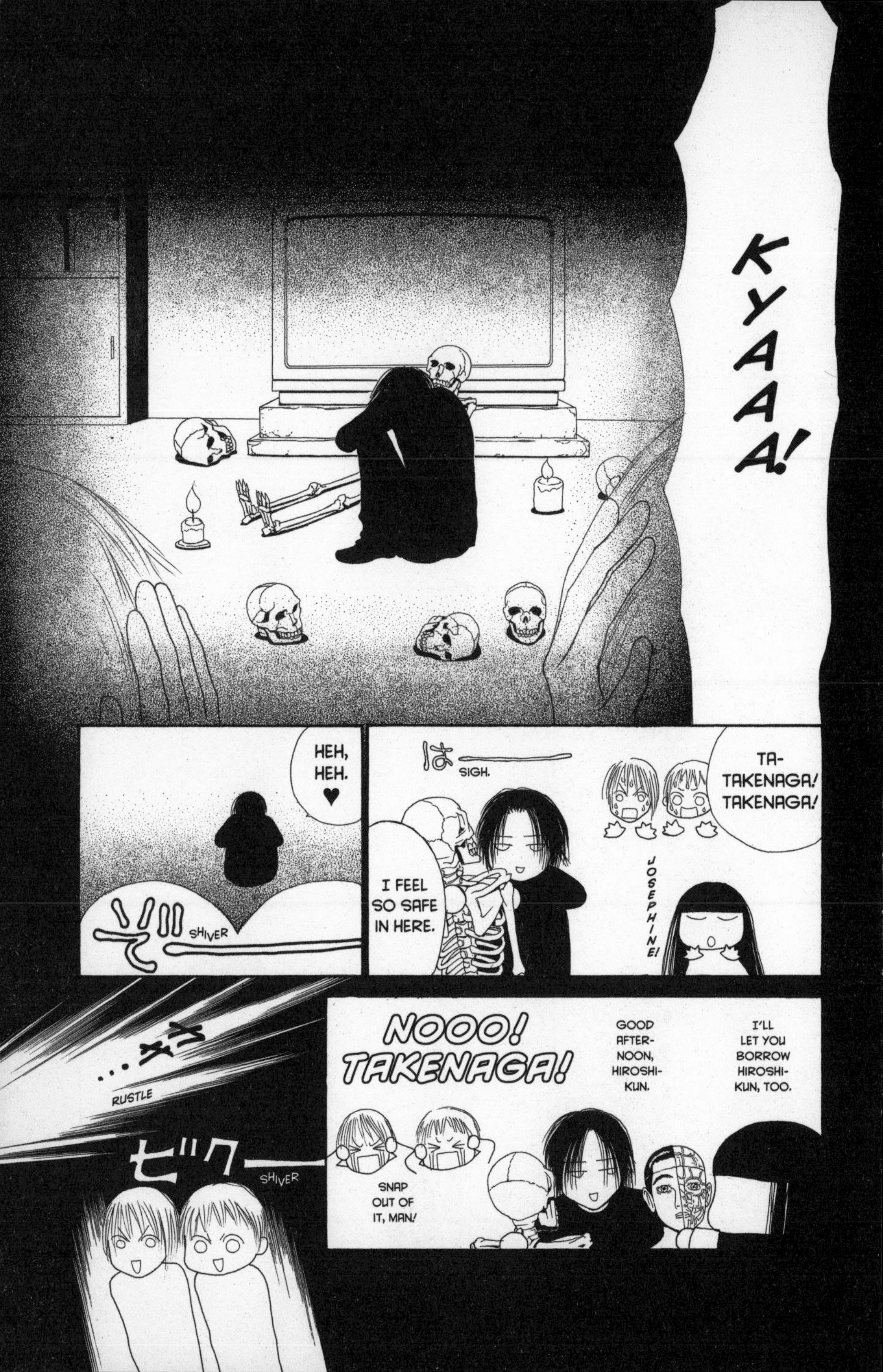
KYAAAA!
TA-TAKENAGA! TAKENAGA!
JOSEPHINE!
は——
SIGH.
I FEEL SO SAFE IN HERE.
HEH, HEH. ♥
SHIVER
I'LL LET YOU BORROW HIROSHI-KUN, TOO.
GOOD AFTER-NOON, HIROSHI-KUN.
NOOO! TAKENAGA!
SNAP OUT OF IT, MAN!
RUSTLE
SHIVER

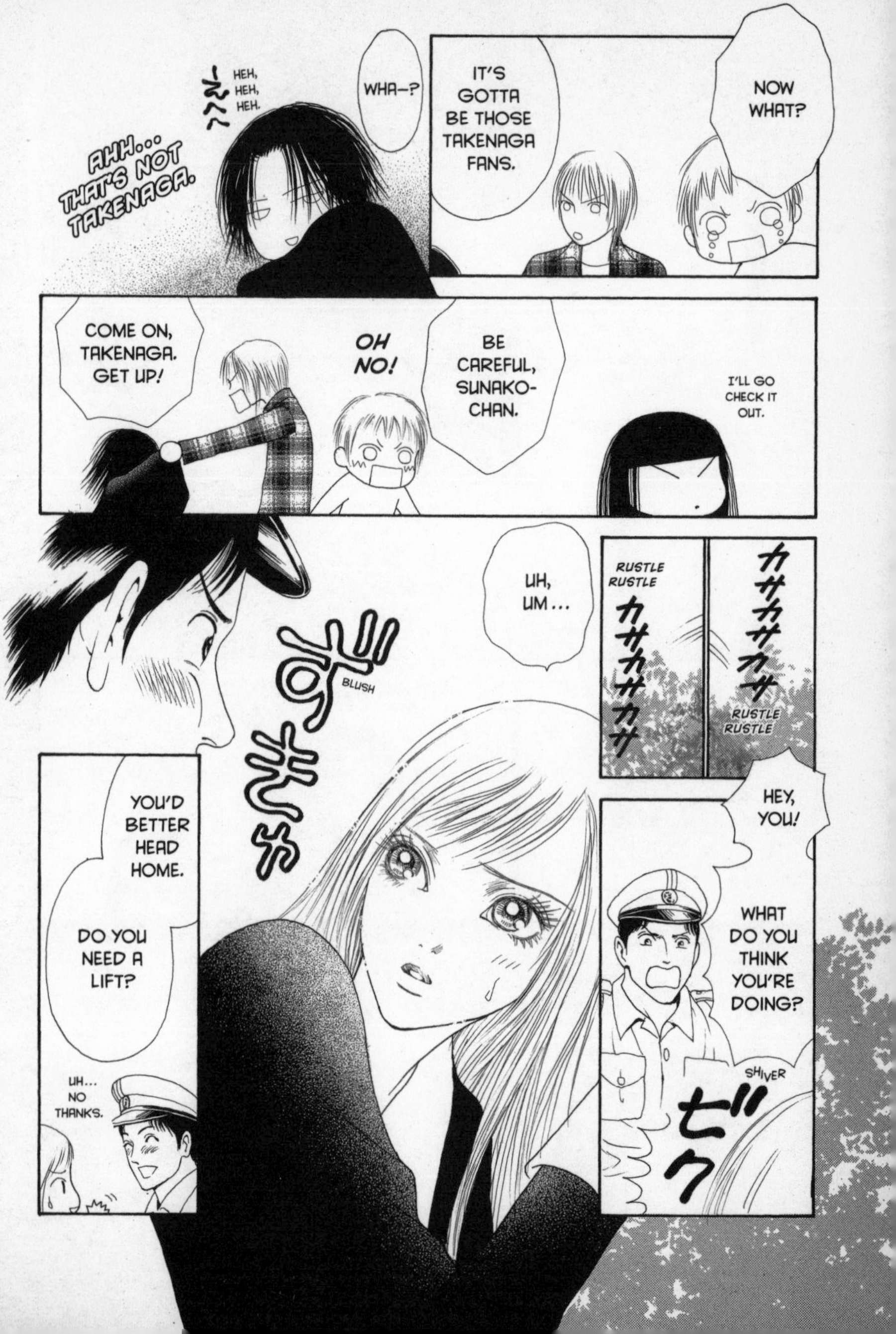
NOW WHAT?
IT'S GOTTA BE THOSE TAKENAGA FANS.
WHA—?
HEH, HEH, HEH.
AHH... THAT'S NOT TAKENAGA.
I'LL GO CHECK IT OUT.
BE CAREFUL, SUNAKO-CHAN.
OH NO!
COME ON, TAKENAGA. GET UP!
RUSTLE RUSTLE
RUSTLE RUSTLE
HEY, YOU!
WHAT DO YOU THINK YOU'RE DOING?
SHIVER
UH, UM...
BLUSH
YOU'D BETTER HEAD HOME.
DO YOU NEED A LIFT?
UH... NO THANKS.

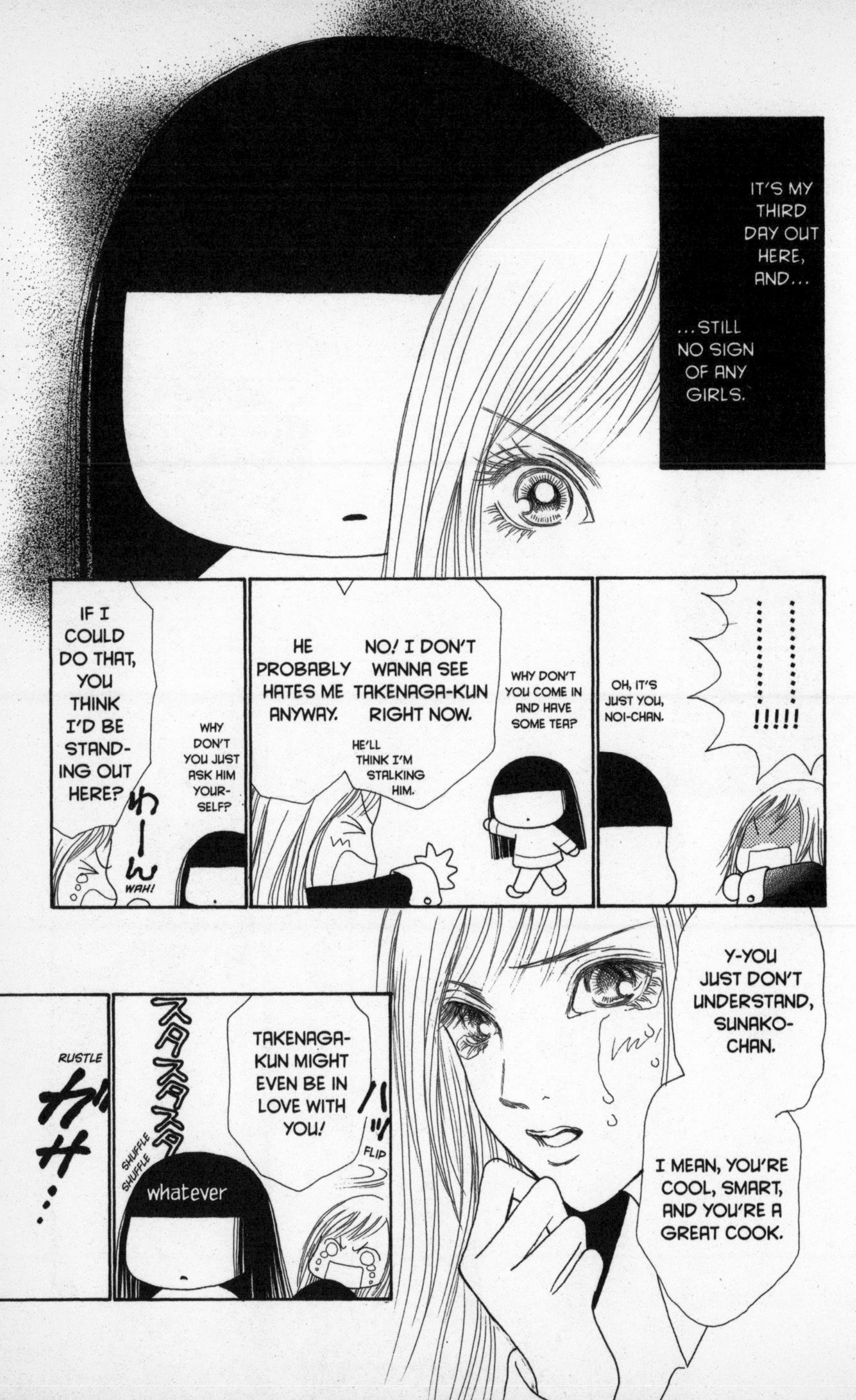
IT'S MY THIRD DAY OUT HERE, AND...
...STILL NO SIGN OF ANY GIRLS.
!!!!!
OH, IT'S JUST YOU, NOI-CHAN.
WHY DON'T YOU COME IN AND HAVE SOME TEA?
NO! I DON'T WANNA SEE TAKENAGA-KUN RIGHT NOW.
HE PROBABLY HATES ME ANYWAY.
HE'LL THINK I'M STALKING HIM.
WHY DON'T YOU JUST ASK HIM YOURSELF?
IF I COULD DO THAT, YOU THINK I'D BE STANDING OUT HERE?
わーん
WAH!
Y-YOU JUST DON'T UNDERSTAND, SUNAKO-CHAN.
I MEAN, YOU'RE COOL, SMART, AND YOU'RE A GREAT COOK.
TAKENAGA-KUN MIGHT EVEN BE IN LOVE WITH YOU!
FLIP
スタスタスタ
SHUFFLE SHUFFLE
whatever
ガサ…
RUSTLE

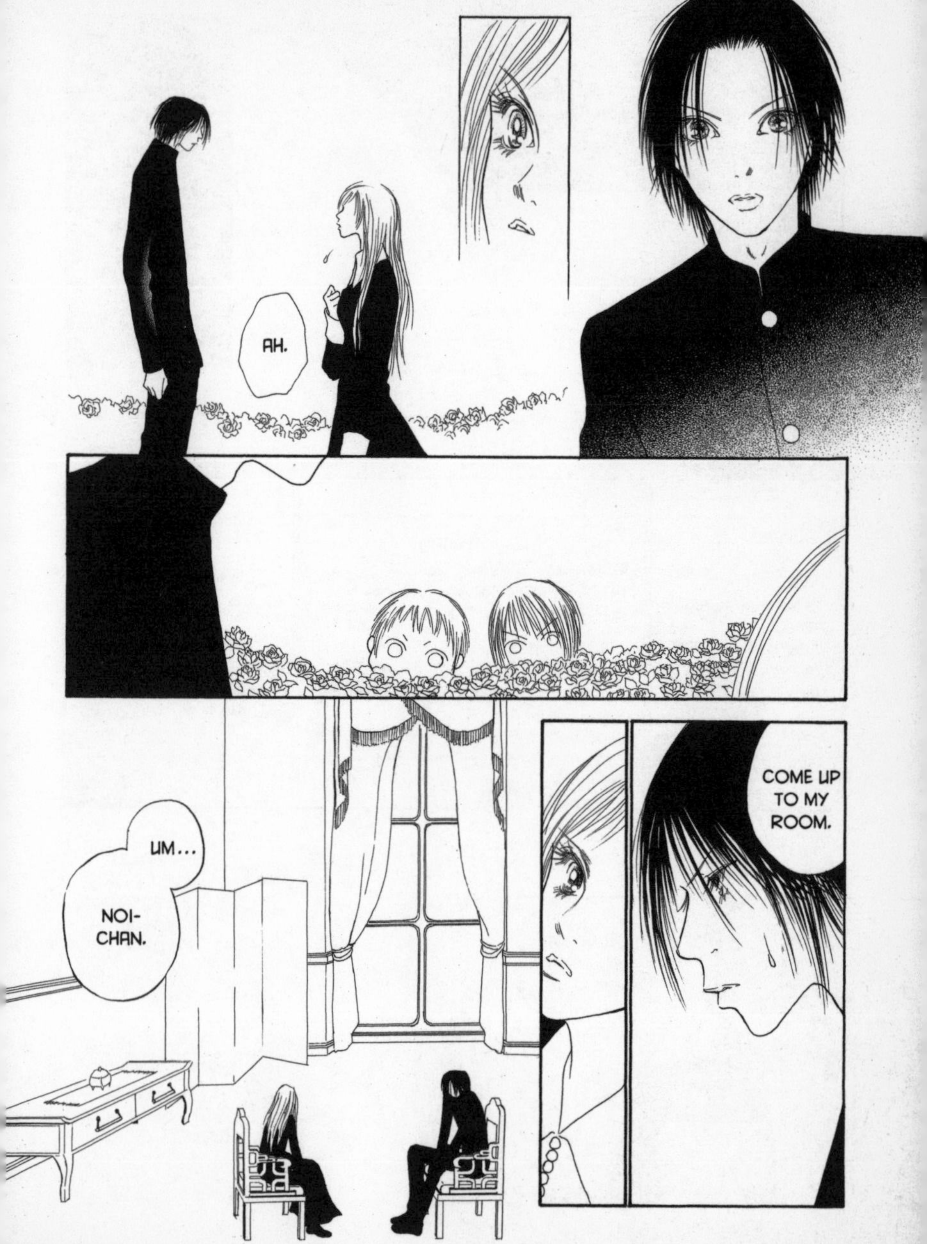
AH.
COME UP TO MY ROOM.
UM...
NOI-CHAN.

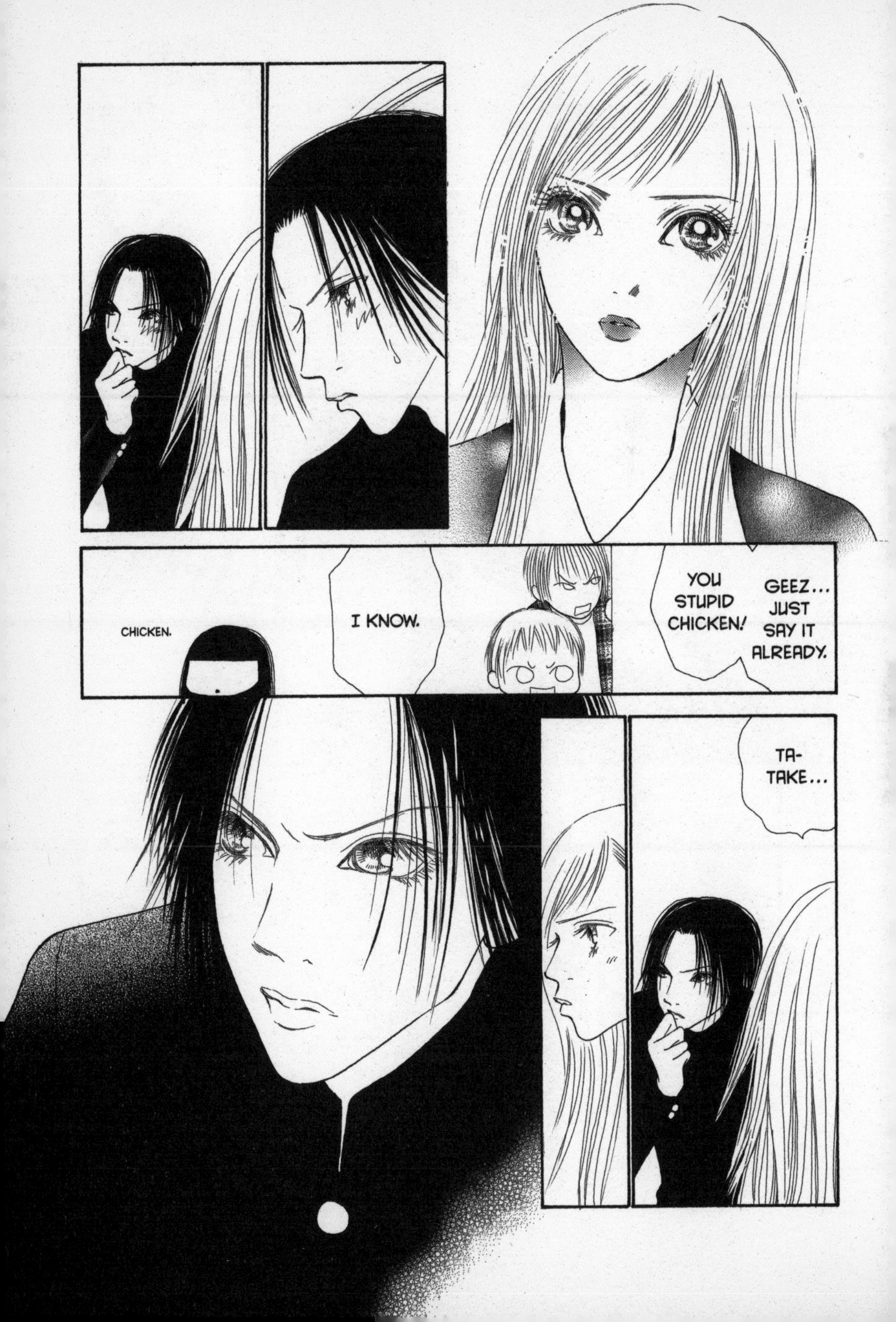
GEEZ... JUST SAY IT ALREADY.
YOU STUPID CHICKEN!
I KNOW.
CHICKEN.
TA-TAKE...

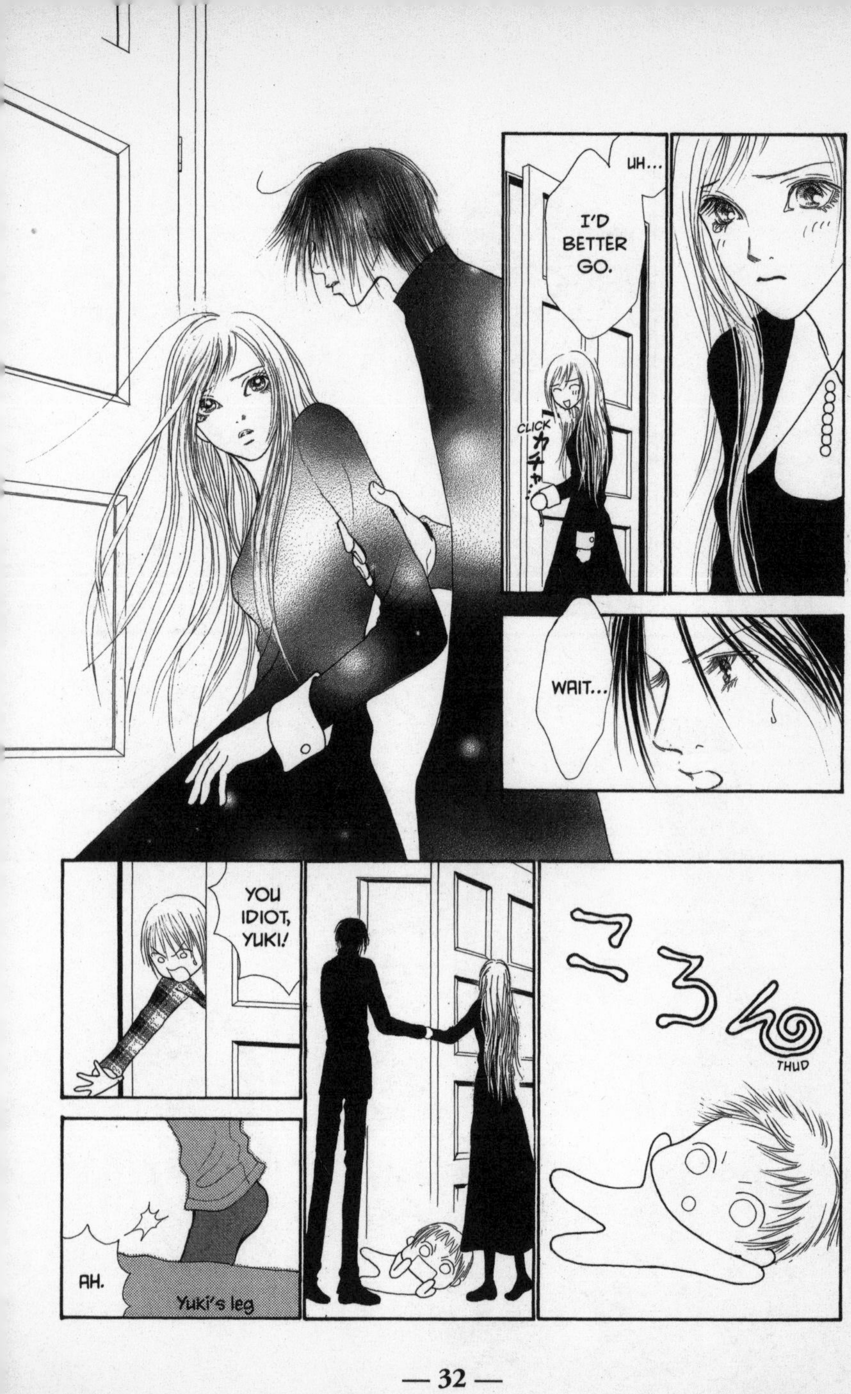
UH...
I'D BETTER GO.
CLICK
カチャ…
WAIT...
ころん
THUD
YOU IDIOT, YUKI!
AH.
Yuki's leg

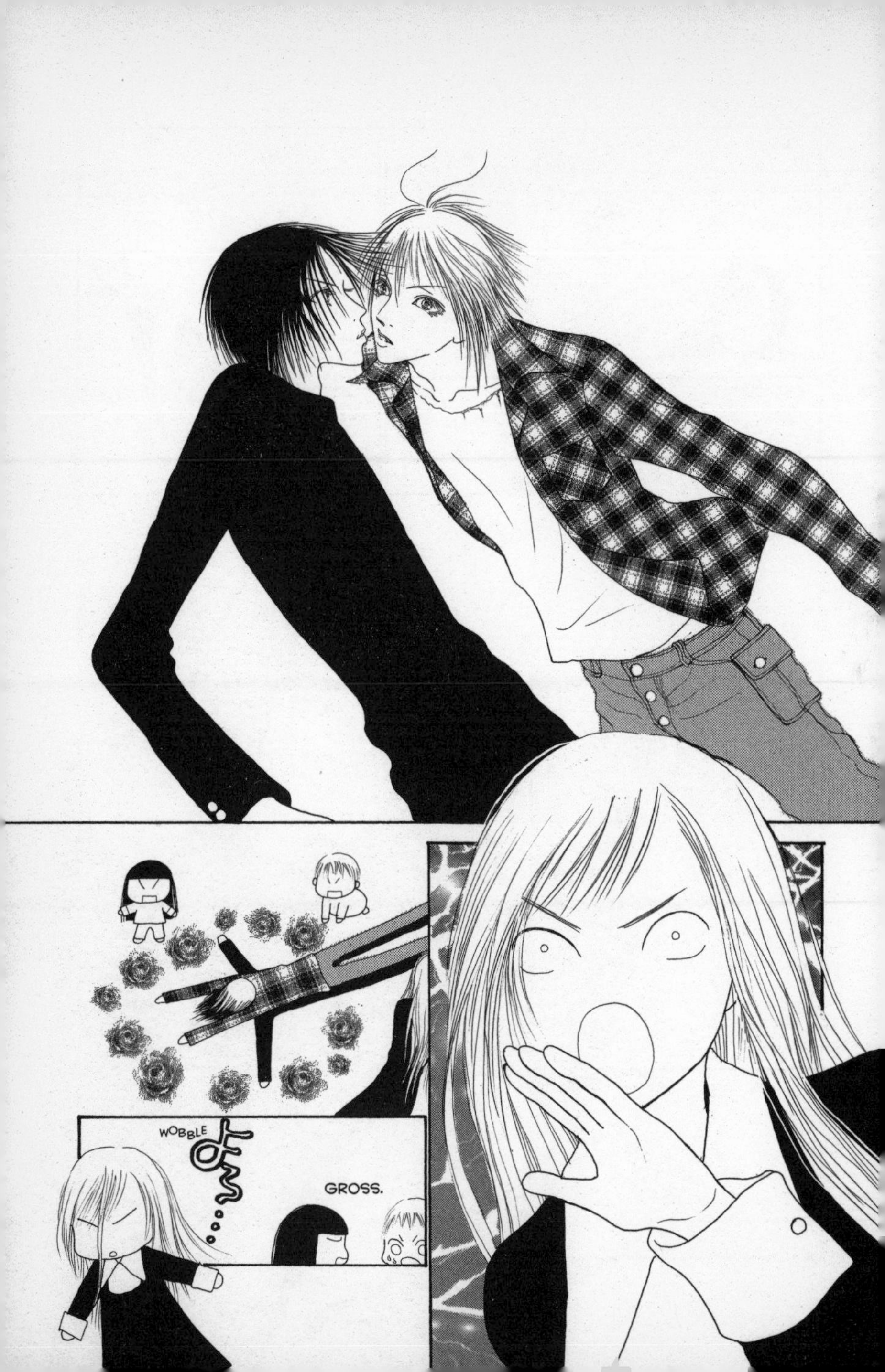
WOBBLE
GROSS.

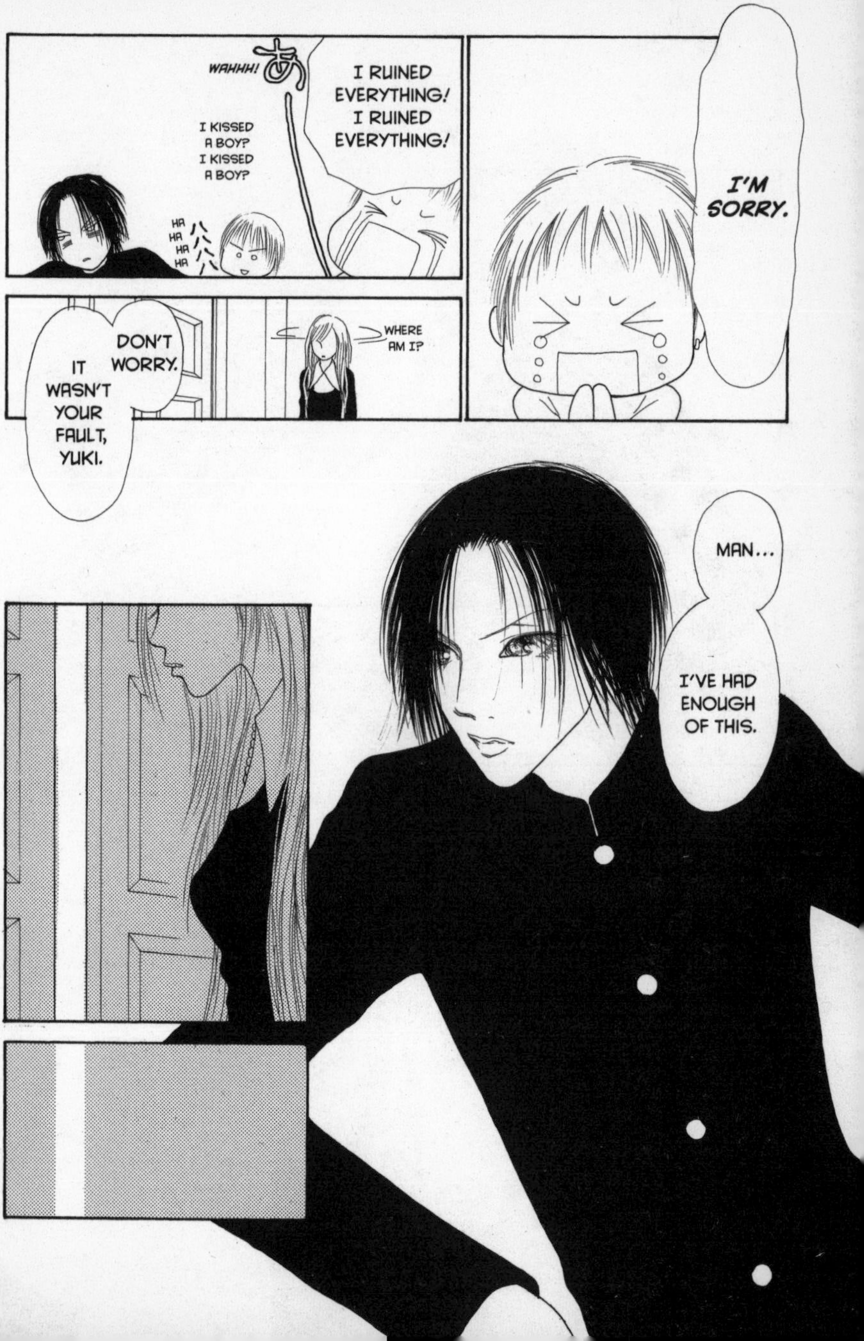
I'M SORRY.
I RUINED EVERYTHING! I RUINED EVERYTHING!
あ
WAHHH!
I KISSED A BOY? I KISSED A BOY?
HA HA HA HA
WHERE AM I?
DON'T WORRY.
IT WASN'T YOUR FAULT, YUKI.
MAN...
I'VE HAD ENOUGH OF THIS.

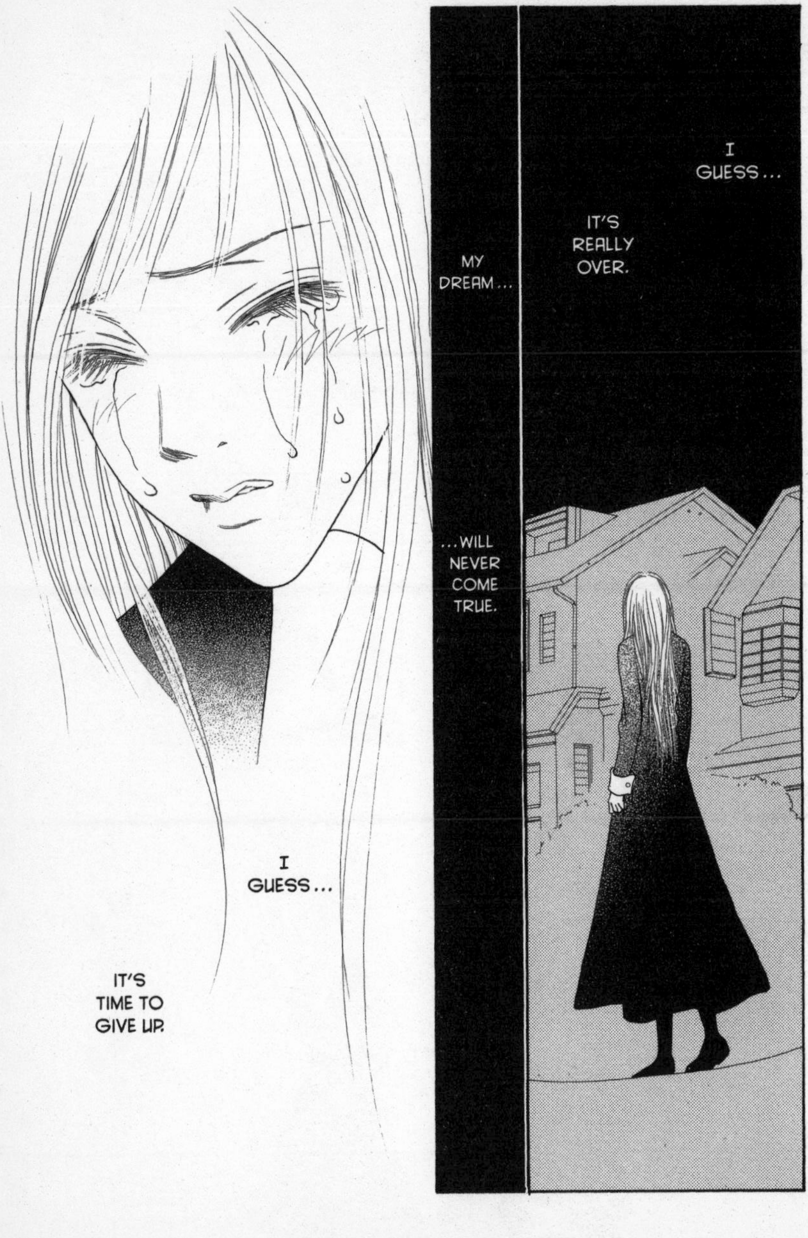
I GUESS...
IT'S REALLY OVER.
MY DREAM...
...WILL NEVER COME TRUE.
I GUESS...
IT'S TIME TO GIVE UP.

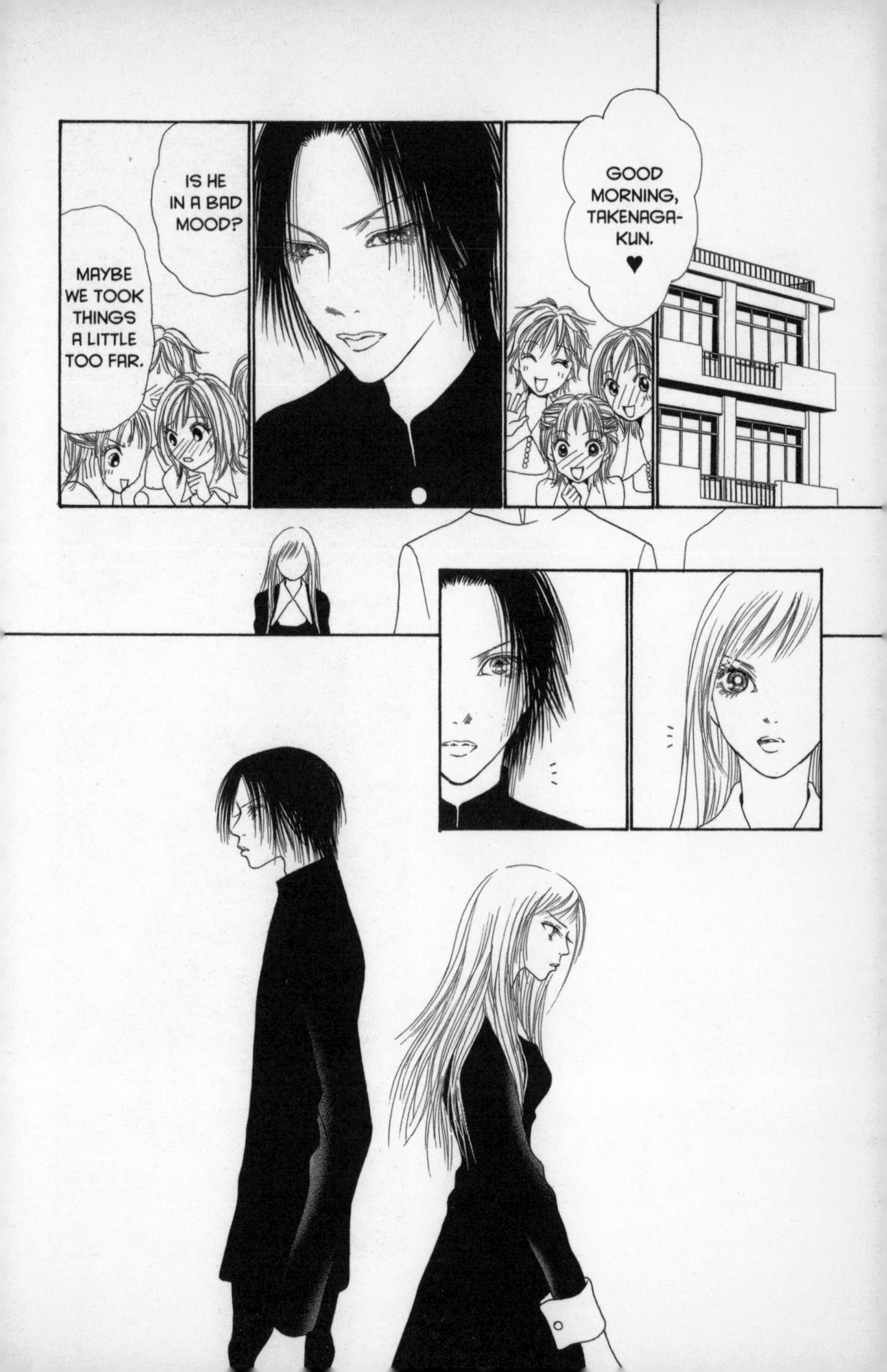
GOOD MORNING, TAKENAGA-KUN. ♥
IS HE IN A BAD MOOD?
MAYBE WE TOOK THINGS A LITTLE TOO FAR.

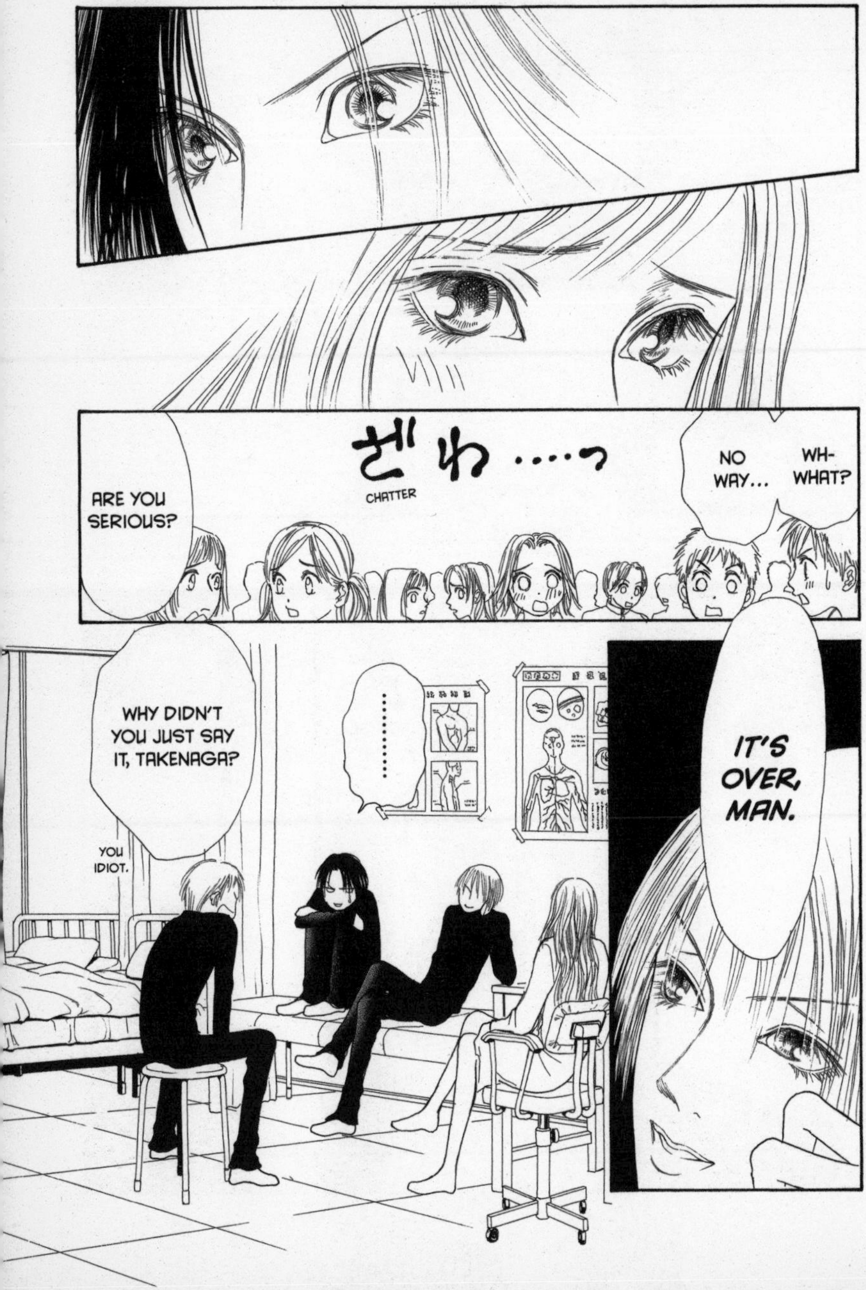
WH-WHAT?
NO WAY...
ざわ…っ
CHATTER
ARE YOU SERIOUS?
IT'S OVER, MAN.
......
WHY DIDN'T YOU JUST SAY IT, TAKENAGA?
YOU IDIOT.

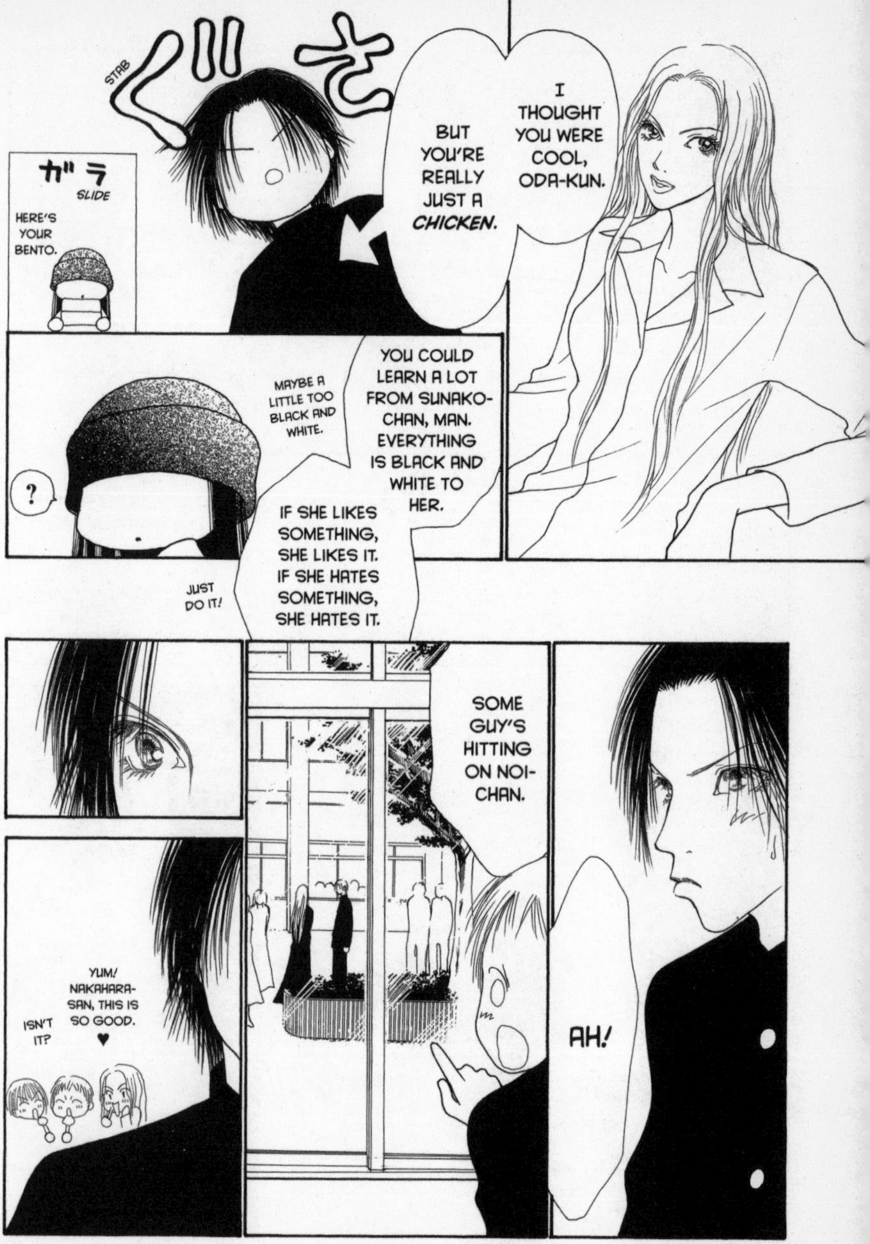
I THOUGHT YOU WERE COOL, ODA-KUN.
BUT YOU'RE REALLY JUST A *CHICKEN*.
STAB
ガラ
SLIDE
HERE'S YOUR BENTO.
YOU COULD LEARN A LOT FROM SUNAKO-CHAN, MAN. EVERYTHING IS BLACK AND WHITE TO HER.
MAYBE A LITTLE TOO BLACK AND WHITE.
?
IF SHE LIKES SOMETHING, SHE LIKES IT. IF SHE HATES SOMETHING, SHE HATES IT.
JUST DO IT!
SOME GUY'S HITTING ON NOI-CHAN.
AH!
YUM! NAKAHARA-SAN, THIS IS SO GOOD. ♥
ISN'T IT?

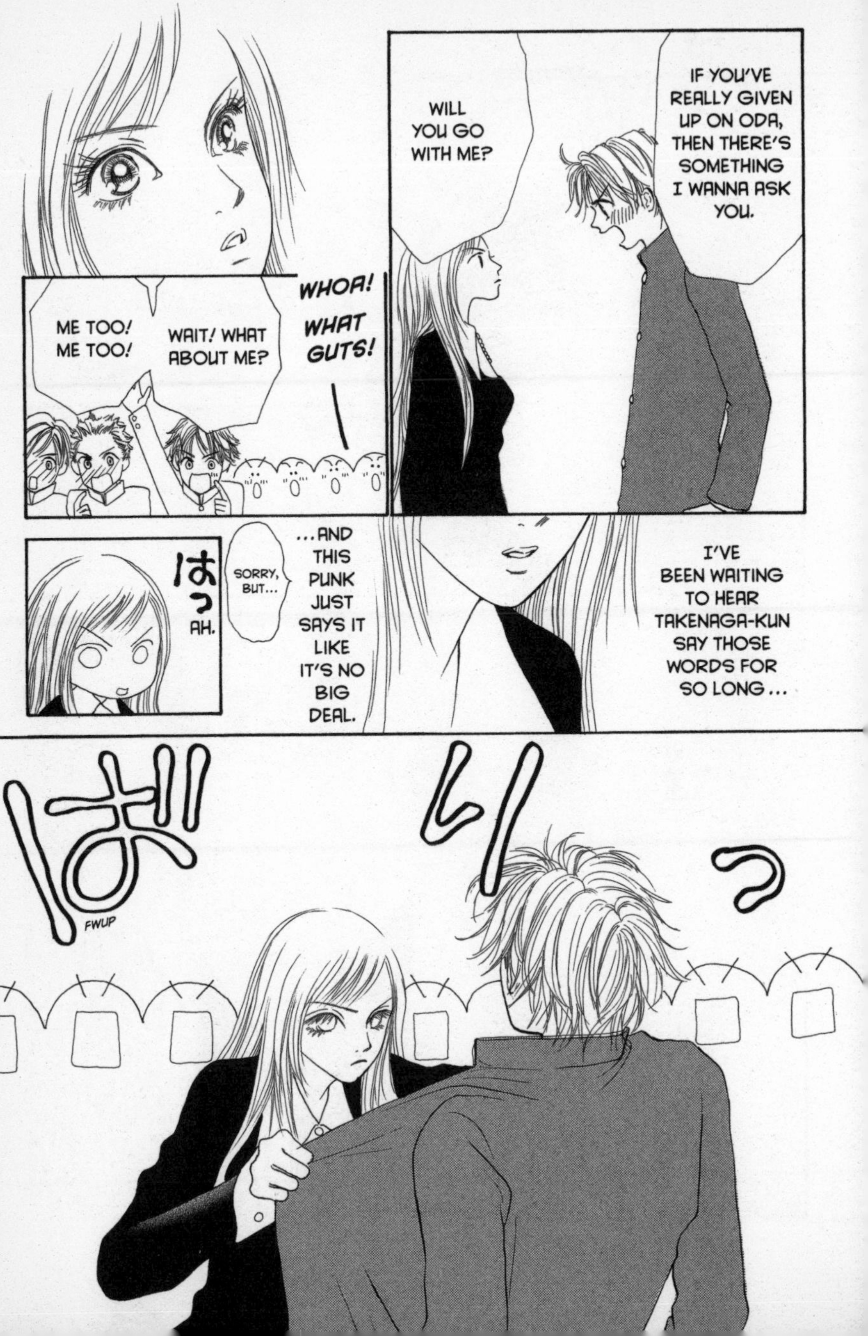
IF YOU'VE REALLY GIVEN UP ON ODA, THEN THERE'S SOMETHING I WANNA ASK YOU.
WILL YOU GO WITH ME?
WHOA! WHAT GUTS!
WAIT! WHAT ABOUT ME?
ME TOO! ME TOO!
I'VE BEEN WAITING TO HEAR TAKENAGA-KUN SAY THOSE WORDS FOR SO LONG...
...AND THIS PUNK JUST SAYS IT LIKE IT'S NO BIG DEAL.
SORRY, BUT...
はっ
AH.
ばしっ
FWUP

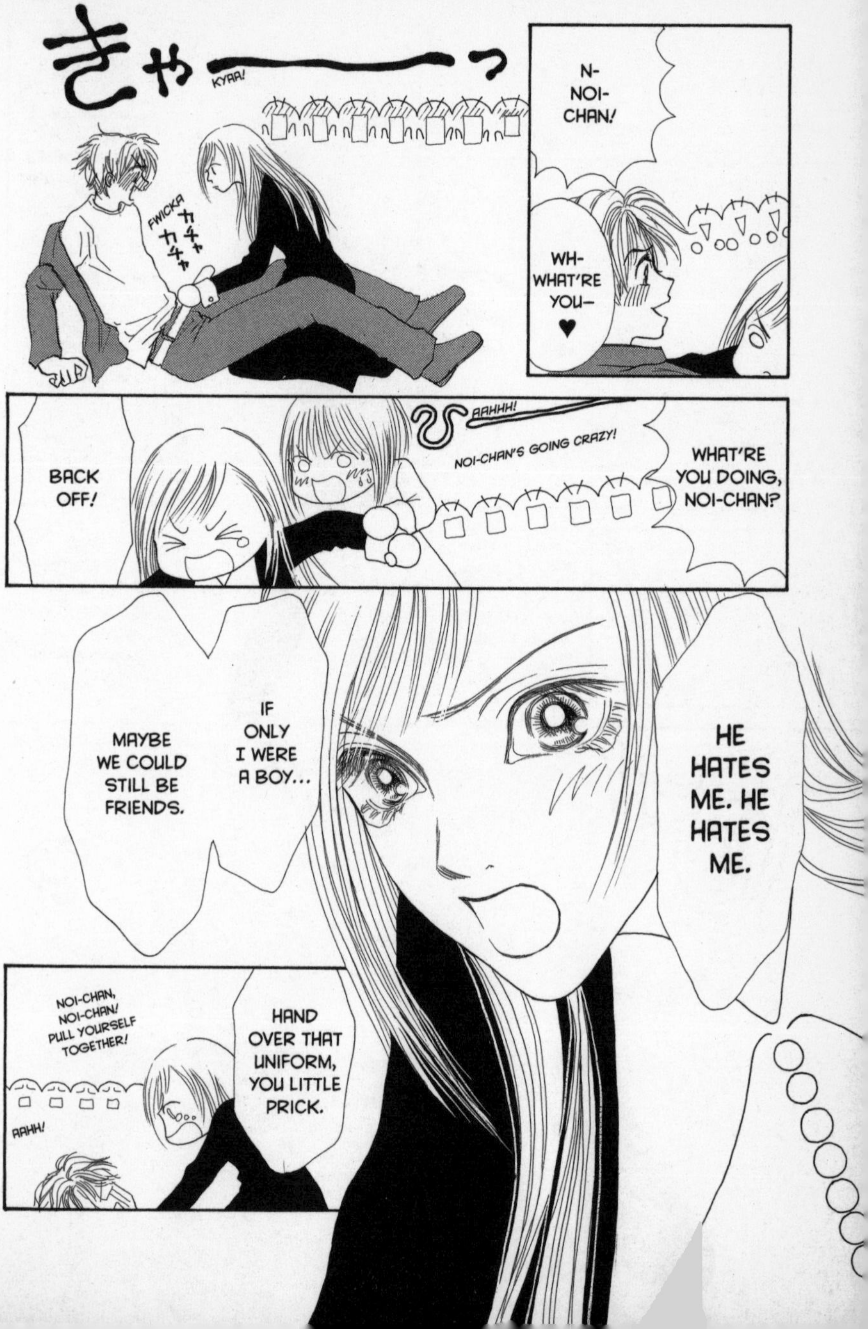
N-NOI-CHAN!
WH-WHAT'RE YOU—♥
きゃーーっ
KYAA!
FWICKA
カチャカチャ
WHAT'RE YOU DOING, NOI-CHAN?
NOI-CHAN'S GOING CRAZY!
AAHHH!
BACK OFF!
HE HATES ME. HE HATES ME.
IF ONLY I WERE A BOY...
MAYBE WE COULD STILL BE FRIENDS.
HAND OVER THAT UNIFORM, YOU LITTLE PRICK.
NOI-CHAN, NOI-CHAN! PULL YOURSELF TOGETHER!
AAHH!

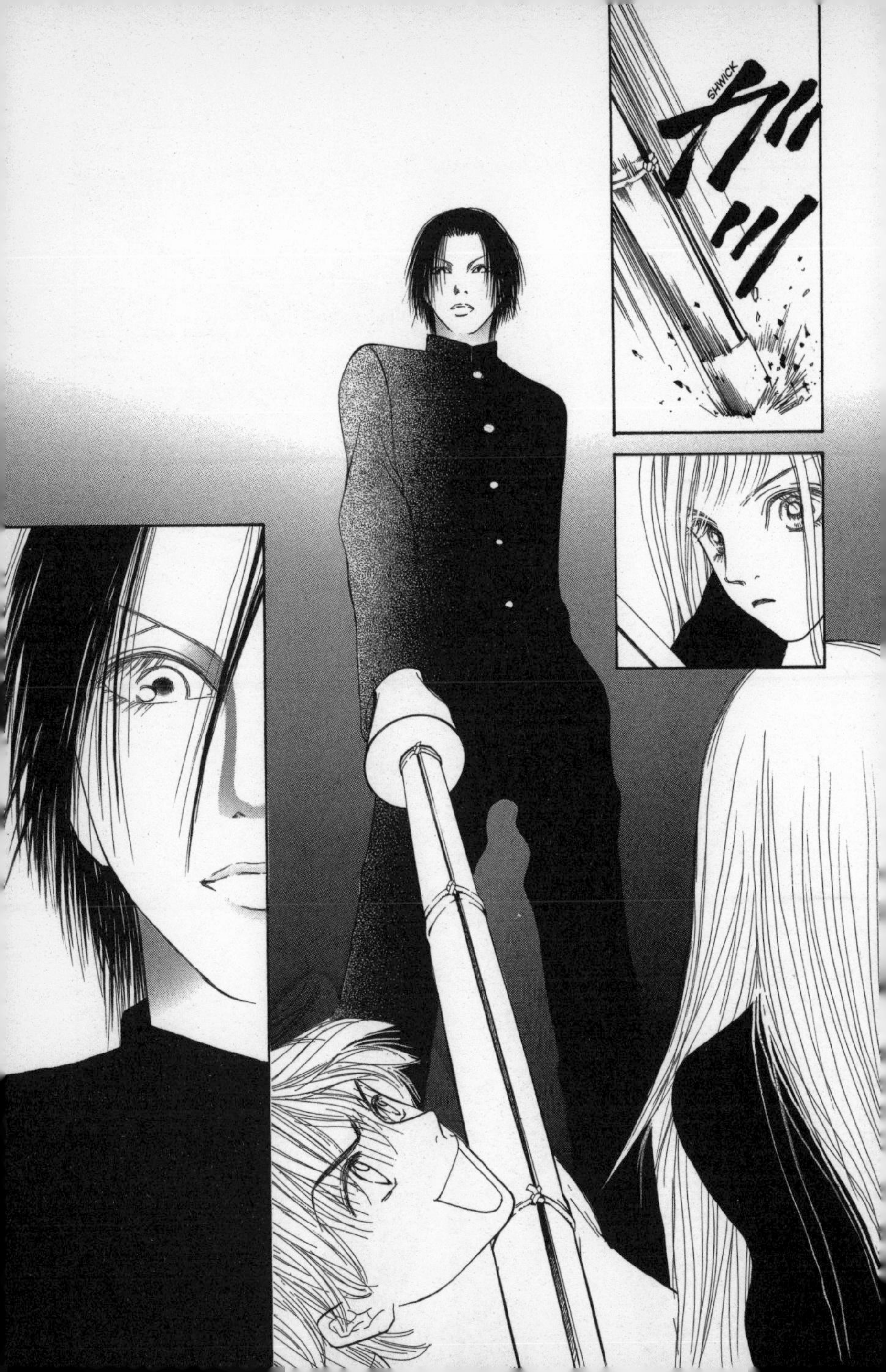
SHWICK

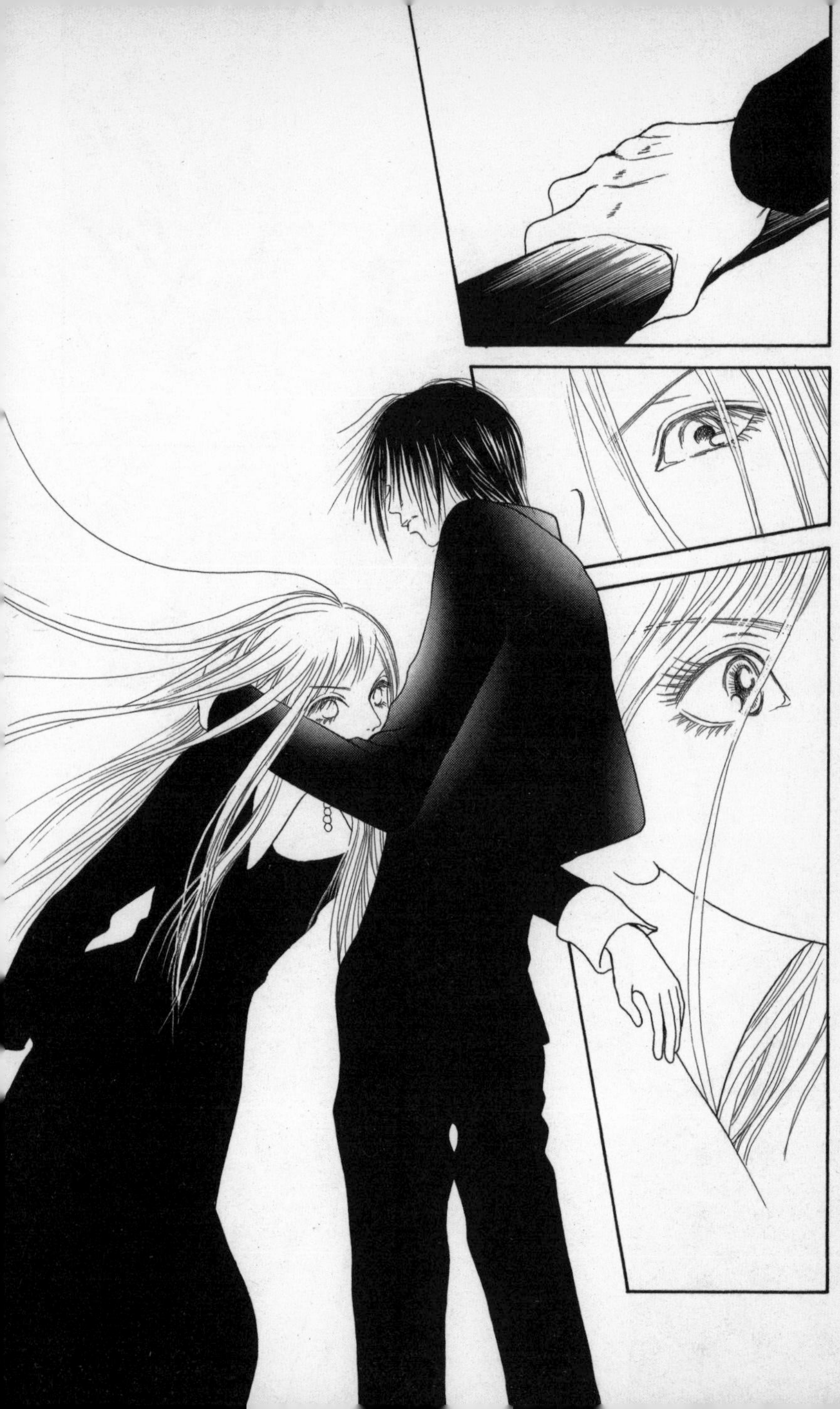

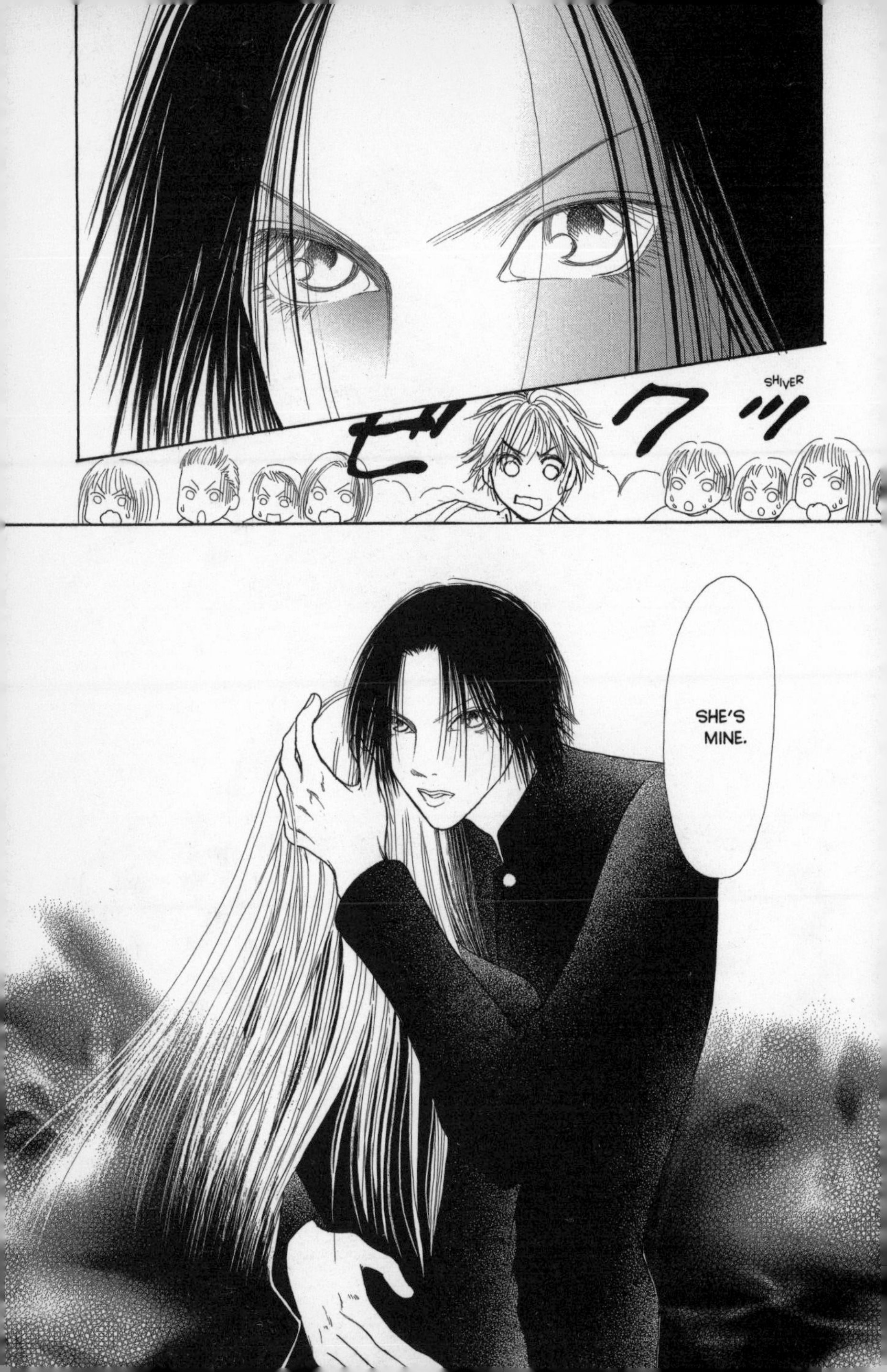
SHIVER
ビクッ
SHE'S MINE.

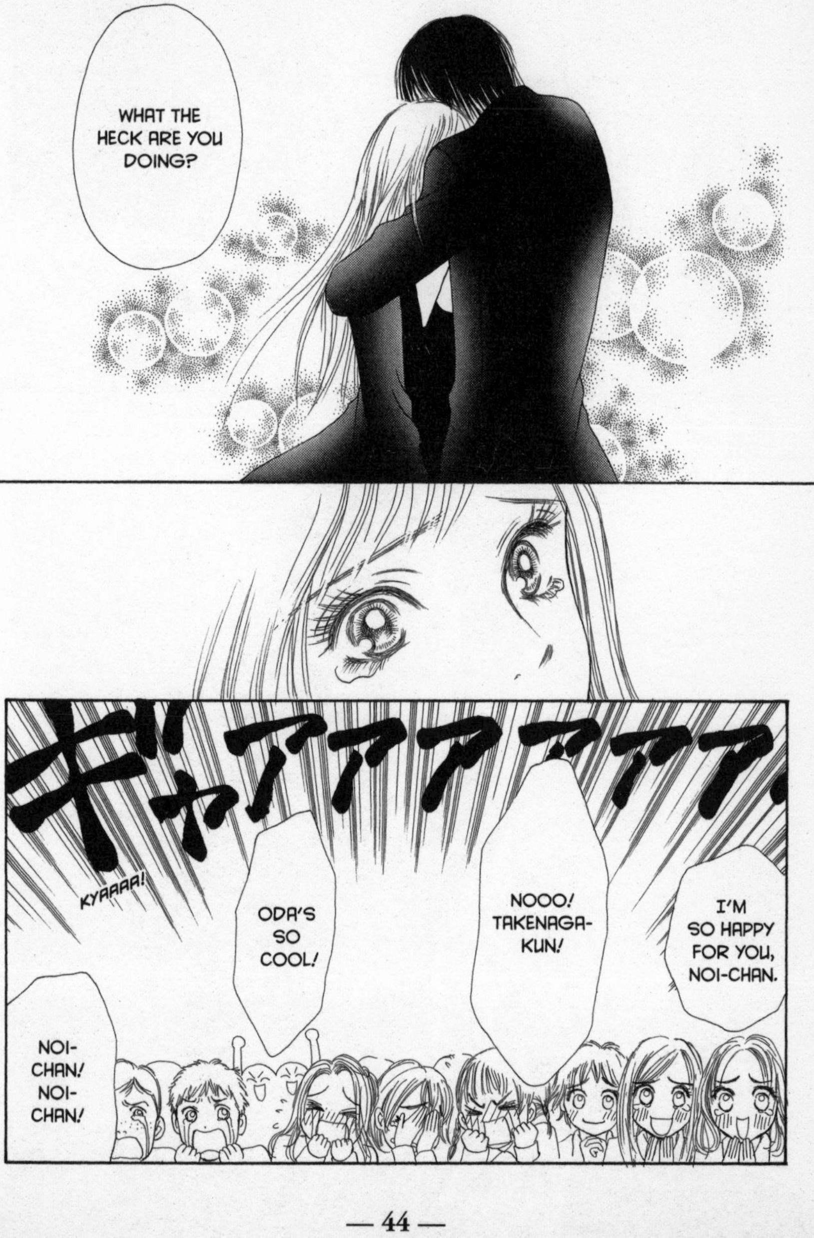
WHAT THE HECK ARE YOU DOING?
ギャアアアアア
I'M SO HAPPY FOR YOU, NOI-CHAN.
NOOO! TAKENAGA-KUN!
ODA'S SO COOL!
KYAAAA!
NOI-CHAN! NOI-CHAN!

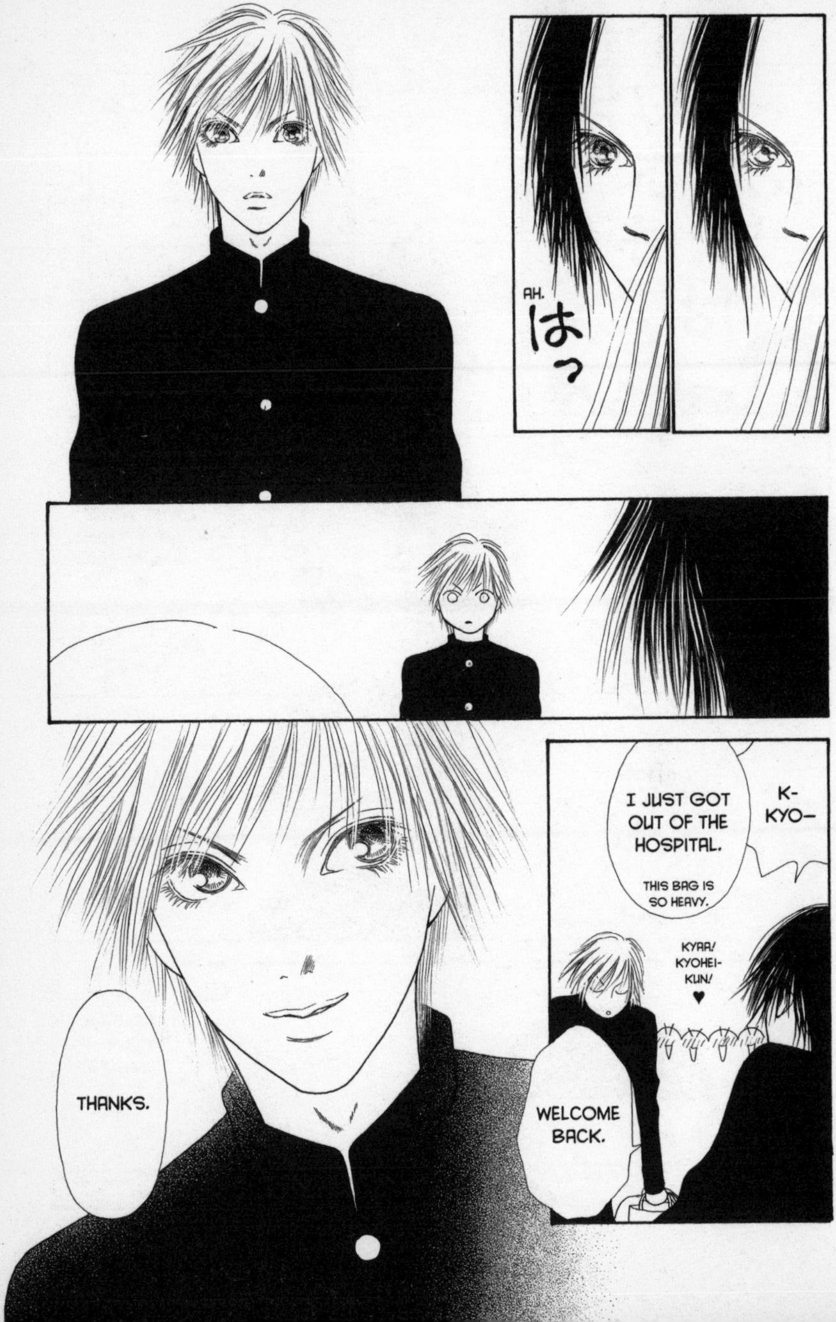

AH.
はっ
K-KYO—
I JUST GOT OUT OF THE HOSPITAL.
THIS BAG IS SO HEAVY.
KYAA! KYOHEI-KUN! ♥
WELCOME BACK.
THANKS.

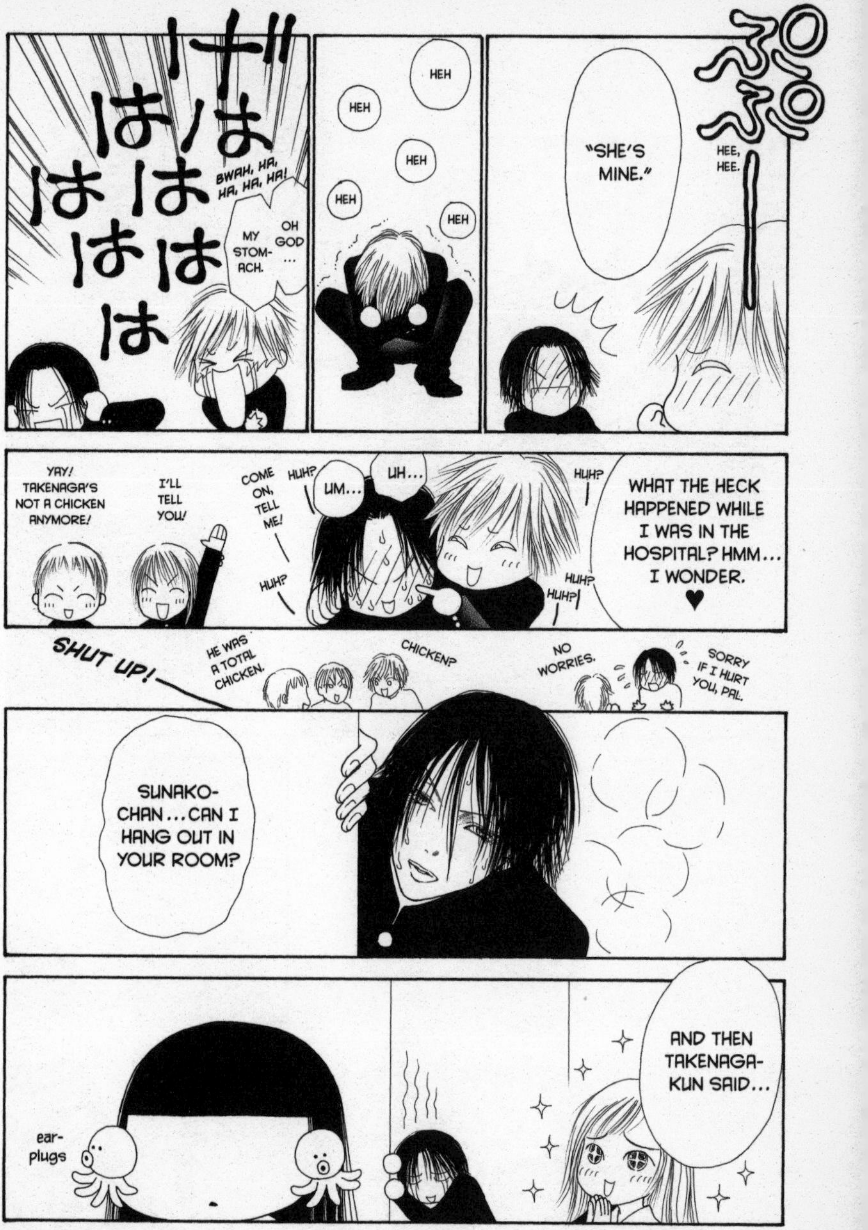
HEE, HEE.
"SHE'S MINE."
HEH
HEH
HEH
HEH
HEH
OH GOD ...
MY STOM-ACH.
BWAH, HA, HA, HA, HA!
WHAT THE HECK HAPPENED WHILE I WAS IN THE HOSPITAL? HMM... I WONDER. ♥
HUH?
HUH?
HUH?
UH...
UM...
HUH?
COME ON, TELL ME!
HUH?
I'LL TELL YOU!
YAY! TAKENAGA'S NOT A CHICKEN ANYMORE!
SORRY IF I HURT YOU, PAL.
NO WORRIES.
CHICKEN?
HE WAS A TOTAL CHICKEN.
SHUT UP!
SUNAKO-CHAN... CAN I HANG OUT IN YOUR ROOM?
AND THEN TAKENAGA-KUN SAID...
ear-plugs

Chapter 32

Queen of Horror: Battle for the Crown

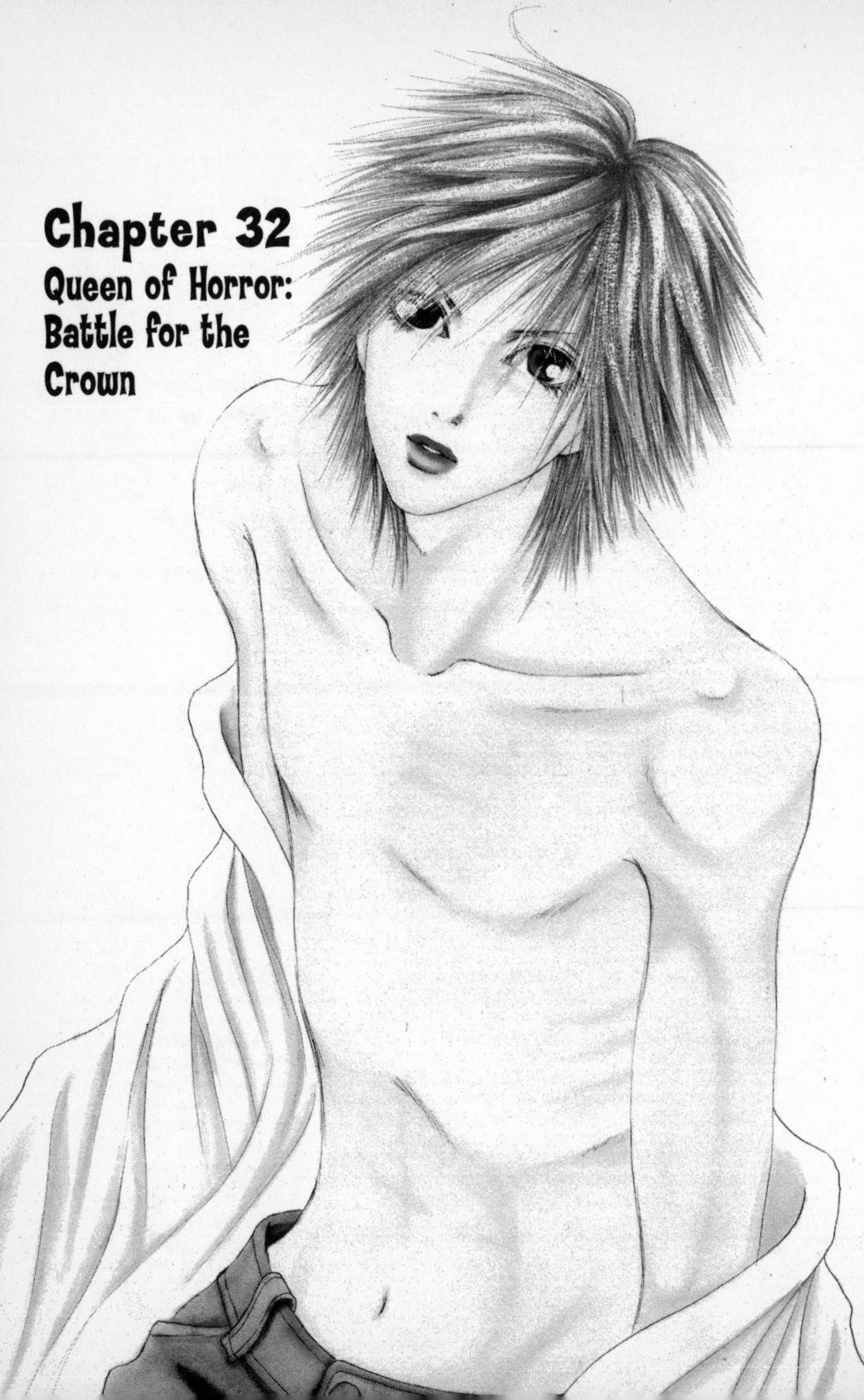

THINGS THAT MAKE ME HAPPY ♥

I FINALLY GOT TO MEET MAYUMI KURATA-SAMA, AUTHOR OF THE MANGA *DAMEN'S WALKER* ♥.

I MET YOOKO-SAMA TOO ♥ (AT THE KODANSHA PARTY).

WE ALL TOOK A PHOTO TOGETHER.

KURATA-SAMA

ME

YOOKO-SAMA.

THIS ACTUALLY LOOKS JUST LIKE THE PHOTO.

I'M SMALL SO MY FACE LOOKS REALLY BIG.

THOSE TWO WERE BOTH SO PRETTY. ♥♥♥

KURATA IS A REALLY SMART AND BEAUTIFUL GIRL, AT LEAST THAT'S THE IMPRESSION SHE MADE ON ME. SHE'S REALLY FUN TO TALK TO. ♥ I WISH WE COULD'VE TALKED EVEN LONGER.

YOOKO-SAN WAS SO CUTE. ♥ SHE WAS SO SKINNY THAT IT MADE ME JEALOUS. SHE WAS BUSY TALKING TO OTHER PEOPLE SO WE REALLY ONLY SAID HI, BUT...

I TOTALLY RELATE TO *DAMEN'S WALKER*, AND SO DO A LOT OF PEOPLE I KNOW.

IN HER BOOKS SHE ALWAYS WRITES THAT SHE'S FAT SO I WAS THINKING SHE'D LOOK JUST LIKE ME, BUT... ACTUALLY I'M WAY FATTER.

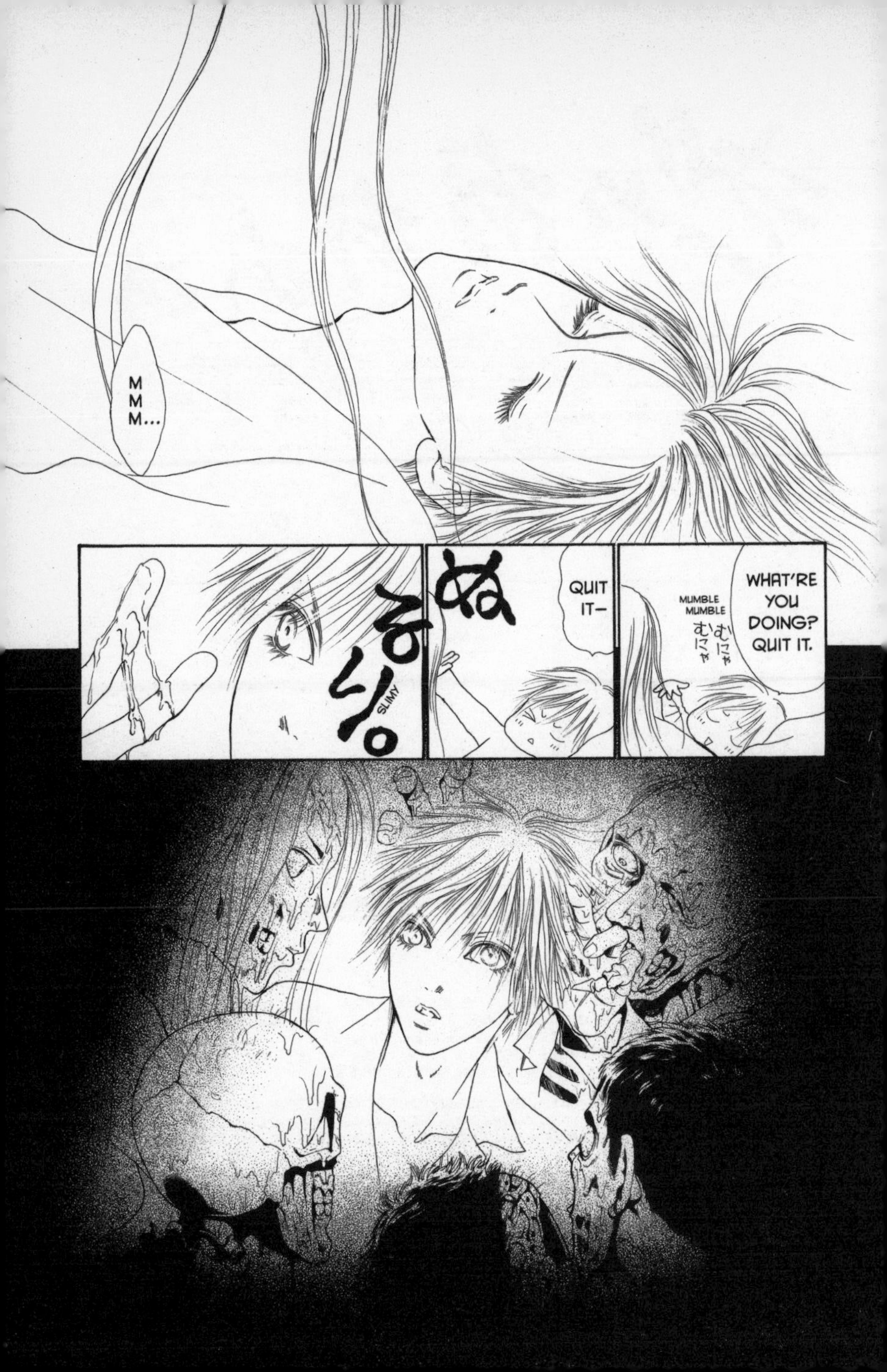
MMM...
WHAT'RE YOU DOING? QUIT IT.
MUMBLE MUMBLE
むにゃむにゃ
QUIT IT—
ぬるり。
SLIMY

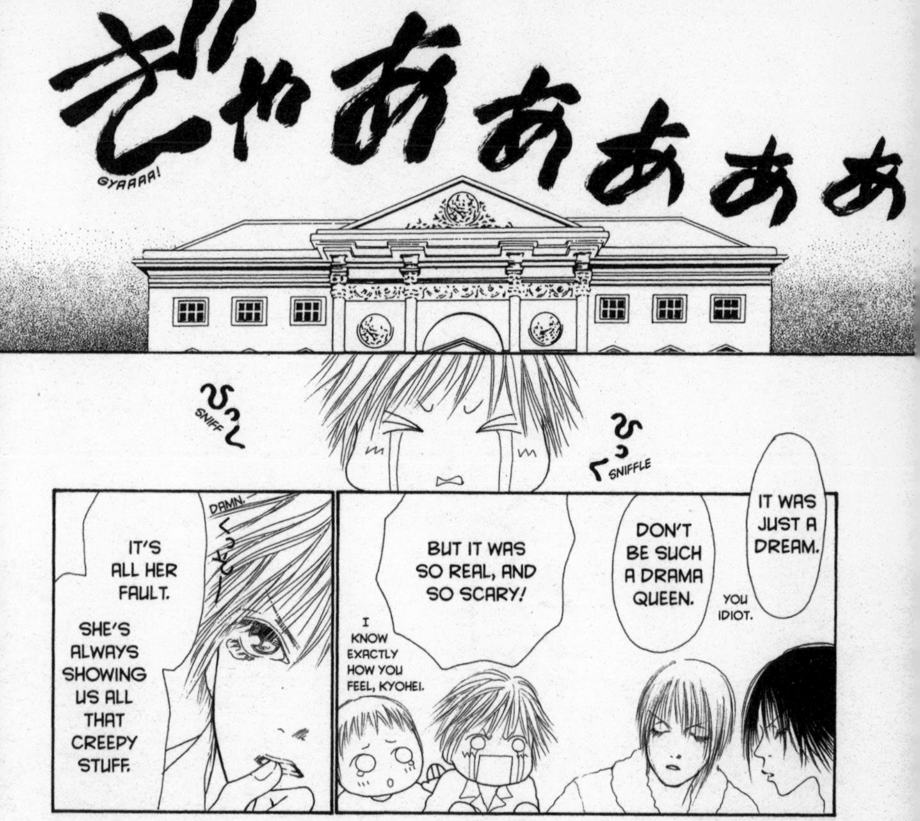
ぎゃあああああ
GYAAAAA!
ぐすっ
SNIFF
ぐすっ
SNIFFLE
IT WAS JUST A DREAM.
YOU IDIOT.
DON'T BE SUCH A DRAMA QUEEN.
BUT IT WAS SO REAL, AND SO SCARY!
I KNOW EXACTLY HOW YOU FEEL, KYOHEI.
DAMN.
IT'S ALL HER FAULT.
SHE'S ALWAYS SHOWING US ALL THAT CREEPY STUFF.

BEHIND THE SCENES

I GUESS A LOT OF PEOPLE THOUGHT THE OLD LADY IN THIS STORY WAS RELATED TO SUNAKO, BUT SHE'S NOT. SORRY FOR THE CONFUSION. THEY'RE DEFINITELY NOT RELATED.

I CAN HARDLY EVEN REMEMBER DOING THESE STORYBOARDS. MY EDITOR REJECTED THE WHOLE THING JUST A WEEK BEFORE MY DEADLINE. THE STORYBOARDS MUST'VE BEEN REALLY BAD FOR MY EDITOR TO COMPLETELY REJECT THEM. I DON'T EVEN REMEMBER ANYTHING ABOUT THOSE ORIGINAL STORYBOARDS.

MY BRAIN JUST TOTALLY OVERLOADED. IN MY MIND I WAS DANCING AROUND WITH LITTLE *FAIRIES*. KYA, HA, HA. ♥ I STARTED PLAYING WITH THE FAIRIES JUST AROUND DUSK, AND BY 3 A.M., MY STORYBOARDS WERE ALL FINISHED. IT WAS A REAL MYSTERY. THE FAIRIES MUST'VE FINISHED THEM FOR ME.

MY EDITOR, INO-SAMA, WENT TO AOMORI, AND BROUGHT ME BACK SOME DELICIOUS AOMORI SALMON ROE. I WAS EATING SALMON ROE OVER RICE EVERY DAY, THAT'S WHAT GAVE ME THE IDEA TO WRITE ABOUT IT. IT WAS SO DELICIOUS. ♥

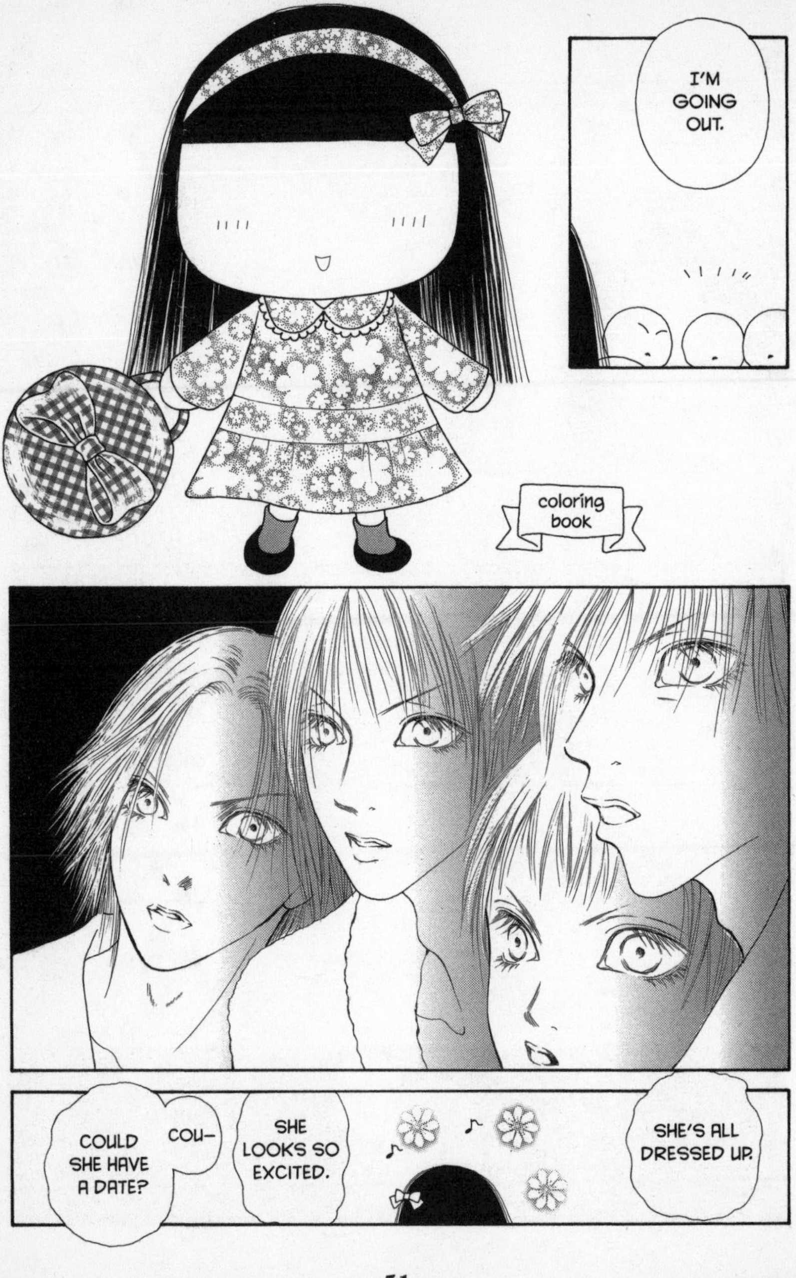
I'M GOING OUT.
coloring book
SHE'S ALL DRESSED UP.
SHE LOOKS SO EXCITED.
COU-
COULD SHE HAVE A DATE?

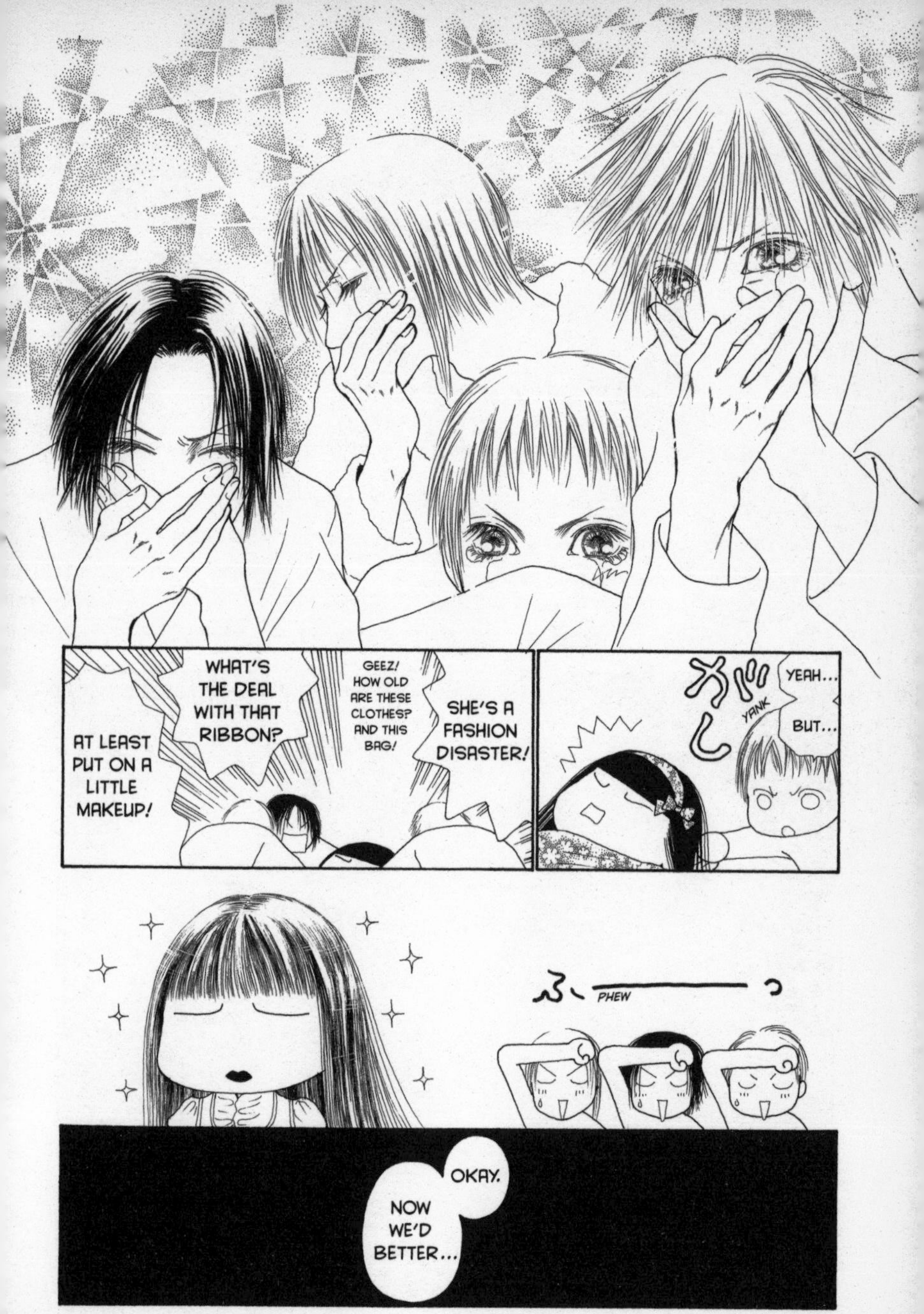
がし
YANK
YEAH... BUT...
SHE'S A FASHION DISASTER!
GEEZ! HOW OLD ARE THESE CLOTHES? AND THIS BAG!
WHAT'S THE DEAL WITH THAT RIBBON?
AT LEAST PUT ON A LITTLE MAKEUP!
ふーーっ
PHEW
OKAY.
NOW WE'D BETTER...

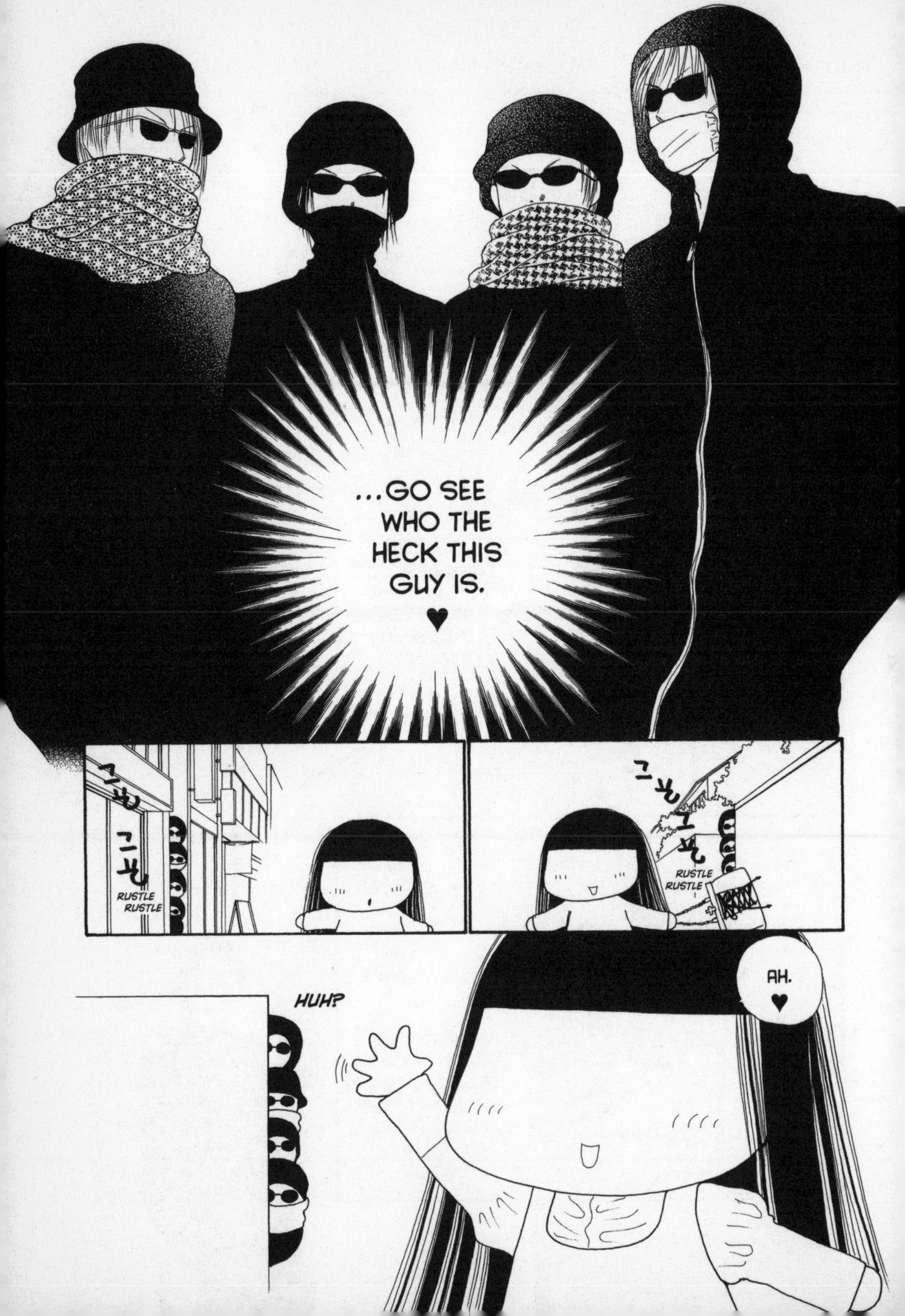
...GO SEE WHO THE HECK THIS GUY IS. ♥
RUSTLE RUSTLE
RUSTLE RUSTLE
AH. ♥
HUH?

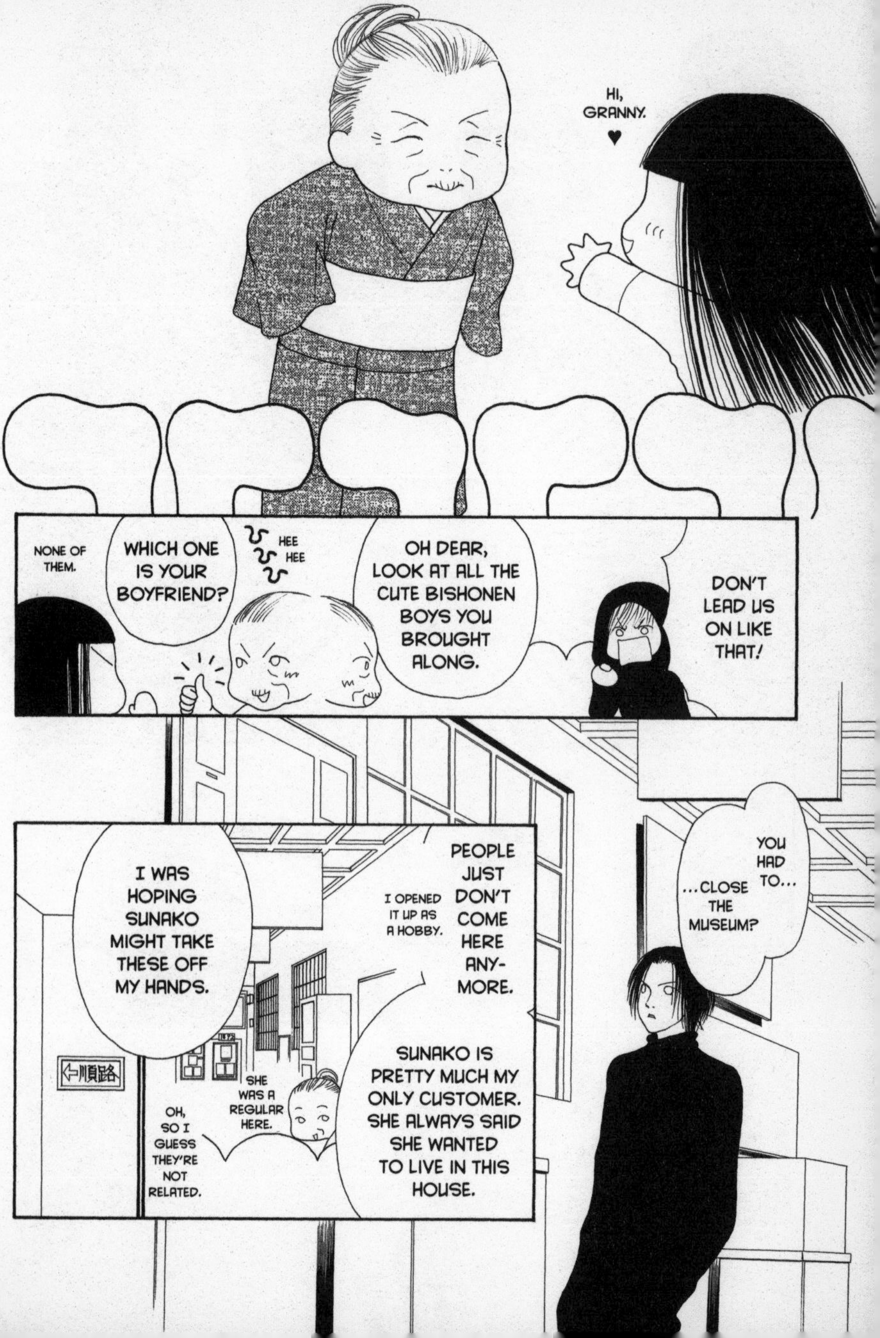
HI, GRANNY. ♥
DON'T LEAD US ON LIKE THAT!
OH DEAR, LOOK AT ALL THE CUTE BISHONEN BOYS YOU BROUGHT ALONG.
HEE HEE
WHICH ONE IS YOUR BOYFRIEND?
NONE OF THEM.
YOU HAD TO...
...CLOSE THE MUSEUM?
PEOPLE JUST DON'T COME HERE ANYMORE.
I OPENED IT UP AS A HOBBY.
I WAS HOPING SUNAKO MIGHT TAKE THESE OFF MY HANDS.
SUNAKO IS PRETTY MUCH MY ONLY CUSTOMER. SHE ALWAYS SAID SHE WANTED TO LIVE IN THIS HOUSE.
SHE WAS A REGULAR HERE.
OH, SO I GUESS THEY'RE NOT RELATED.
順路

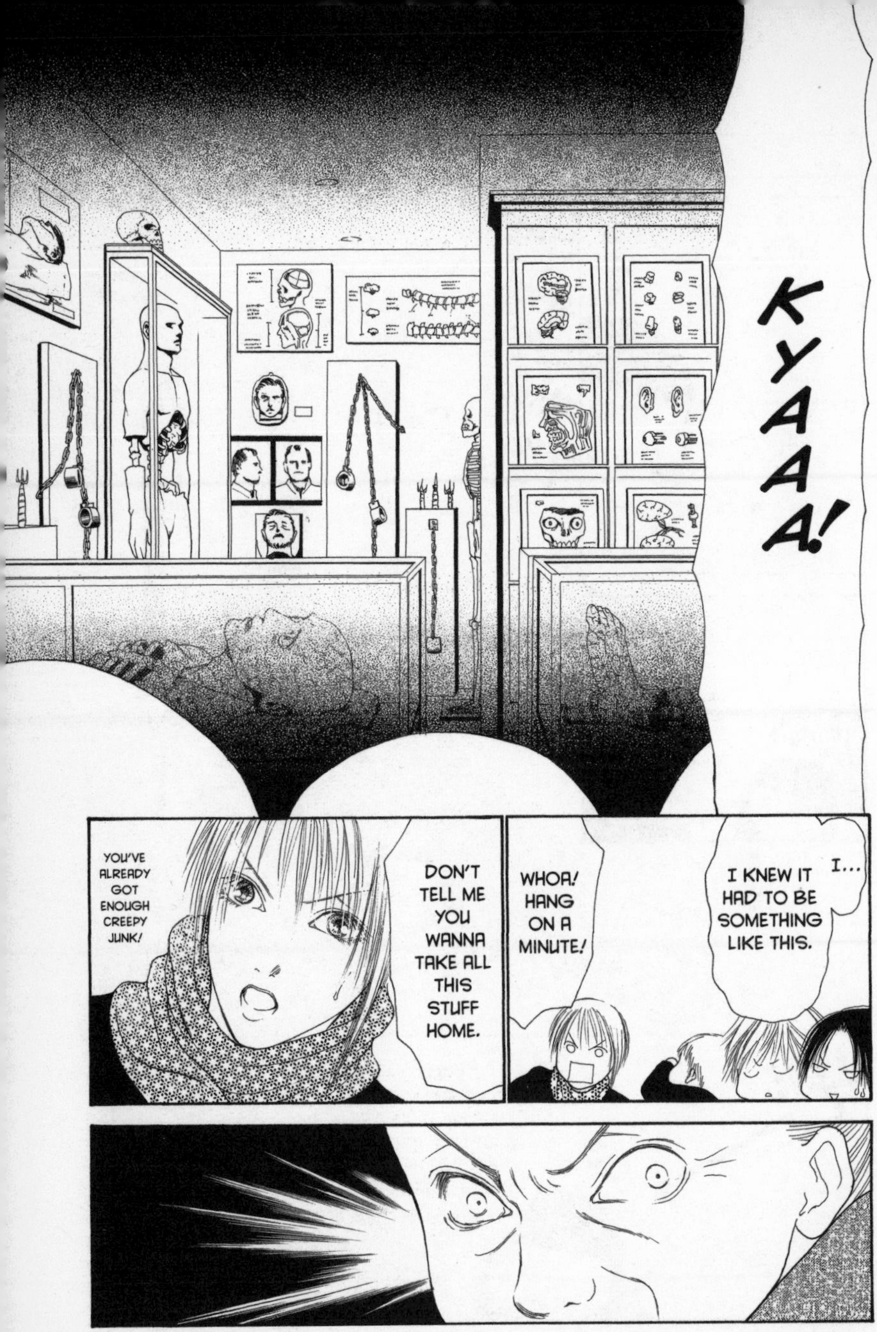
KYAAA!
I...
I KNEW IT HAD TO BE SOMETHING LIKE THIS.
WHOA! HANG ON A MINUTE!
DON'T TELL ME YOU WANNA TAKE ALL THIS STUFF HOME.
YOU'VE ALREADY GOT ENOUGH CREEPY JUNK!

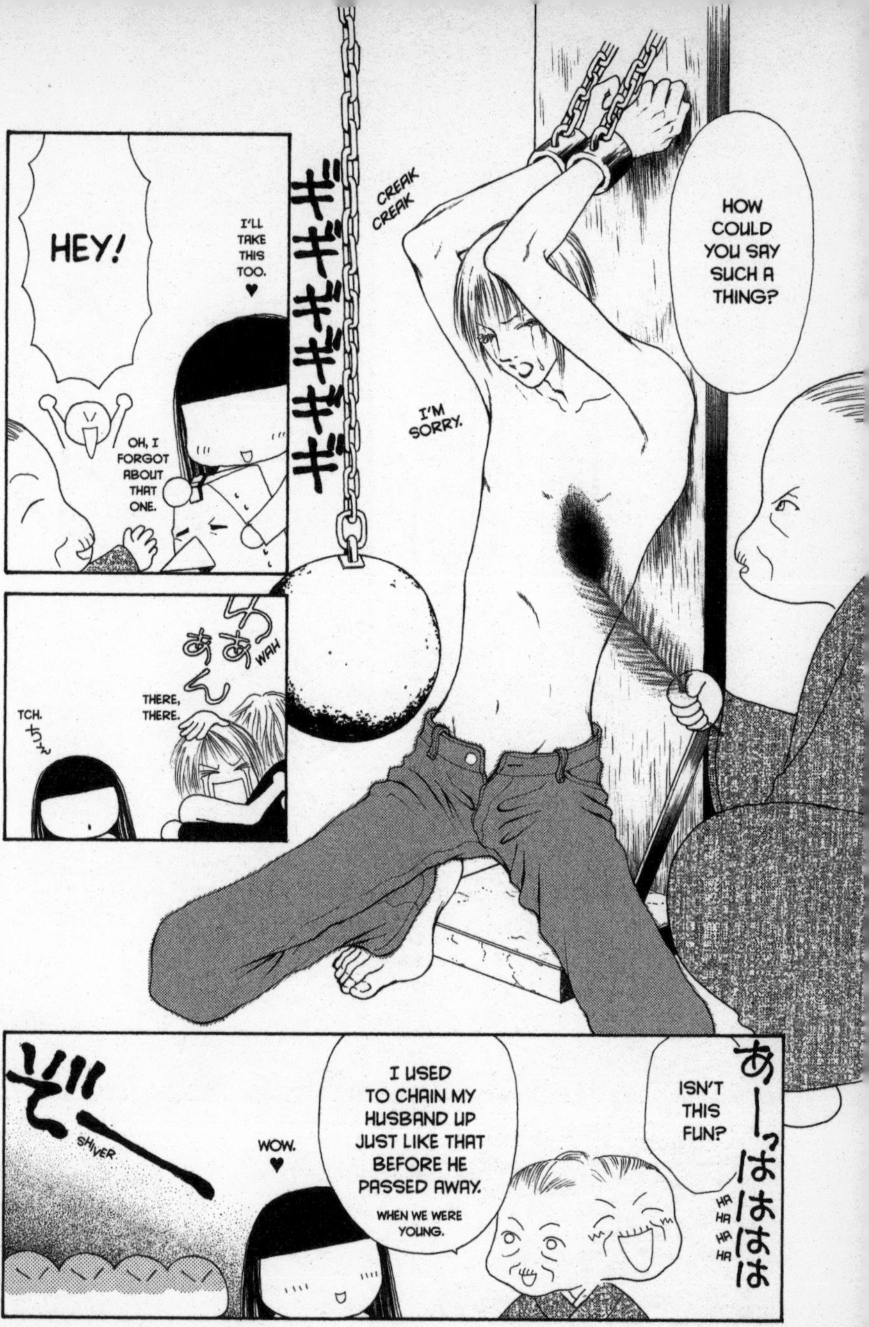
HOW COULD YOU SAY SUCH A THING?
ギギギギギ
CREAK CREAK
I'M SORRY.
I'LL TAKE THIS TOO. ♥
HEY!
OH, I FORGOT ABOUT THAT ONE.
わああん
WAH
THERE, THERE.
TCH.
ちぇ
あーっははは
HA HA HA HA
ISN'T THIS FUN?
I USED TO CHAIN MY HUSBAND UP JUST LIKE THAT BEFORE HE PASSED AWAY.
WHEN WE WERE YOUNG.
WOW. ♥
ぞ〜
SHIVER

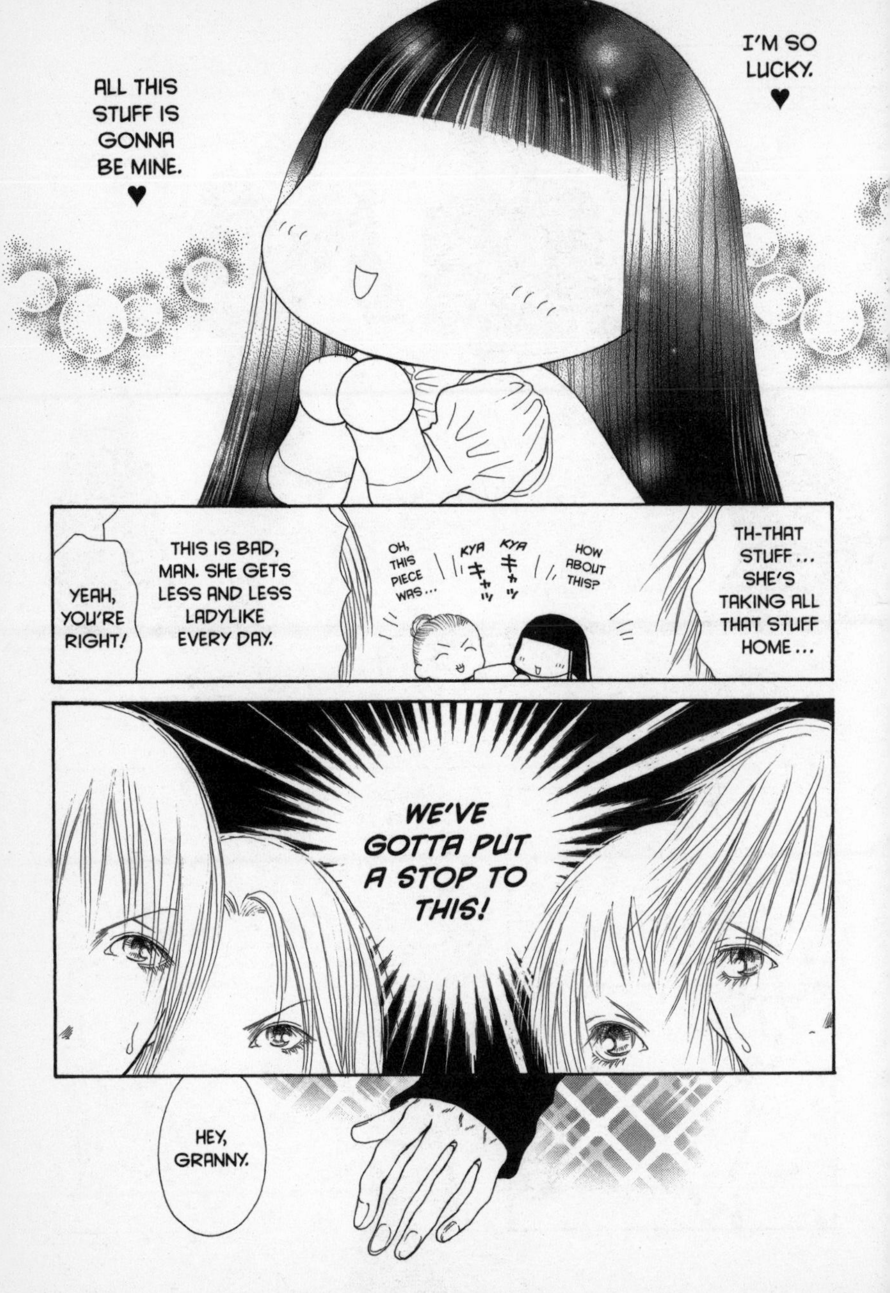
I'M SO LUCKY. ♥
ALL THIS STUFF IS GONNA BE MINE. ♥
TH-THAT STUFF... SHE'S TAKING ALL THAT STUFF HOME...
HOW ABOUT THIS?
KYA キャッ
KYA キャッ
OH, THIS PIECE WAS...
THIS IS BAD, MAN. SHE GETS LESS AND LESS LADYLIKE EVERY DAY.
YEAH, YOU'RE RIGHT!
WE'VE GOTTA PUT A STOP TO THIS!
HEY, GRANNY.

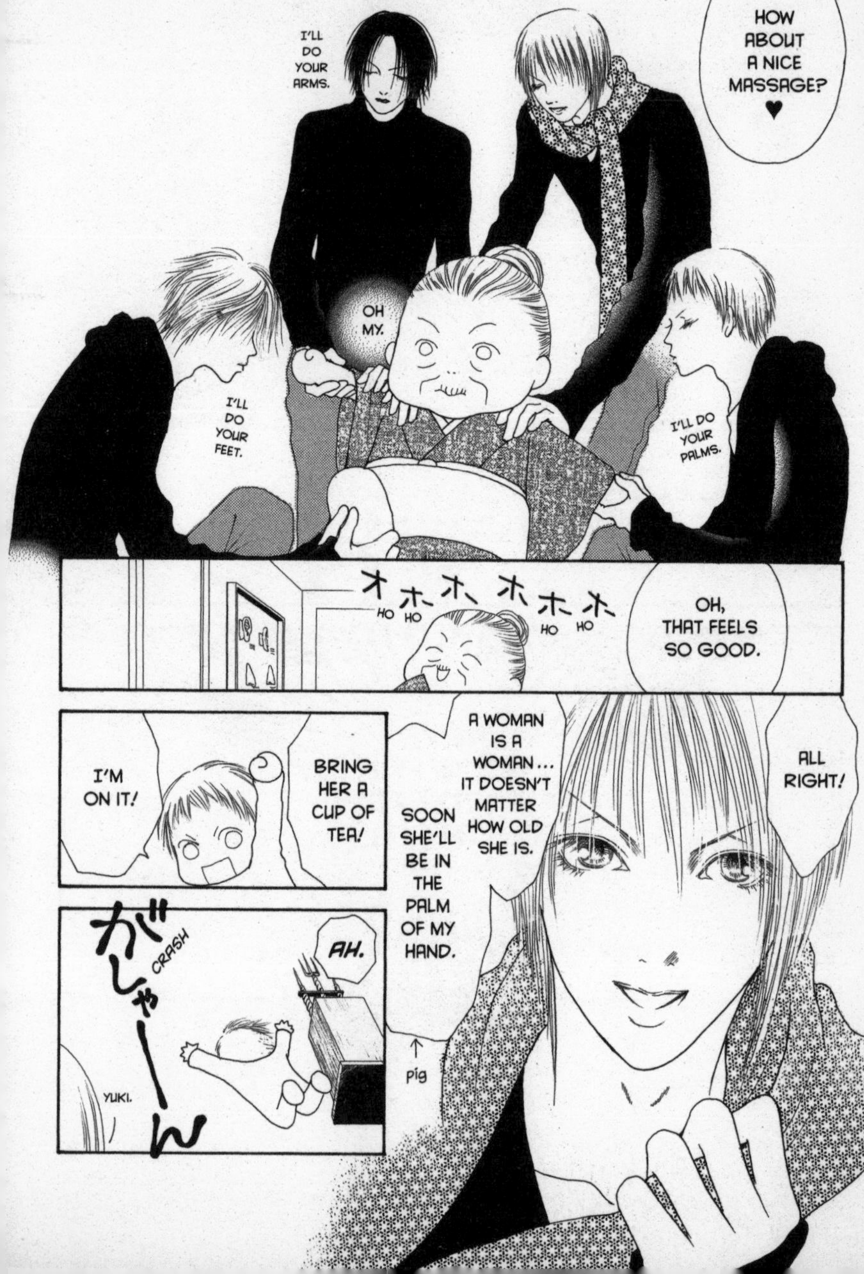
HOW ABOUT A NICE MASSAGE? ♥
I'LL DO YOUR ARMS.
OH MY.
I'LL DO YOUR PALMS.
I'LL DO YOUR FEET.
OH, THAT FEELS SO GOOD.
オホホ、ホホホ
HO HO HO HO
ALL RIGHT!
A WOMAN IS A WOMAN... IT DOESN'T MATTER HOW OLD SHE IS.
SOON SHE'LL BE IN THE PALM OF MY HAND.
↑ pig
BRING HER A CUP OF TEA!
I'M ON IT!
AH.
がしゃーん
CRASH
YUKI.

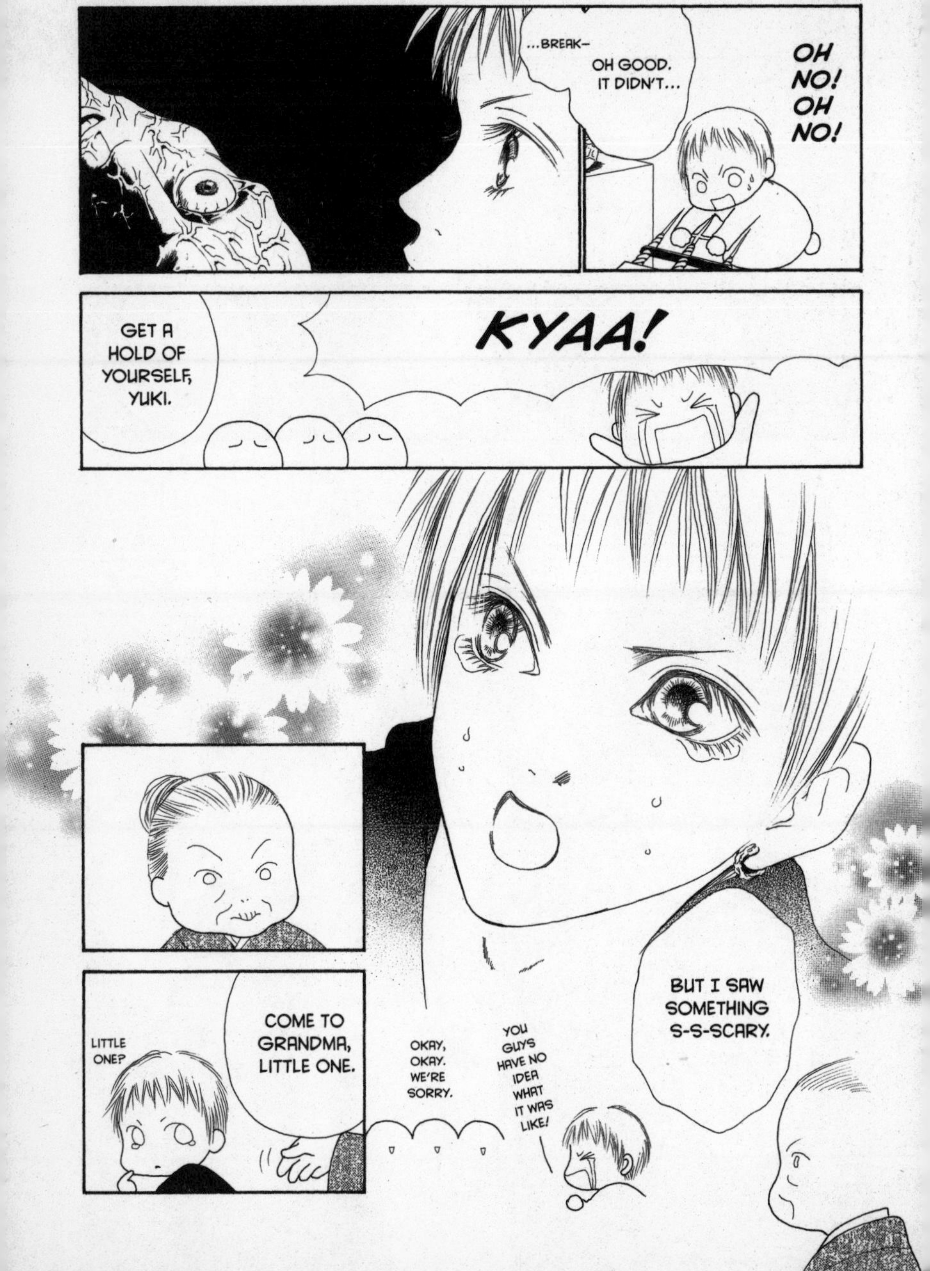
OH NO! OH NO!
...BREAK— OH GOOD. IT DIDN'T...
KYAA!
GET A HOLD OF YOURSELF, YUKI.
BUT I SAW SOMETHING S-S-SCARY.
YOU GUYS HAVE NO IDEA WHAT IT WAS LIKE!
OKAY, OKAY. WE'RE SORRY.
COME TO GRANDMA, LITTLE ONE.
LITTLE ONE?

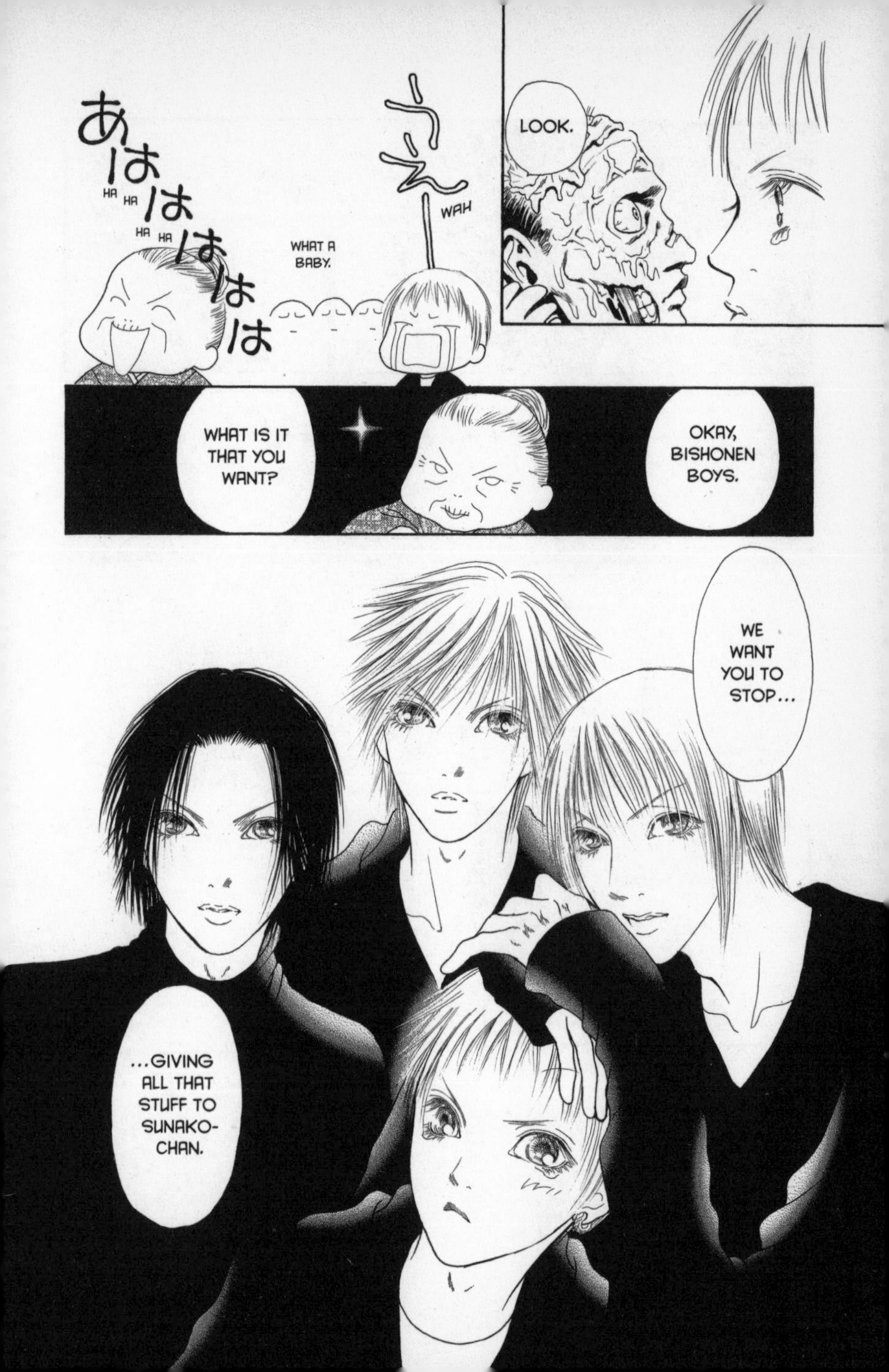
LOOK.
うえ
WAH
WHAT A BABY.
あははは
HA HA HA HA
OKAY, BISHONEN BOYS.
WHAT IS IT THAT YOU WANT?
WE WANT YOU TO STOP...
...GIVING ALL THAT STUFF TO SUNAKO-CHAN.

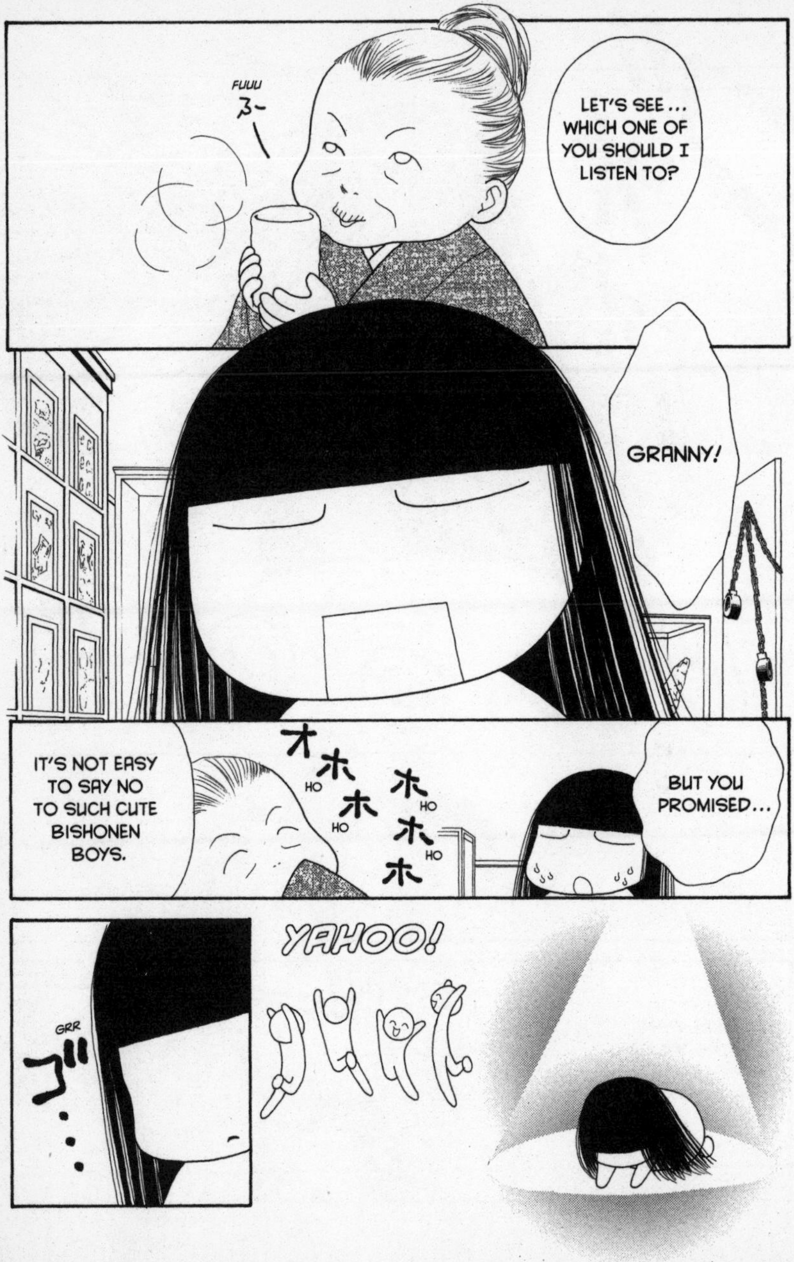
FUUU
ふー
LET'S SEE... WHICH ONE OF YOU SHOULD I LISTEN TO?
GRANNY!
BUT YOU PROMISED...
オホホホホ
HO HO HO HO
IT'S NOT EASY TO SAY NO TO SUCH CUTE BISHONEN BOYS.
YAHOO!
GRR
ゴ...

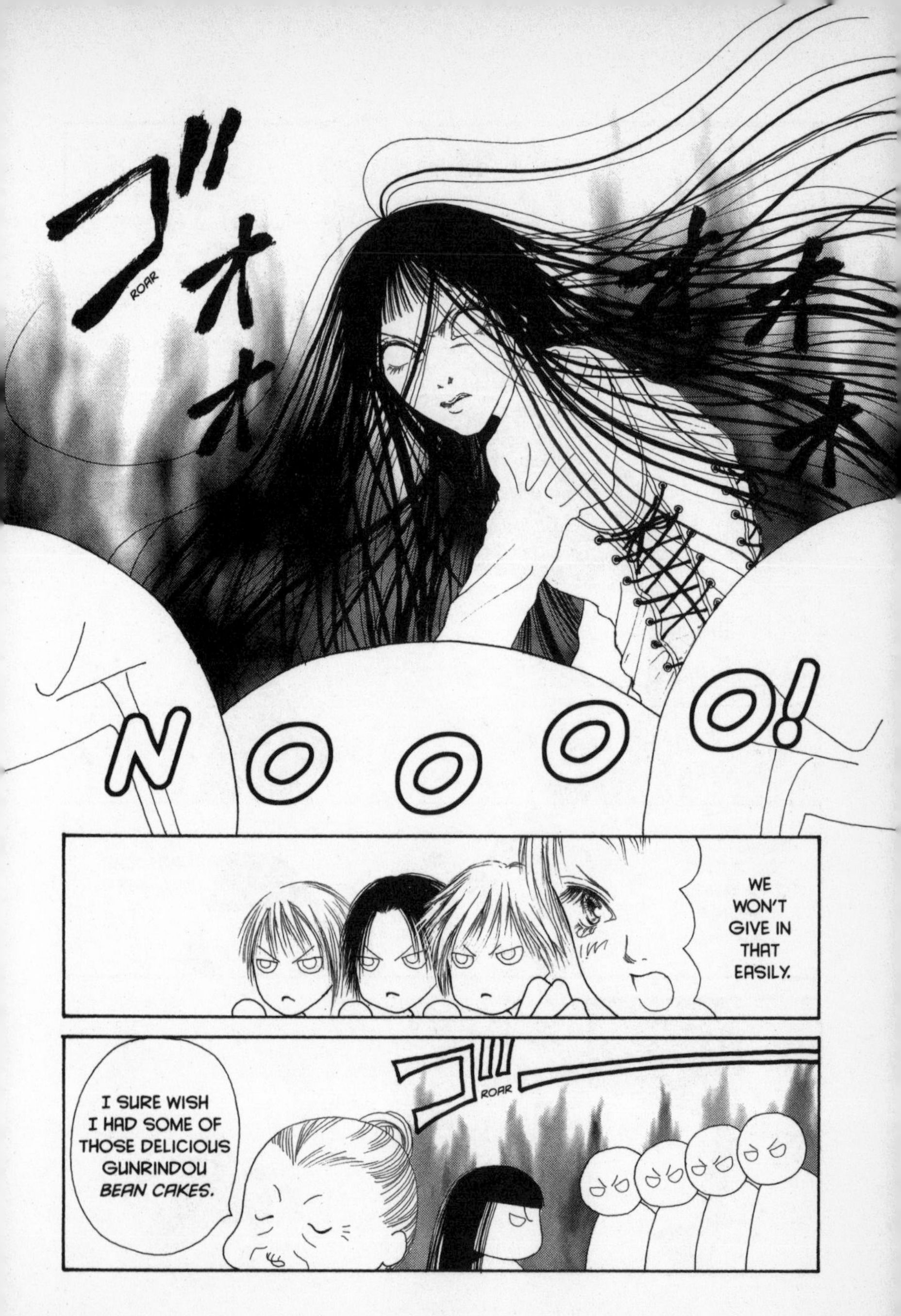
ゴオオオオオ
ROAR
NOOOOO!
WE WON'T GIVE IN THAT EASILY.
ゴー
ROAR
I SURE WISH I HAD SOME OF THOSE DELICIOUS GUNRINDOU *BEAN CAKES.*

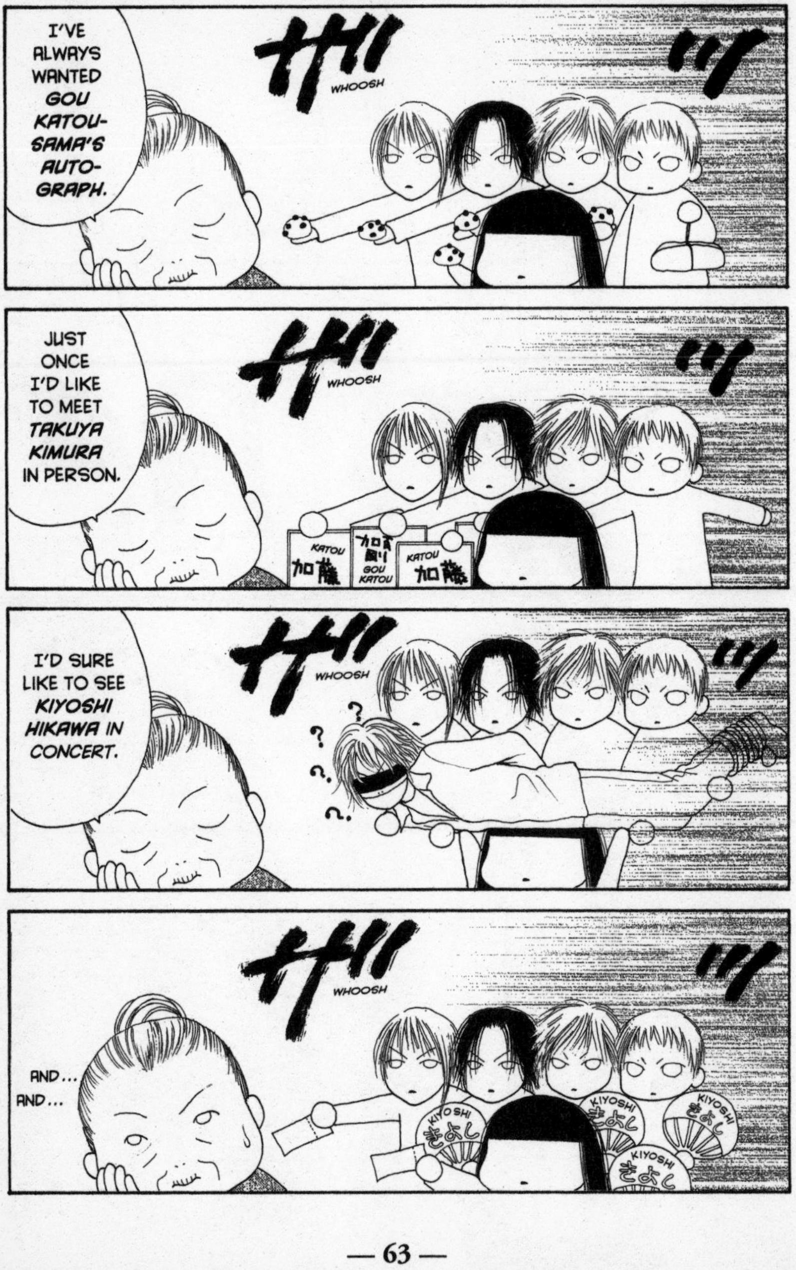
WHOOSH
I'VE ALWAYS WANTED GOU KATOU-SAMA'S AUTOGRAPH.
WHOOSH
JUST ONCE I'D LIKE TO MEET TAKUYA KIMURA IN PERSON.
KATOU 加藤
GOU KATOU
KATOU 加藤
WHOOSH
I'D SURE LIKE TO SEE KIYOSHI HIKAWA IN CONCERT.
WHOOSH
AND...
AND...
KIYOSHI きよし
KIYOSHI きよし
KIYOSHI きよし
KIYOSHI きよし

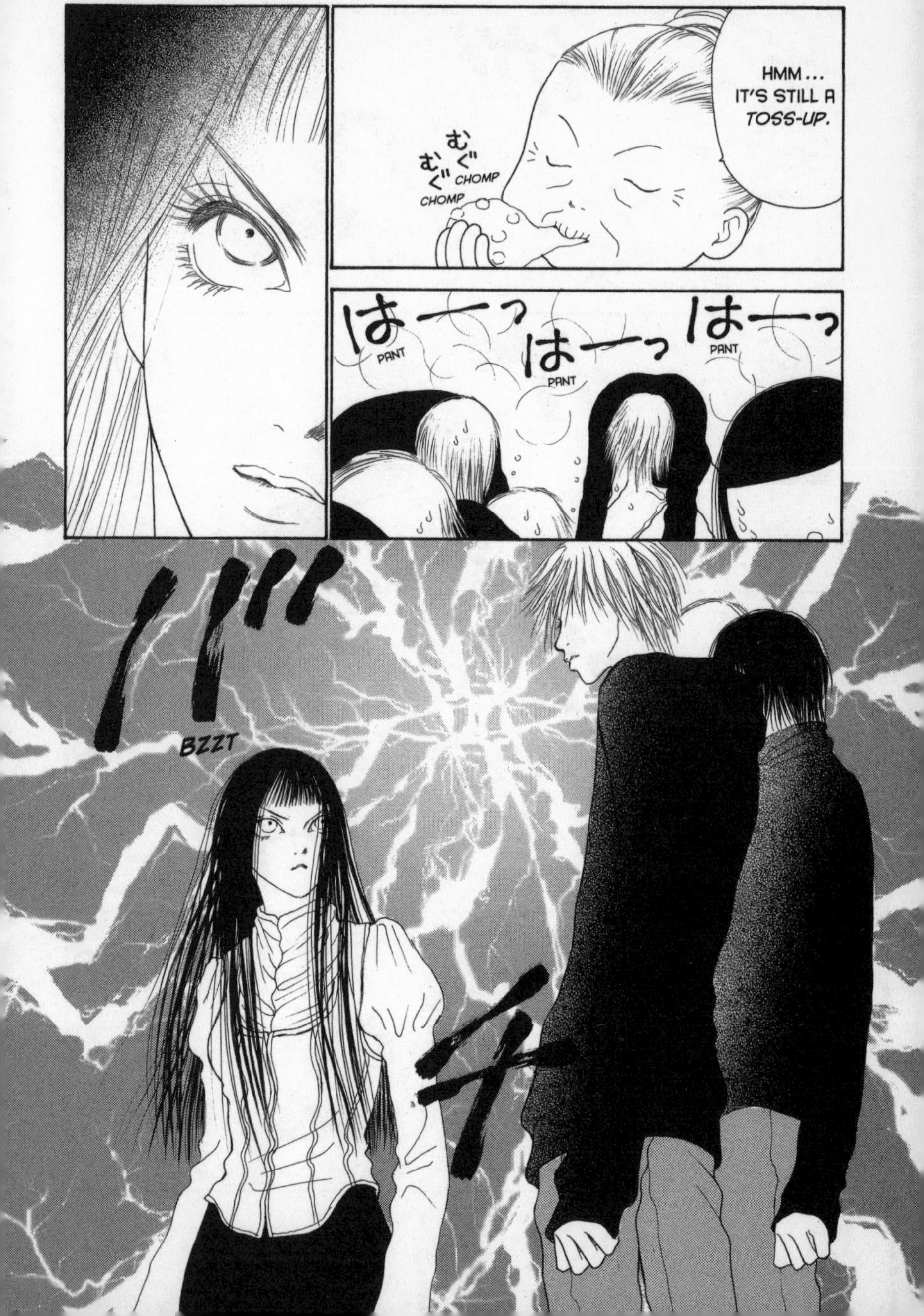
HMM... IT'S STILL A TOSS-UP.
むぐむぐ
CHOMP CHOMP
はーっ はーっ はーっ
PANT PANT PANT
バ
BZZT

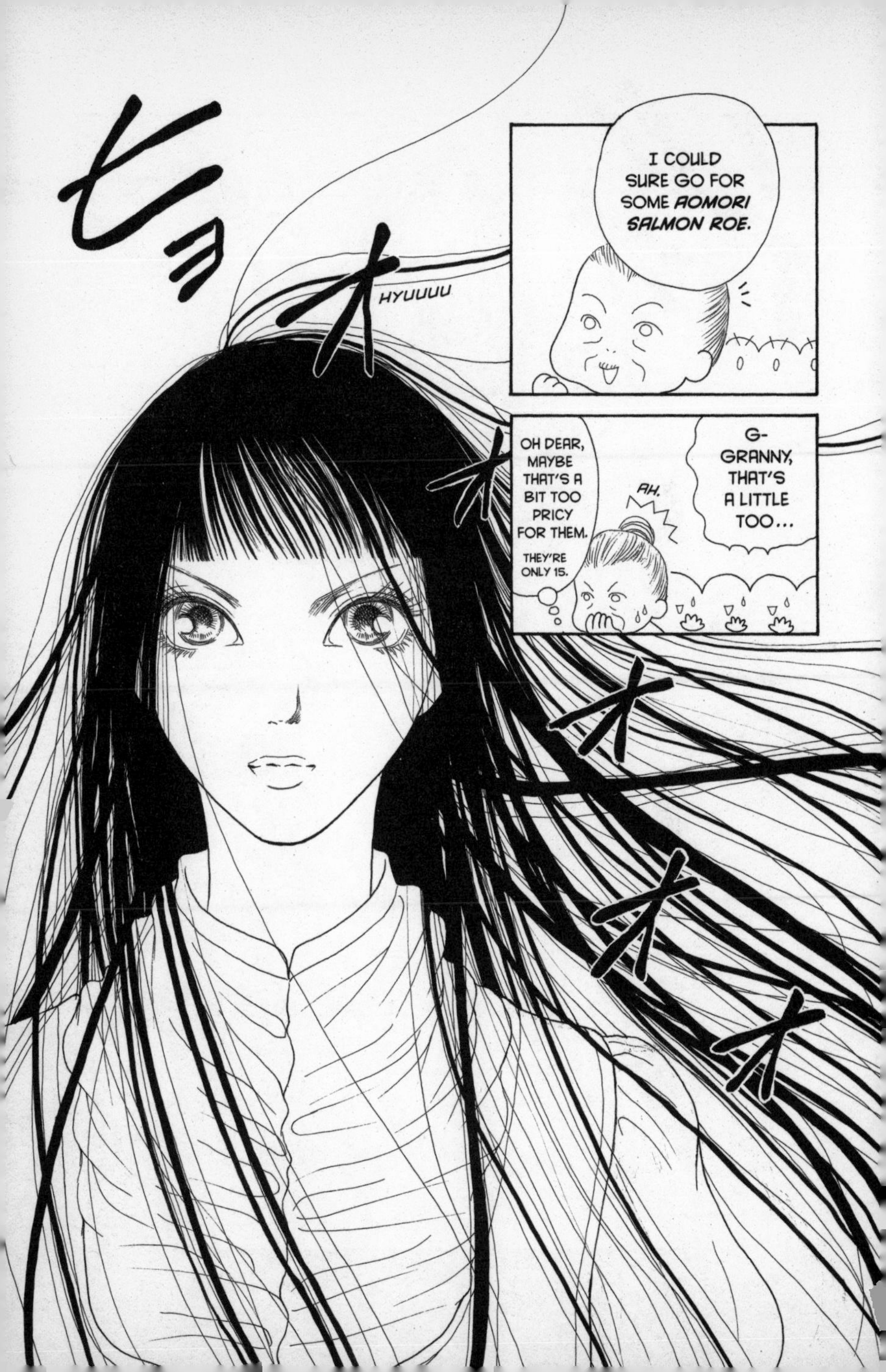
I COULD SURE GO FOR SOME *AOMORI SALMON ROE.*
G-GRANNY, THAT'S A LITTLE TOO...
AH.
OH DEAR, MAYBE THAT'S A BIT TOO PRICY FOR THEM.
THEY'RE ONLY 15.
ヒョオオオオオ
HYUUUU

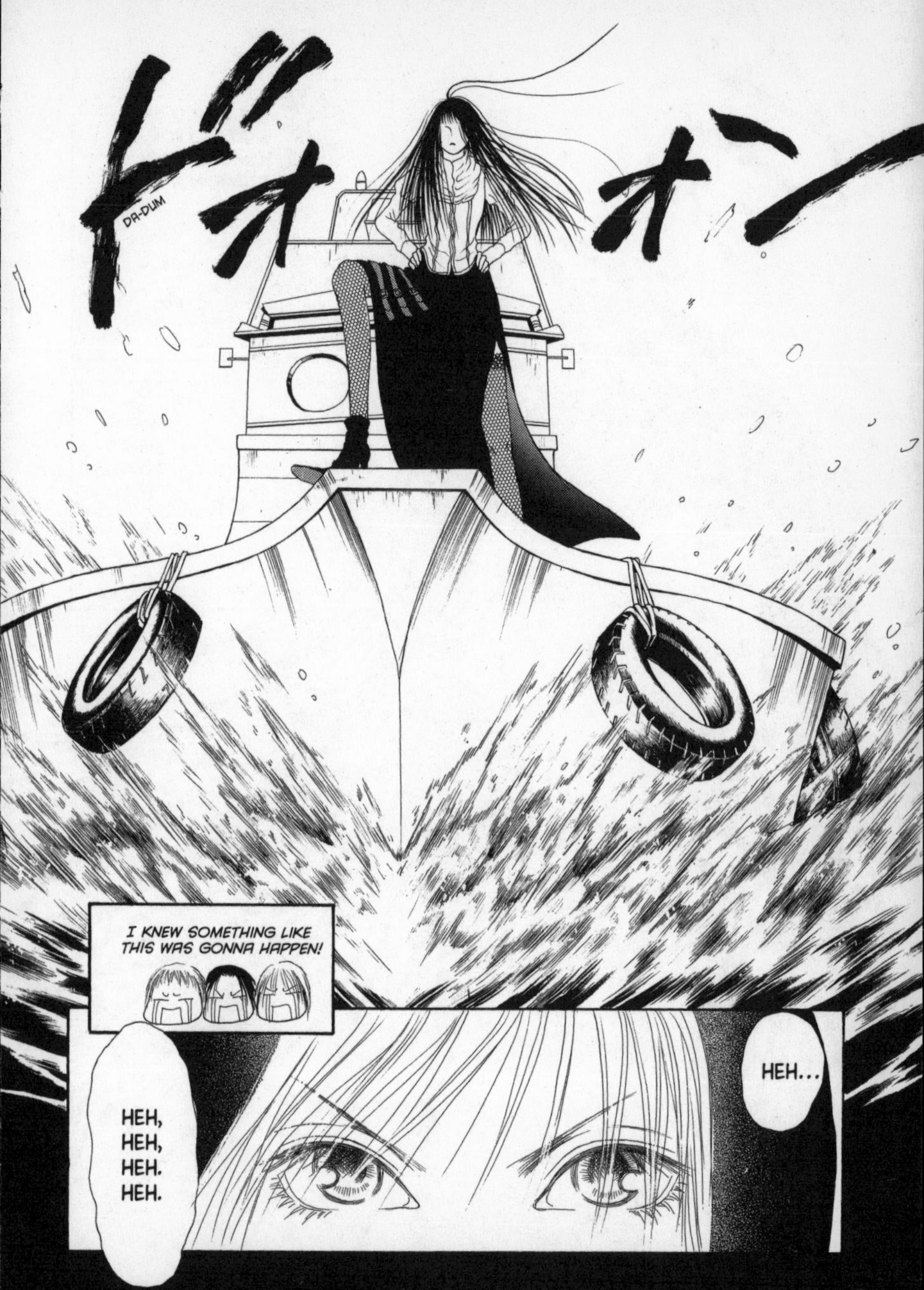
ドオン
DA-DUM
I KNEW SOMETHING LIKE THIS WAS GONNA HAPPEN!
HEH...
HEH, HEH, HEH. HEH.

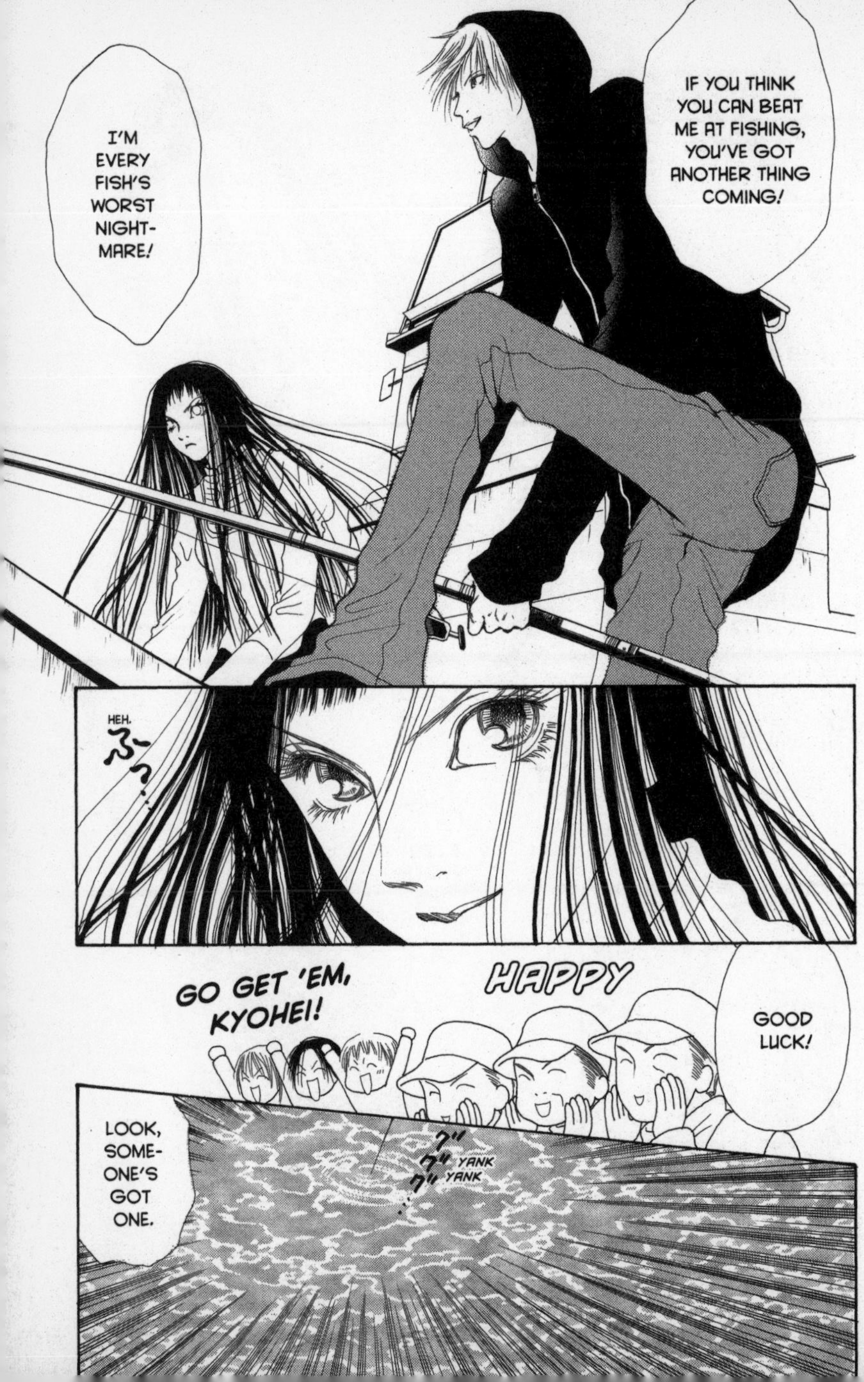
IF YOU THINK YOU CAN BEAT ME AT FISHING, YOU'VE GOT ANOTHER THING COMING!
I'M EVERY FISH'S WORST NIGHT-MARE!
HEH.
ふっ
GOOD LUCK!
HAPPY
GO GET 'EM, KYOHEI!
YANK YANK
LOOK, SOME-ONE'S GOT ONE.

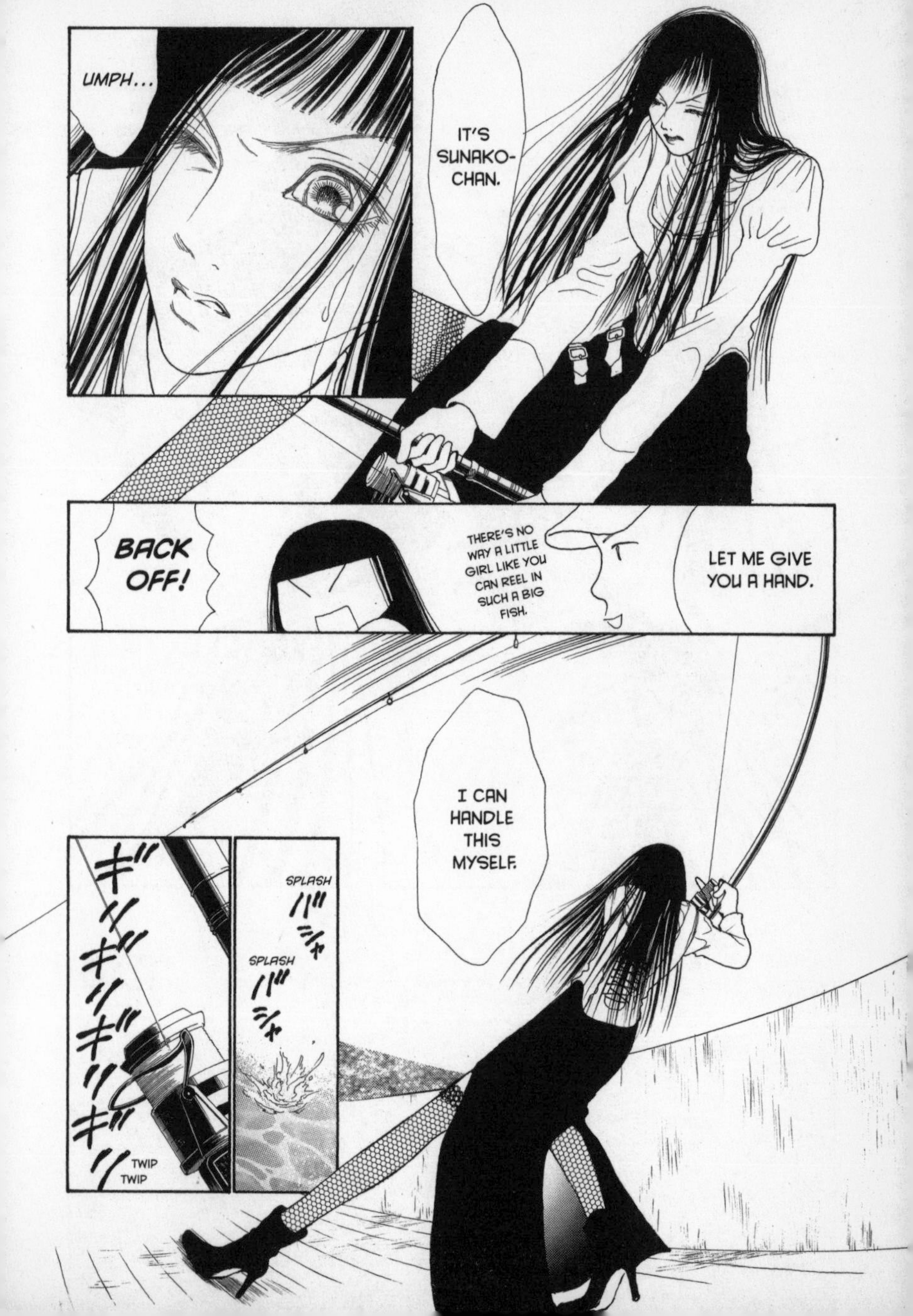
IT'S SUNAKO-CHAN.
UMPH...
LET ME GIVE YOU A HAND.
THERE'S NO WAY A LITTLE GIRL LIKE YOU CAN REEL IN SUCH A BIG FISH.
BACK OFF!
I CAN HANDLE THIS MYSELF.
SPLASH
バシャ
SPLASH
バシャ
ギリギリギリギリ
TWIP
TWIP

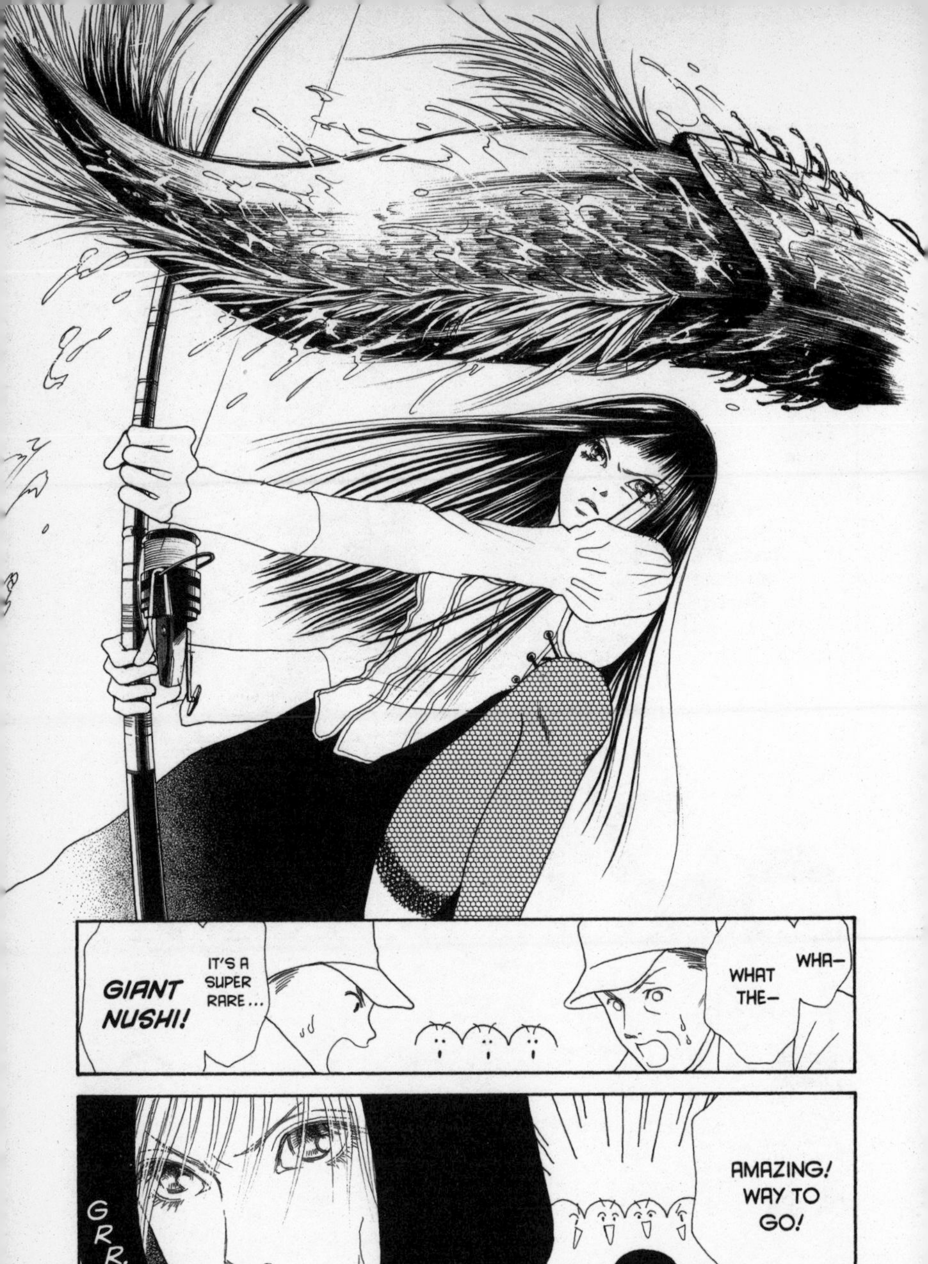
WHA-
WHAT THE-
IT'S A SUPER RARE...
GIANT NUSHI!
AMAZING! WAY TO GO!
GRR.

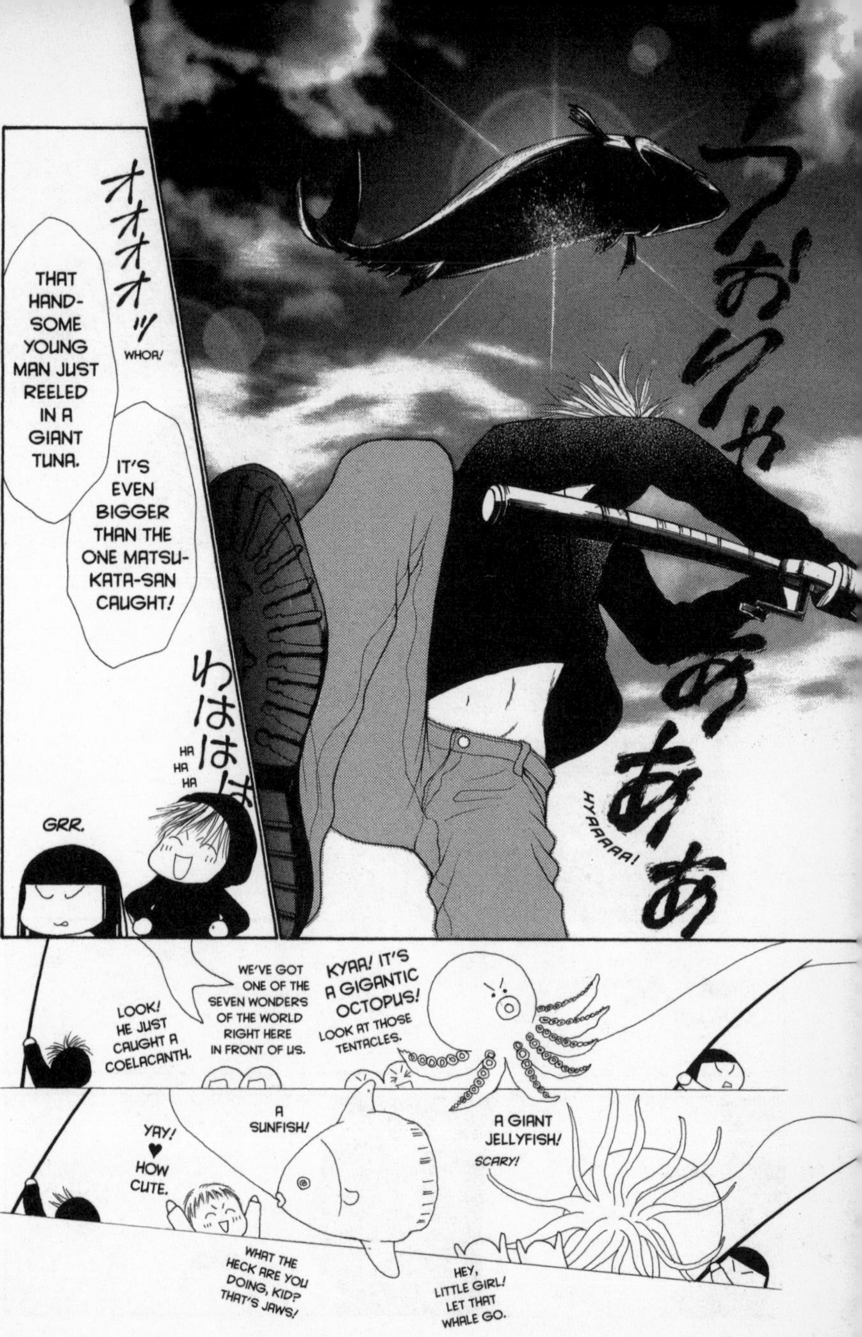
うおりゃあああ
HYAAAAAA!
オオオオッ
WHOA!
THAT HANDSOME YOUNG MAN JUST REELED IN A GIANT TUNA.
IT'S EVEN BIGGER THAN THE ONE MATSUKATA-SAN CAUGHT!
わははは
HA HA HA
GRR.
KYAA! IT'S A GIGANTIC OCTOPUS!
LOOK AT THOSE TENTACLES.
WE'VE GOT ONE OF THE SEVEN WONDERS OF THE WORLD RIGHT HERE IN FRONT OF US.
LOOK! HE JUST CAUGHT A COELACANTH.
A GIANT JELLYFISH!
SCARY!
A SUNFISH!
YAY! ♥ HOW CUTE.
HEY, LITTLE GIRL! LET THAT WHALE GO.
WHAT THE HECK ARE YOU DOING, KID? THAT'S JAWS!

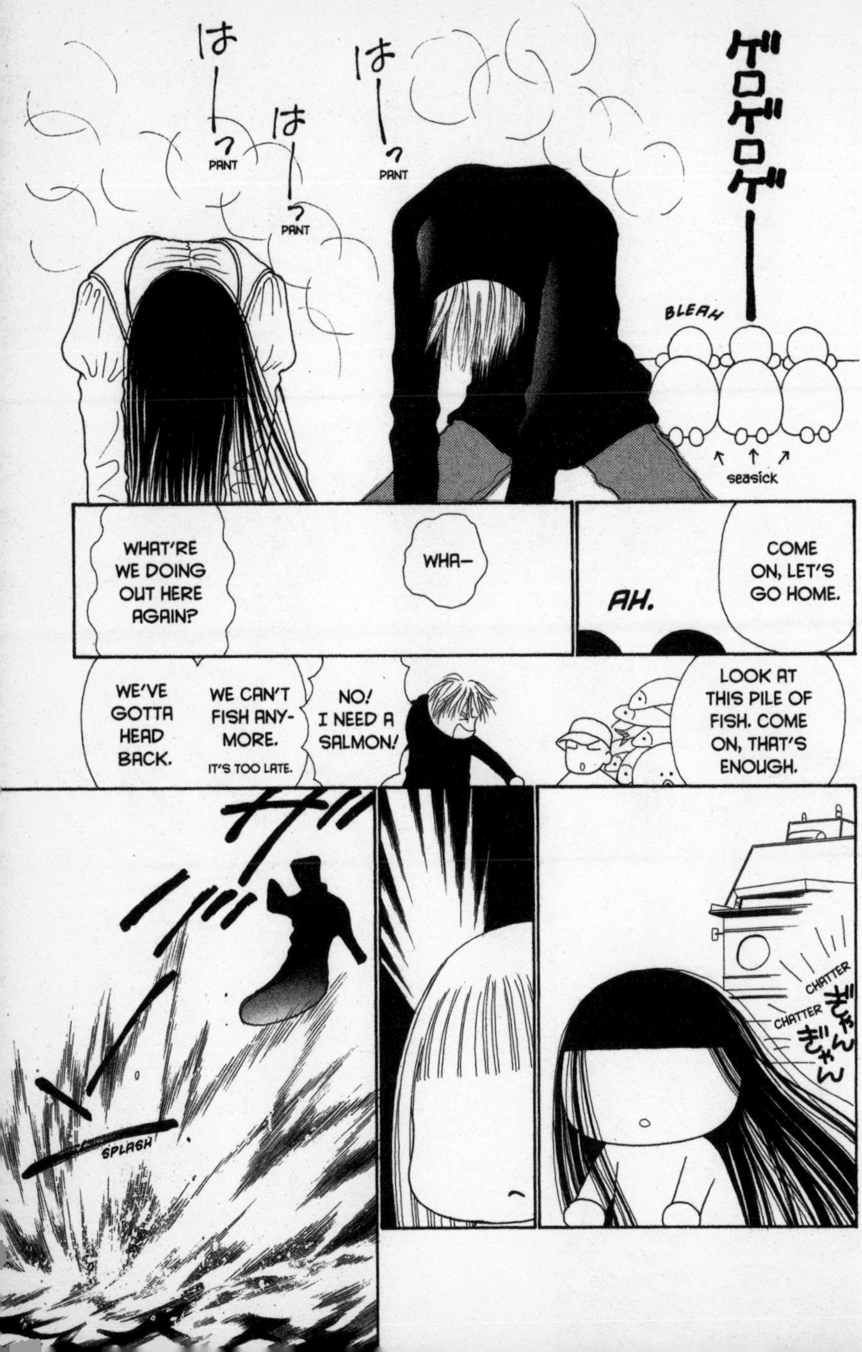
ゲロゲロゲーー
BLEAH
seasick
はーっ
PANT
はーっ
PANT
はーっ
PANT
COME ON, LET'S GO HOME.
AH.
WHA—
WHAT'RE WE DOING OUT HERE AGAIN?
LOOK AT THIS PILE OF FISH. COME ON, THAT'S ENOUGH.
NO! I NEED A SALMON!
WE CAN'T FISH ANY-MORE.
IT'S TOO LATE.
WE'VE GOTTA HEAD BACK.
ぎゃんぎゃん
CHATTER CHATTER
SPLASH

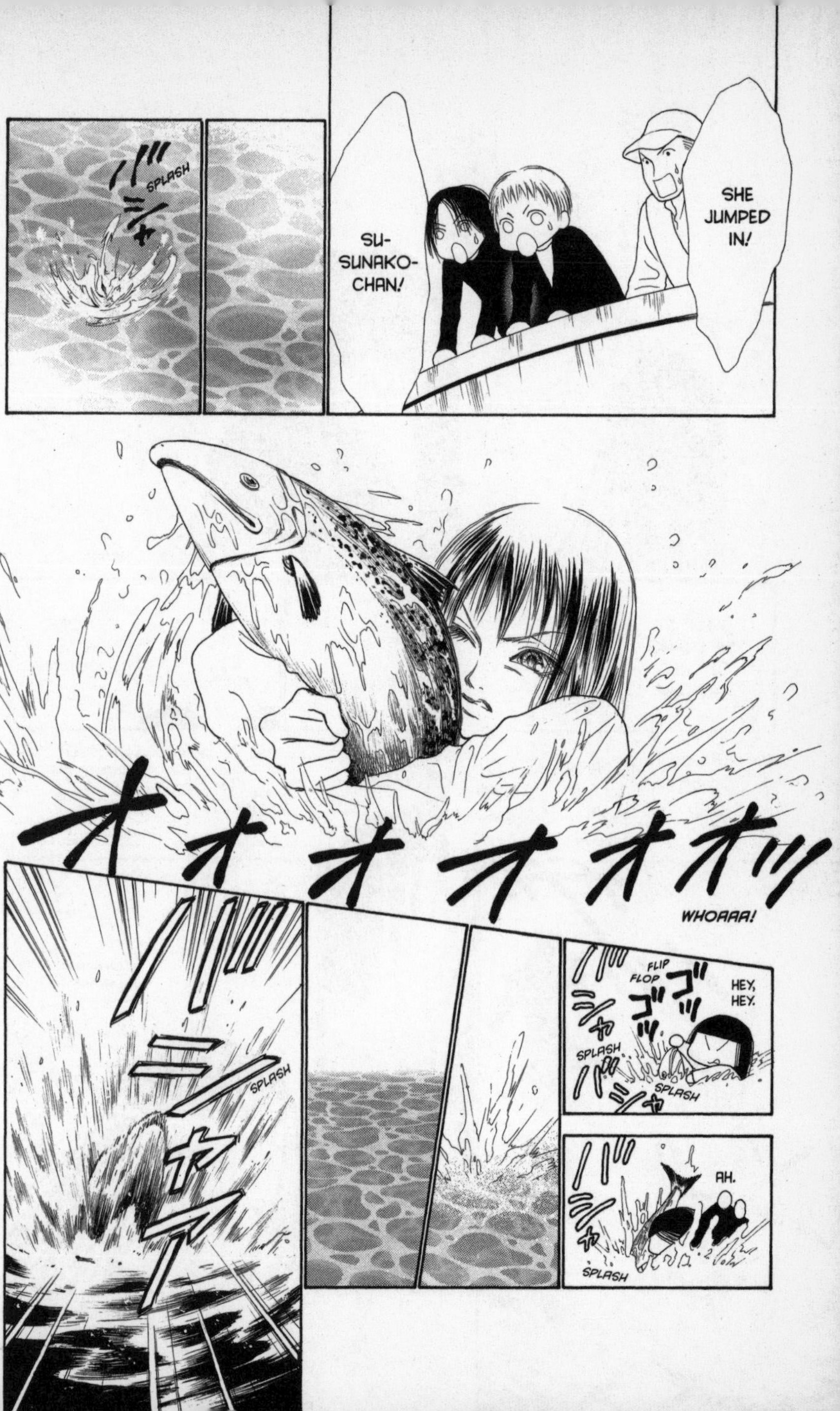
SHE JUMPED IN!
SU- SUNAKO-CHAN!
SPLASH
オオオオオッ
WHOAAA!
FLIP FLOP
HEY, HEY.
SPLASH
SPLASH
AH.
SPLASH
SPLASH

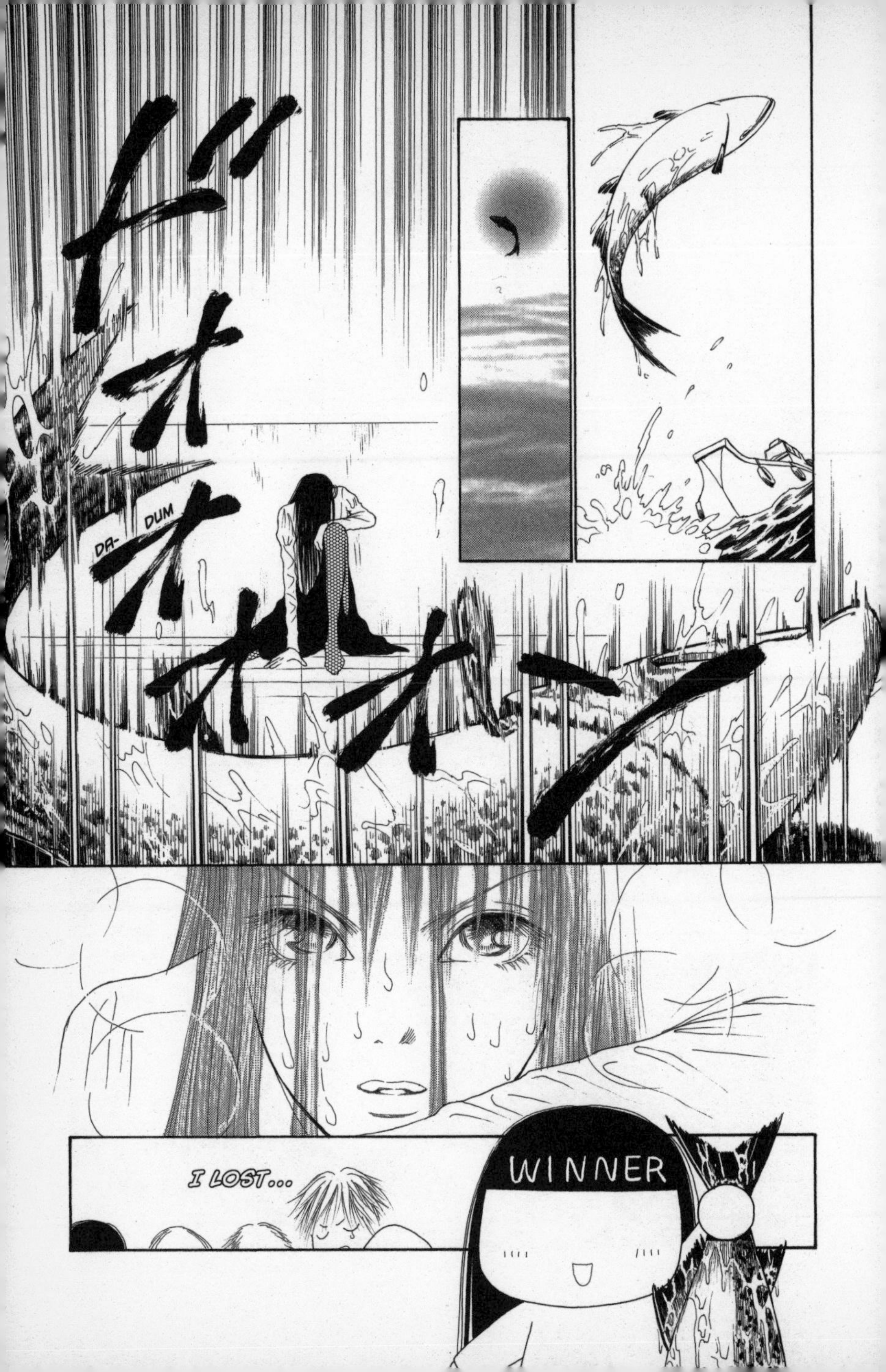
DA-
DUM
WINNER
I LOST...

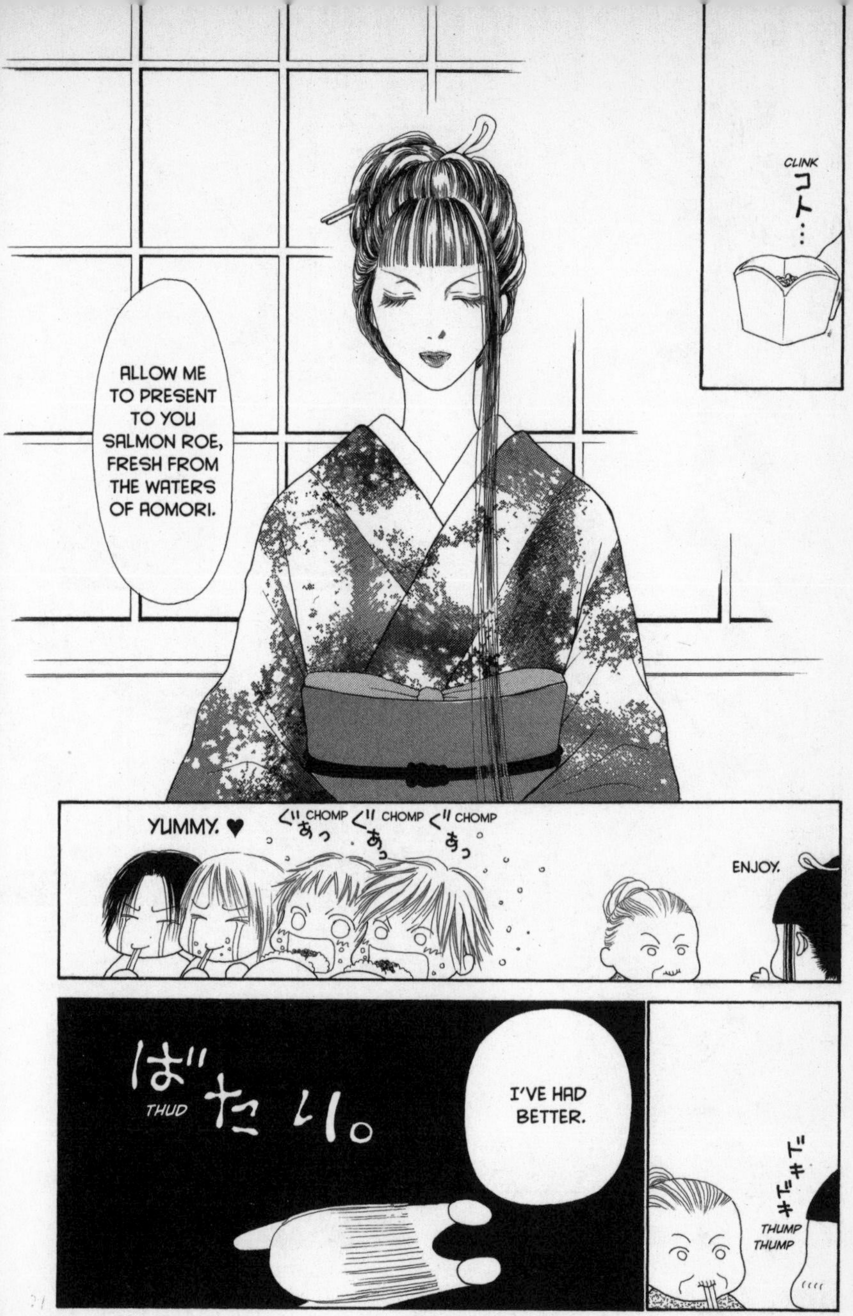
CLINK
コト…
ALLOW ME TO PRESENT TO YOU SALMON ROE, FRESH FROM THE WATERS OF AOMORI.
ENJOY.
ぐあっ CHOMP
ぐあっ CHOMP
ぐあっ CHOMP
YUMMY. ♥
ドキドキ
THUMP THUMP
I'VE HAD BETTER.
ばたり。
THUD

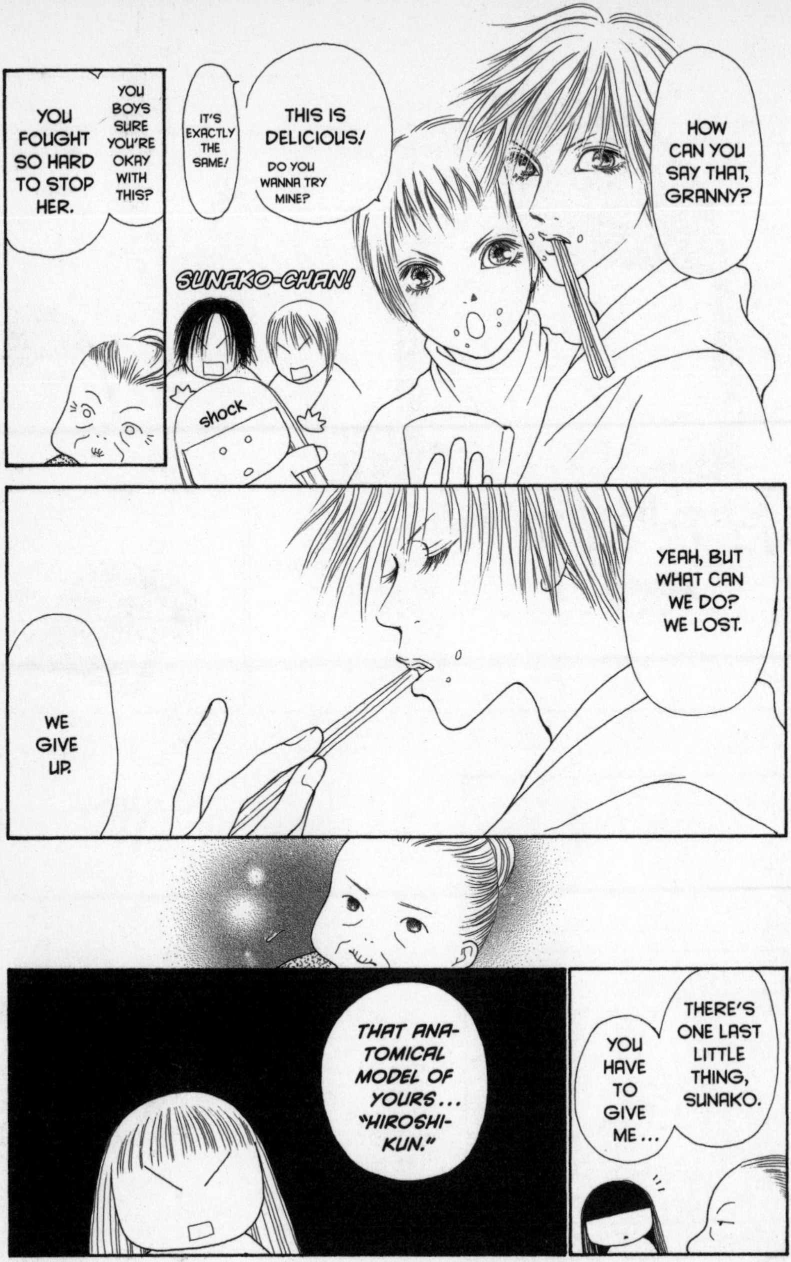
HOW CAN YOU SAY THAT, GRANNY?
THIS IS DELICIOUS! DO YOU WANNA TRY MINE?
IT'S EXACTLY THE SAME!
SUNAKO-CHAN!
shock
YOU BOYS SURE YOU'RE OKAY WITH THIS?
YOU FOUGHT SO HARD TO STOP HER.
YEAH, BUT WHAT CAN WE DO? WE LOST.
WE GIVE UP.
THERE'S ONE LAST LITTLE THING, SUNAKO.
YOU HAVE TO GIVE ME...
THAT ANATOMICAL MODEL OF YOURS... "HIROSHI-KUN."

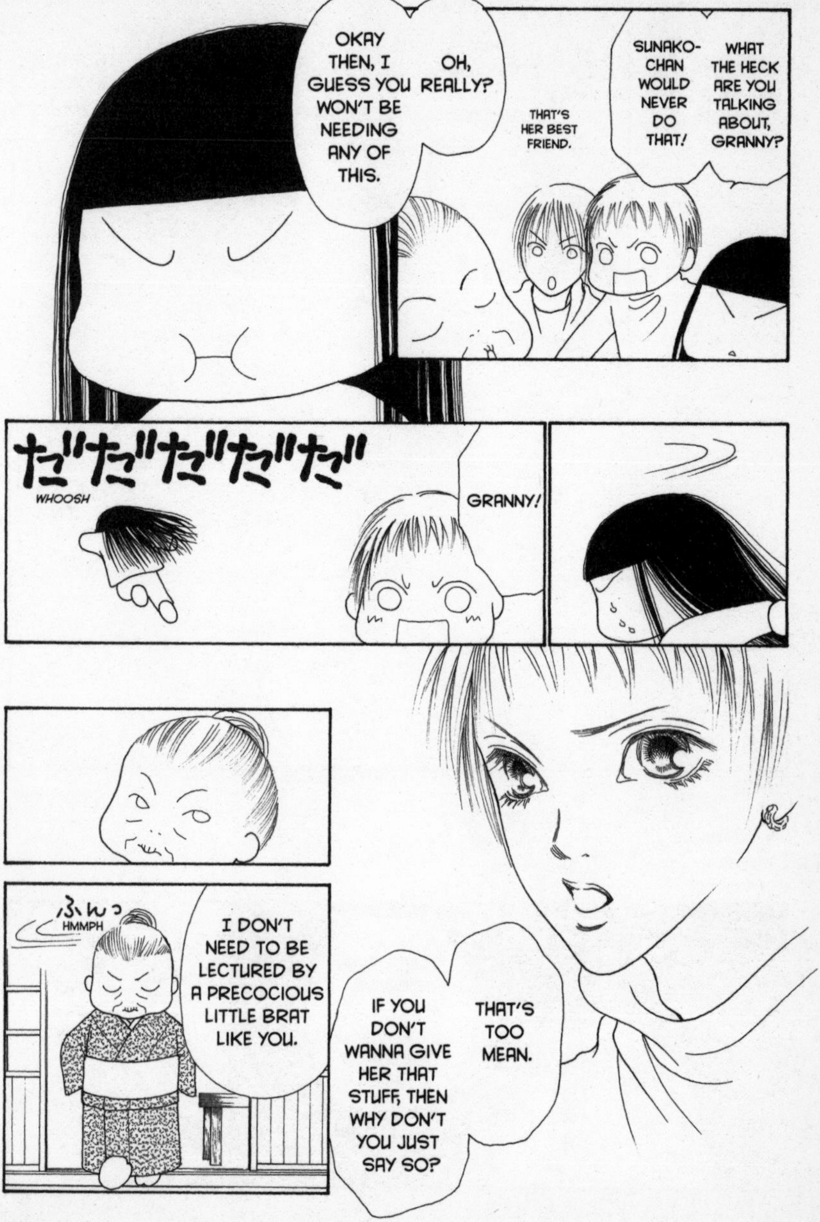
WHAT THE HECK ARE YOU TALKING ABOUT, GRANNY?
SUNAKO-CHAN WOULD NEVER DO THAT!
THAT'S HER BEST FRIEND.
OH, REALLY?
OKAY THEN, I GUESS YOU WON'T BE NEEDING ANY OF THIS.
GRANNY!
だだだだだ
WHOOSH
THAT'S TOO MEAN.
IF YOU DON'T WANNA GIVE HER THAT STUFF, THEN WHY DON'T YOU JUST SAY SO?
ふんっ
HMMPH
I DON'T NEED TO BE LECTURED BY A PRECOCIOUS LITTLE BRAT LIKE YOU.

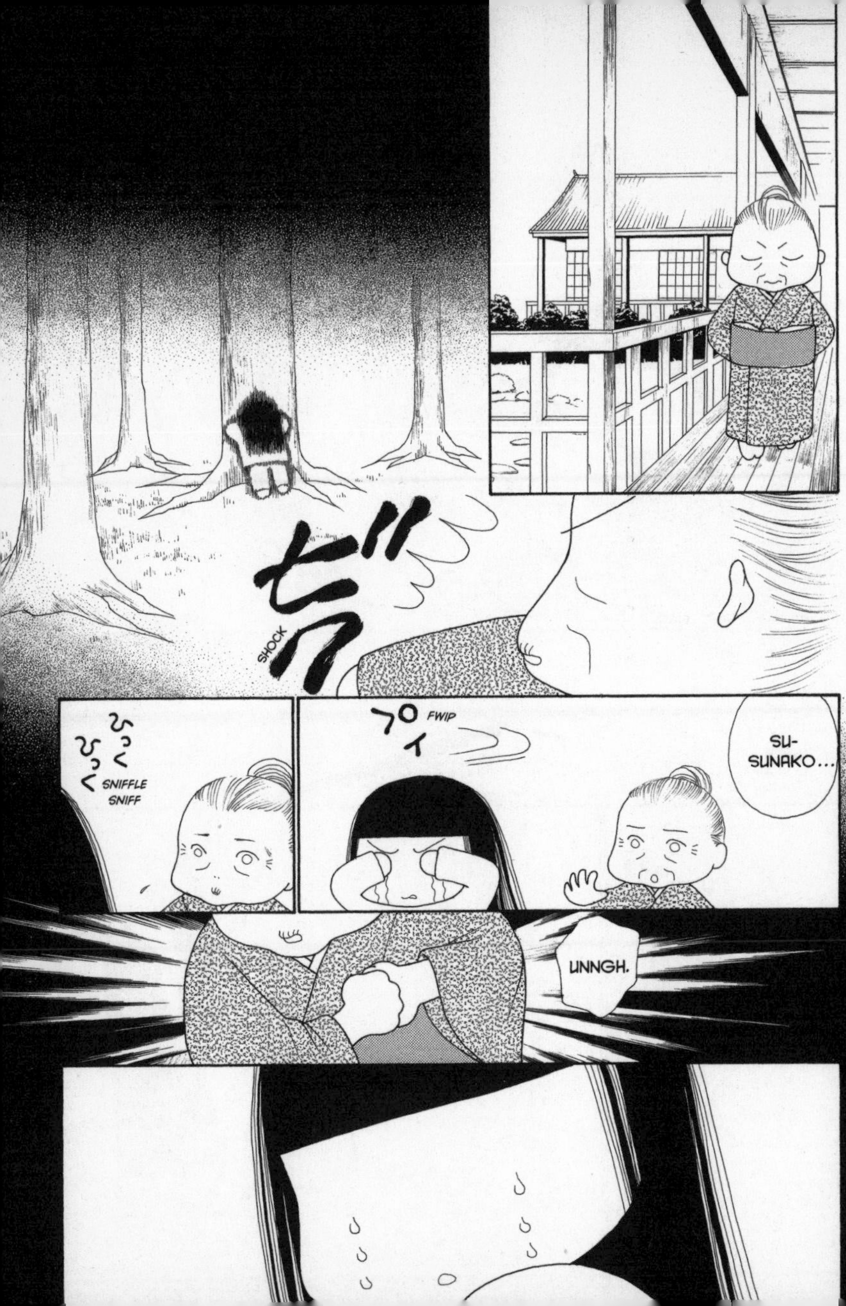
SHOCK
SU-SUNAKO...
プイ
FWIP
ひっく ひっく
SNIFFLE SNIFF
UNNGH.

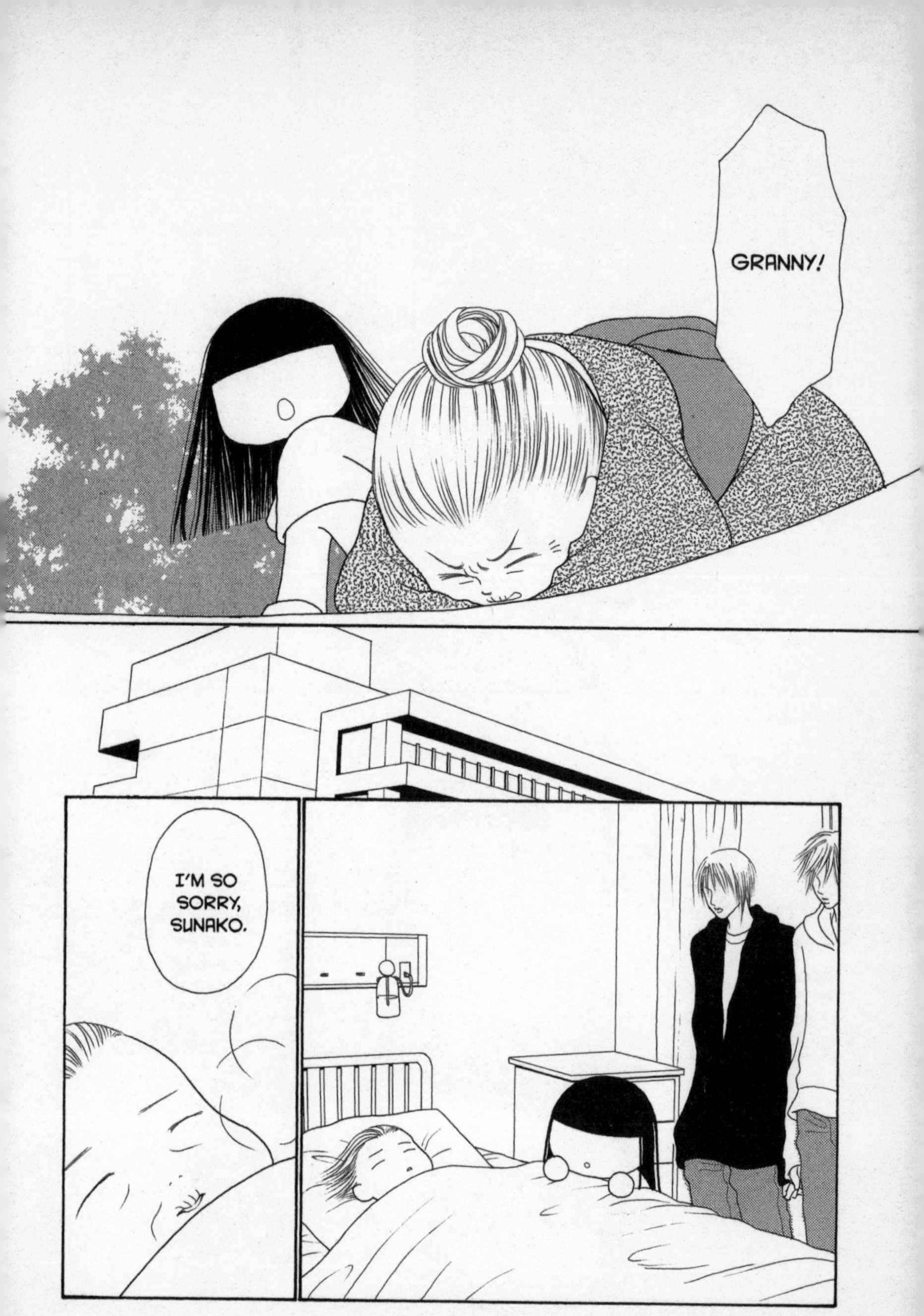
GRANNY!
I'M SO SORRY, SUNAKO.

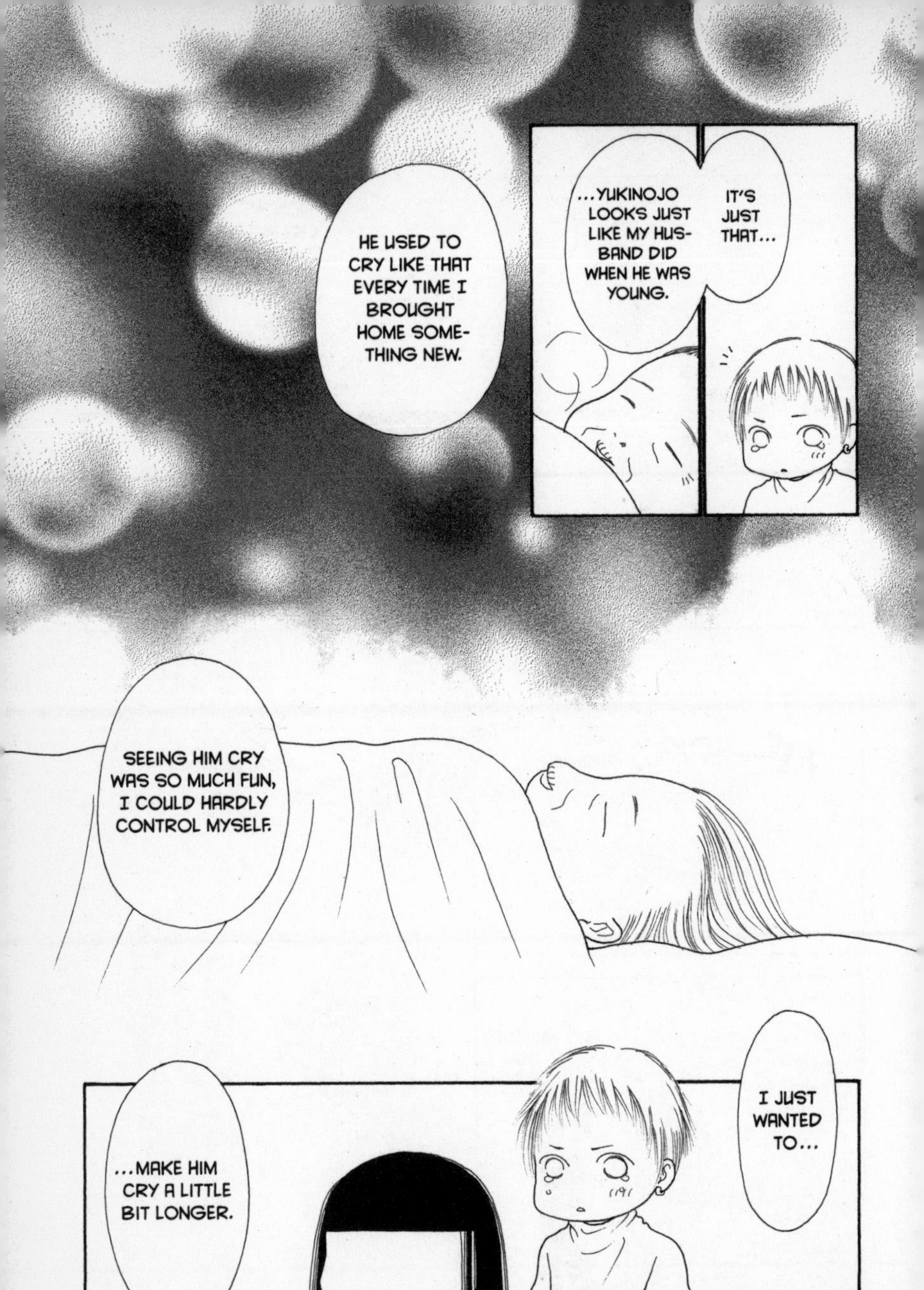
IT'S JUST THAT...
...YUKINOJO LOOKS JUST LIKE MY HUS-BAND DID WHEN HE WAS YOUNG.
HE USED TO CRY LIKE THAT EVERY TIME I BROUGHT HOME SOME-THING NEW.
SEEING HIM CRY WAS SO MUCH FUN, I COULD HARDLY CONTROL MYSELF.
I JUST WANTED TO...
...MAKE HIM CRY A LITTLE BIT LONGER.

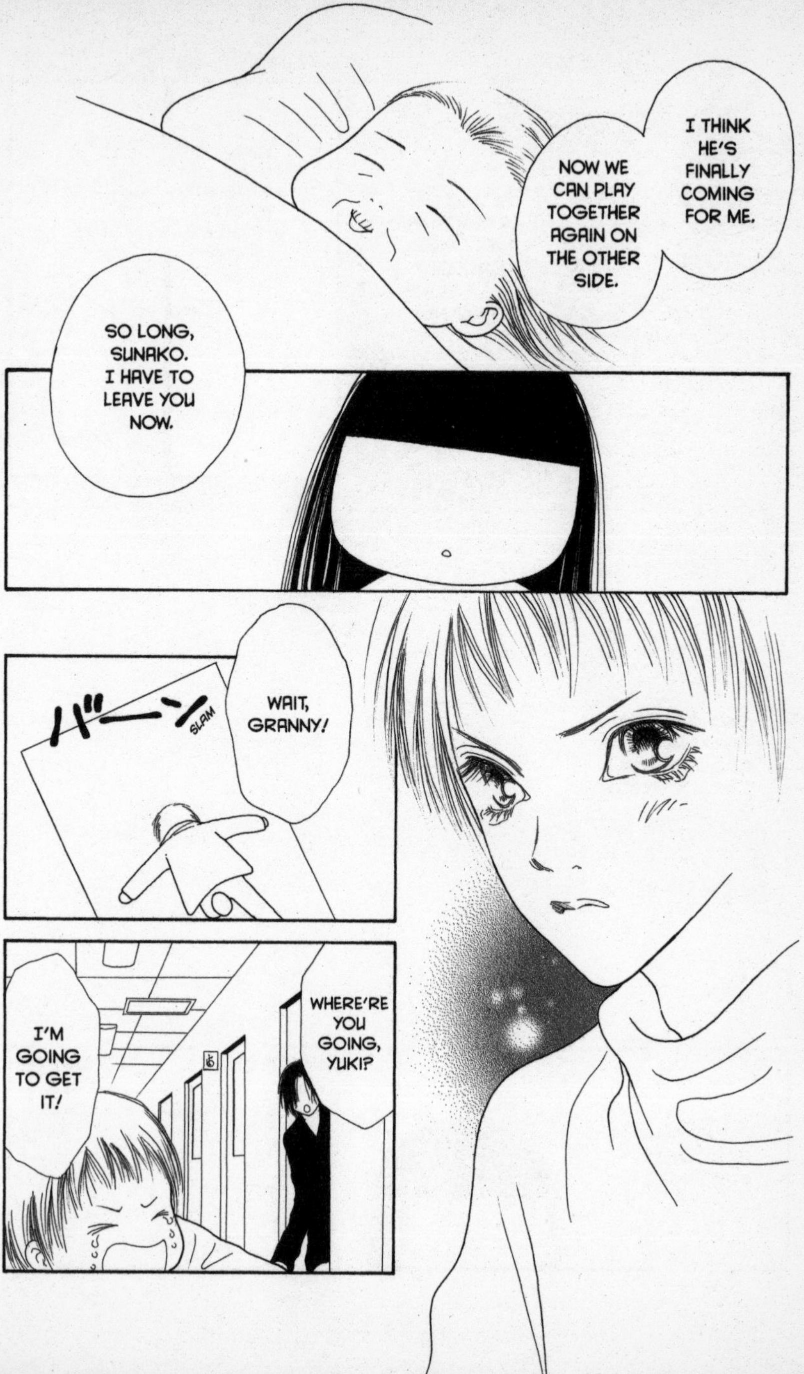
I THINK HE'S FINALLY COMING FOR ME.
NOW WE CAN PLAY TOGETHER AGAIN ON THE OTHER SIDE.
SO LONG, SUNAKO. I HAVE TO LEAVE YOU NOW.
WAIT, GRANNY!
バーン
SLAM
WHERE'RE YOU GOING, YUKI?
I'M GOING TO GET IT!

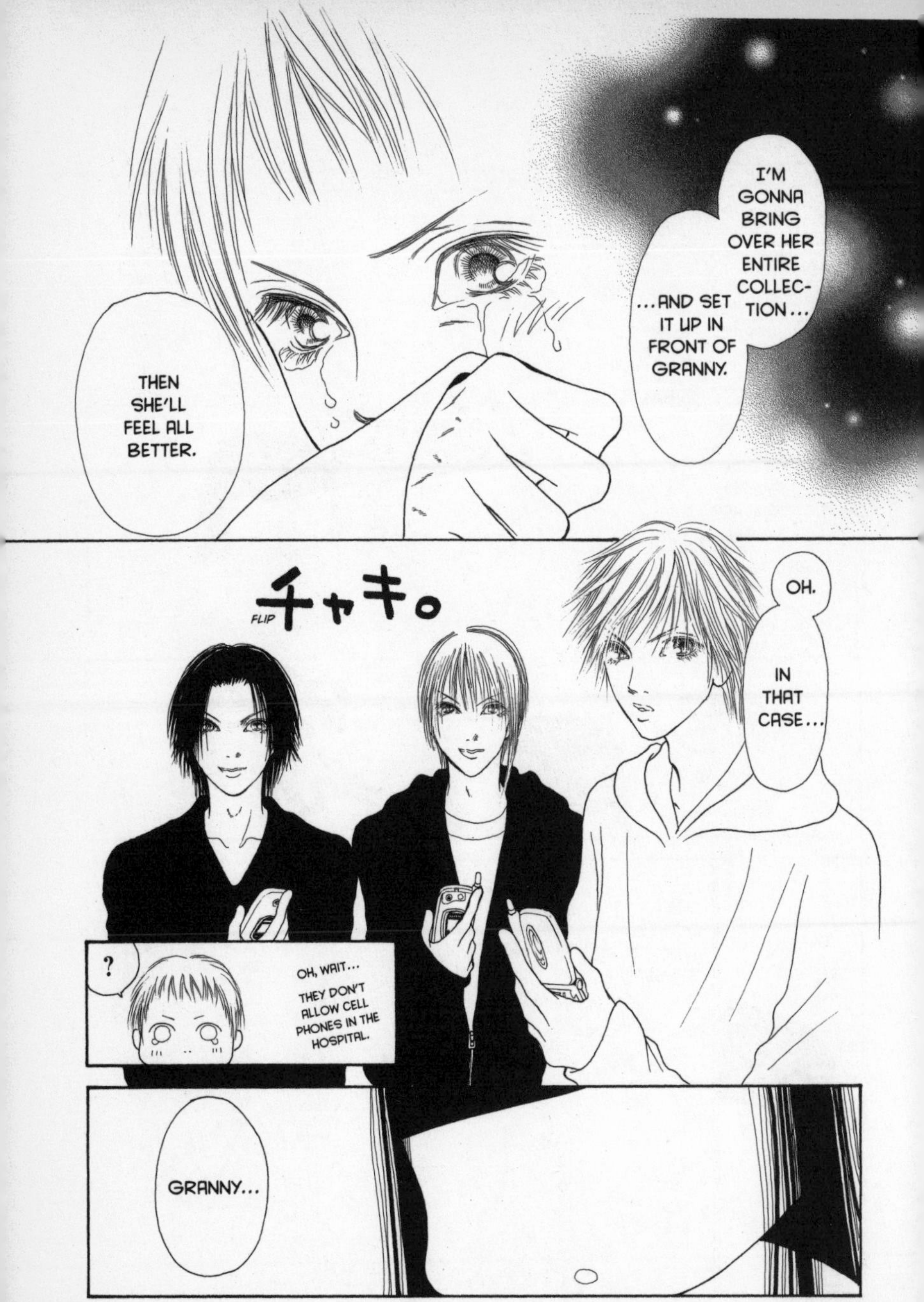
I'M GONNA BRING OVER HER ENTIRE COLLECTION...
...AND SET IT UP IN FRONT OF GRANNY.
THEN SHE'LL FEEL ALL BETTER.
OH.
IN THAT CASE...
FLIP チャキ。
?
OH, WAIT... THEY DON'T ALLOW CELL PHONES IN THE HOSPITAL.
GRANNY...

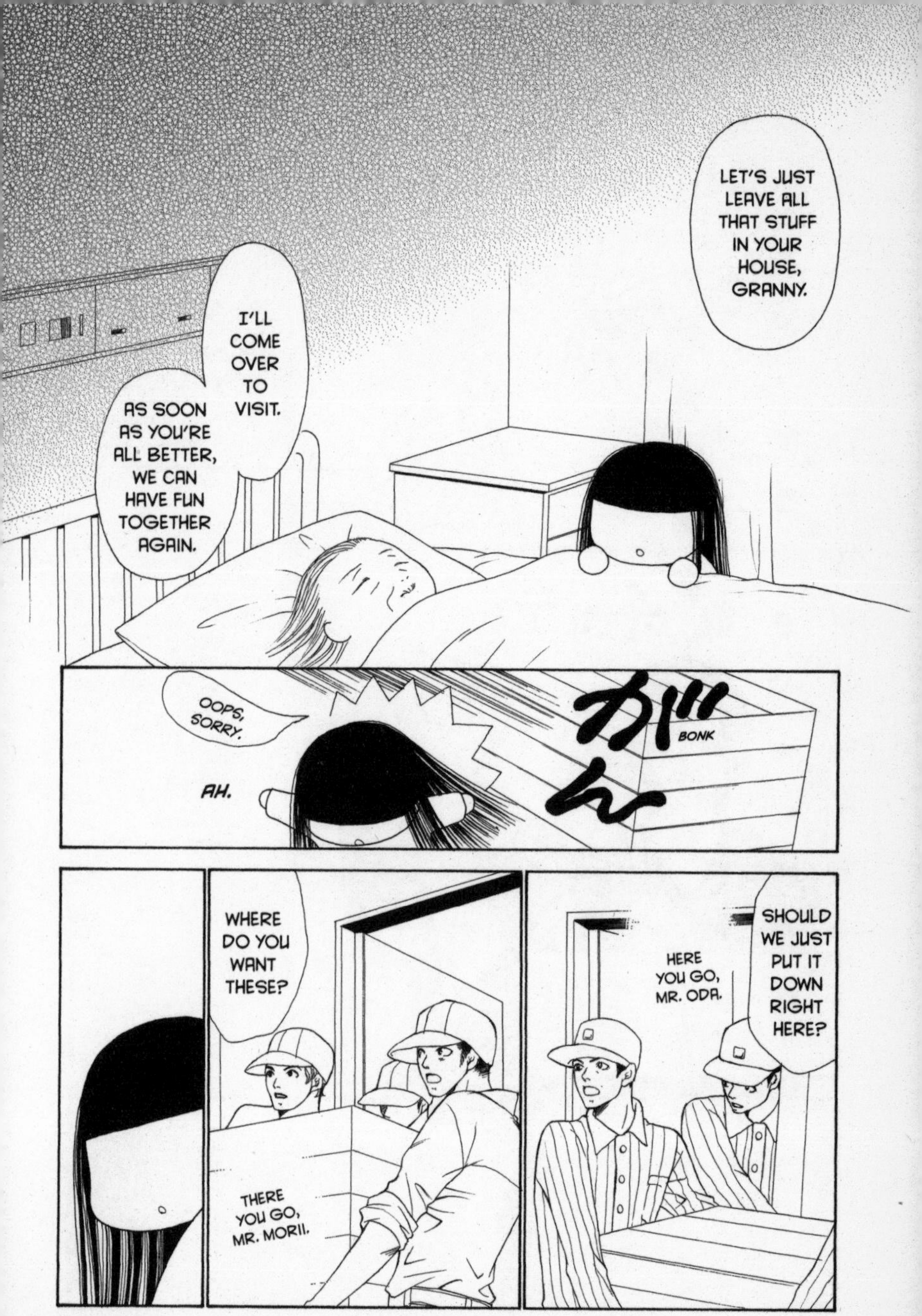
LET'S JUST LEAVE ALL THAT STUFF IN YOUR HOUSE, GRANNY.
I'LL COME OVER TO VISIT.
AS SOON AS YOU'RE ALL BETTER, WE CAN HAVE FUN TOGETHER AGAIN.
がん
BONK
OOPS, SORRY.
AH.
SHOULD WE JUST PUT IT DOWN RIGHT HERE?
HERE YOU GO, MR. ODA.
WHERE DO YOU WANT THESE?
THERE YOU GO, MR. MORII.

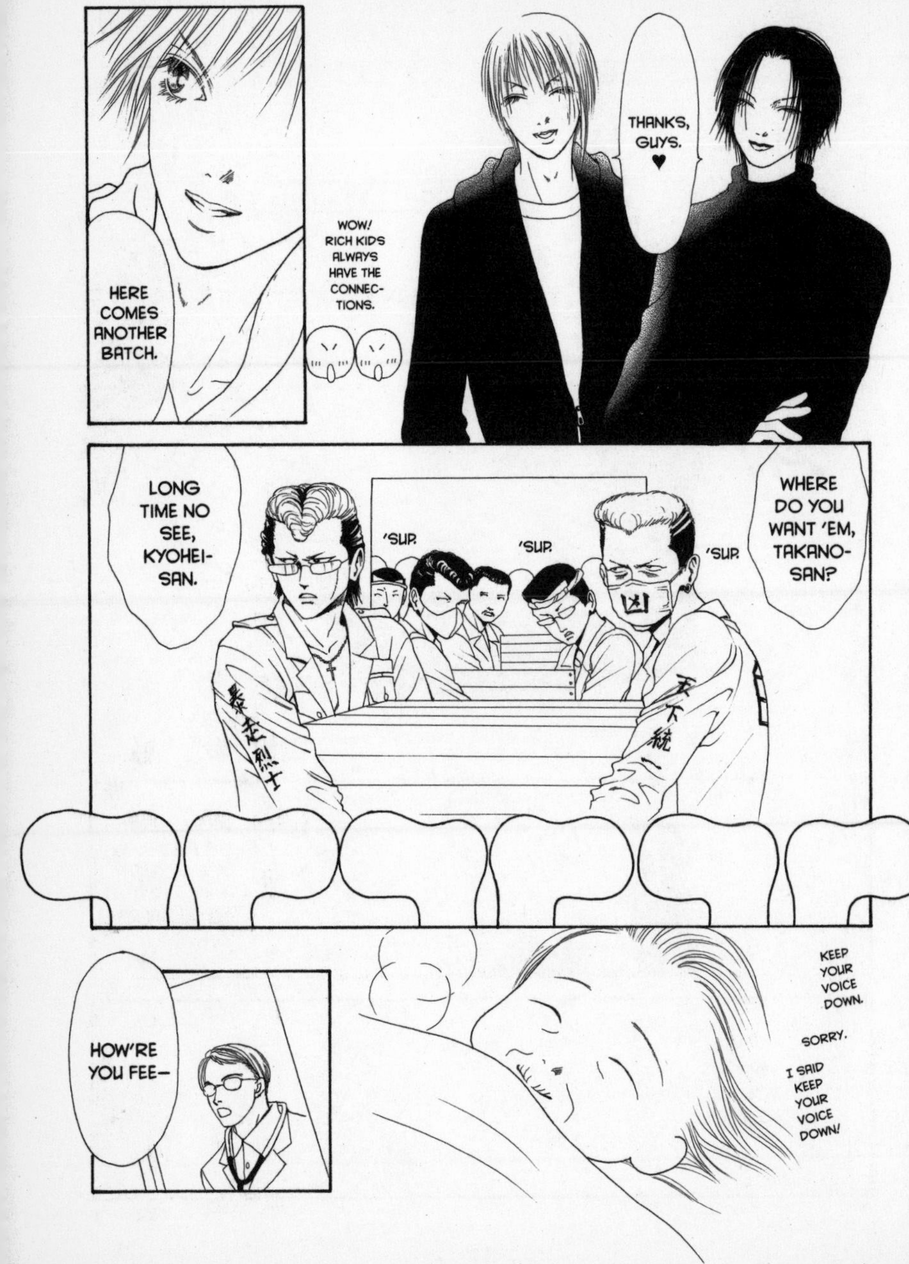
THANKS, GUYS. ♥
WOW! RICH KIDS ALWAYS HAVE THE CONNECTIONS.
HERE COMES ANOTHER BATCH.
WHERE DO YOU WANT 'EM, TAKANO-SAN?
'SUP.
天下統一
'SUP.
'SUP.
暴走烈士
LONG TIME NO SEE, KYOHEI-SAN.
KEEP YOUR VOICE DOWN.
SORRY.
I SAID KEEP YOUR VOICE DOWN!
HOW'RE YOU FEE—

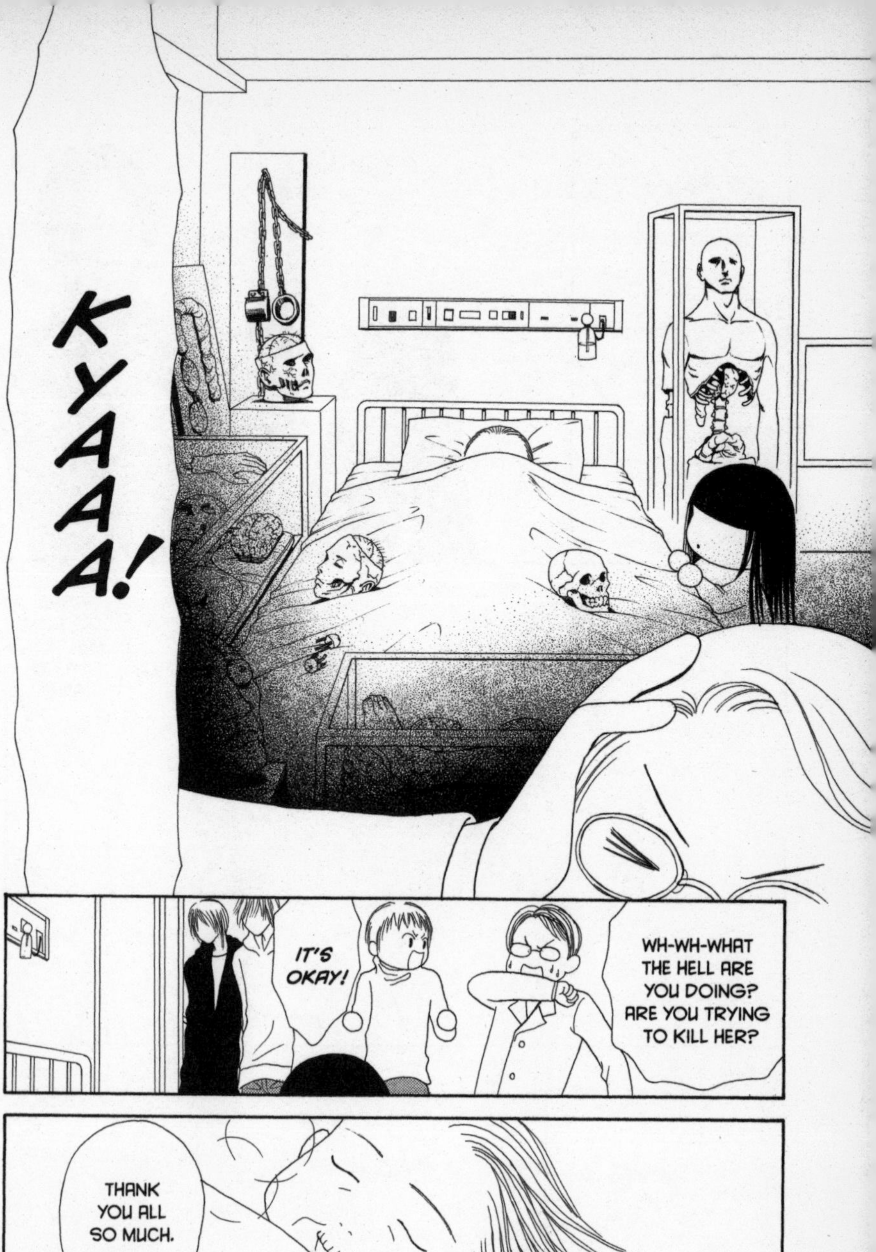
KYAAAA!
WH-WH-WHAT THE HELL ARE YOU DOING? ARE YOU TRYING TO KILL HER?
IT'S OKAY!
THANK YOU ALL SO MUCH.

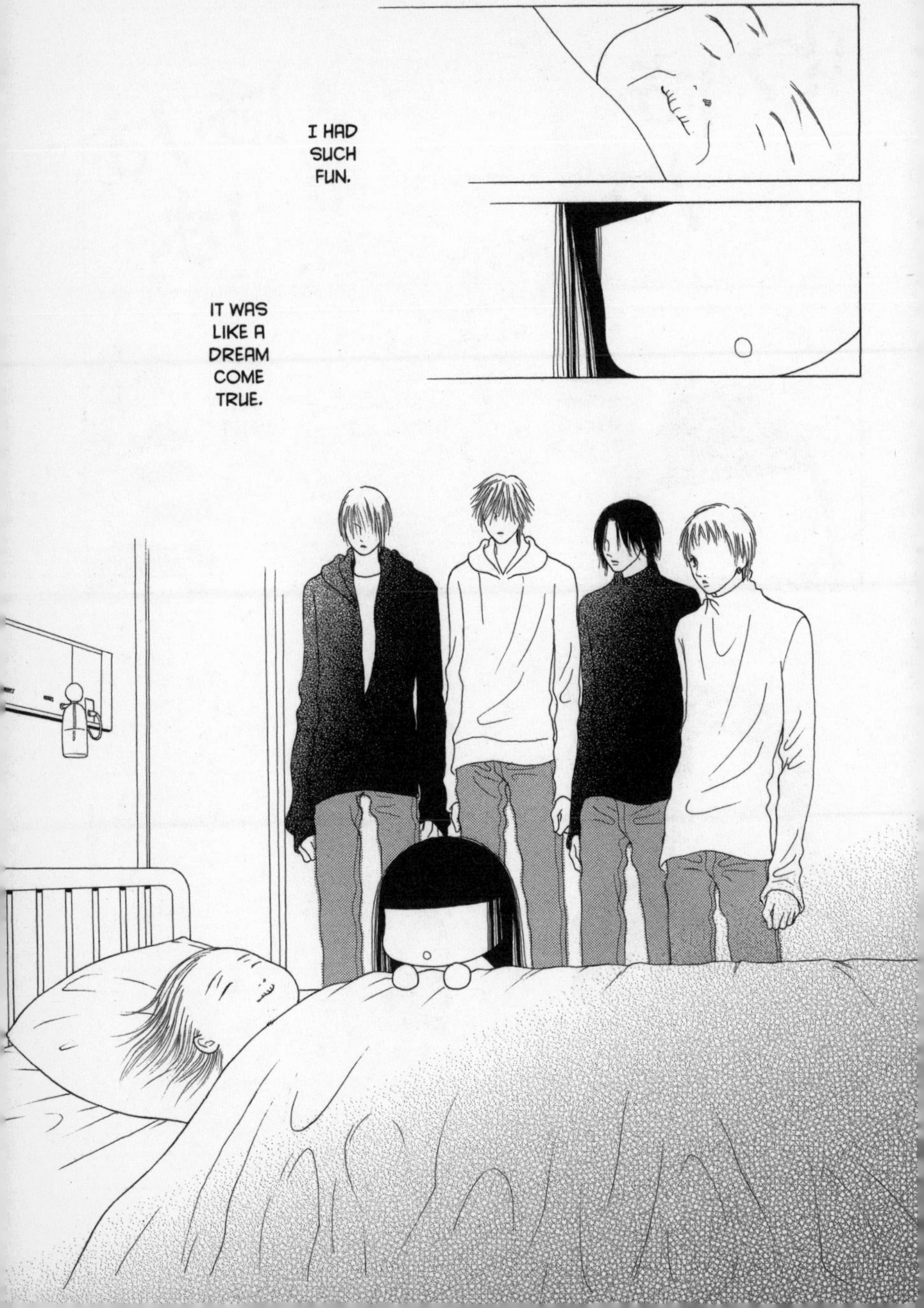
I HAD SUCH FUN.
IT WAS LIKE A DREAM COME TRUE.

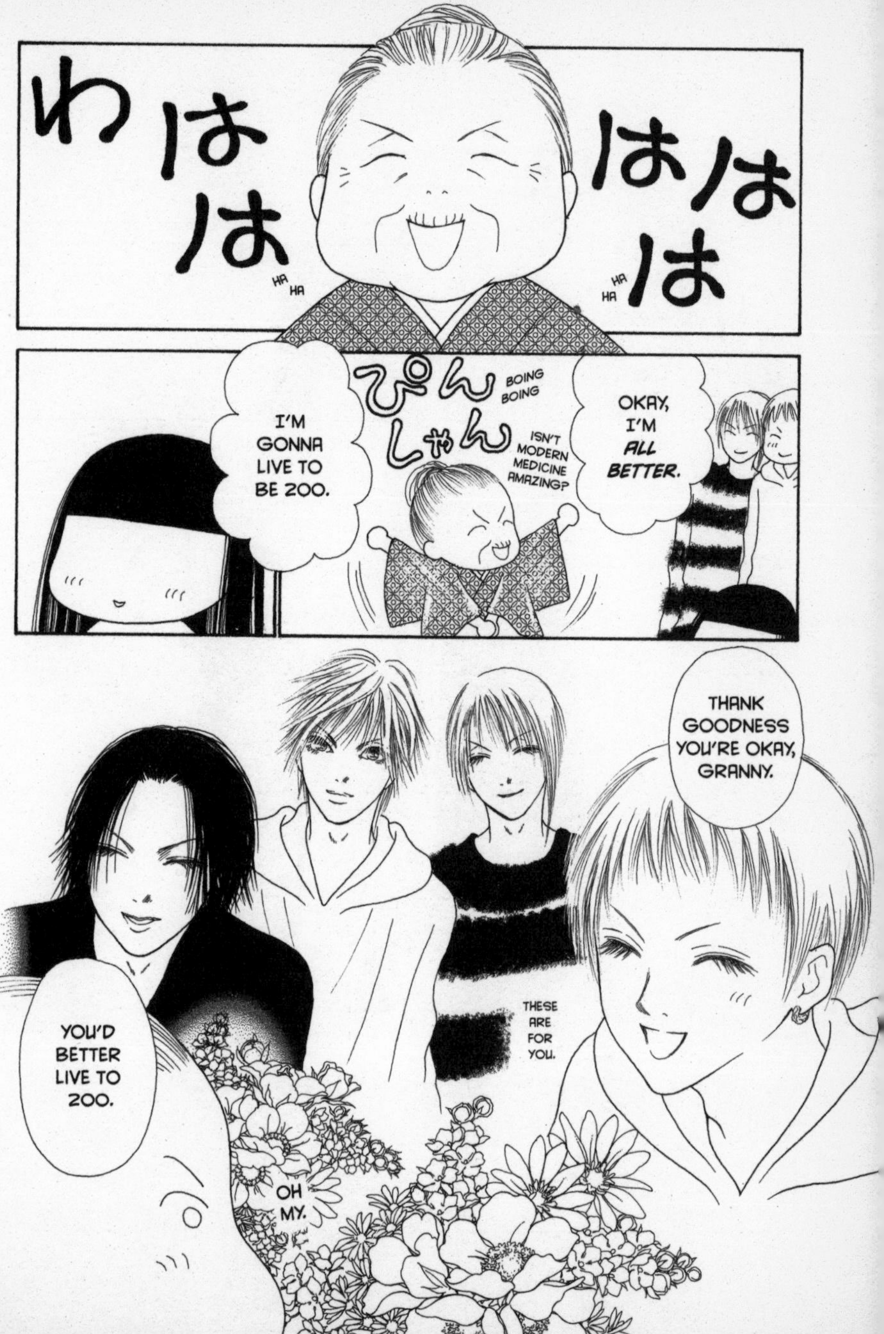
ははは
HA HA
わはは
HA HA
OKAY, I'M ALL BETTER.
ISN'T MODERN MEDICINE AMAZING?
ぴんしゃん
BOING BOING
I'M GONNA LIVE TO BE 200.
THANK GOODNESS YOU'RE OKAY, GRANNY.
THESE ARE FOR YOU.
YOU'D BETTER LIVE TO 200.
OH MY.

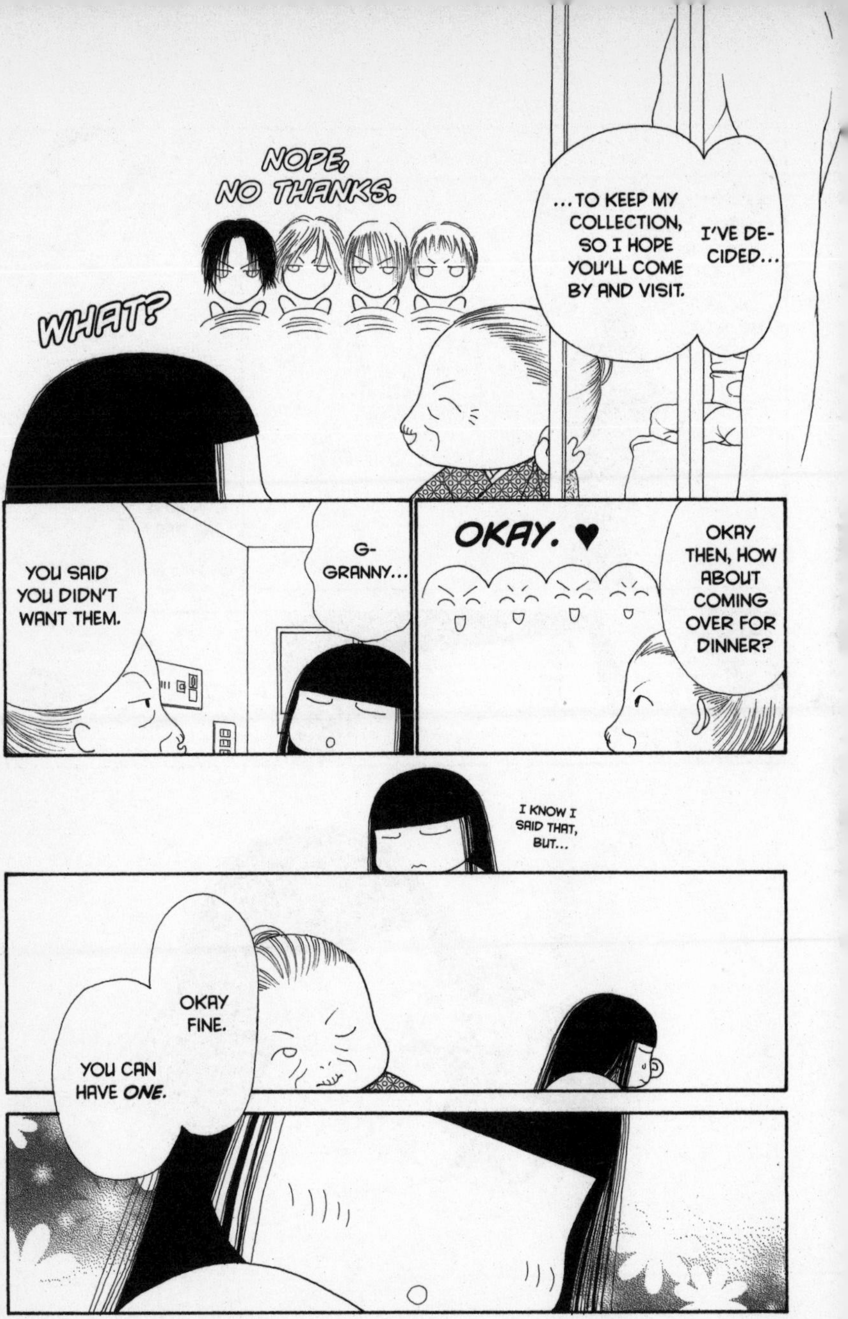
I'VE DECIDED...
...TO KEEP MY COLLECTION, SO I HOPE YOU'LL COME BY AND VISIT.
NOPE, NO THANKS.
WHAT?
OKAY THEN, HOW ABOUT COMING OVER FOR DINNER?
OKAY. ♥
G-GRANNY...
YOU SAID YOU DIDN'T WANT THEM.
I KNOW I SAID THAT, BUT...
OKAY FINE.
YOU CAN HAVE *ONE*.

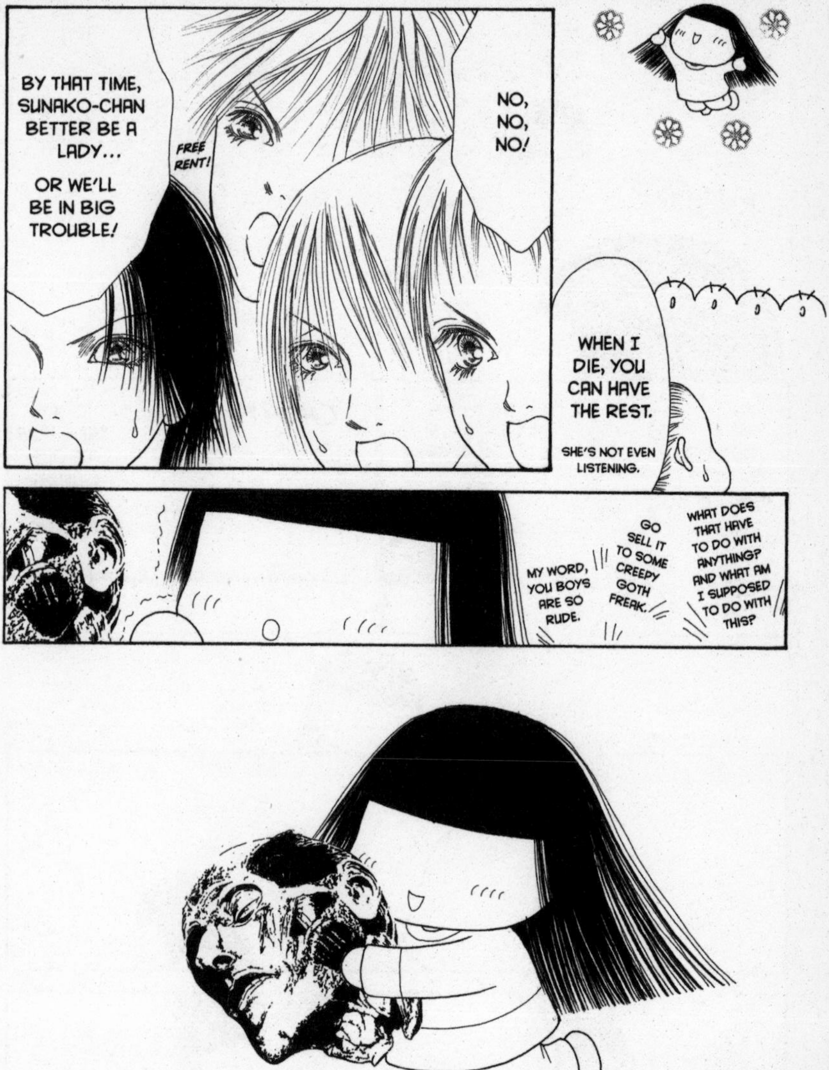
WHEN I DIE, YOU CAN HAVE THE REST.
SHE'S NOT EVEN LISTENING.
NO, NO, NO!
FREE RENT!
BY THAT TIME, SUNAKO-CHAN BETTER BE A LADY...
OR WE'LL BE IN BIG TROUBLE!
WHAT DOES THAT HAVE TO DO WITH ANYTHING? AND WHAT AM I SUPPOSED TO DO WITH THIS?
GO SELL IT TO SOME CREEPY GOTH FREAK.
MY WORD, YOU BOYS ARE SO RUDE.

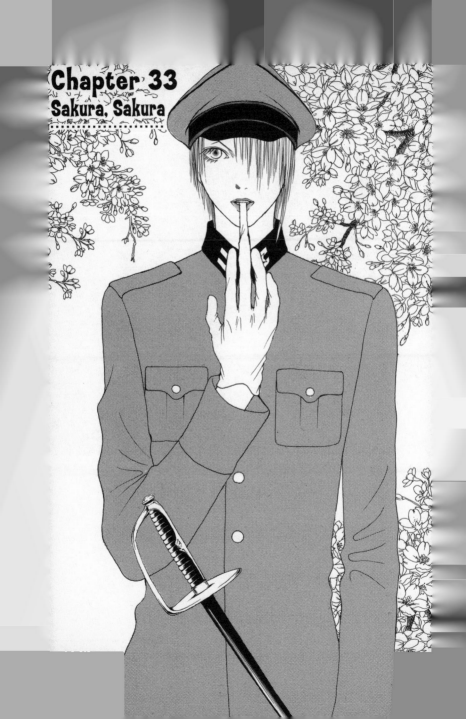

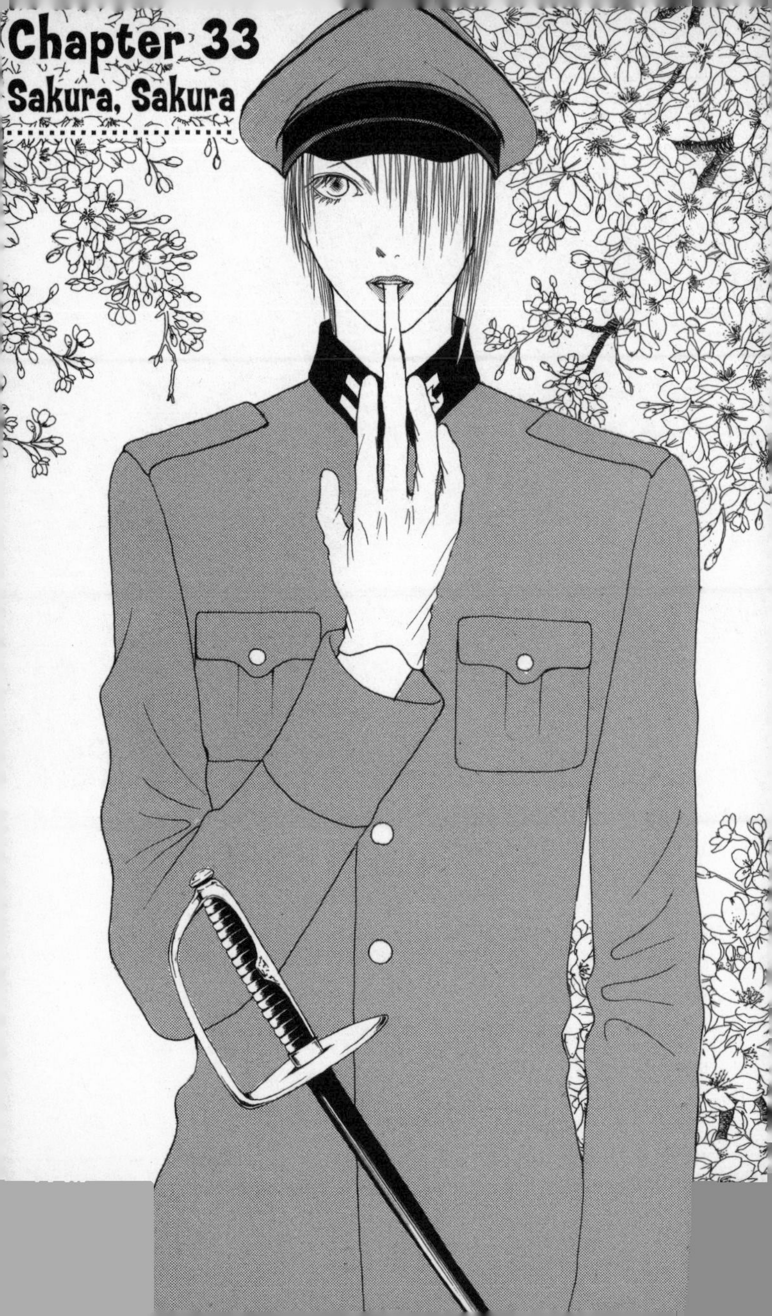
Chapter 33
Sakura, Sakura

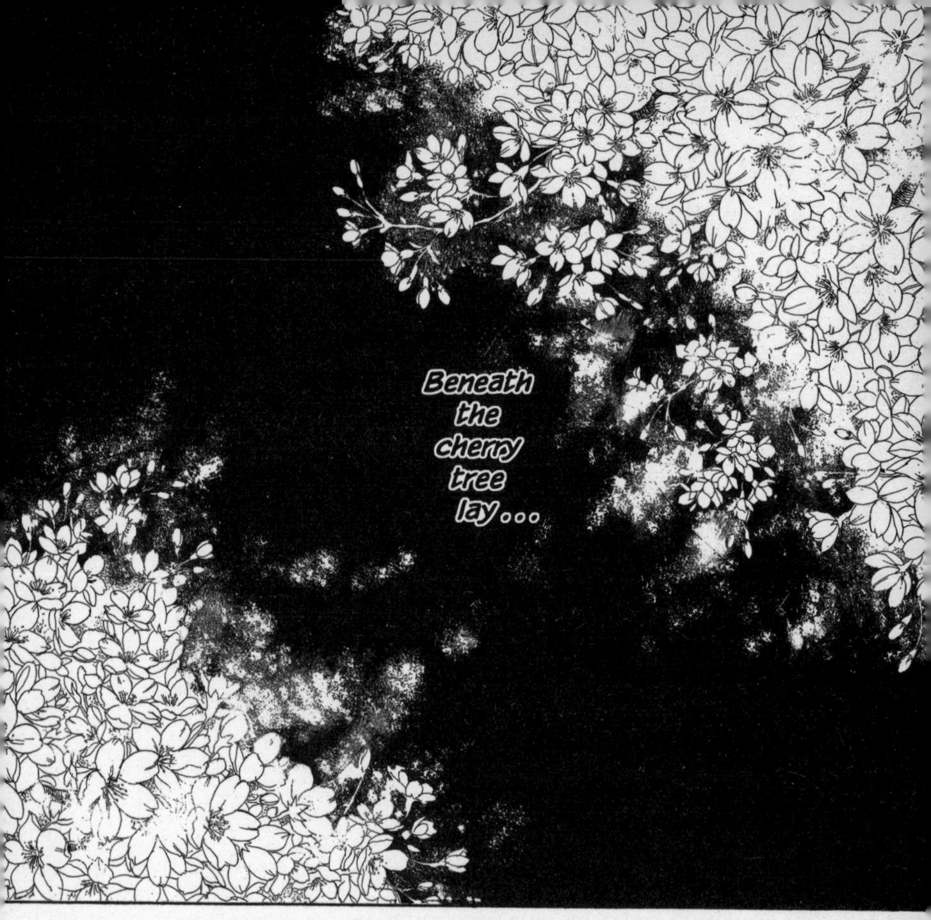
Beneath the cherry tree lay...

BEHIND THE SCENES

WHILE WORKING ON THESE STORYBOARDS, SOMETHING TRULY TERRIBLE HAPPENED TO ME. MY EDITOR SENT ME A COPY OF THE NEWLY PRINTED VOLUME 7, AND WELL... YOU CAN READ ALL ABOUT IT AT THE END OF THE BOOK. YOU MIGHT NOT THINK IT WAS A BIG DEAL, BUT IT SURE WAS TO ME. I COULD BARELY FINISH WRITING THIS STORY.

I REALLY CAN'T BELIEVE THAT I ACTUALLY MANAGED TO FINISH THE STORY WHILE IN SUCH AN UNSTABLE MENTAL STATE. AS FOR WHETHER THE STORY WAS ANY GOOD OR NOT... YOU CAN BE THE JUDGE OF THAT.

OH, DON'T WORRY. I'M ALL BETTER NOW.

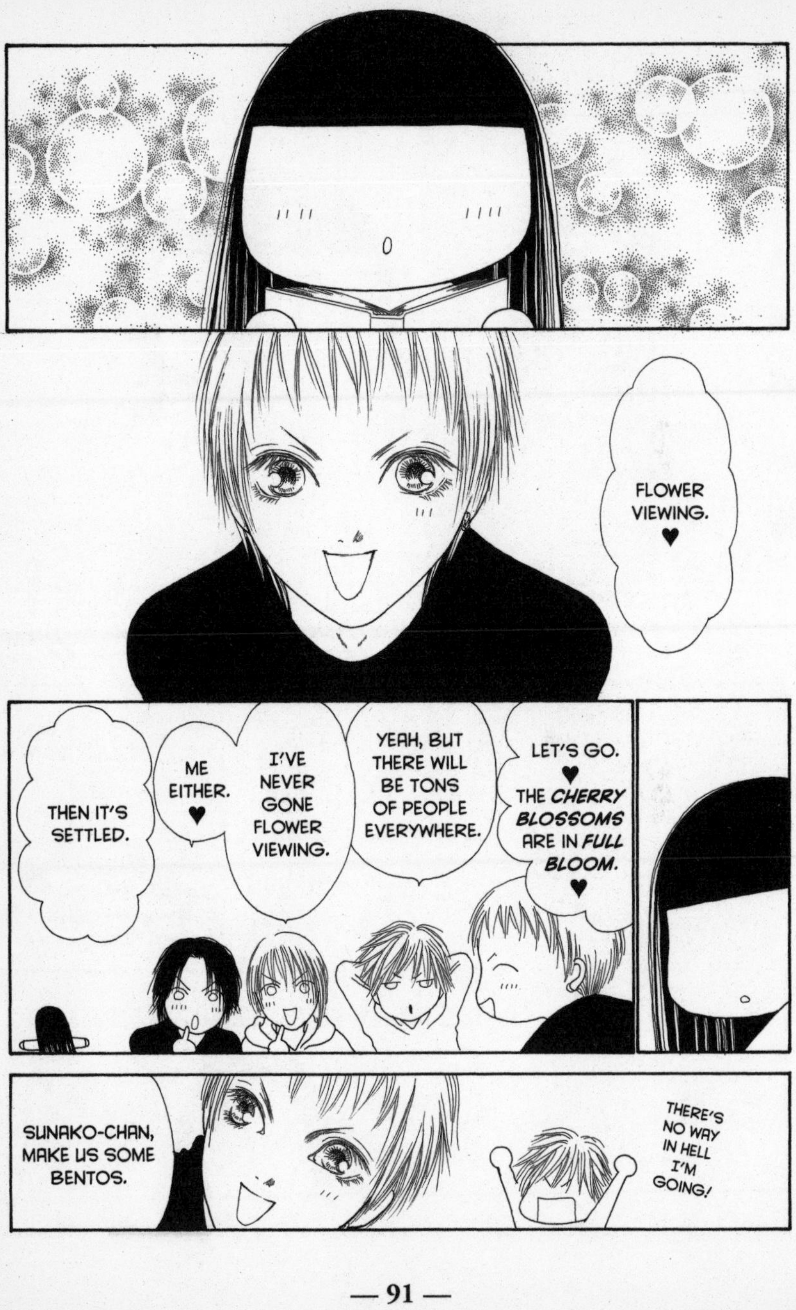
FLOWER VIEWING. ♥
LET'S GO. ♥ THE *CHERRY BLOSSOMS* ARE IN *FULL BLOOM*. ♥
YEAH, BUT THERE WILL BE TONS OF PEOPLE EVERYWHERE.
I'VE NEVER GONE FLOWER VIEWING.
ME EITHER. ♥
THEN IT'S SETTLED.
THERE'S NO WAY IN HELL I'M GOING!
SUNAKO-CHAN, MAKE US SOME BENTOS.

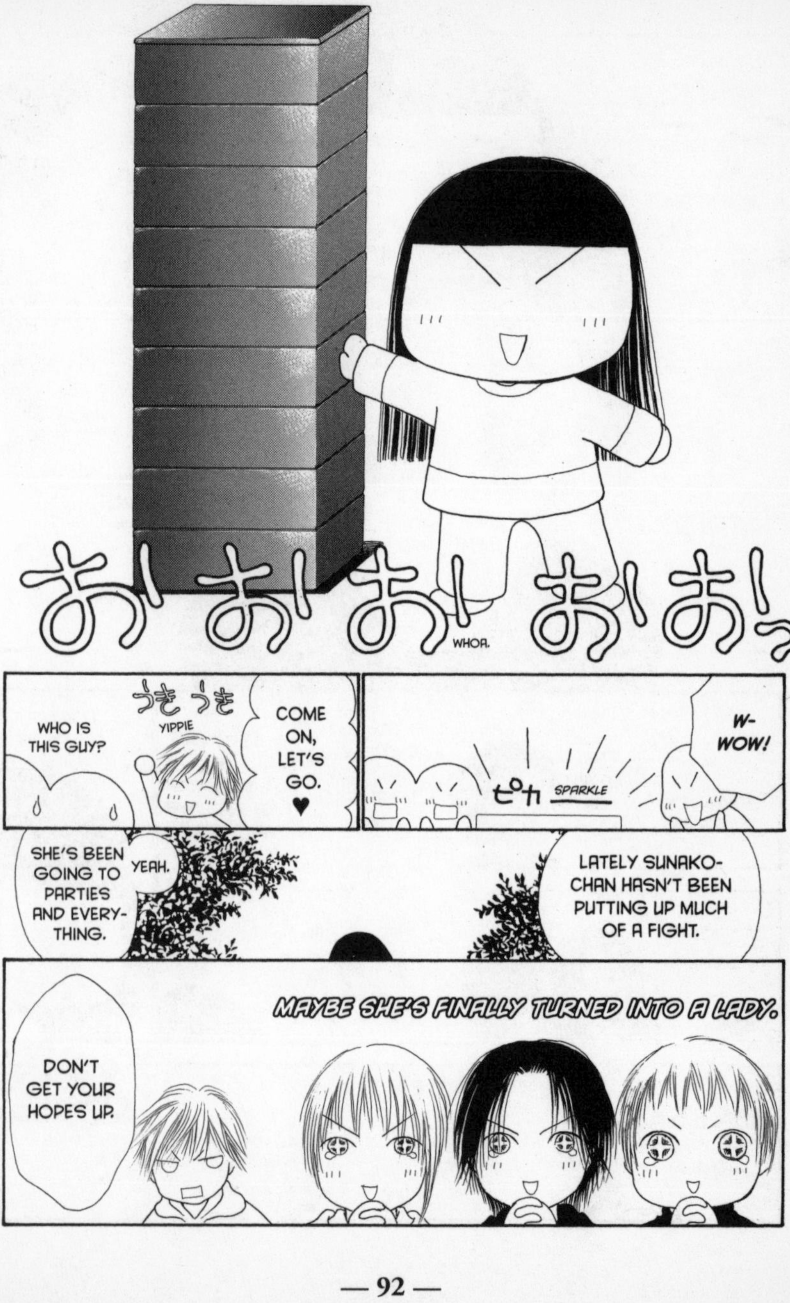
WHOA.
W-WOW!
ピカ
SPARKLE
COME ON, LET'S GO. ♥
うきうき
YIPPIE
WHO IS THIS GUY?
LATELY SUNAKO-CHAN HASN'T BEEN PUTTING UP MUCH OF A FIGHT.
SHE'S BEEN GOING TO PARTIES AND EVERY-THING.
YEAH.
MAYBE SHE'S FINALLY TURNED INTO A LADY.
DON'T GET YOUR HOPES UP.

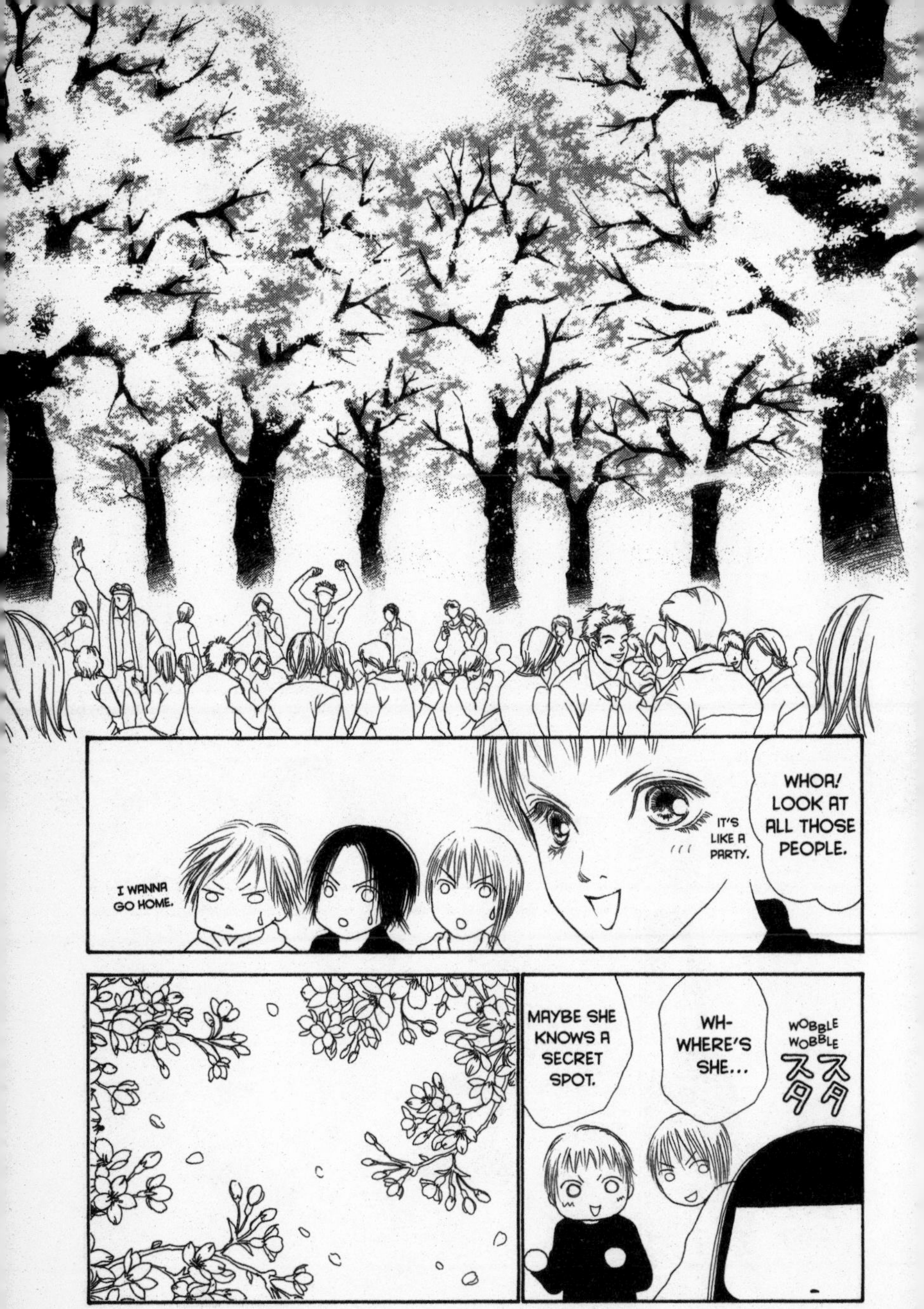
WHOA! LOOK AT ALL THOSE PEOPLE.
IT'S LIKE A PARTY.
I WANNA GO HOME.
WOBBLE WOBBLE
スタスタ
WH- WHERE'S SHE...
MAYBE SHE KNOWS A SECRET SPOT.

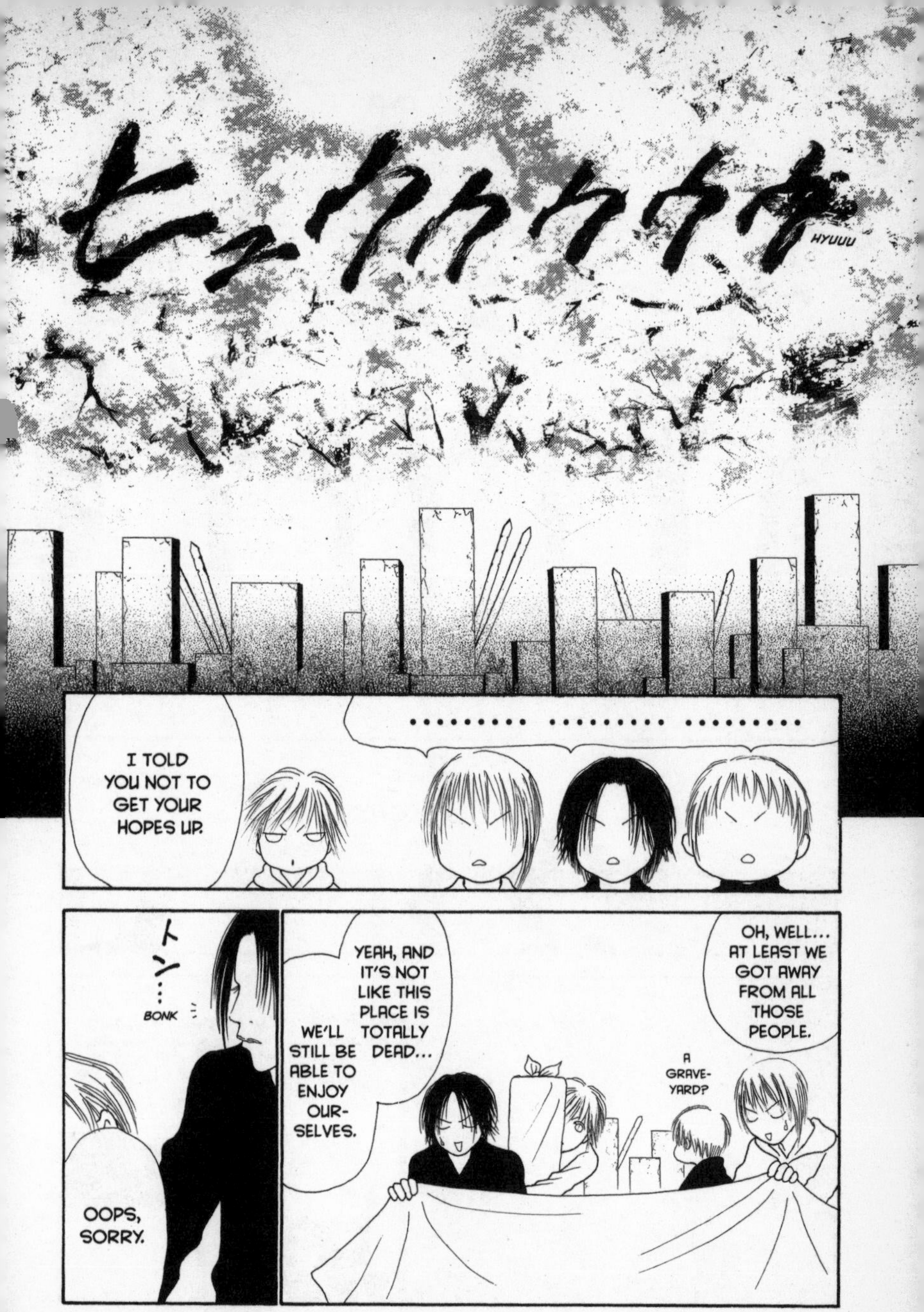
ヒュウウウウ
HYUUU
....
I TOLD YOU NOT TO GET YOUR HOPES UP.
OH, WELL... AT LEAST WE GOT AWAY FROM ALL THOSE PEOPLE.
A GRAVEYARD?
YEAH, AND IT'S NOT LIKE THIS PLACE IS TOTALLY DEAD... WE'LL STILL BE ABLE TO ENJOY OURSELVES.
トン…
BONK
OOPS, SORRY.

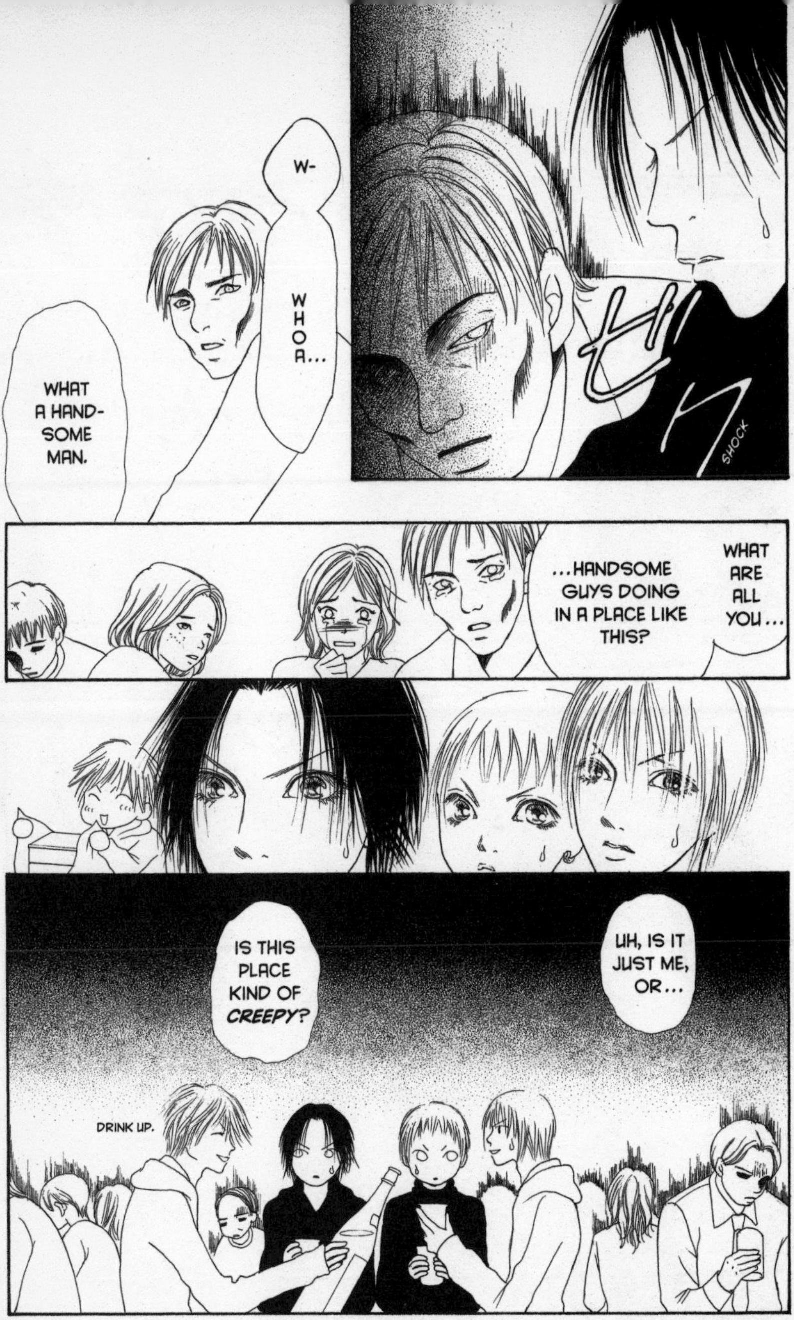
SHOCK
W-
WHOA...
WHAT A HANDSOME MAN.
WHAT ARE ALL YOU...
...HANDSOME GUYS DOING IN A PLACE LIKE THIS?
UH, IS IT JUST ME, OR...
IS THIS PLACE KIND OF *CREEPY*?
DRINK UP.

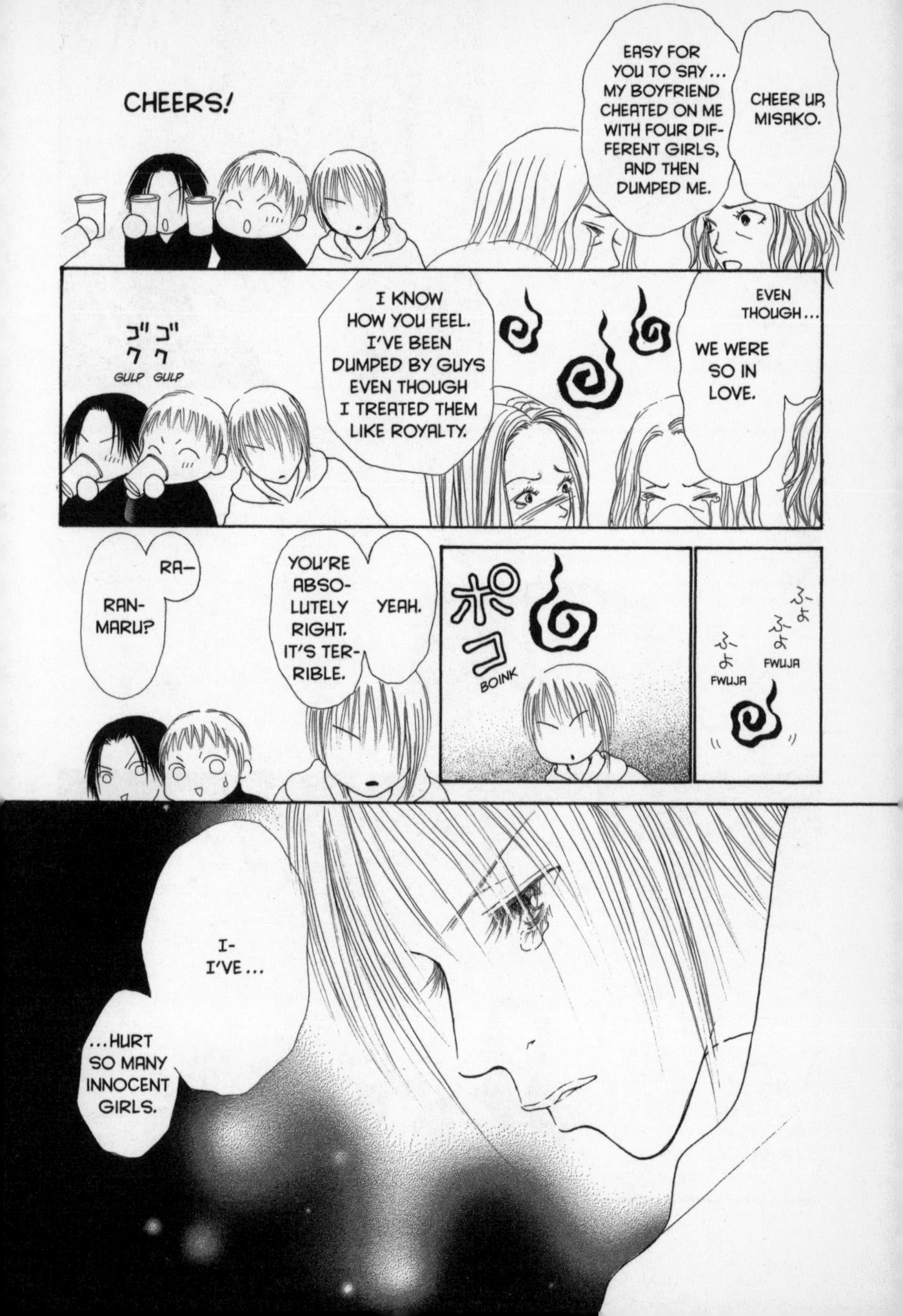
CHEER UP, MISAKO.
EASY FOR YOU TO SAY... MY BOYFRIEND CHEATED ON ME WITH FOUR DIFFERENT GIRLS, AND THEN DUMPED ME.
CHEERS!
EVEN THOUGH... WE WERE SO IN LOVE.
I KNOW HOW YOU FEEL. I'VE BEEN DUMPED BY GUYS EVEN THOUGH I TREATED THEM LIKE ROYALTY.
ゴクゴク
GULP GULP
ふよふよふよ
FWUJA FWUJA
ポコ
BOINK
YEAH.
YOU'RE ABSOLUTELY RIGHT. IT'S TERRIBLE.
RA- RAN-MARU?
I- I'VE...
...HURT SO MANY INNOCENT GIRLS.

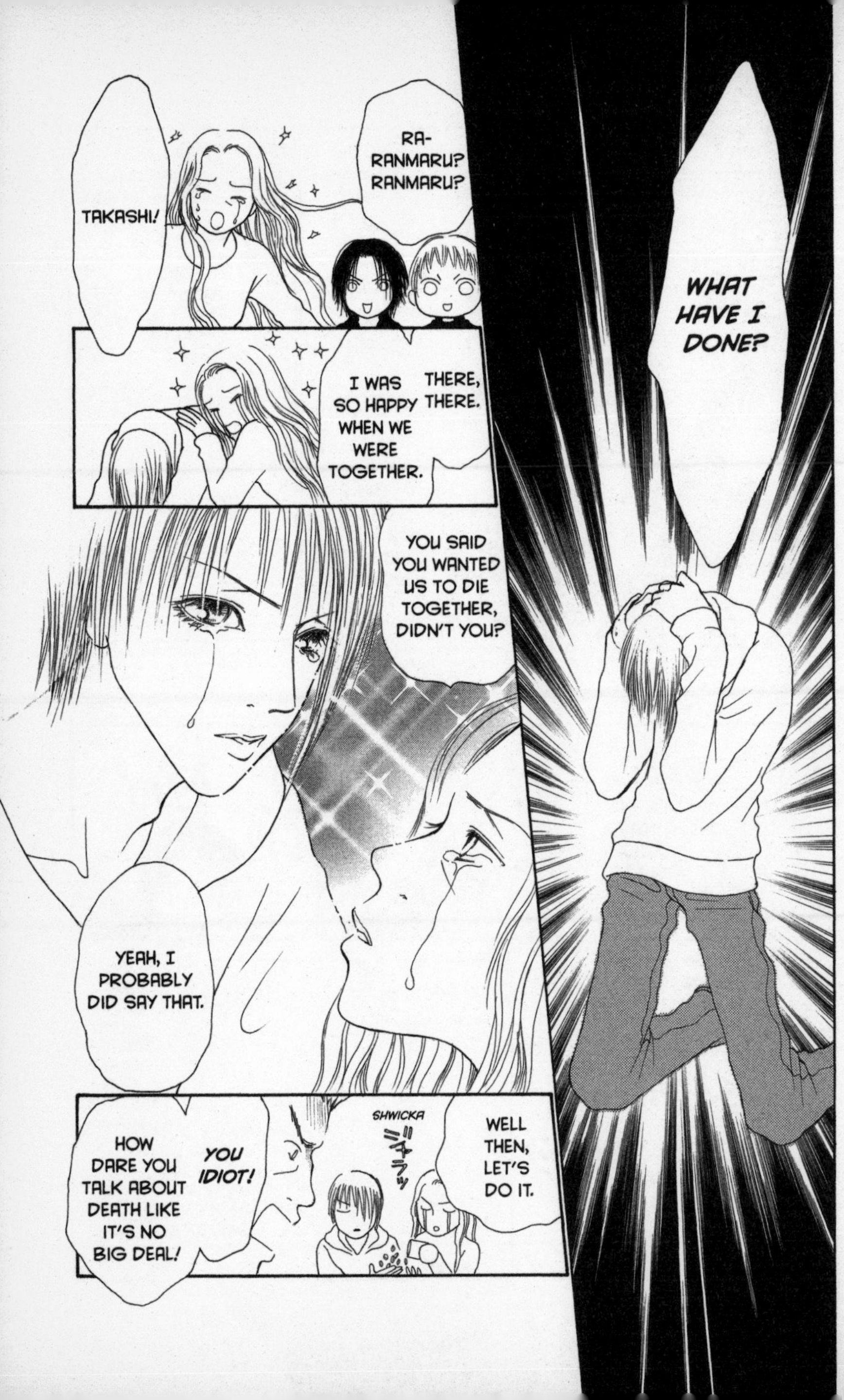
WHAT HAVE I DONE?
RA- RANMARU? RANMARU?
TAKASHI!
THERE, THERE.
I WAS SO HAPPY WHEN WE WERE TOGETHER.
YOU SAID YOU WANTED US TO DIE TOGETHER, DIDN'T YOU?
YEAH, I PROBABLY DID SAY THAT.
WELL THEN, LET'S DO IT.
SHWICKA
YOU IDIOT!
HOW DARE YOU TALK ABOUT DEATH LIKE IT'S NO BIG DEAL!

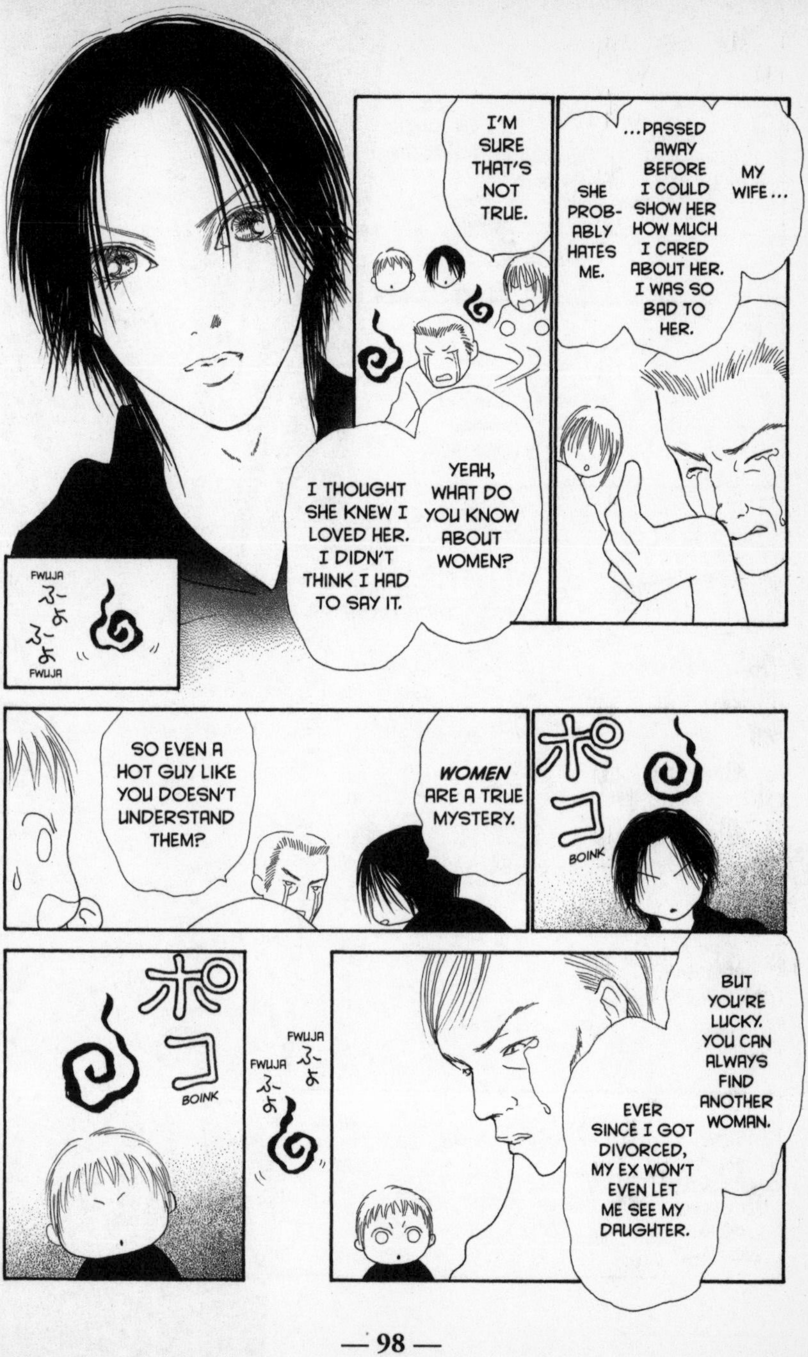
MY WIFE...
...PASSED AWAY BEFORE I COULD SHOW HER HOW MUCH I CARED ABOUT HER. I WAS SO BAD TO HER.
SHE PROBABLY HATES ME.
I'M SURE THAT'S NOT TRUE.
YEAH, WHAT DO YOU KNOW ABOUT WOMEN?
I THOUGHT SHE KNEW I LOVED HER. I DIDN'T THINK I HAD TO SAY IT.
ふよふよ
FWUJA FWUJA
ポコ
BOINK
WOMEN ARE A TRUE MYSTERY.
SO EVEN A HOT GUY LIKE YOU DOESN'T UNDERSTAND THEM?
BUT YOU'RE LUCKY. YOU CAN ALWAYS FIND ANOTHER WOMAN.
EVER SINCE I GOT DIVORCED, MY EX WON'T EVEN LET ME SEE MY DAUGHTER.
ポコ
BOINK
ふよふよ
FWUJA FWUJA

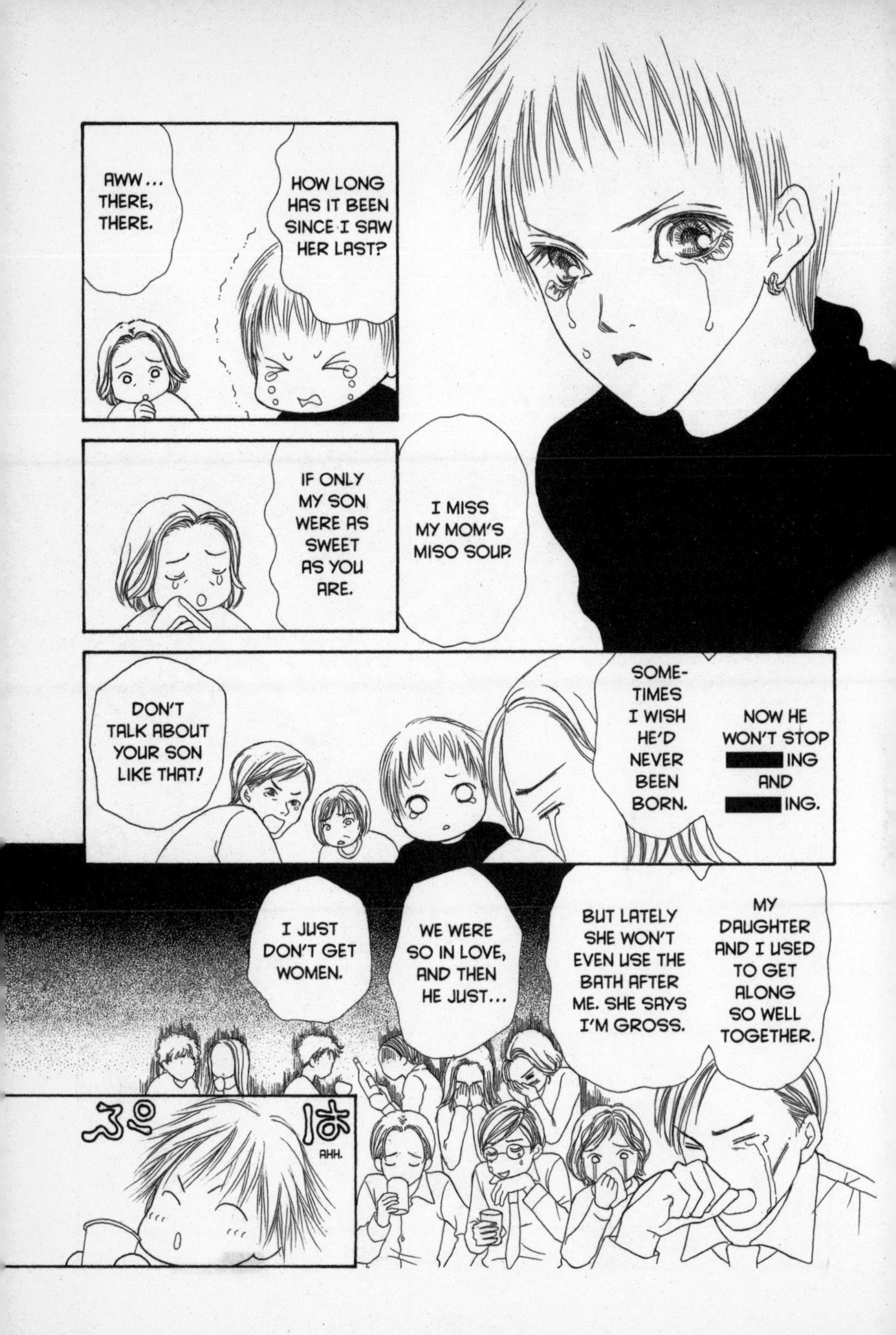
I MISS MY MOM'S MISO SOUP.
HOW LONG HAS IT BEEN SINCE I SAW HER LAST?
AWW... THERE, THERE.
IF ONLY MY SON WERE AS SWEET AS YOU ARE.
NOW HE WON'T STOP [redacted]ING AND [redacted]ING.
SOME-TIMES I WISH HE'D NEVER BEEN BORN.
DON'T TALK ABOUT YOUR SON LIKE THAT!
MY DAUGHTER AND I USED TO GET ALONG SO WELL TOGETHER.
BUT LATELY SHE WON'T EVEN USE THE BATH AFTER ME. SHE SAYS I'M GROSS.
WE WERE SO IN LOVE, AND THEN HE JUST...
I JUST DON'T GET WOMEN.
ぷは
AHH.

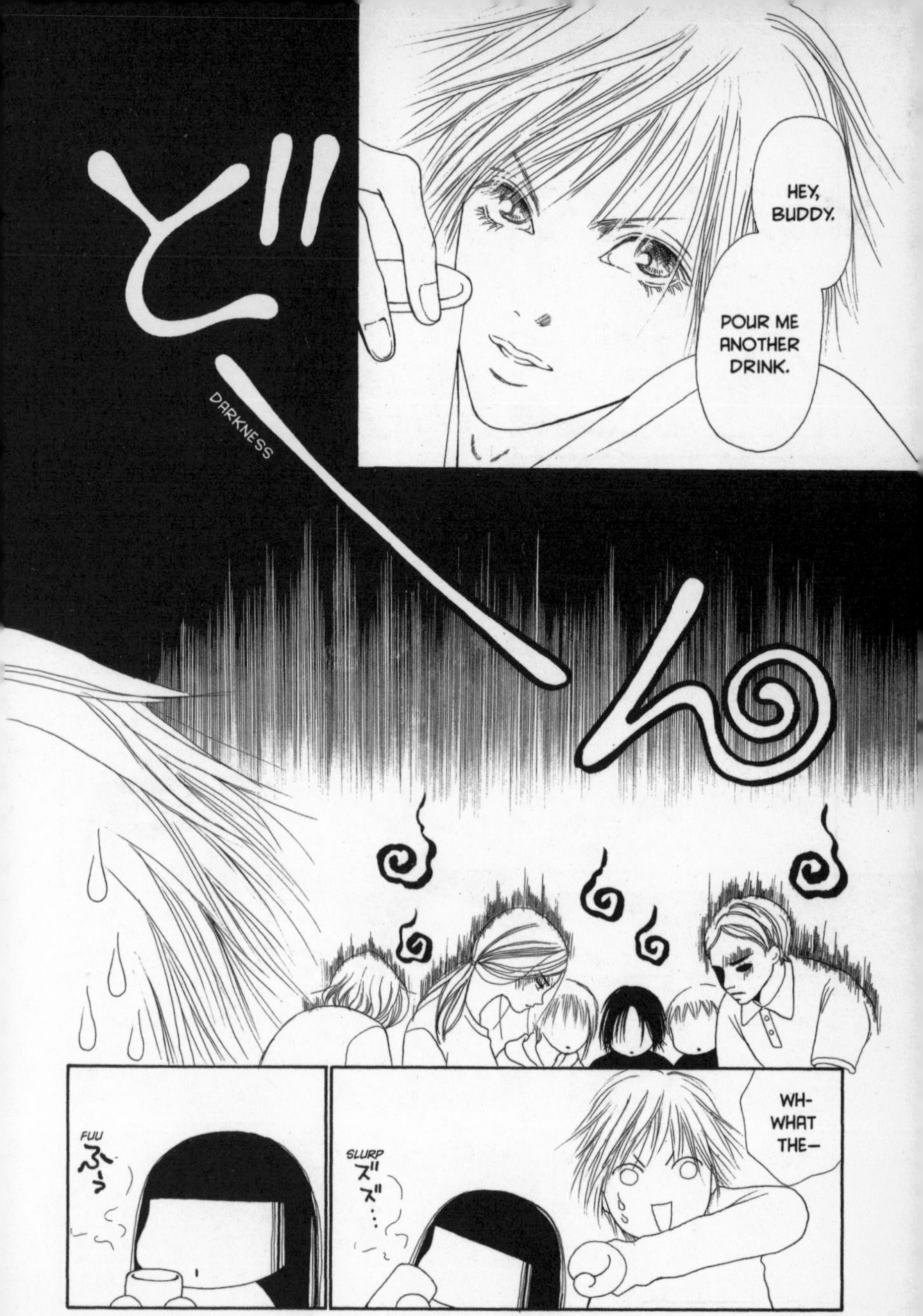
HEY, BUDDY.
POUR ME ANOTHER DRINK.
どーん
DARKNESS
WH- WHAT THE—
SLURP
ズズ…
FUU
ふ～

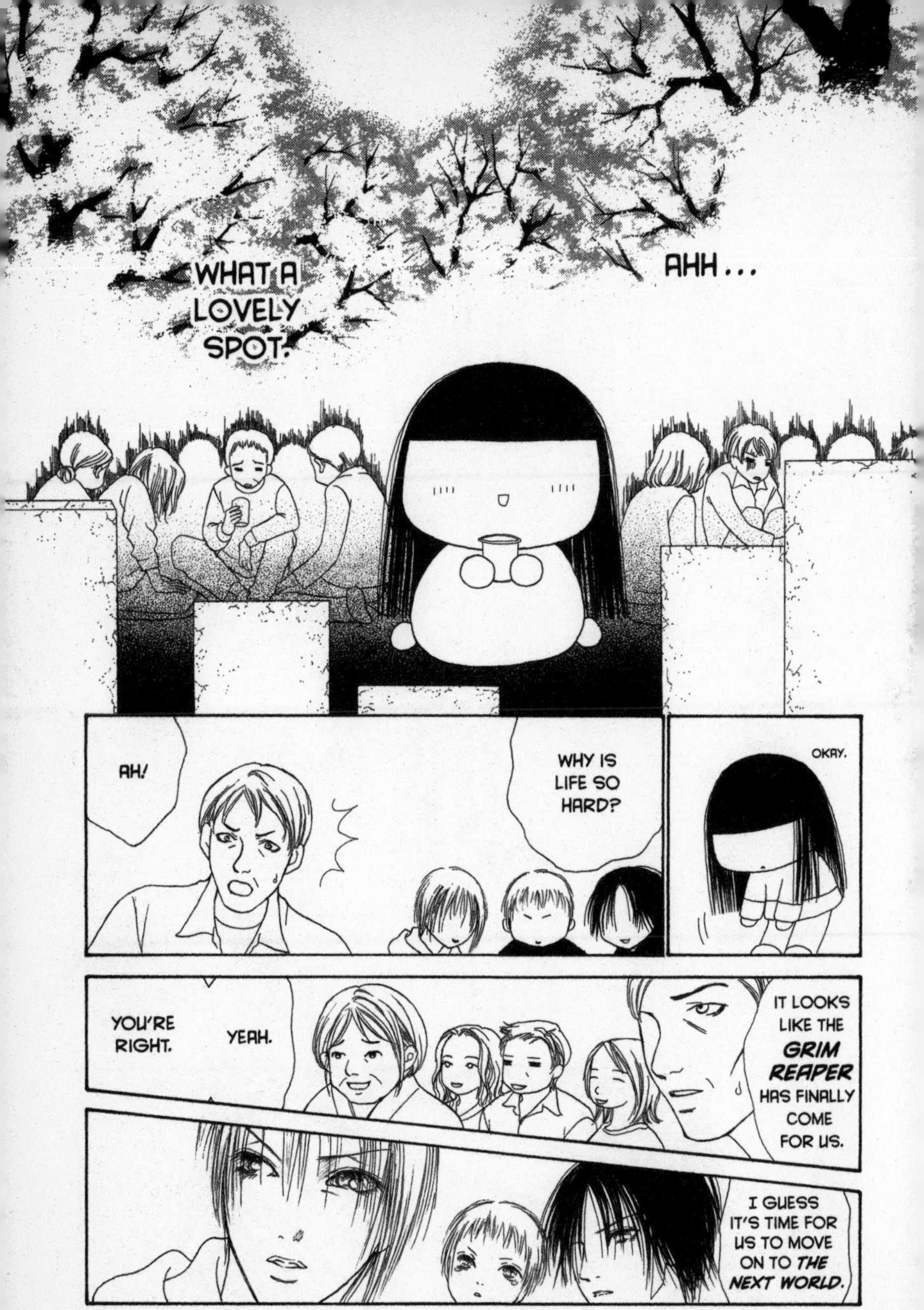
AHH...
WHAT A LOVELY SPOT.
OKAY.
WHY IS LIFE SO HARD?
AH!
IT LOOKS LIKE THE ***GRIM REAPER*** HAS FINALLY COME FOR US.
YEAH.
YOU'RE RIGHT.
I GUESS IT'S TIME FOR US TO MOVE ON TO ***THE NEXT WORLD***.

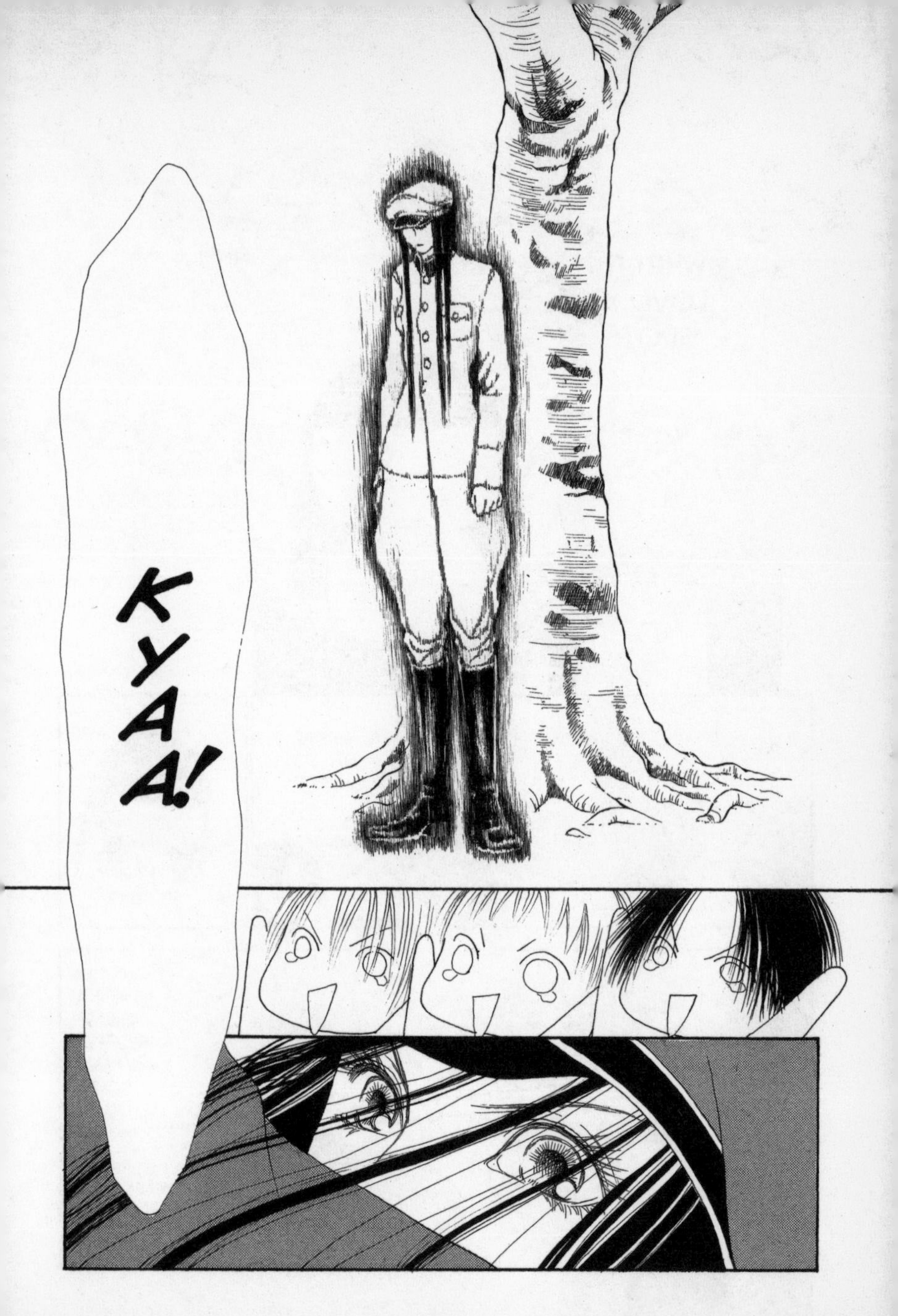
KYAA!

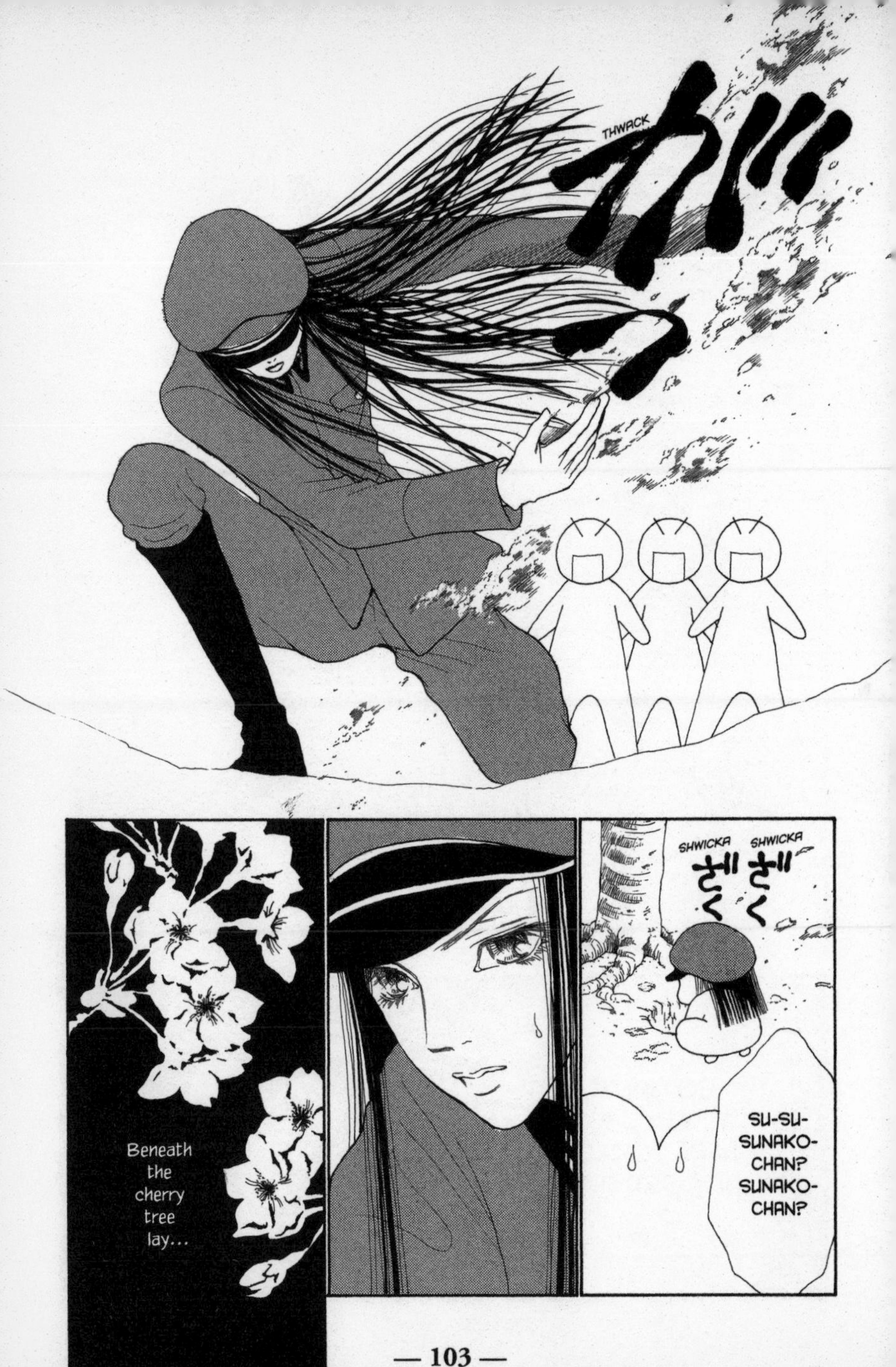
THWACK
ガッ
SHWICKA SHWICKA
ざく ざく
SU-SU-SUNAKO-CHAN? SUNAKO-CHAN?
Beneath the cherry tree lay...

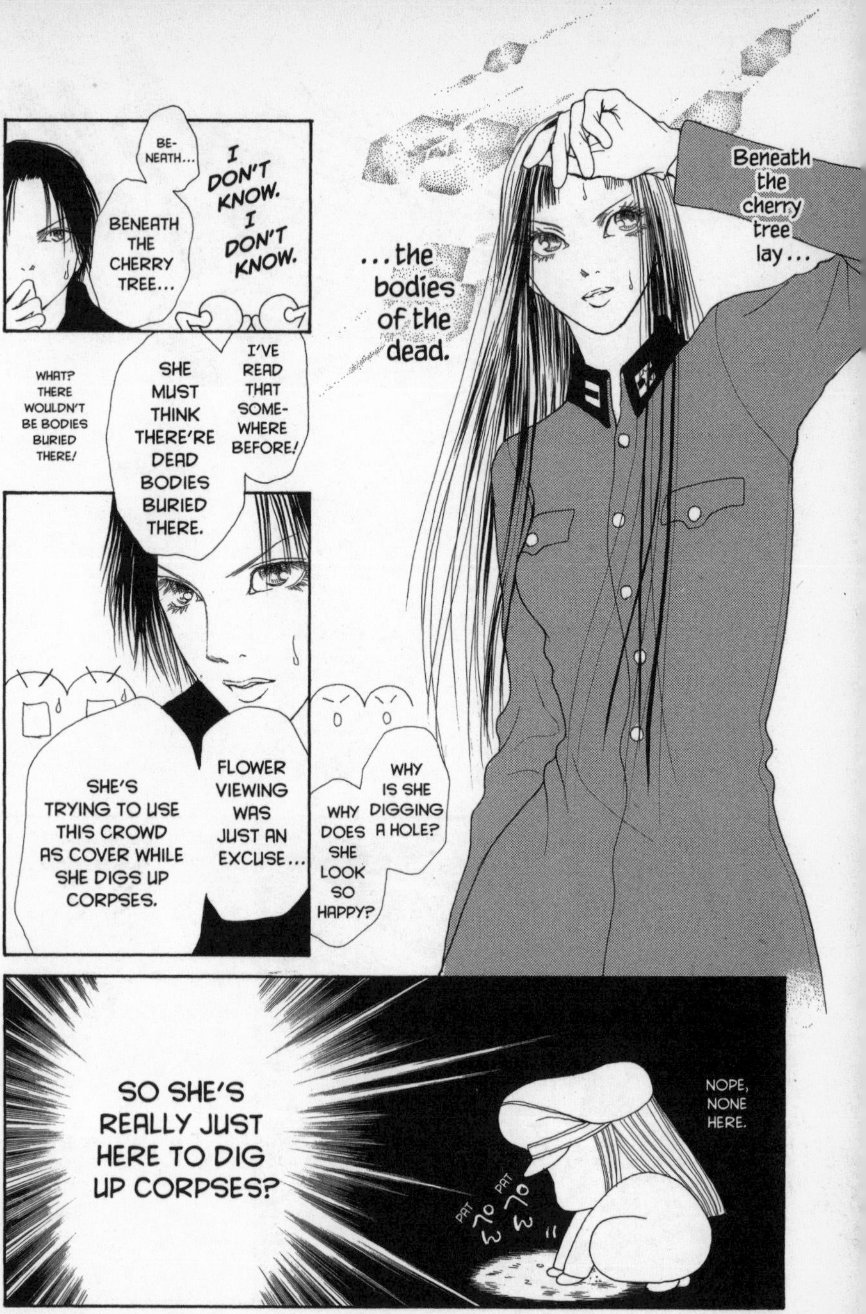
Beneath the cherry tree lay...
...the bodies of the dead.
I DON'T KNOW. I DON'T KNOW.
BE-NEATH...
BENEATH THE CHERRY TREE...
I'VE READ THAT SOME-WHERE BEFORE!
SHE MUST THINK THERE'RE DEAD BODIES BURIED THERE.
WHAT? THERE WOULDN'T BE BODIES BURIED THERE!
WHY IS SHE DIGGING A HOLE?
WHY DOES SHE LOOK SO HAPPY?
FLOWER VIEWING WAS JUST AN EXCUSE...
SHE'S TRYING TO USE THIS CROWD AS COVER WHILE SHE DIGS UP CORPSES.
NOPE, NONE HERE.
PAT PAT
SO SHE'S REALLY JUST HERE TO DIG UP CORPSES?

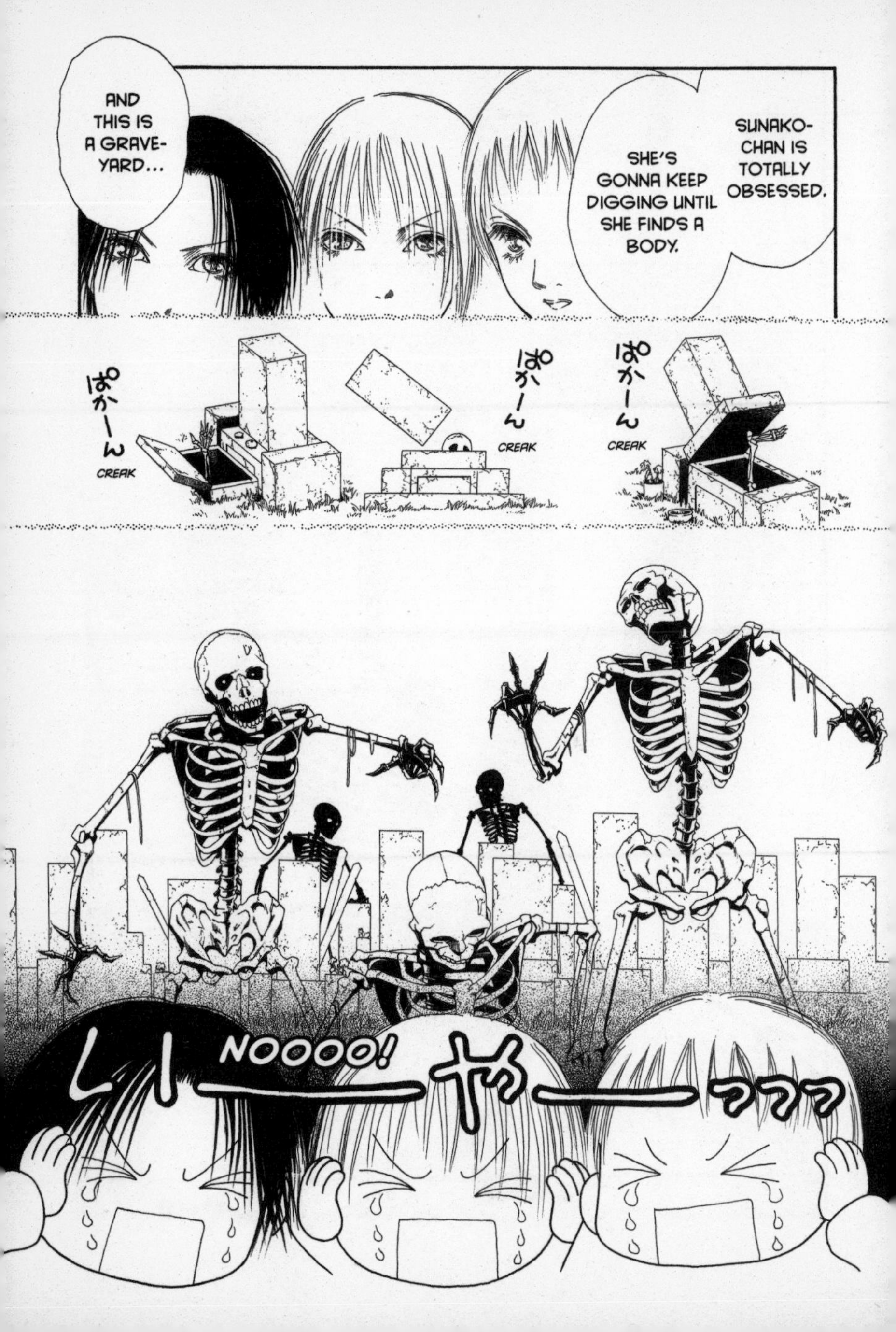
SUNAKO-CHAN IS TOTALLY OBSESSED.
SHE'S GONNA KEEP DIGGING UNTIL SHE FINDS A BODY.
AND THIS IS A GRAVE-YARD...
ぱかーん
CREAK
ぱかーん
CREAK
ぱかーん
CREAK
いーやーっっっ
NOOOO!

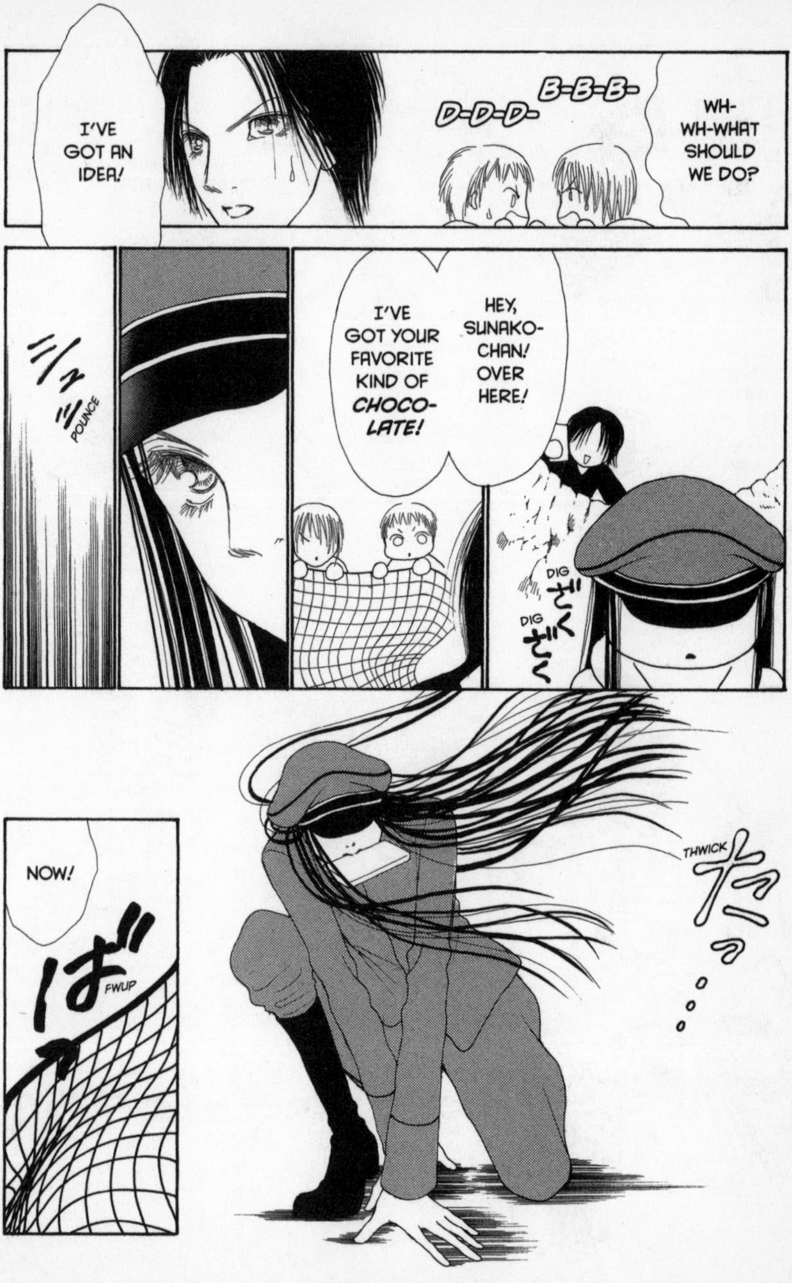
WH- WH-WHAT SHOULD WE DO?
B-B-B-
D-D-D-
I'VE GOT AN IDEA!
HEY, SUNAKO-CHAN! OVER HERE!
I'VE GOT YOUR FAVORITE KIND OF *CHOCOLATE!*
DIG ざく
DIG ざく
シュッ
POUNCE
THWICK
たっ
NOW!
ばっ
FWUP

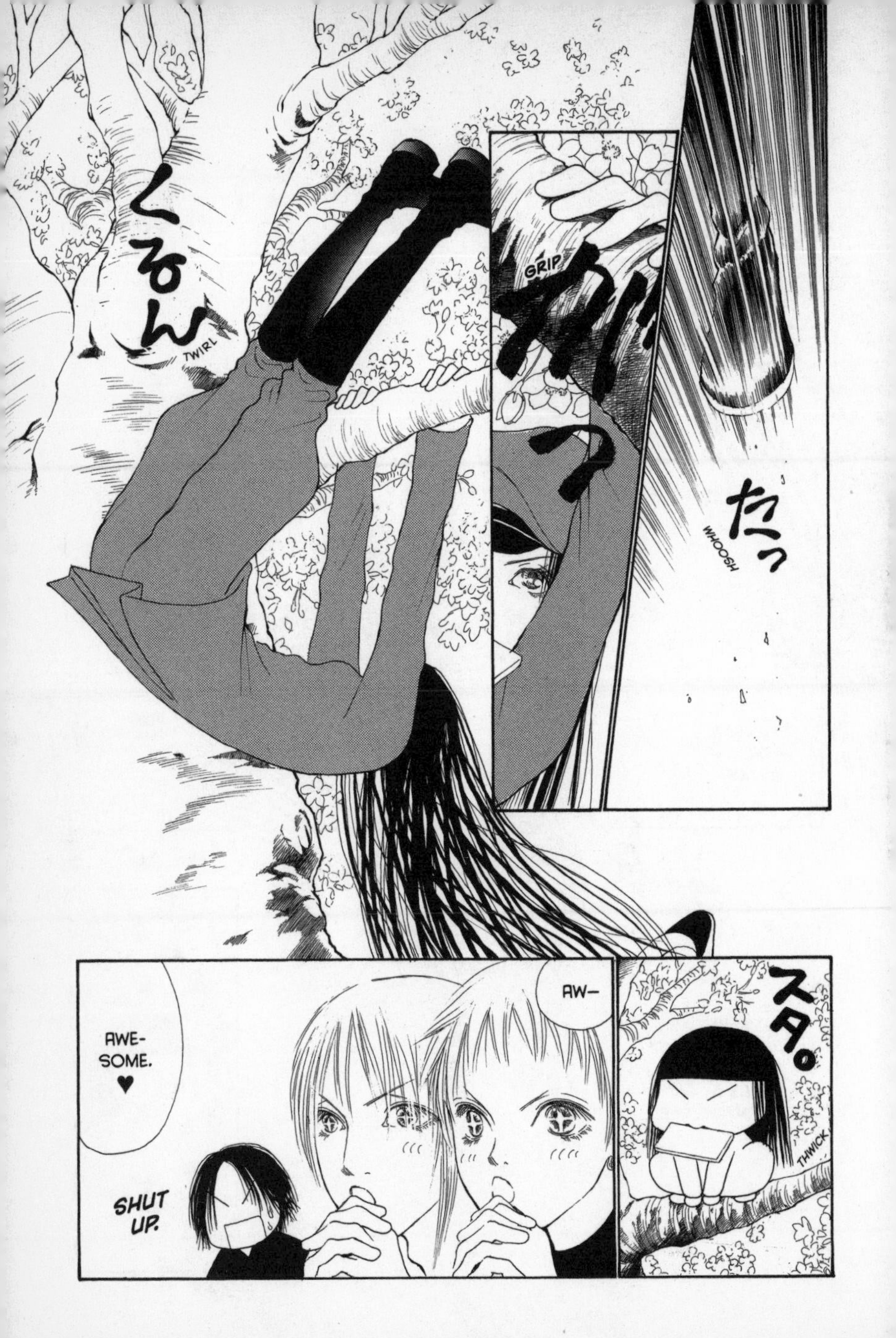

たっ
WHOOSH
ガッ
GRIP
くるん
TWIRL
スタ。
THWICK
AW—
AWE-SOME. ♥
SHUT UP.

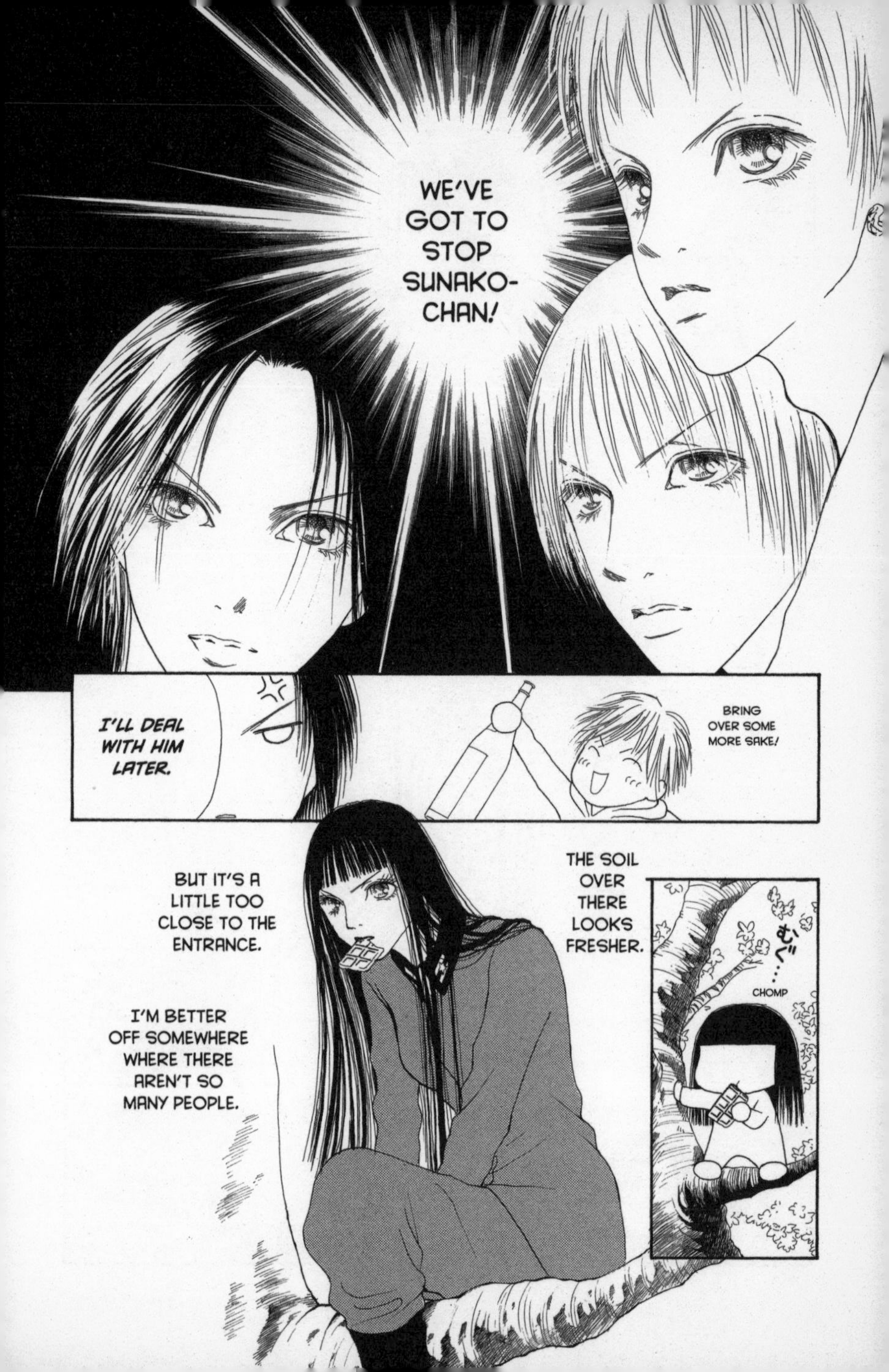
WE'VE GOT TO STOP SUNAKO-CHAN!
BRING OVER SOME MORE SAKE!
I'LL DEAL WITH HIM LATER.
THE SOIL OVER THERE LOOKS FRESHER.
むぐ…
CHOMP
BUT IT'S A LITTLE TOO CLOSE TO THE ENTRANCE.
I'M BETTER OFF SOMEWHERE WHERE THERE AREN'T SO MANY PEOPLE.

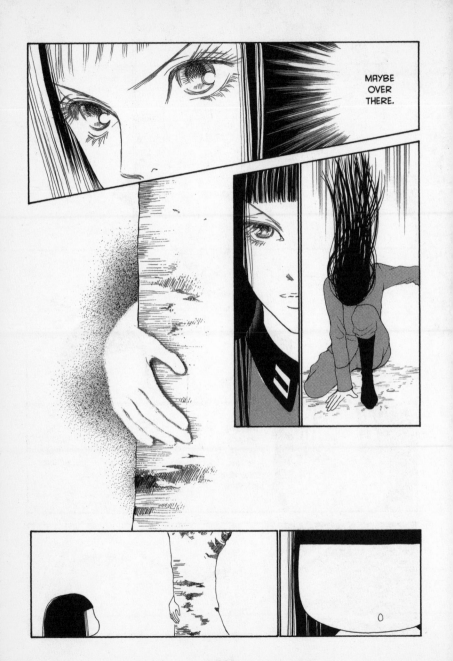

MAYBE
OVER
THERE.

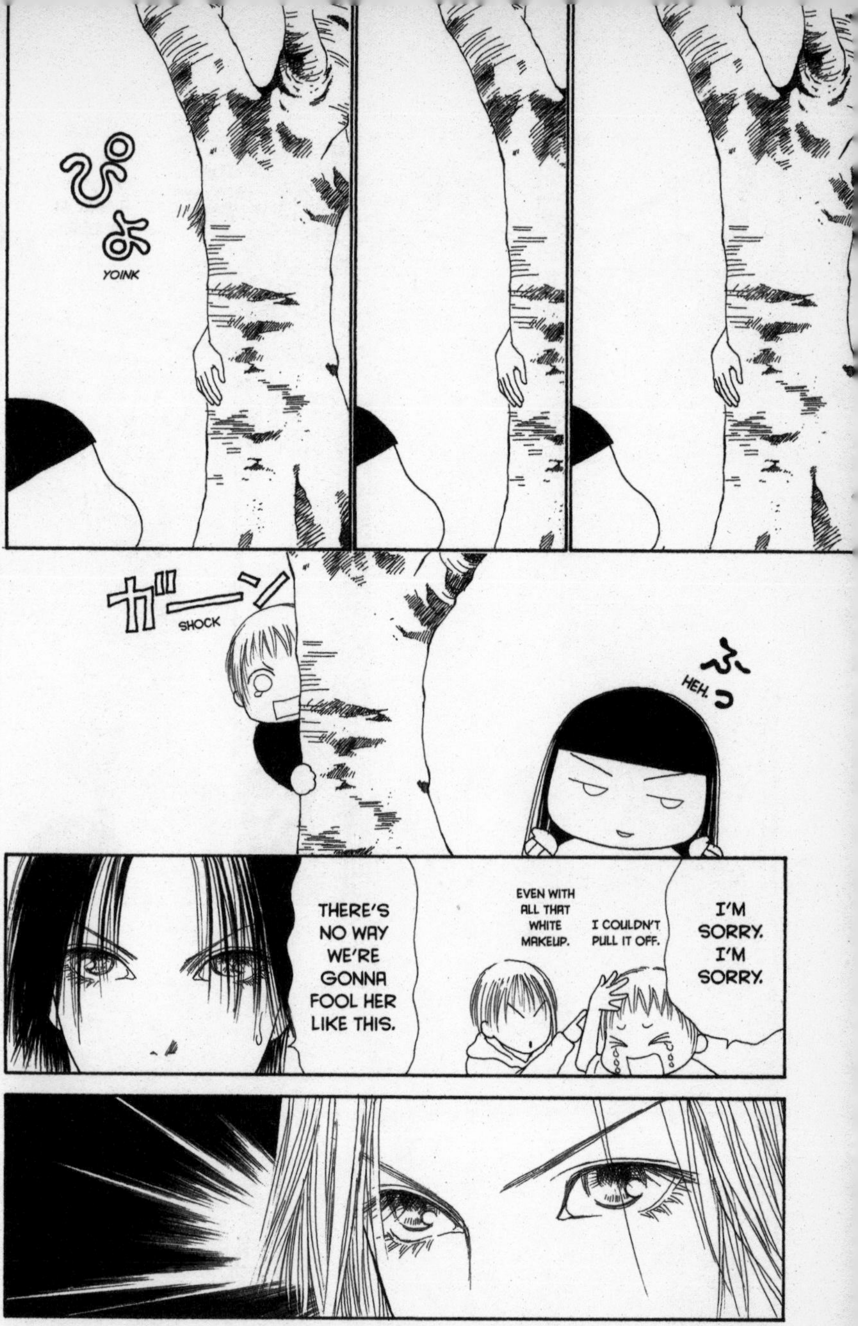
ぴょ
YOINK
ふっ
HEH.
ガーン
SHOCK
I'M SORRY. I'M SORRY.
I COULDN'T PULL IT OFF.
EVEN WITH ALL THAT WHITE MAKEUP.
THERE'S NO WAY WE'RE GONNA FOOL HER LIKE THIS.

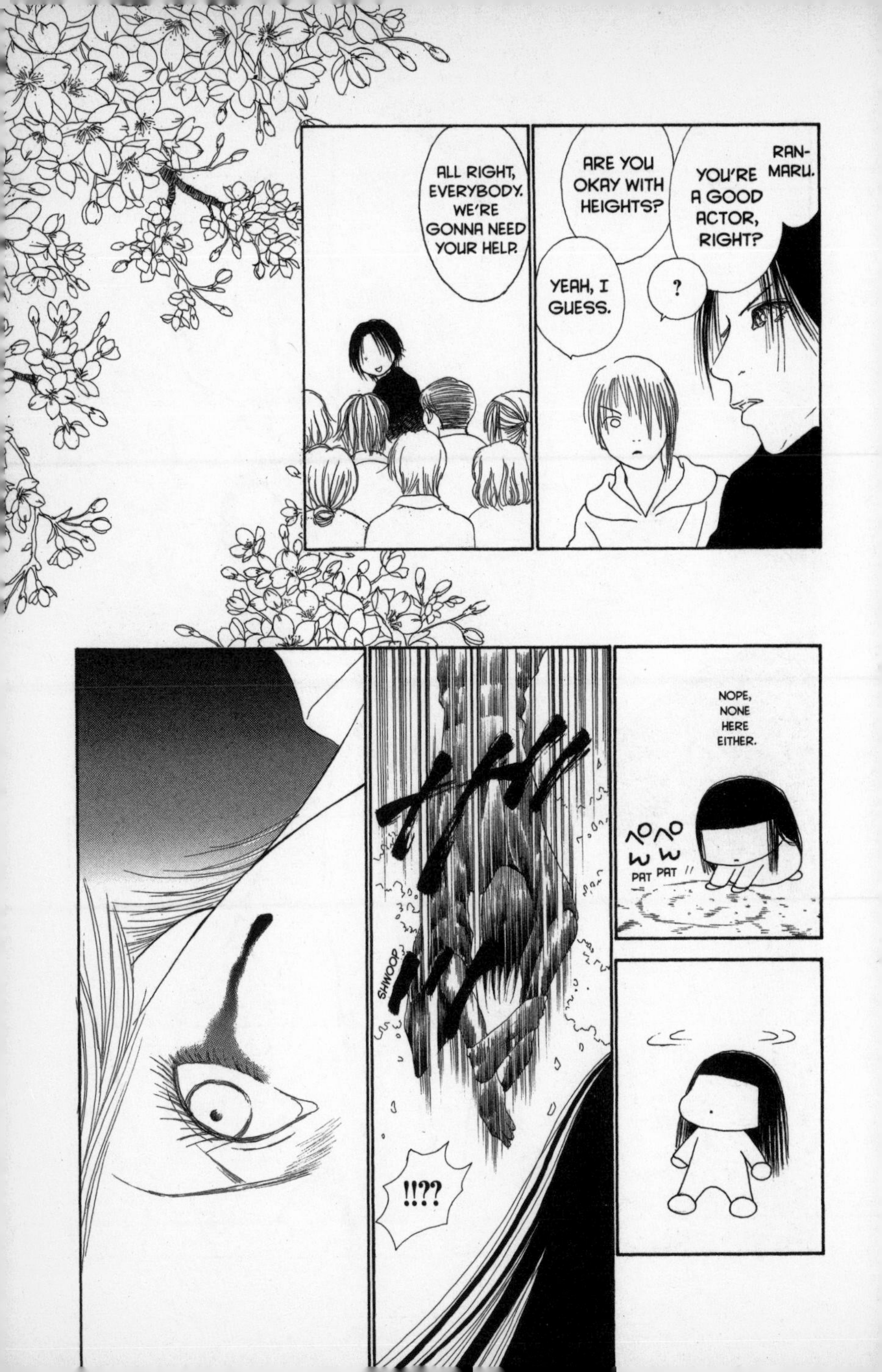
RAN-MARU.
YOU'RE A GOOD ACTOR, RIGHT?
?
ARE YOU OKAY WITH HEIGHTS?
YEAH, I GUESS.
ALL RIGHT, EVERYBODY. WE'RE GONNA NEED YOUR HELP.
NOPE, NONE HERE EITHER.
PAT PAT
SHWOOP
!!??

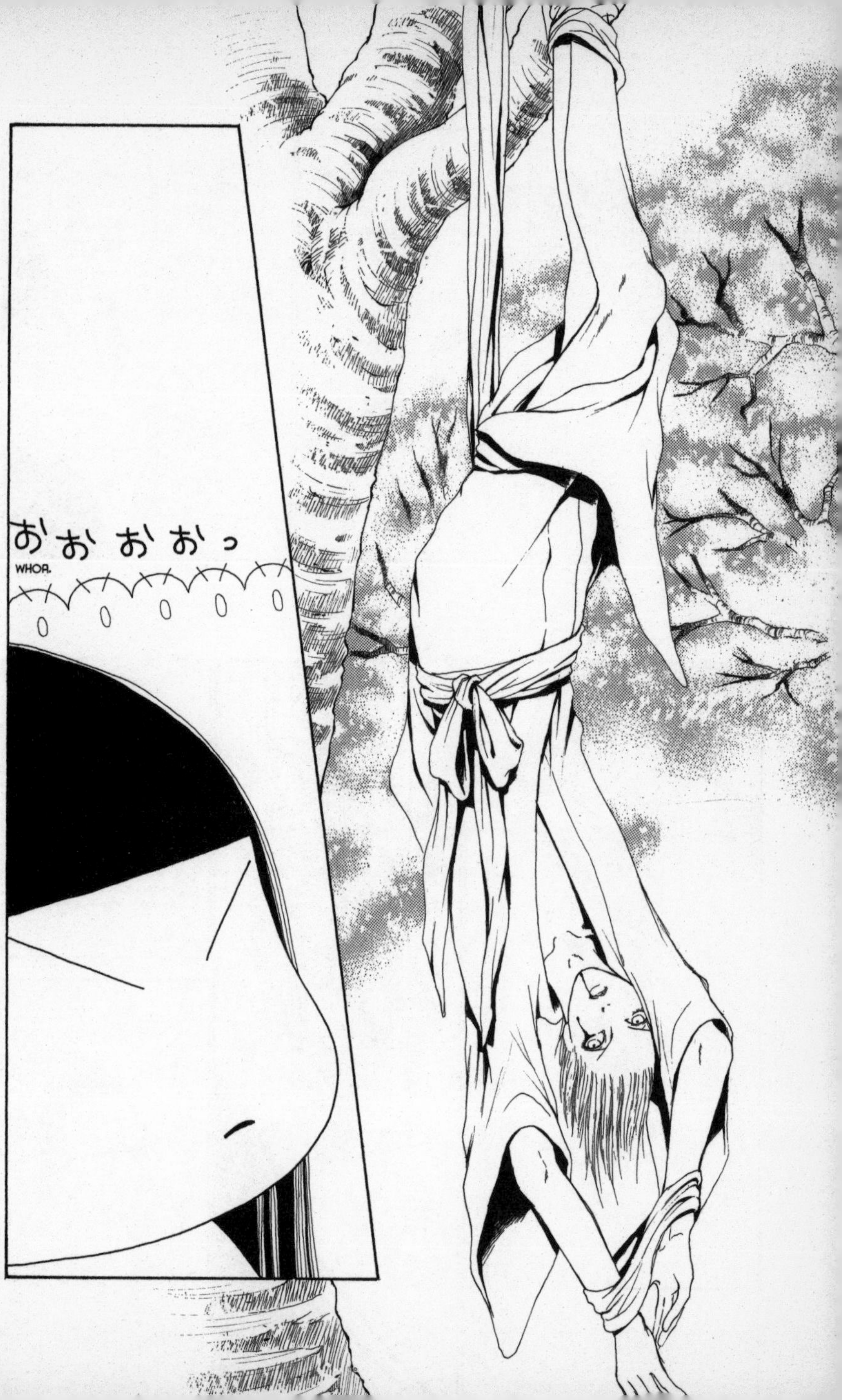
おぉおおっ
WHOA.

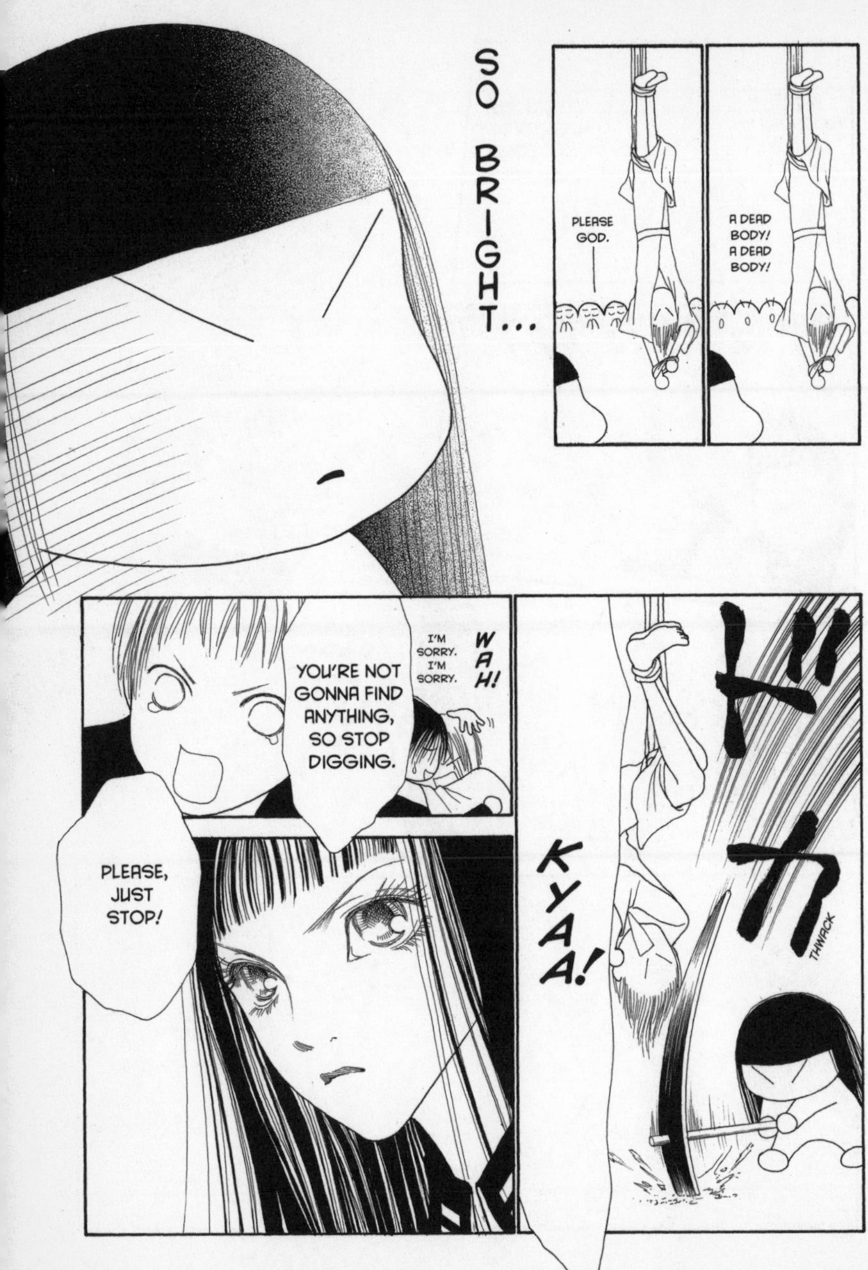
A DEAD BODY! A DEAD BODY!
PLEASE GOD.
SO BRIGHT...
ドカ
THWACK
KYAA!
WAH!
I'M SORRY. I'M SORRY.
YOU'RE NOT GONNA FIND ANYTHING, SO STOP DIGGING.
PLEASE, JUST STOP!

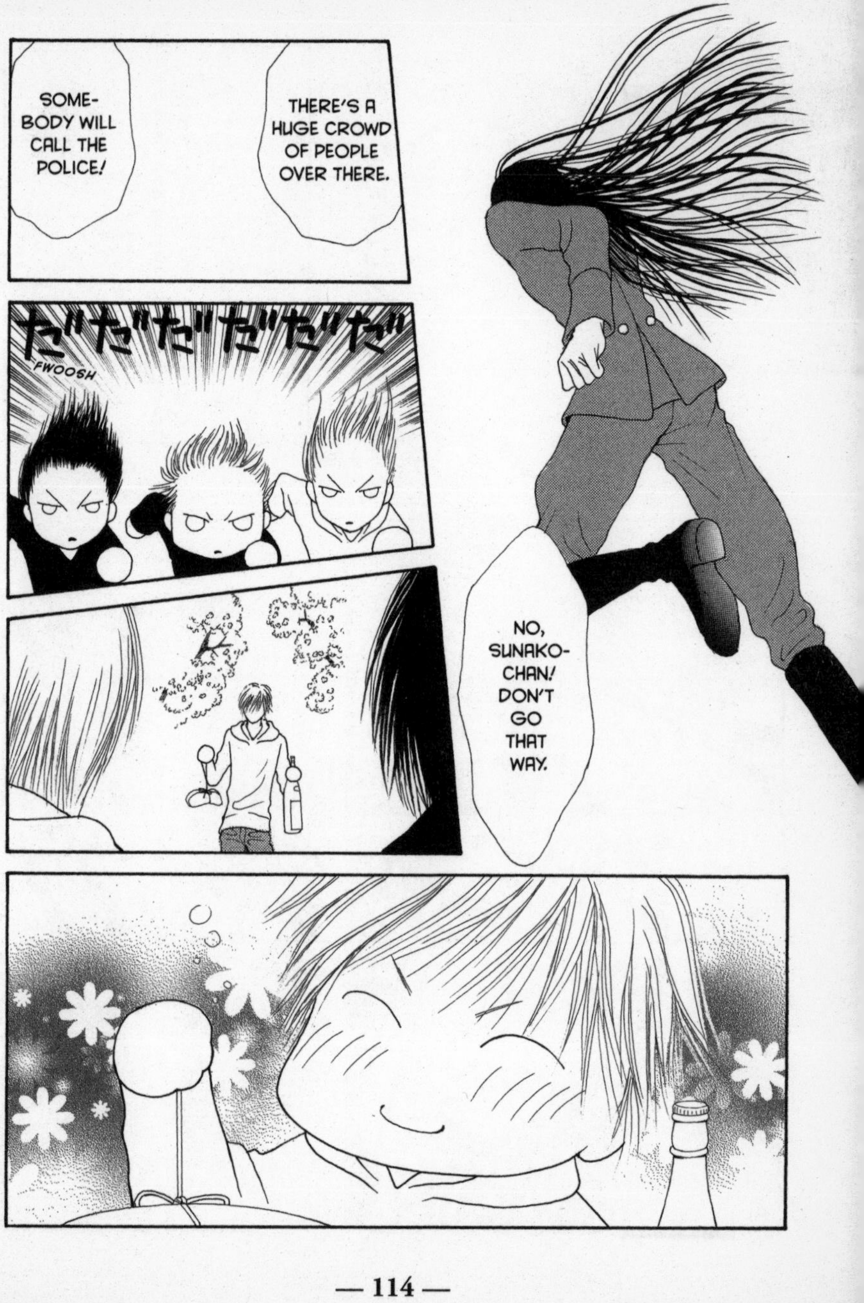
NO, SUNAKO-CHAN! DON'T GO THAT WAY.
THERE'S A HUGE CROWD OF PEOPLE OVER THERE.
SOMEBODY WILL CALL THE POLICE!
だ"だ"だ"だ"だ"だ"
FWOOSH

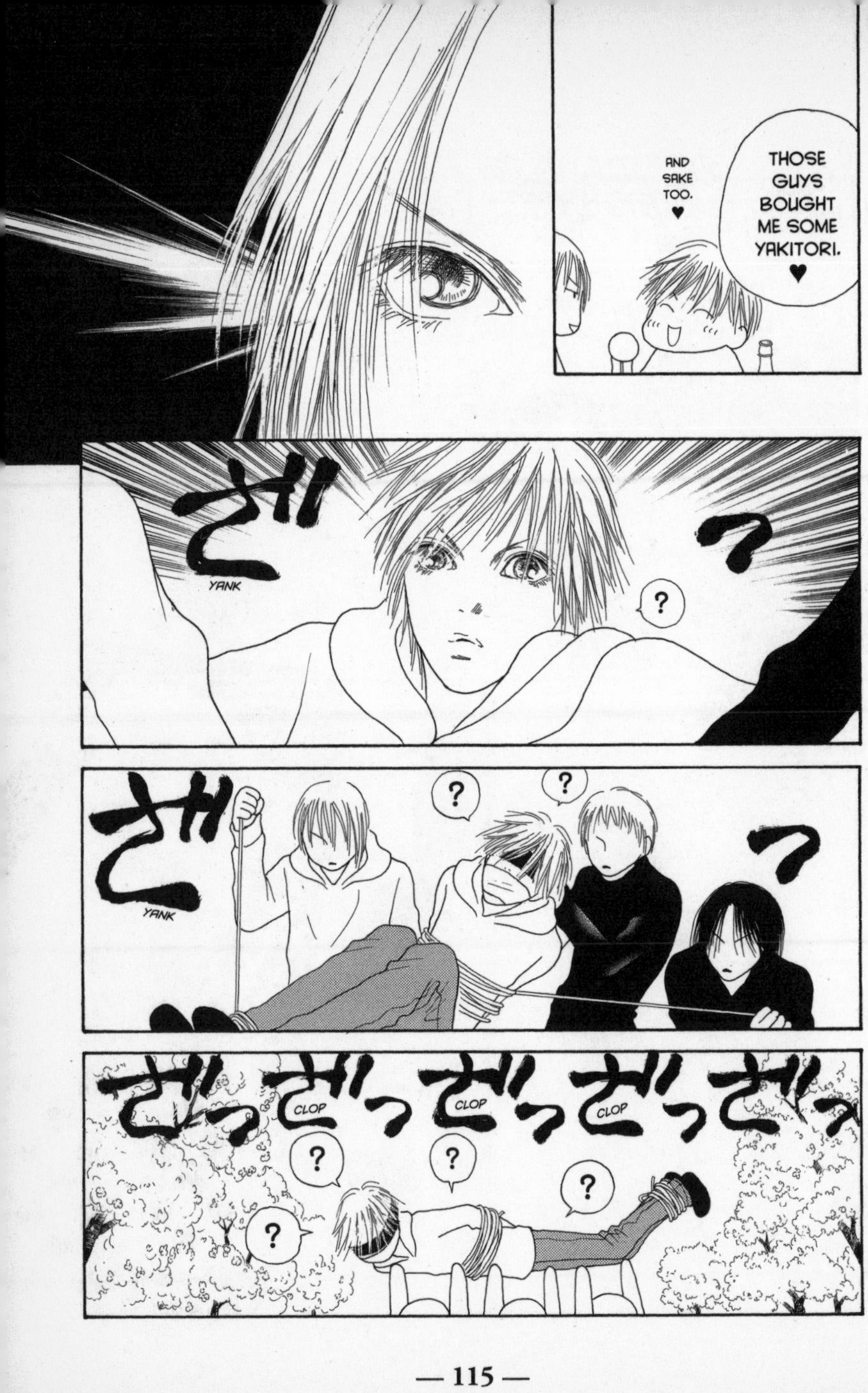
THOSE GUYS BOUGHT ME SOME YAKITORI. ♥
AND SAKE TOO. ♥
?
YANK
?
?
YANK
CLOP
CLOP
CLOP
?
?
?
?

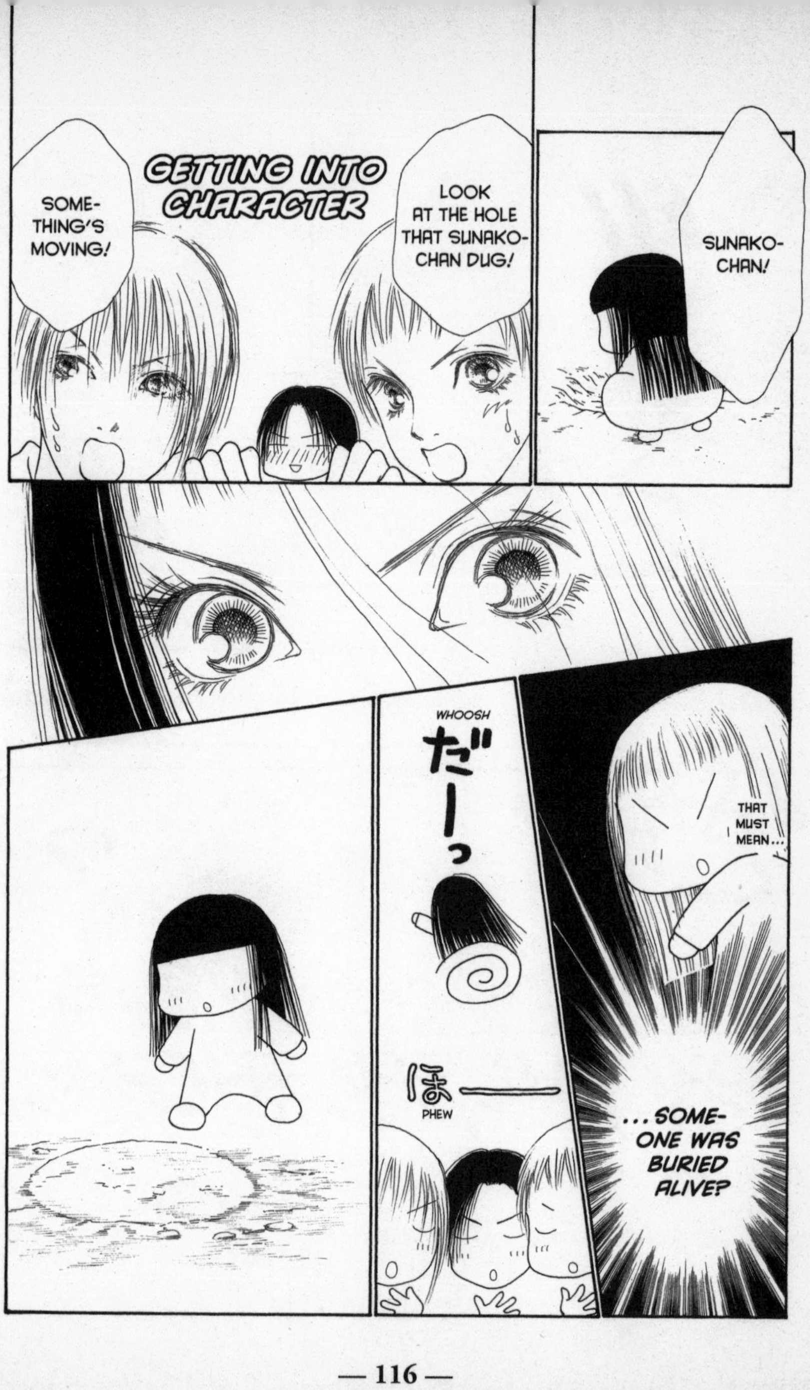
SUNAKO-CHAN!
LOOK AT THE HOLE THAT SUNAKO-CHAN DUG!
GETTING INTO CHARACTER
SOME-THING'S MOVING!
THAT MUST MEAN...
...SOME-ONE WAS BURIED ALIVE?
WHOOSH
だーっ
ほーー
PHEW

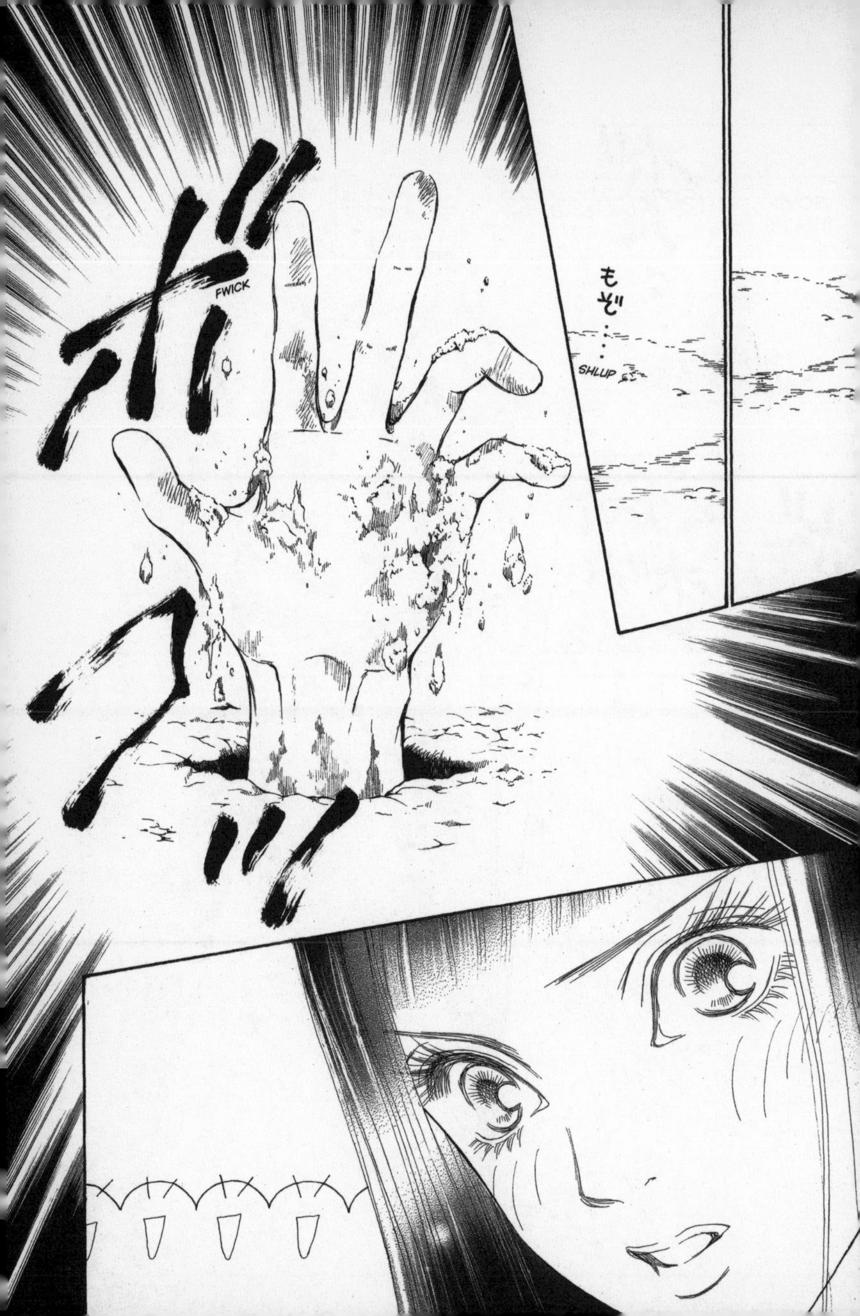
もぞ・・・
SHLUP
ガバッ
FWICK

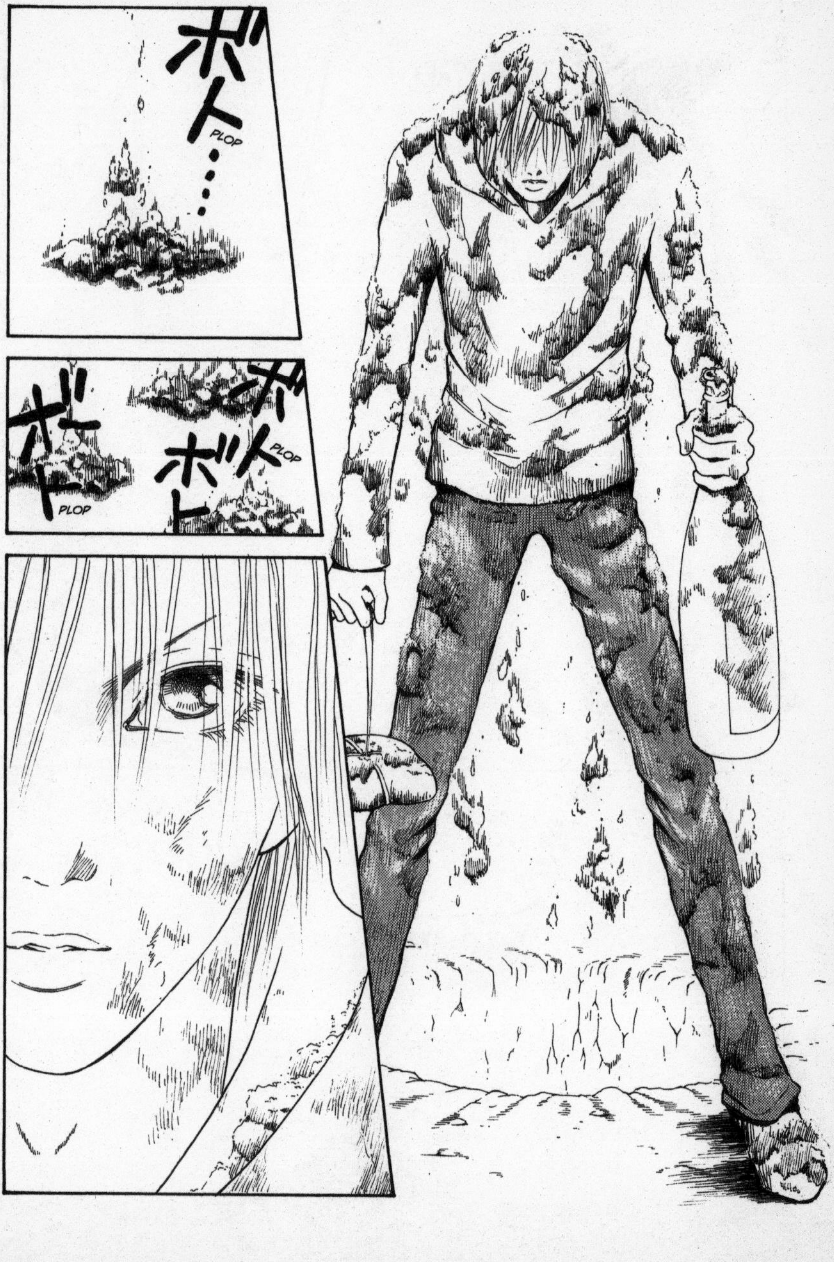
ボト……
PLOP
ボトボト
PLOP
ボト
PLOP

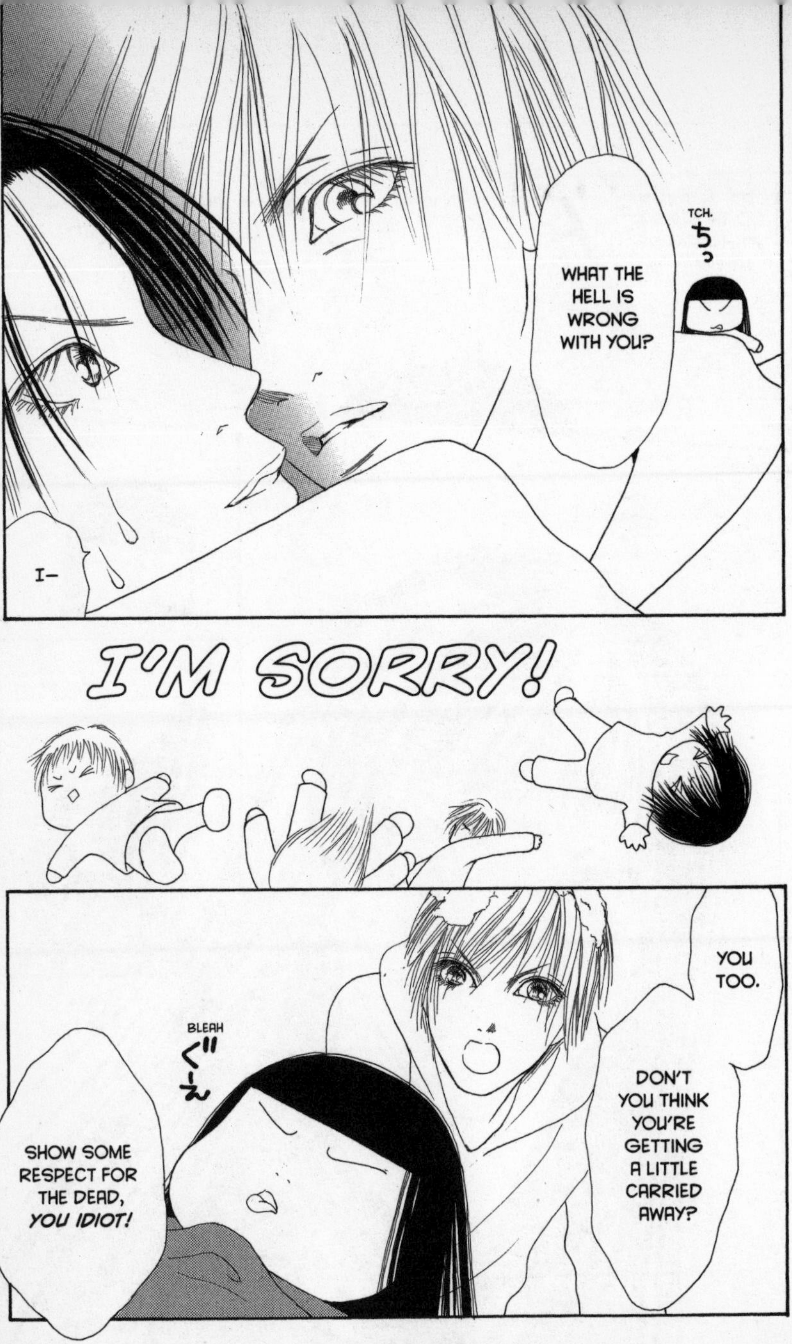
TCH.
ちっ
WHAT THE HELL IS WRONG WITH YOU?
I–
I'M SORRY!
YOU TOO.
DON'T YOU THINK YOU'RE GETTING A LITTLE CARRIED AWAY?
BLEAH
SHOW SOME RESPECT FOR THE DEAD, *YOU IDIOT!*

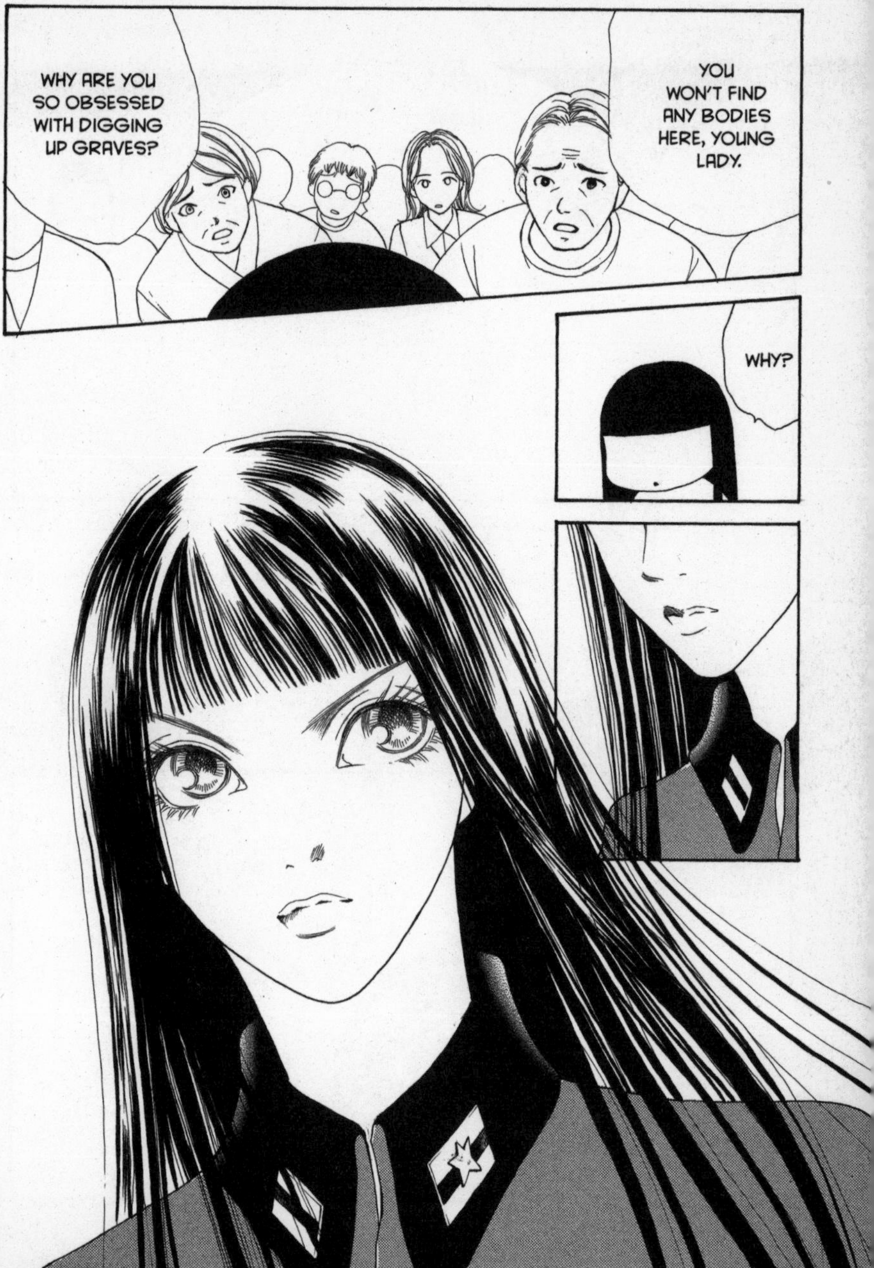
YOU WON'T FIND ANY BODIES HERE, YOUNG LADY.
WHY ARE YOU SO OBSESSED WITH DIGGING UP GRAVES?
WHY?

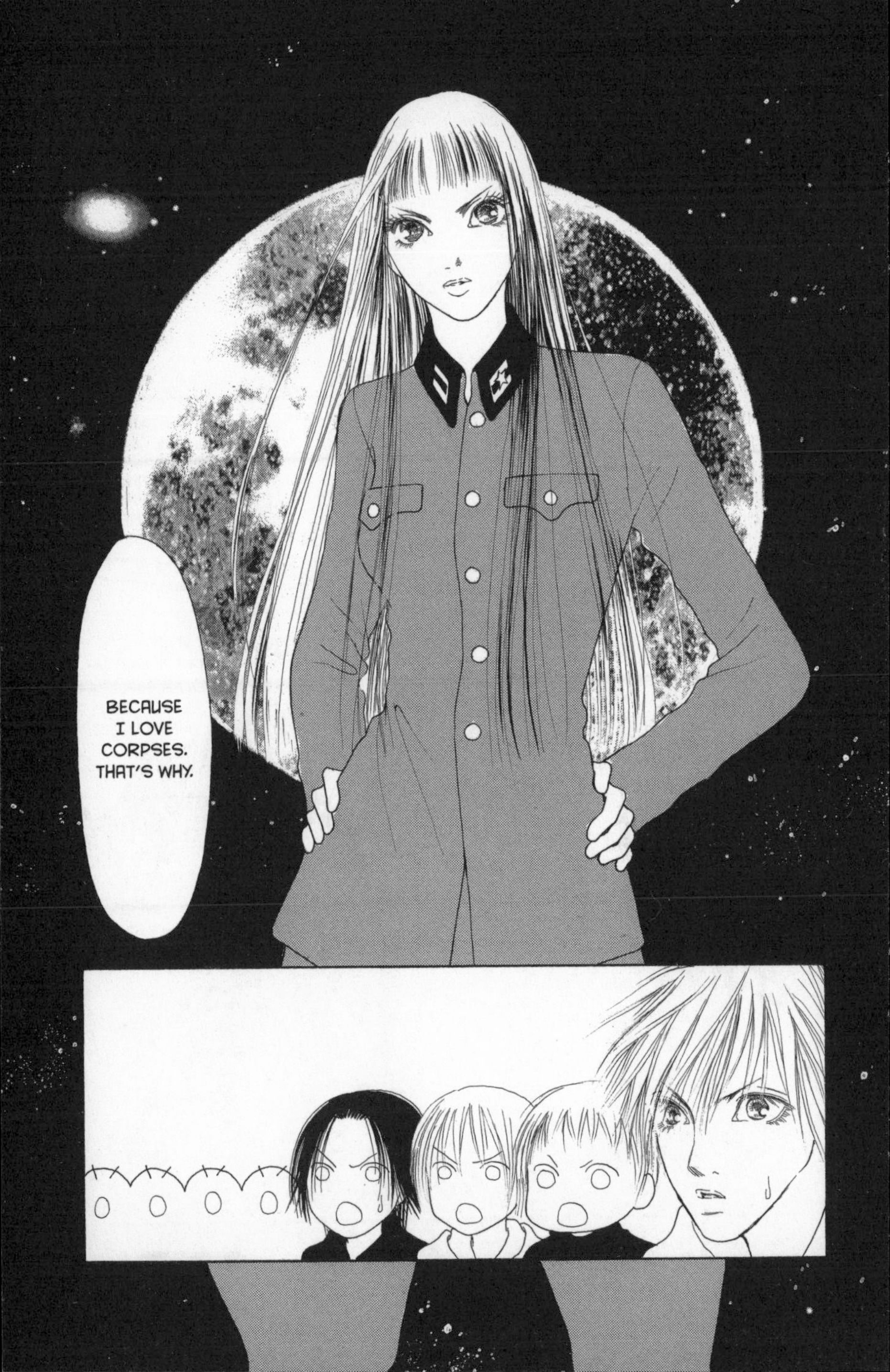
BECAUSE I LOVE CORPSES. THAT'S WHY.

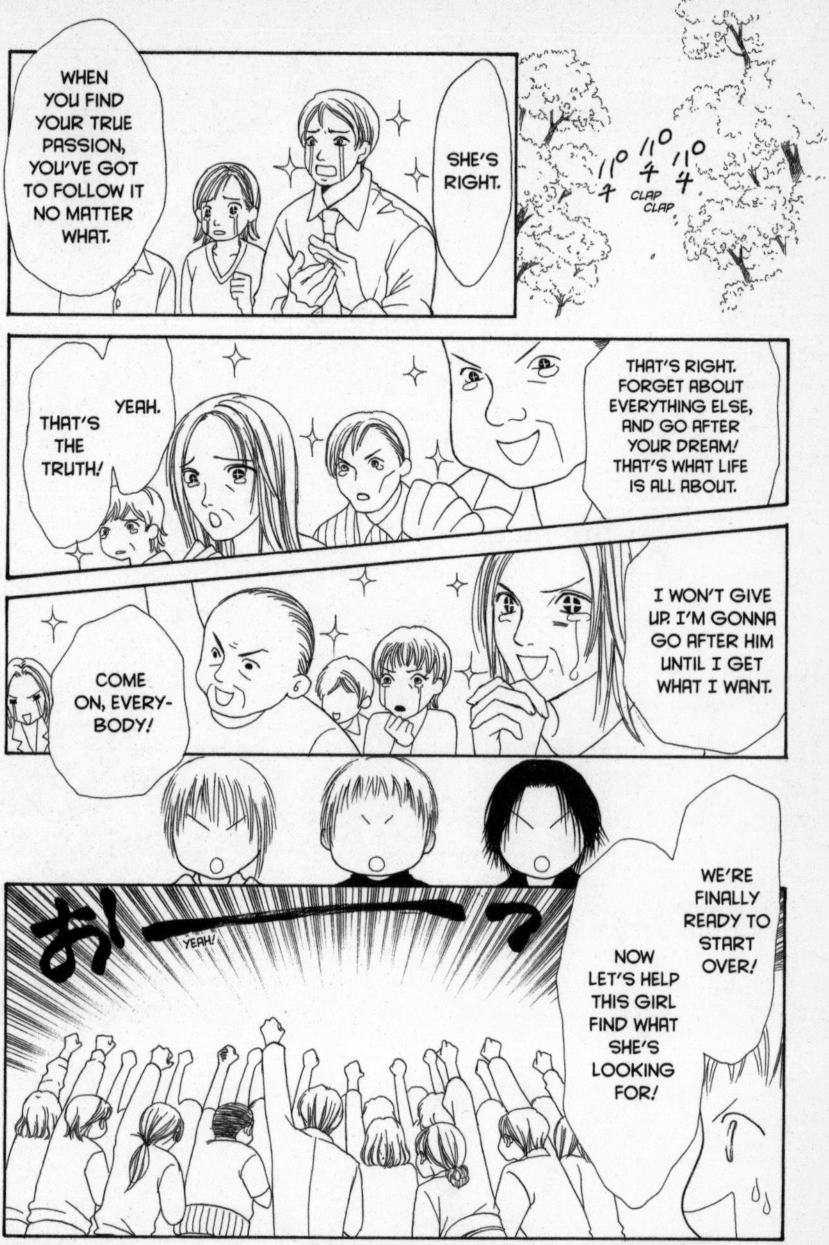
CLAP CLAP
SHE'S RIGHT.
WHEN YOU FIND YOUR TRUE PASSION, YOU'VE GOT TO FOLLOW IT NO MATTER WHAT.
THAT'S RIGHT. FORGET ABOUT EVERYTHING ELSE, AND GO AFTER YOUR DREAM! THAT'S WHAT LIFE IS ALL ABOUT.
YEAH.
THAT'S THE TRUTH!
I WON'T GIVE UP. I'M GONNA GO AFTER HIM UNTIL I GET WHAT I WANT.
COME ON, EVERY-BODY!
WE'RE FINALLY READY TO START OVER!
NOW LET'S HELP THIS GIRL FIND WHAT SHE'S LOOKING FOR!
お!————っ
YEAH!

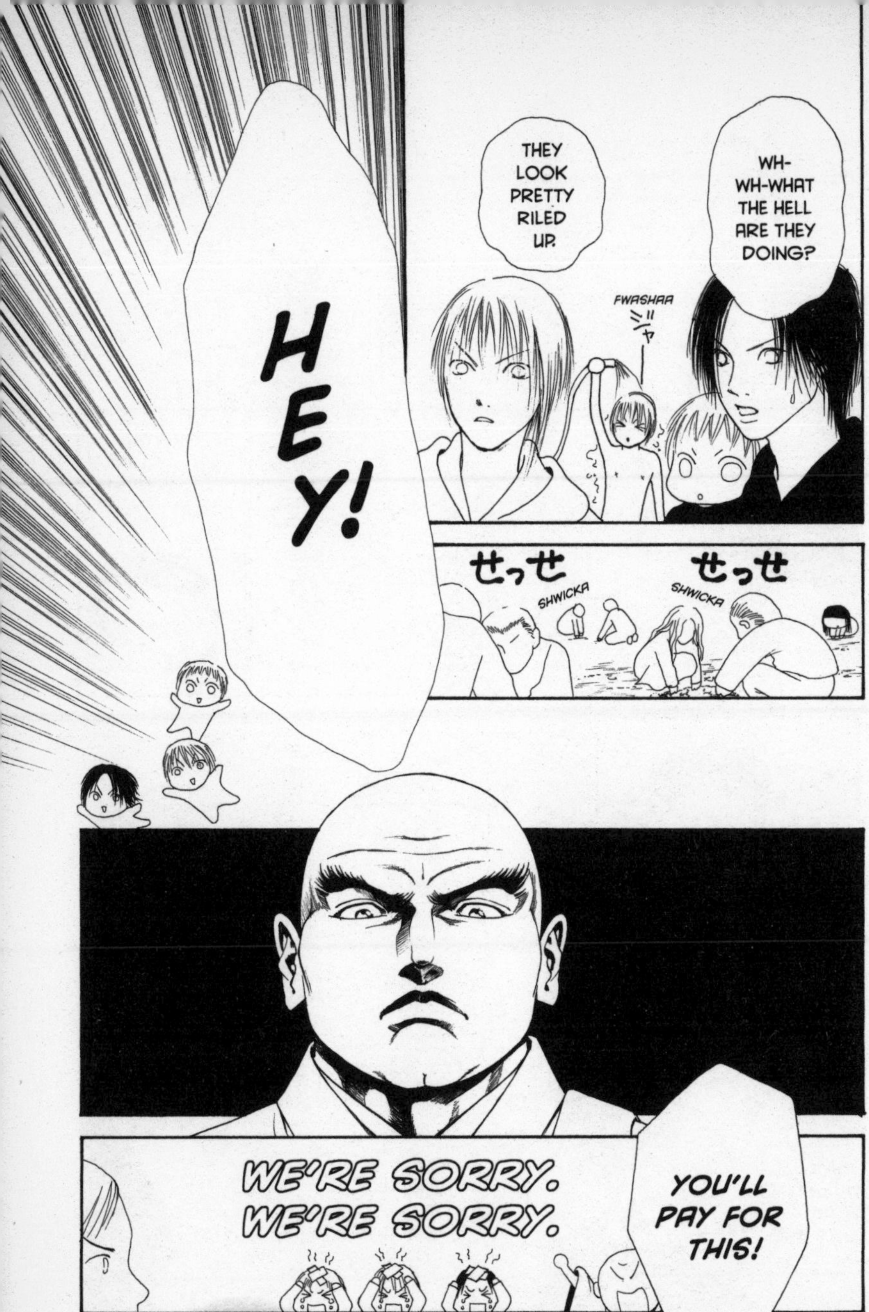
WH-WH-WHAT THE HELL ARE THEY DOING?
THEY LOOK PRETTY RILED UP.
FWASHAA
ジャー
せっせ
SHWICKA
せっせ
SHWICKA
HEY!
YOU'LL PAY FOR THIS!
WE'RE SORRY. WE'RE SORRY.

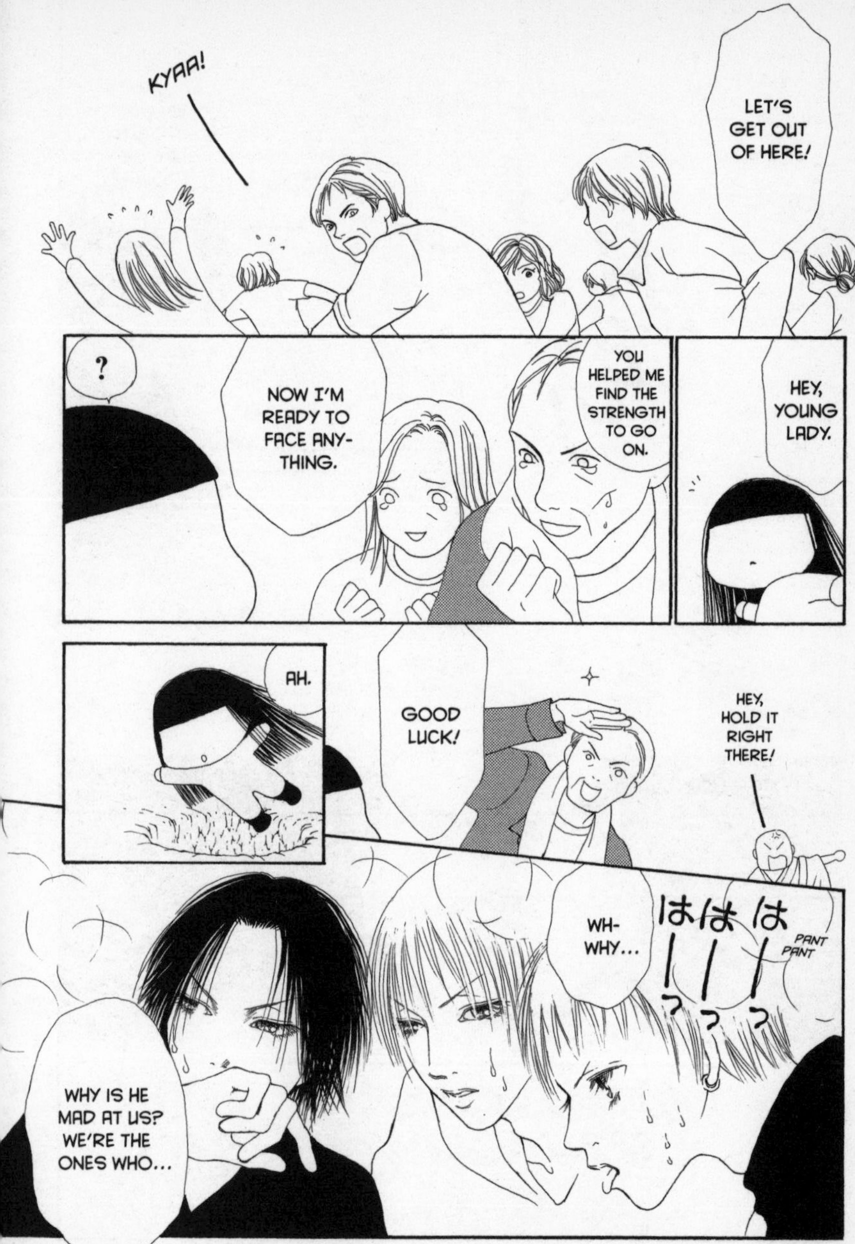
LET'S GET OUT OF HERE!
KYAA!
HEY, YOUNG LADY.
YOU HELPED ME FIND THE STRENGTH TO GO ON.
NOW I'M READY TO FACE ANY-THING.
?
HEY, HOLD IT RIGHT THERE!
GOOD LUCK!
AH.
はーっ はーっ はーっ
PANT PANT
WH- WHY...
WHY IS HE MAD AT US? WE'RE THE ONES WHO...

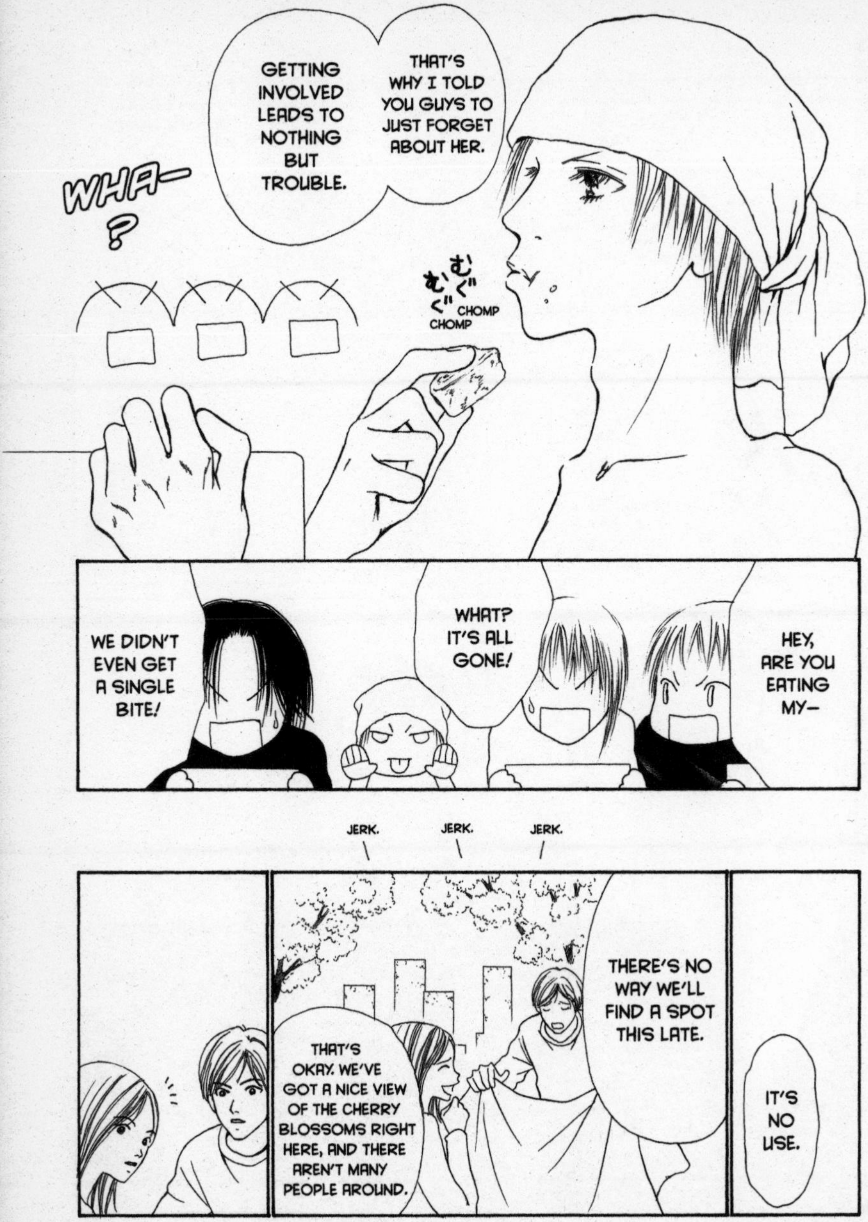
THAT'S WHY I TOLD YOU GUYS TO JUST FORGET ABOUT HER.
GETTING INVOLVED LEADS TO NOTHING BUT TROUBLE.
WHA- ?
むぐむぐ CHOMP CHOMP
HEY, ARE YOU EATING MY—
WHAT? IT'S ALL GONE!
WE DIDN'T EVEN GET A SINGLE BITE!
JERK.
JERK.
JERK.
IT'S NO USE.
THERE'S NO WAY WE'LL FIND A SPOT THIS LATE.
THAT'S OKAY. WE'VE GOT A NICE VIEW OF THE CHERRY BLOSSOMS RIGHT HERE, AND THERE AREN'T MANY PEOPLE AROUND.

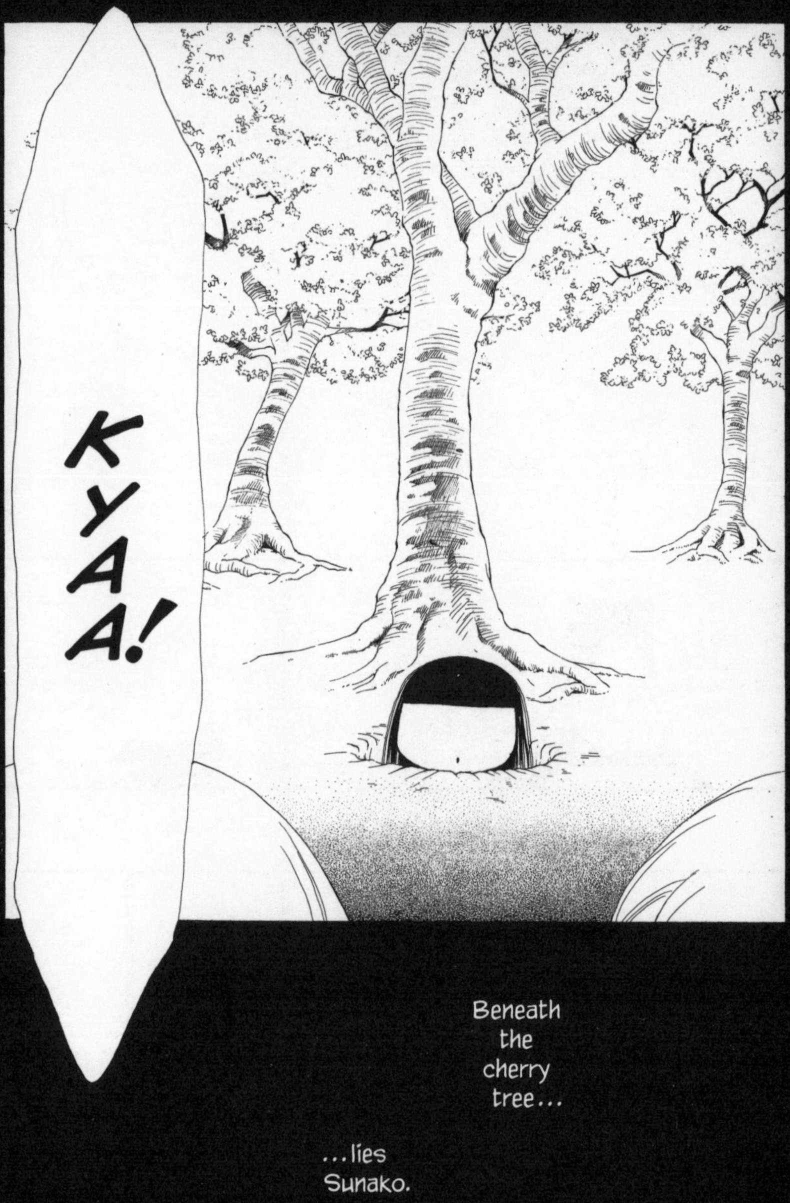
KYAA!
Beneath the cherry tree...
...lies Sunako.

Chapter 34
Five-Star Restaurant

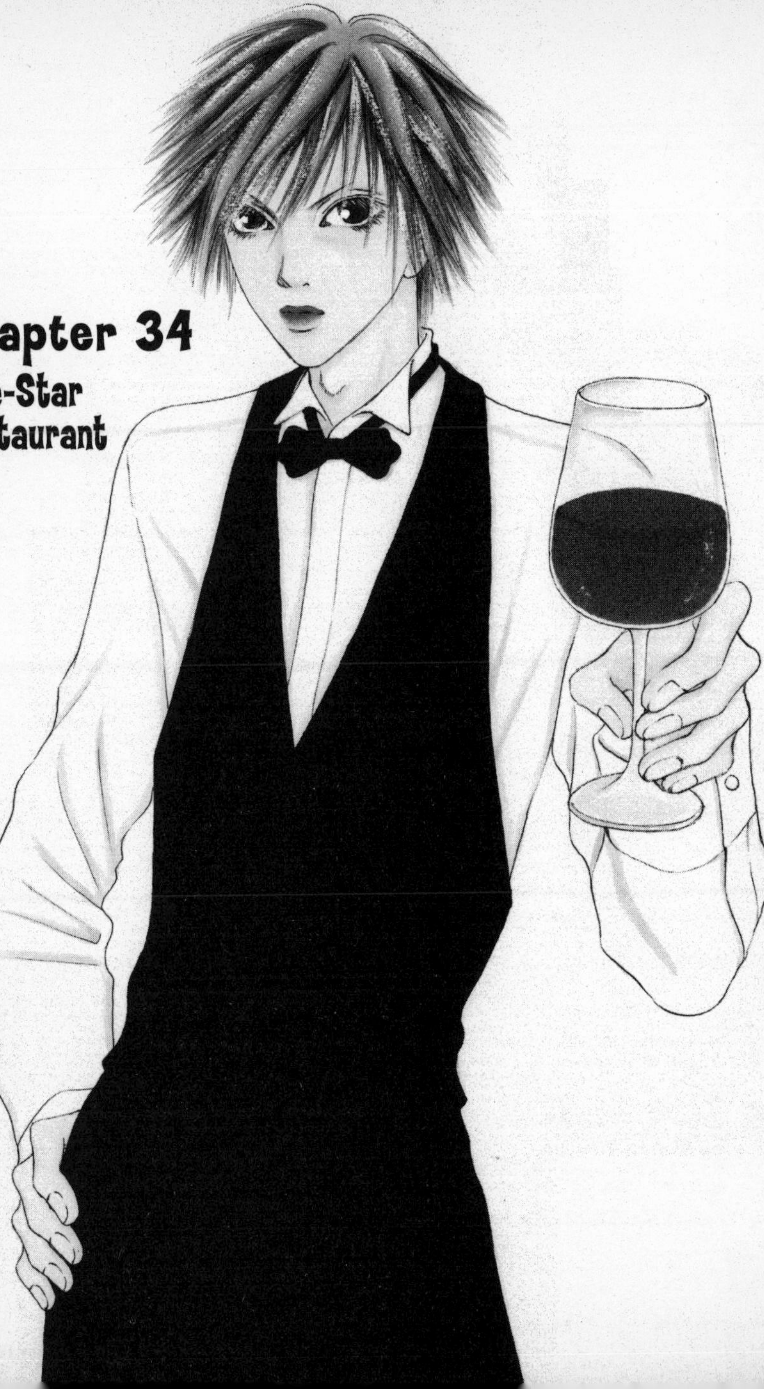

MY RECENT ACTIVITIES

THIS IS ALL ABOUT CONCERTS, SO IF YOU'RE NOT INTERESTED, PLEASE JUST SKIP IT.

BAROQUE
THEY DID NINE SHOWS, BUT UNFORTUNATELY I ONLY MADE IT TO SIX OF THEM. BANSAKU-KUN IS ALWAYS HOT, NO MATTER WHEN OR WHERE I SEE HIM. ♥ AWESOME. ♥ I WAS SO HAPPY WHEN I FINALLY GOT TO SPEAK WITH REI-KUN AT NHK HALL. ♥ HE WAS SO CUTE. ♥ I WISH I HAD A CHANCE TO WRITE ABOUT HIM IN THE BONUS PAGES.

SOFT BALLET
THEY WERE SO COOL! ♥ ENDO IS SUCH A HOTTIE. ♥ I LOVE HIS VOICE, HIS FACE, AND HIS ENTIRE BODY. ♥

NEW ROTE'KA
I LOVE THEM. ♥ I'VE BEEN A FAN FOR OVER TEN YEARS, AND THEY HAVEN'T CHANGED AT ALL. ♥ AWESOME. ♥ THEY'RE SO MUCH FUN. ♥

ANIMETAL
THANKS TO THE DRUMMER, SHINKI KITAOKA, I GOT TO SEE THEIR CONCERT. I HAD LOTS OF FUN. I'VE KNOWN HIM FOR OVER TEN YEARS NOW.

WYSE
I JUST WENT BECAUSE MY FRIEND ASKED ME TO, BUT THEY WERE PRETTY COOL.

MOI DIX MOIS
THANKS TO THE DRUMMER, TORU-SAN, WHO'S CURRENTLY PLAYING WITH THIS BAND, I GOT TO SEE THEIR SHOW. TORU-SAN IS A FRIEND OF A FRIEND. PLEASE TAKE ME TO THE KIREEK CONCERT TOO.

COLOR
I WENT TO MARY-SAN'S FAREWELL CONCERT. ♥ TOMMY WAS REALLY COOL. ♥ THEY'RE STILL ROCKING AFTER ALL THESE YEARS! ♥♥♥

WRISK
THIS WAS ALMOST LIKE A COMEBACK CONCERT FOR THEM. THEY HADN'T PERFORMED FOR SIX MONTHS! I'VE BEEN FRIENDS WITH THE SINGER TAKENAGA FOR SIX OR SEVEN YEARS. I SAW ANOTHER BAND AT THIS SHOW CALLED PRIVATE BLACK BERRY. THE SINGER WAS HOT. I DIDN'T GET TO SEE THE BAND CHOCOLATE'S...I WAS TOO LATE. THERE WAS A GIRL THERE WHO SPOTTED ME, AND ASKED FOR MY AUTOGRAPH. SORRY I HAD TO SAY NO...I GET A LITTLE NERVOUS.

GENTLE
I'VE BEEN SEEING THIS BAND A LOT THESE DAYS. THE BASSIST YUJI IS SO CUTE, AND HE'S MY FAVORITE. (CHECK OUT BOOK 7. HE'S THE ONE WHO I WENT TO SEE BAROQUE WITH.) I'M SUCH A BIG FAN OF THE DRUMMER YUKI-KUN. ♥ HE'S NOT A REGULAR MEMBER, SO I ONLY GO SEE THEM WHEN HE PLAYS. HE ALSO PLAYS FOR THE BAND HIRO-X.

SHOCKING LEMON
I'M STILL FOLLOWING THEM AROUND ALL OVER THE PLACE.

SADS
THEY RECENTLY HAD A TOUR, BUT I WAS ONLY ABLE TO GO TO THE CONCERT AT THE ZEPP IN TOKYO...I WISH I HAD A CHANCE TO TRAVEL AROUND THE COUNTRY WITH THEM. I HAVE NOTHING ELSE TO SAY. *KIYOHARU IS THE BEST!* ♥♥♥

AS SOON AS I TURN THIS IN, I'M GONNA GO SEE BUG. I'M ALSO PLANNING TO GO SEE SHELLY TRIP REALIZE AND VOGUE IMAGE. I HOPE I GET A CHANCE TO SEE JILS AND MASA-KUN TOO. *AHH, I'D DIE TO SEE BUCK-TICK.* THANKS SO MUCH FOR SENDING ME THE MDS. NOW I'M INTERESTED IN MORE BANDS THAN EVER! THANK YOU ALL. ♥♥♥ *BAROQUE* IS PLAYING AT THE *BUDOUKAN* AROUND THE TIME THIS BOOK COMES OUT. KYAA! ♥♥♥ I CAN HARDLY WAIT! ♥♥♥

FOR THE PAST FEW MONTHS, I'VE BEEN GOING TO A LOT OF CONCERTS. THAT'S PRETTY MUCH ALL I DO. BUT SOMETIMES I CAN'T GO BECAUSE OF WORK. SOFT BALLET! WAH! I REALLY WANTED TO SEE THEM AT THE BLITZ! AND L'ARC~EN~CIEL TOO! THEY WERE DOING SEVEN SHOWS, AND I EVEN HAD TICKETS, DAMN IT!

I WISH I COULD TAKE A TRIP SOMEWHERE. SIGH...

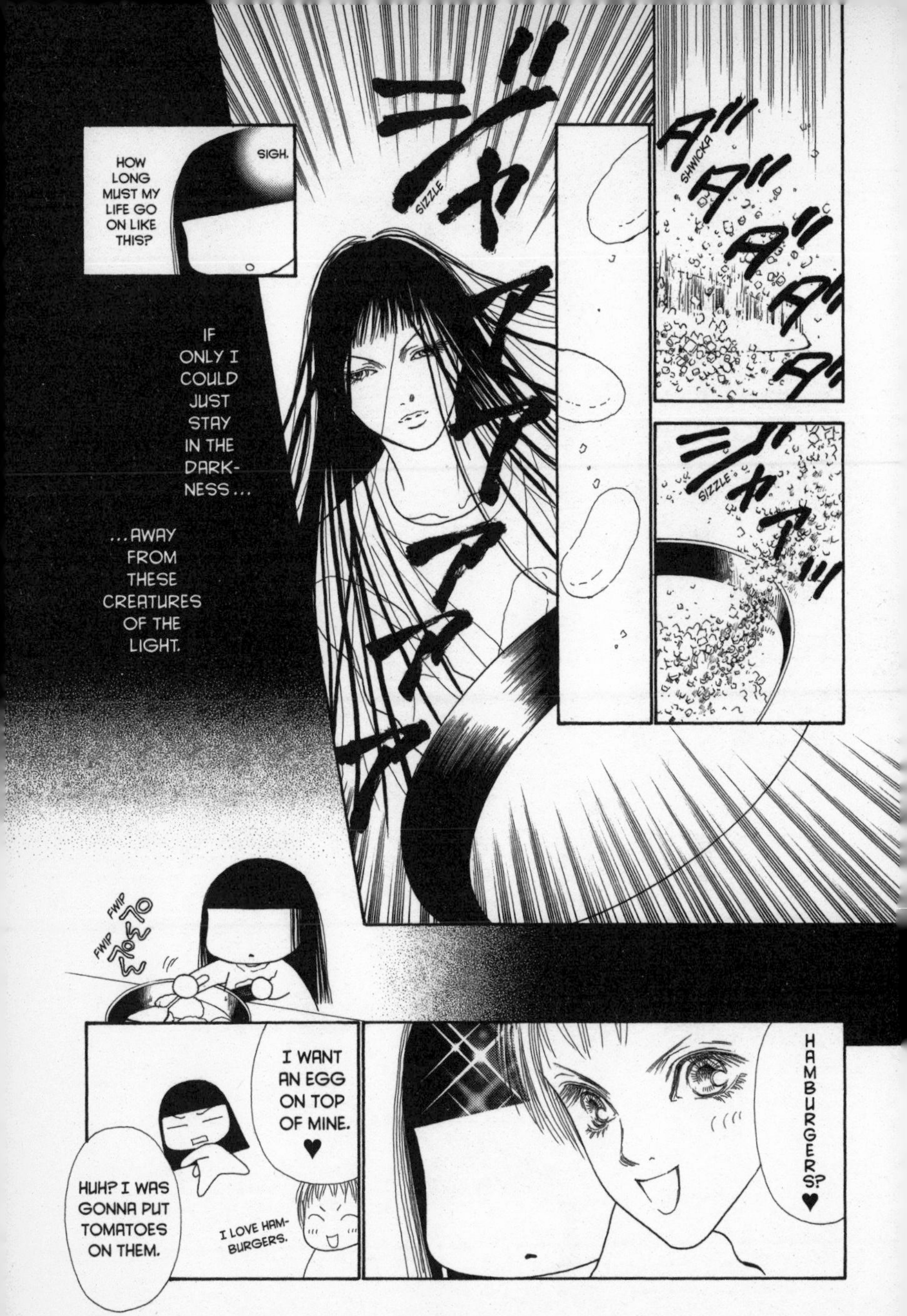
SHWICKA
SIZZLE
SIZZLE
SIGH.
HOW LONG MUST MY LIFE GO ON LIKE THIS?
IF ONLY I COULD JUST STAY IN THE DARKNESS...
...AWAY FROM THESE CREATURES OF THE LIGHT.
FWIP
FWIP
HAMBURGERS? ♥
I WANT AN EGG ON TOP OF MINE. ♥
HUH? I WAS GONNA PUT TOMATOES ON THEM.
I LOVE HAMBURGERS.

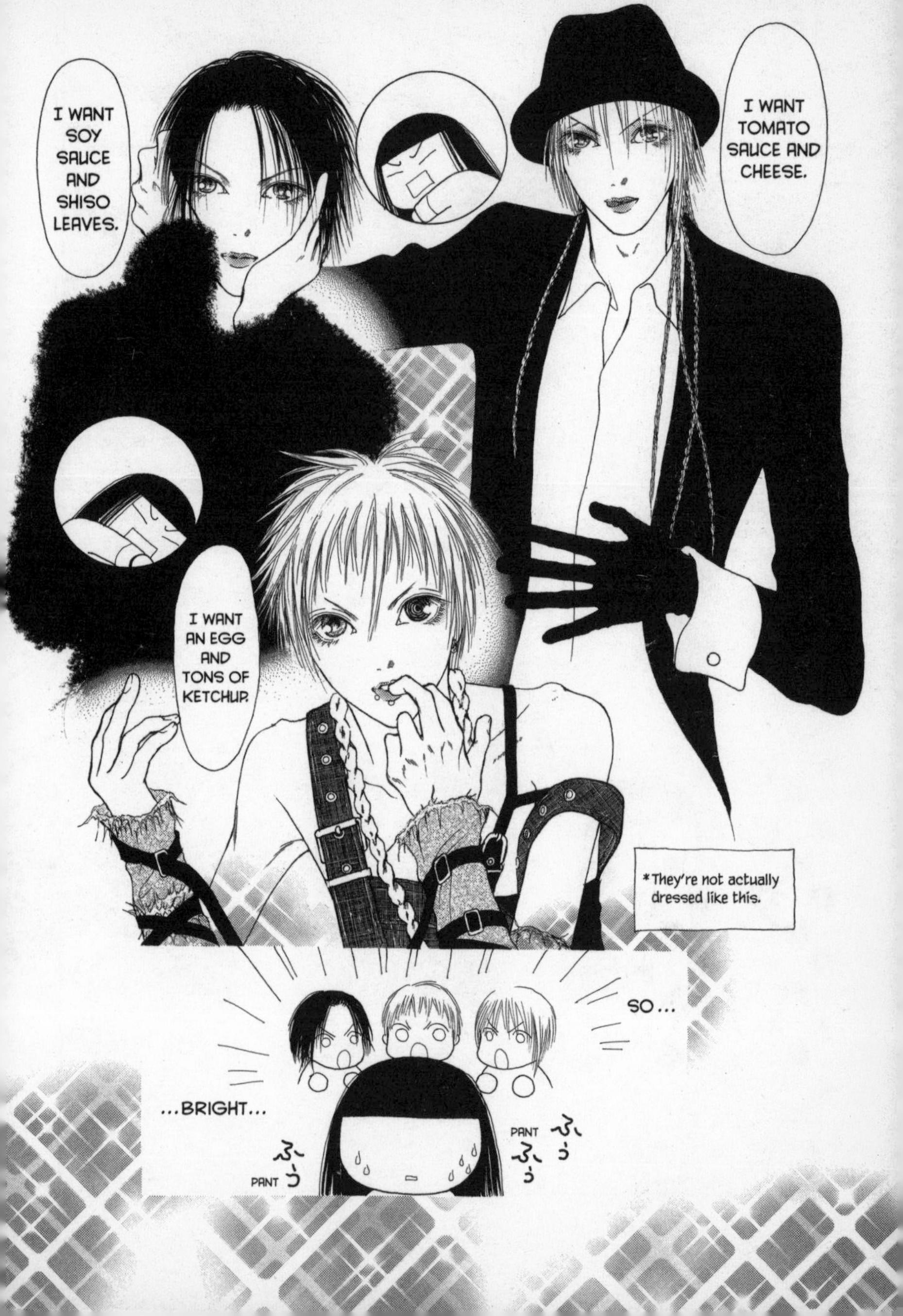
I WANT TOMATO SAUCE AND CHEESE.
I WANT SOY SAUCE AND SHISO LEAVES.
I WANT AN EGG AND TONS OF KETCHUP.
*They're not actually dressed like this.
SO...
...BRIGHT...
PANT
PANT

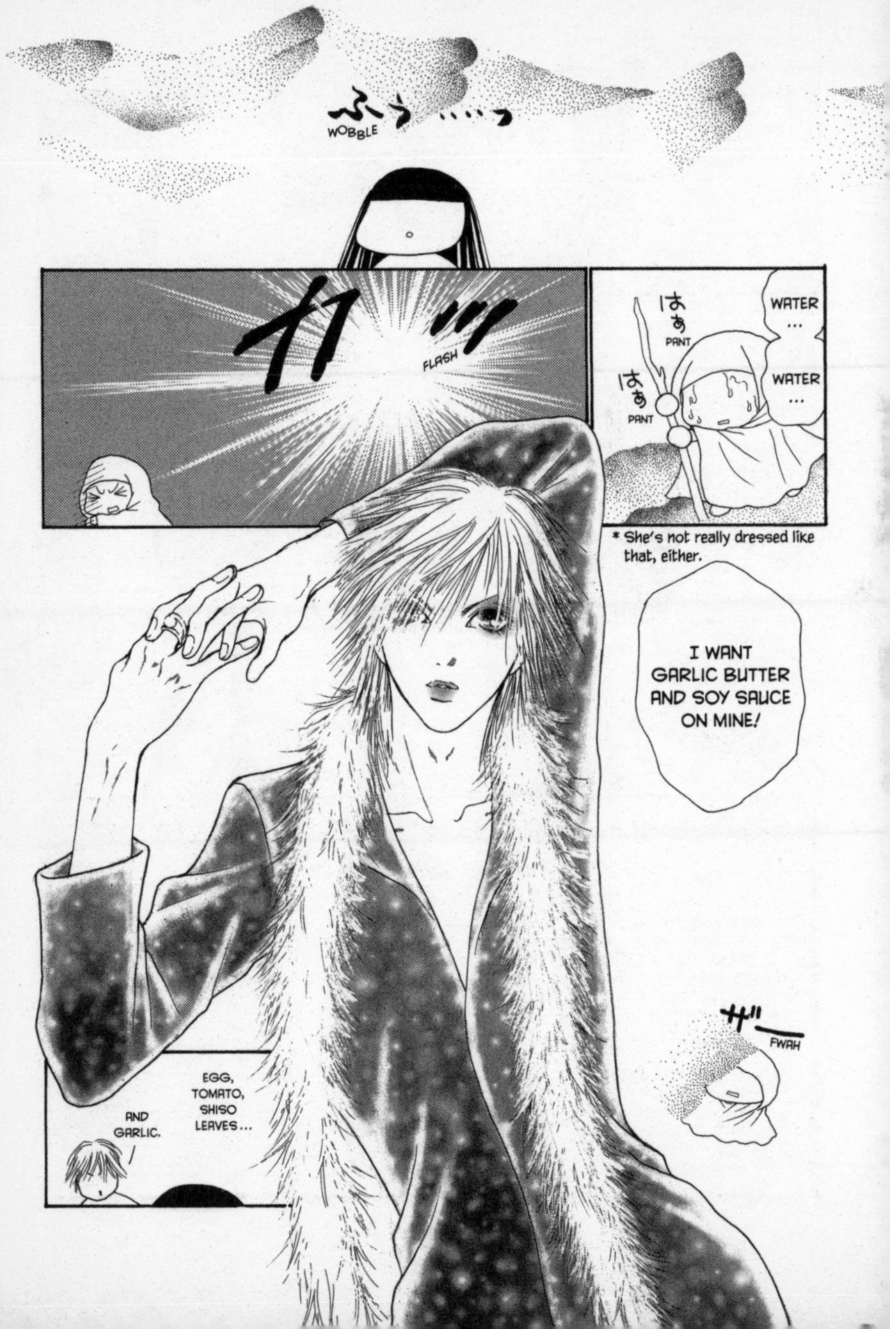
ふぅ…っ
WOBBLE
WATER...
WATER...
はぁ
PANT
はぁ
PANT
カッ
FLASH
* She's not really dressed like that, either.
I WANT GARLIC BUTTER AND SOY SAUCE ON MINE!
ザー
FWAH
EGG, TOMATO, SHISO LEAVES...
AND GARLIC.

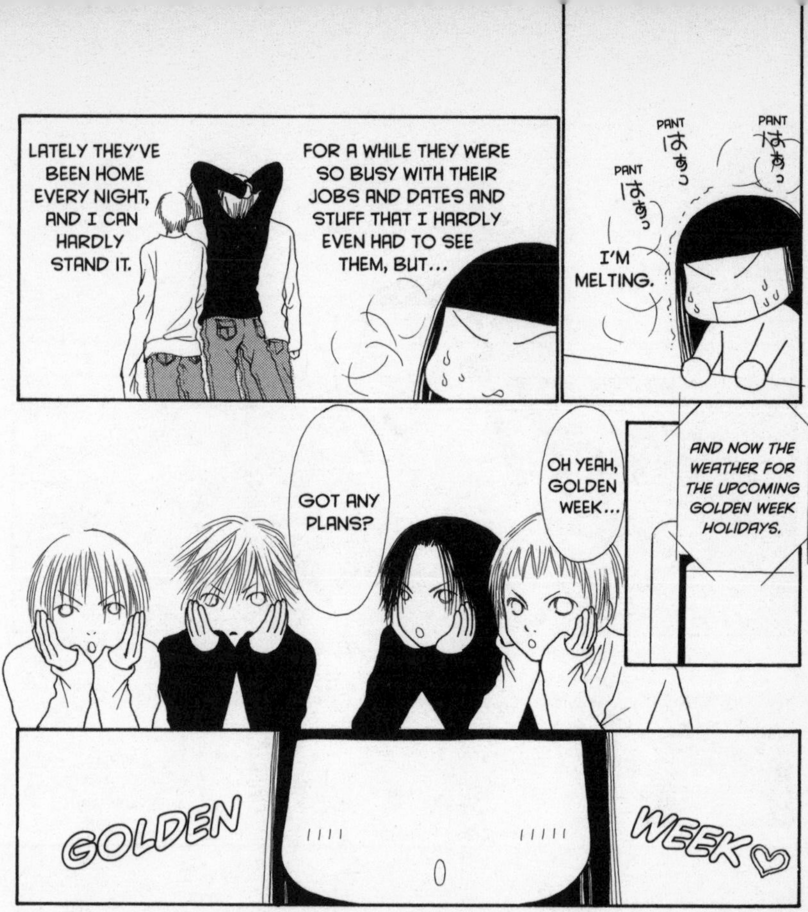
PANT
はあっ
PANT
はあっ
PANT
はあっ
I'M MELTING.
LATELY THEY'VE BEEN HOME EVERY NIGHT, AND I CAN HARDLY STAND IT.
FOR A WHILE THEY WERE SO BUSY WITH THEIR JOBS AND DATES AND STUFF THAT I HARDLY EVEN HAD TO SEE THEM, BUT...
AND NOW THE WEATHER FOR THE UPCOMING GOLDEN WEEK HOLIDAYS.
OH YEAH, GOLDEN WEEK...
GOT ANY PLANS?
GOLDEN
WEEK ♡

BEHIND THE SCENES

I WENT KIND OF CRAZY WHILE I WAS WRITING THIS STORY. I GOT REALLY INTO THAT COMEDY TROUPE "SUMMERS." I KEPT MAKING ALL THESE STUPID JOKES. I WAS ESPECIALLY CRAZY WHEN I WAS FINISHING THE STORY. I GOT SO SLEEPY THAT I ENDED UP WITH A KIND OF NATURAL HIGH. I KEPT PLAYING "NAME THAT TUNE" WITH MY ASSISTANT.

I TOTALLY GOT INTO IT!

MY EDITOR SOTOOKA-SAN TOOK ME OUT FOR BONITO SASHIMI, AND AFTER THAT ALL I COULD THINK ABOUT WAS SASHIMI.

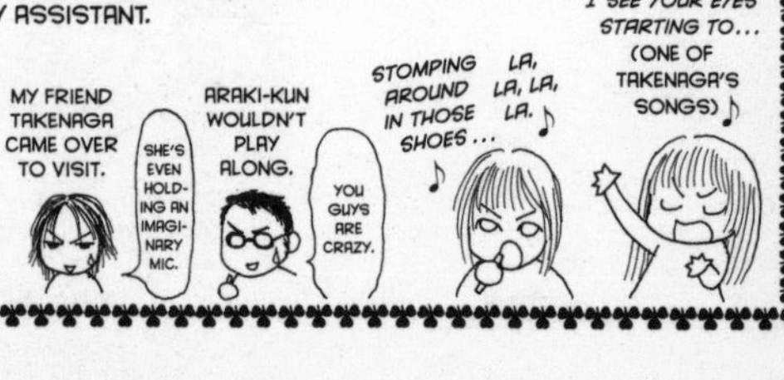
WHEN THOSE BRIGHT FLOWERS FADE, I SEE YOUR EYES STARTING TO... (ONE OF TAKENAGA'S SONGS) ♪
LA, LA, LA, LA. ♪
STOMPING AROUND IN THOSE SHOES... ♪
YOU GUYS ARE CRAZY.
ARAKI-KUN WOULDN'T PLAY ALONG.
SHE'S EVEN HOLDING AN IMAGINARY MIC.
MY FRIEND TAKENAGA CAME OVER TO VISIT.

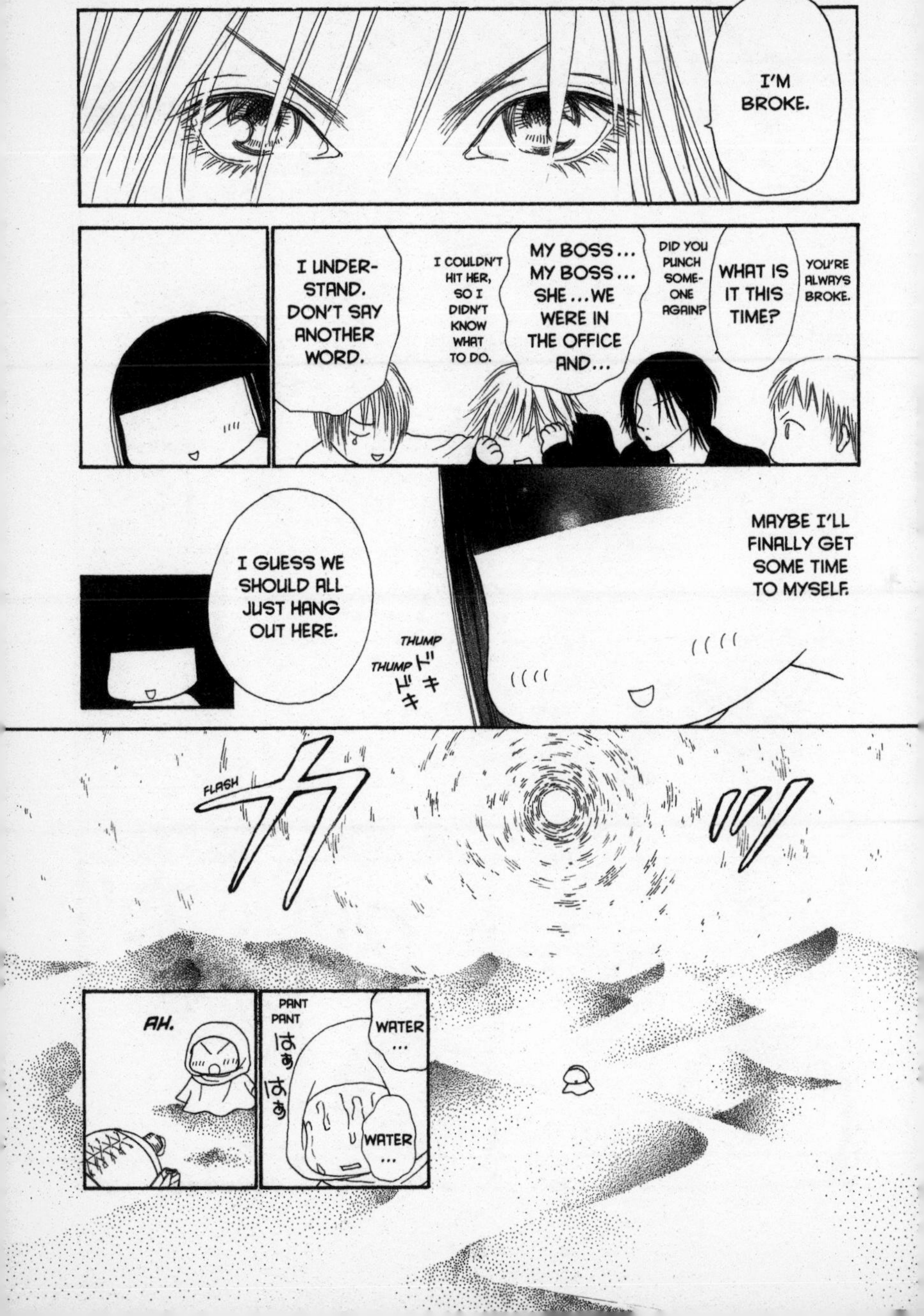
I'M BROKE.
YOU'RE ALWAYS BROKE.
WHAT IS IT THIS TIME?
DID YOU PUNCH SOMEONE AGAIN?
MY BOSS... MY BOSS... SHE... WE WERE IN THE OFFICE AND...
I COULDN'T HIT HER, SO I DIDN'T KNOW WHAT TO DO.
I UNDERSTAND. DON'T SAY ANOTHER WORD.
MAYBE I'LL FINALLY GET SOME TIME TO MYSELF.
THUMP THUMP ドキドキ
I GUESS WE SHOULD ALL JUST HANG OUT HERE.
FLASH カッ
PANT PANT はぁはぁ
WATER...
WATER...
AH.

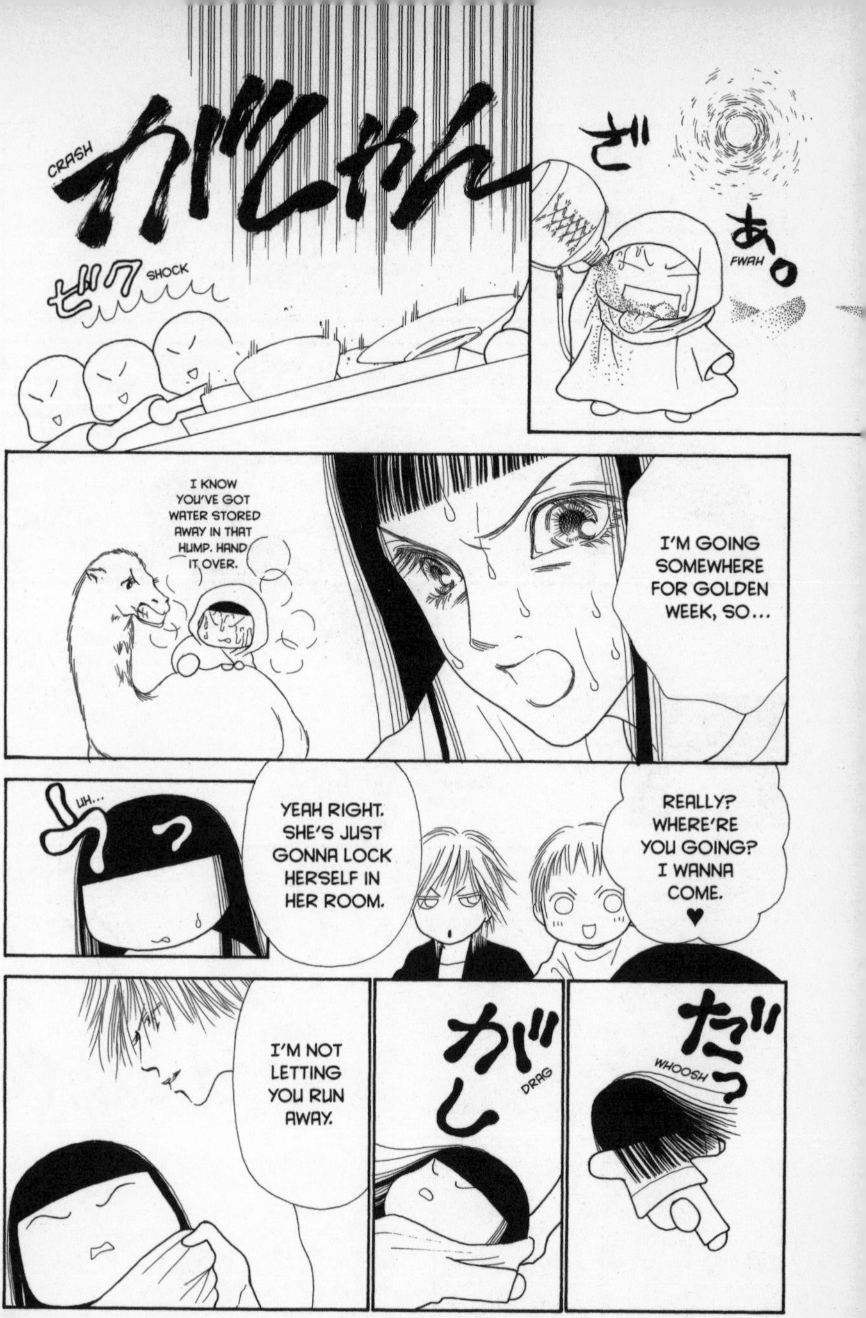

ざ
あ。
FWAH
がしゃん
CRASH
ビクッ
SHOCK
I'M GOING SOMEWHERE FOR GOLDEN WEEK, SO...
I KNOW YOU'VE GOT WATER STORED AWAY IN THAT HUMP. HAND IT OVER.
REALLY? WHERE'RE YOU GOING? I WANNA COME. ♥
YEAH RIGHT. SHE'S JUST GONNA LOCK HERSELF IN HER ROOM.
うっ
UH...
だっ
WHOOSH
がし
DRAG
I'M NOT LETTING YOU RUN AWAY.

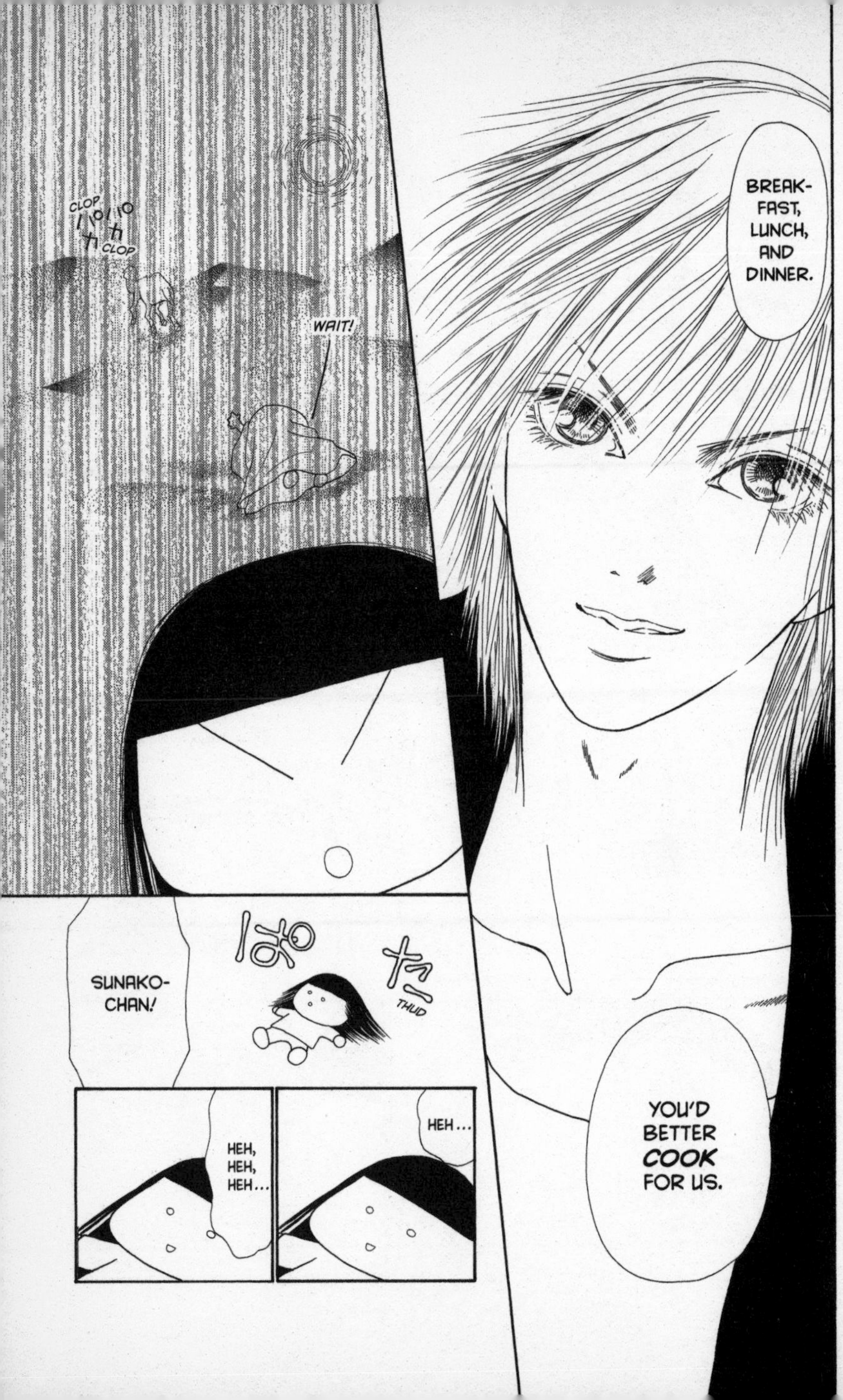
BREAK-FAST, LUNCH, AND DINNER.
YOU'D BETTER **COOK** FOR US.
CLOP CLOP
WAIT!
SUNAKO-CHAN!
THUD
HEH...
HEH, HEH, HEH...

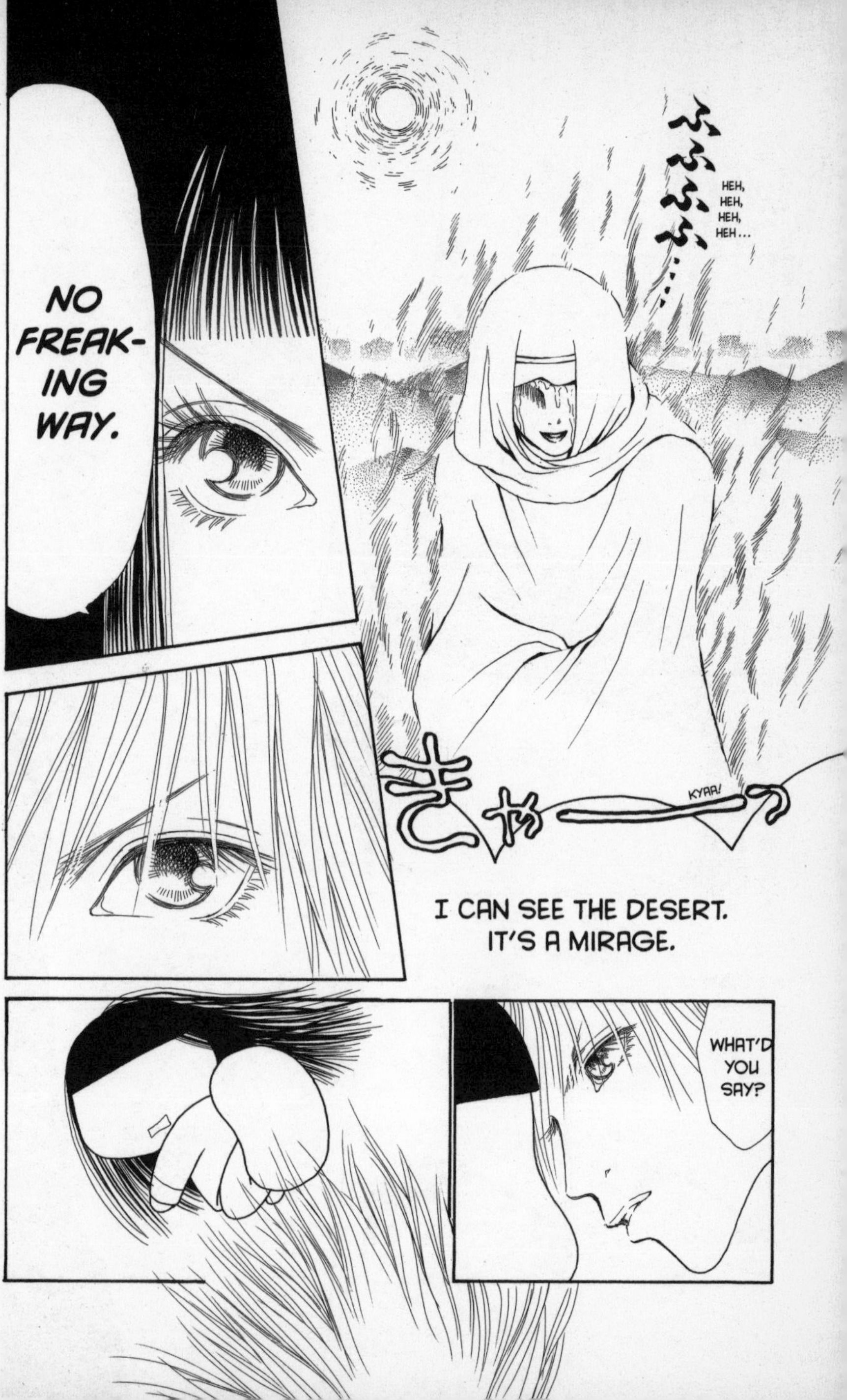
ふふふ…
HEH, HEH, HEH, HEH…
きゃーっ
KYAA!
I CAN SEE THE DESERT. IT'S A MIRAGE.
NO FREAKING-ING WAY.
WHAT'D YOU SAY?

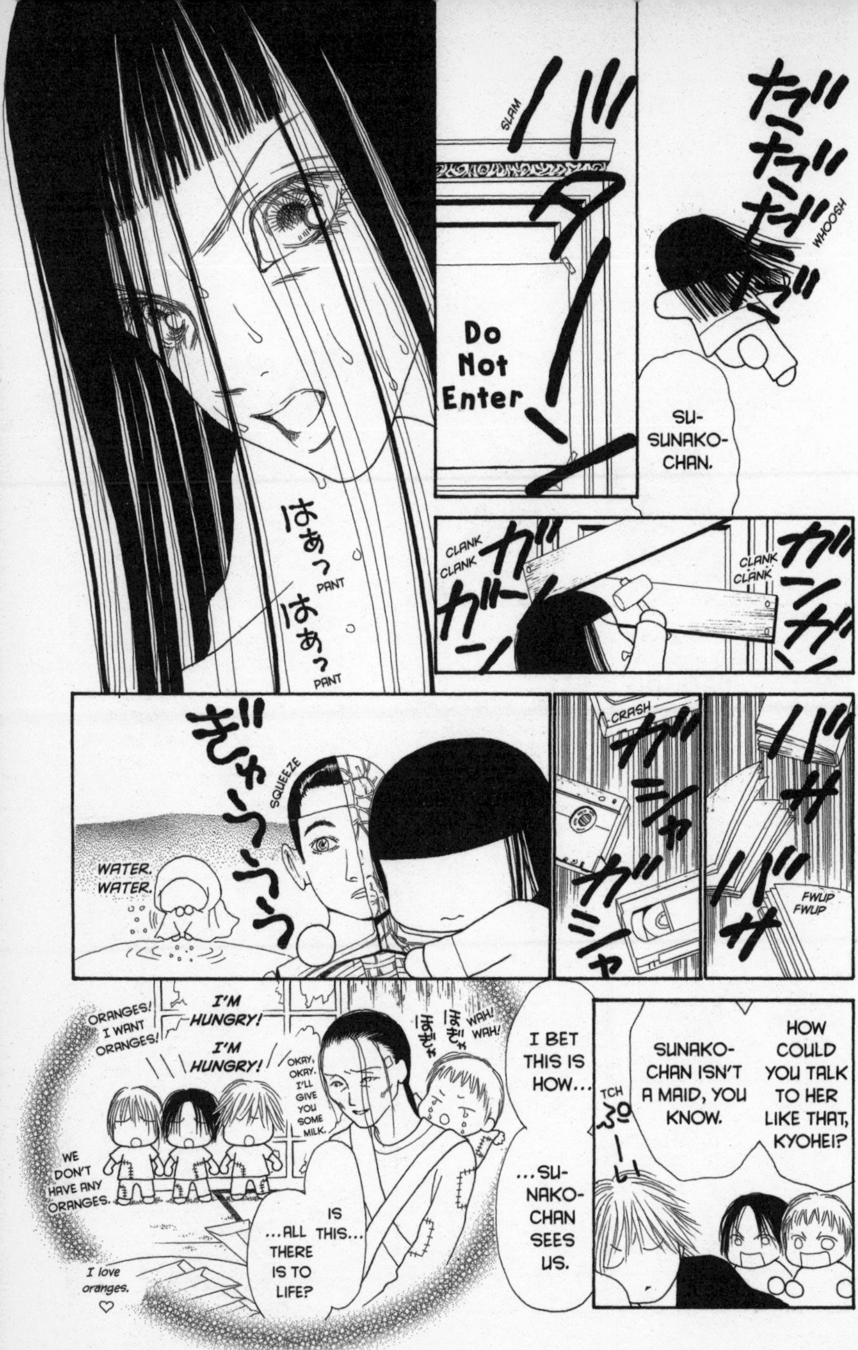

だだだだ
WHOOSH
SU-SUNAKO-CHAN.
バターン
SLAM
Do Not Enter
ガンガン
CLANK CLANK
ガーンガーン
CLANK CLANK
はあっ
PANT
はあっ
PANT
バサバサ
FWUP FWUP
ガシャガシャ
CRASH
ぎゅううう
SQUEEZE
WATER. WATER.
HOW COULD YOU TALK TO HER LIKE THAT, KYOHEI?
SUNAKO-CHAN ISN'T A MAID, YOU KNOW.
ぶー
TCH
I BET THIS IS HOW...
...SU-SUNAKO-CHAN SEES US.
ほぎゃほぎゃ
WAH! WAH!
I'M HUNGRY!
I'M HUNGRY!
ORANGES! I WANT ORANGES!
OKAY, OKAY. I'LL GIVE YOU SOME MILK.
IS THIS...
...ALL THERE IS TO LIFE?
WE DON'T HAVE ANY ORANGES.
I love oranges. ♡

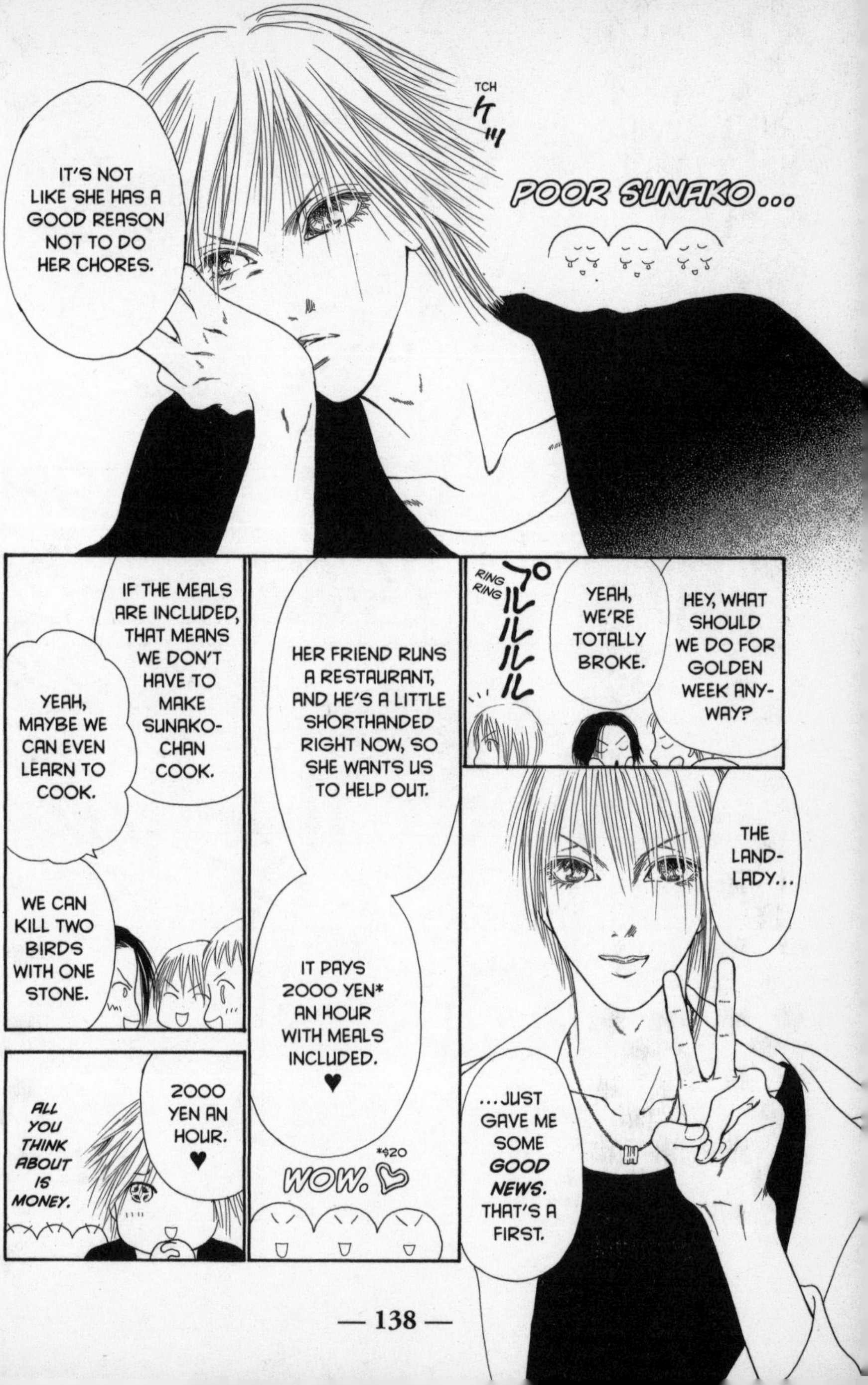
TCH
IT'S NOT LIKE SHE HAS A GOOD REASON NOT TO DO HER CHORES.
POOR SUNAKO...
RING RING
HEY, WHAT SHOULD WE DO FOR GOLDEN WEEK ANY-WAY?
YEAH, WE'RE TOTALLY BROKE.
THE LAND-LADY...
...JUST GAVE ME SOME GOOD NEWS. THAT'S A FIRST.
HER FRIEND RUNS A RESTAURANT, AND HE'S A LITTLE SHORTHANDED RIGHT NOW, SO SHE WANTS US TO HELP OUT.
IT PAYS 2000 YEN* AN HOUR WITH MEALS INCLUDED. ♥
*$20
WOW. ♡
IF THE MEALS ARE INCLUDED, THAT MEANS WE DON'T HAVE TO MAKE SUNAKO-CHAN COOK.
YEAH, MAYBE WE CAN EVEN LEARN TO COOK.
WE CAN KILL TWO BIRDS WITH ONE STONE.
2000 YEN AN HOUR. ♥
ALL YOU THINK ABOUT IS MONEY.

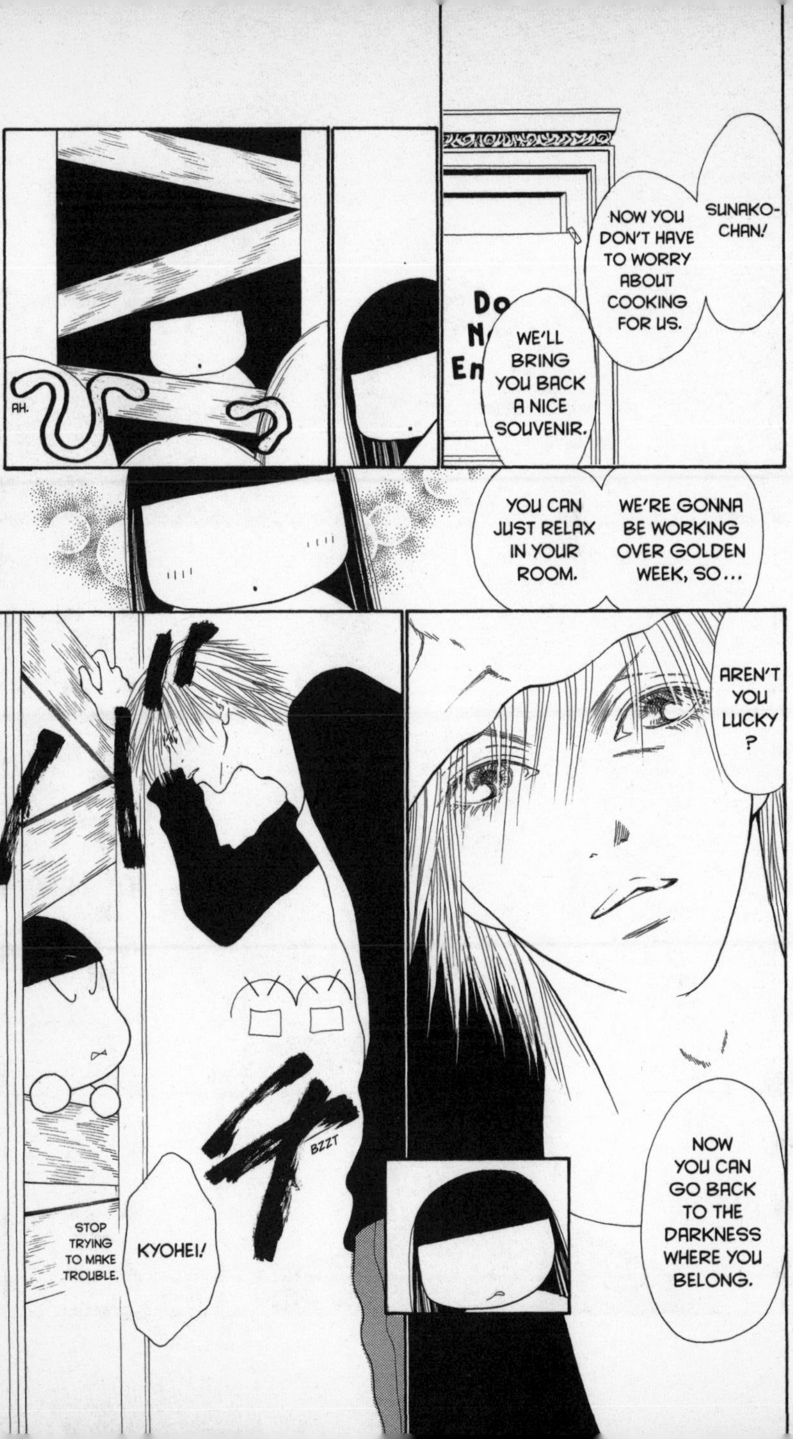
SUNAKO-CHAN!
NOW YOU DON'T HAVE TO WORRY ABOUT COOKING FOR US.
WE'LL BRING YOU BACK A NICE SOUVENIR.
AH.
WE'RE GONNA BE WORKING OVER GOLDEN WEEK, SO...
YOU CAN JUST RELAX IN YOUR ROOM.
AREN'T YOU LUCKY?
NOW YOU CAN GO BACK TO THE DARKNESS WHERE YOU BELONG.
BZZT
KYOHEI!
STOP TRYING TO MAKE TROUBLE.

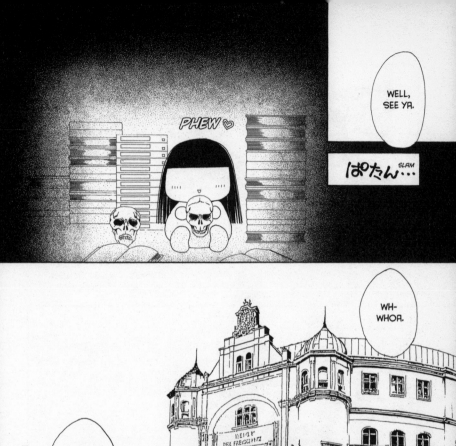

WELL, SEE YA.

PHEW ♡

ぱたん… SLAM

WH-WHOA.

THIS PLACE LOOKS PRETTY FANCY.

WH—

WELL, WHATEVER. WE'LL ONLY BE IN THE KITCHEN ANYWAY.

WHOA!

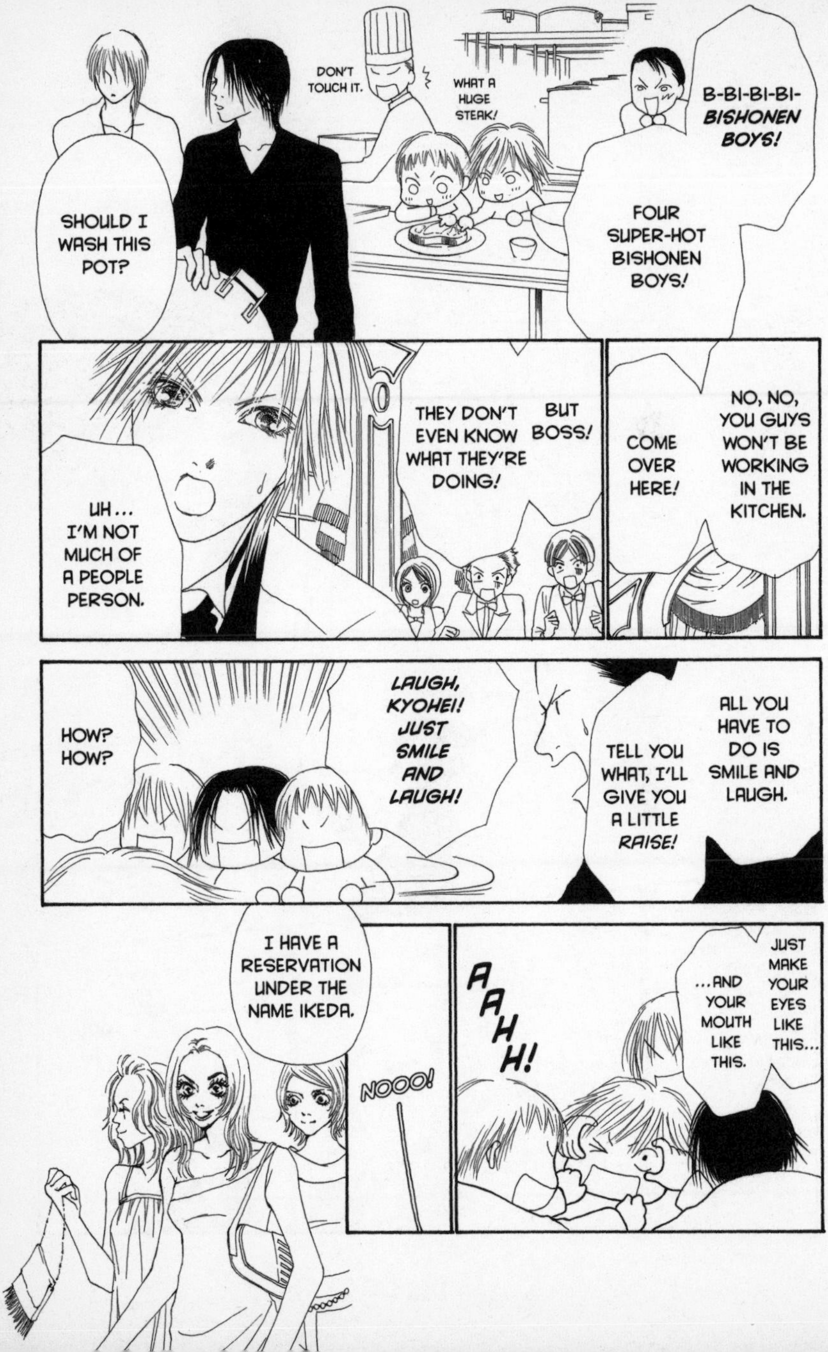
B-BI-BI-BI-BISHONEN BOYS!
FOUR SUPER-HOT BISHONEN BOYS!
WHAT A HUGE STEAK!
DON'T TOUCH IT.
SHOULD I WASH THIS POT?
NO, NO, YOU GUYS WON'T BE WORKING IN THE KITCHEN.
COME OVER HERE!
BUT BOSS!
THEY DON'T EVEN KNOW WHAT THEY'RE DOING!
UH... I'M NOT MUCH OF A PEOPLE PERSON.
ALL YOU HAVE TO DO IS SMILE AND LAUGH.
TELL YOU WHAT, I'LL GIVE YOU A LITTLE *RAISE!*
LAUGH, KYOHEI! JUST SMILE AND LAUGH!
HOW? HOW?
JUST MAKE YOUR EYES LIKE THIS...
...AND YOUR MOUTH LIKE THIS.
AAHH!
NOOO!
I HAVE A RESERVATION UNDER THE NAME IKEDA.

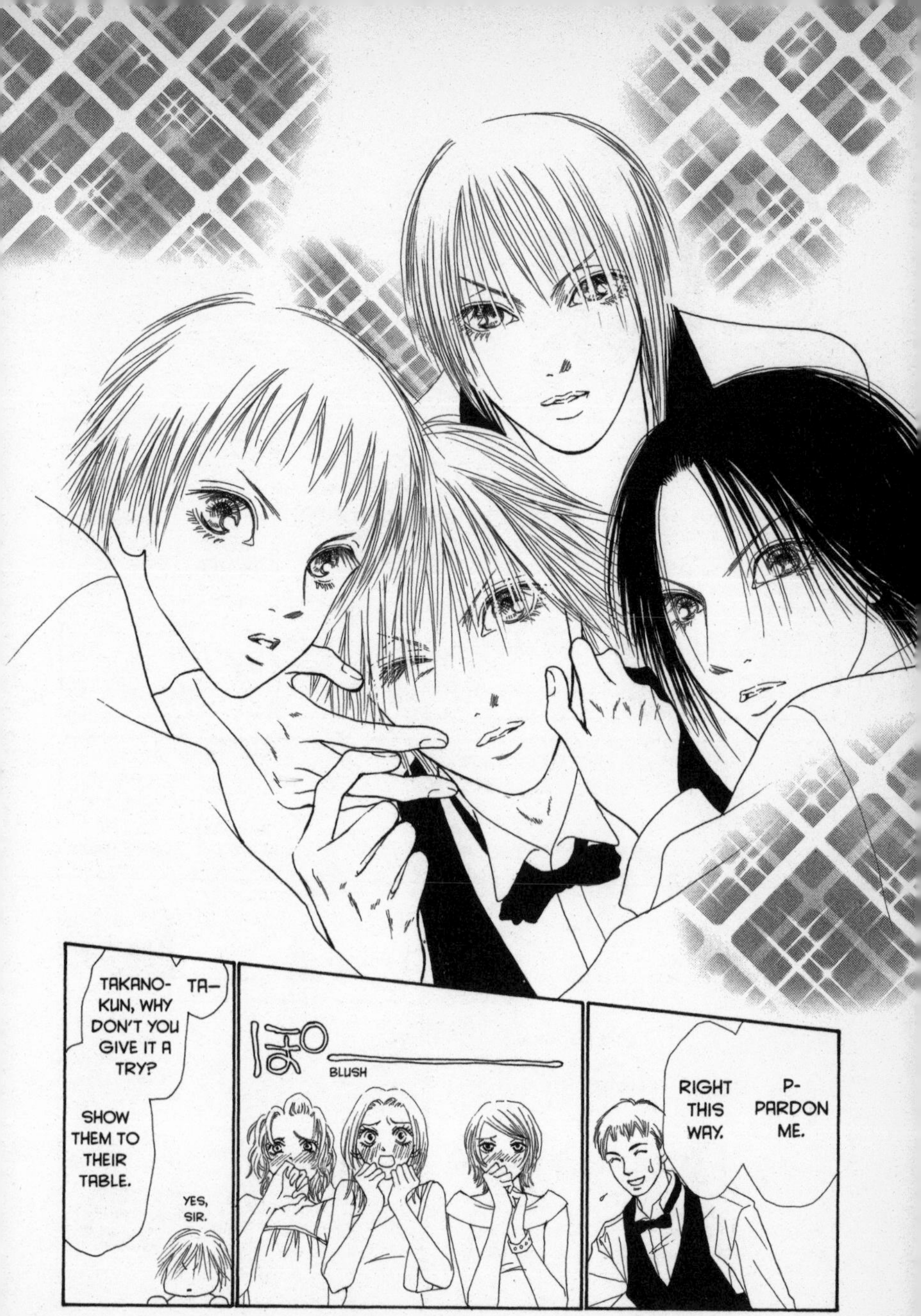
P-PARDON ME.
RIGHT THIS WAY.
ぽ
BLUSH
TA-
TAKANO-KUN, WHY DON'T YOU GIVE IT A TRY?
SHOW THEM TO THEIR TABLE.
YES, SIR.

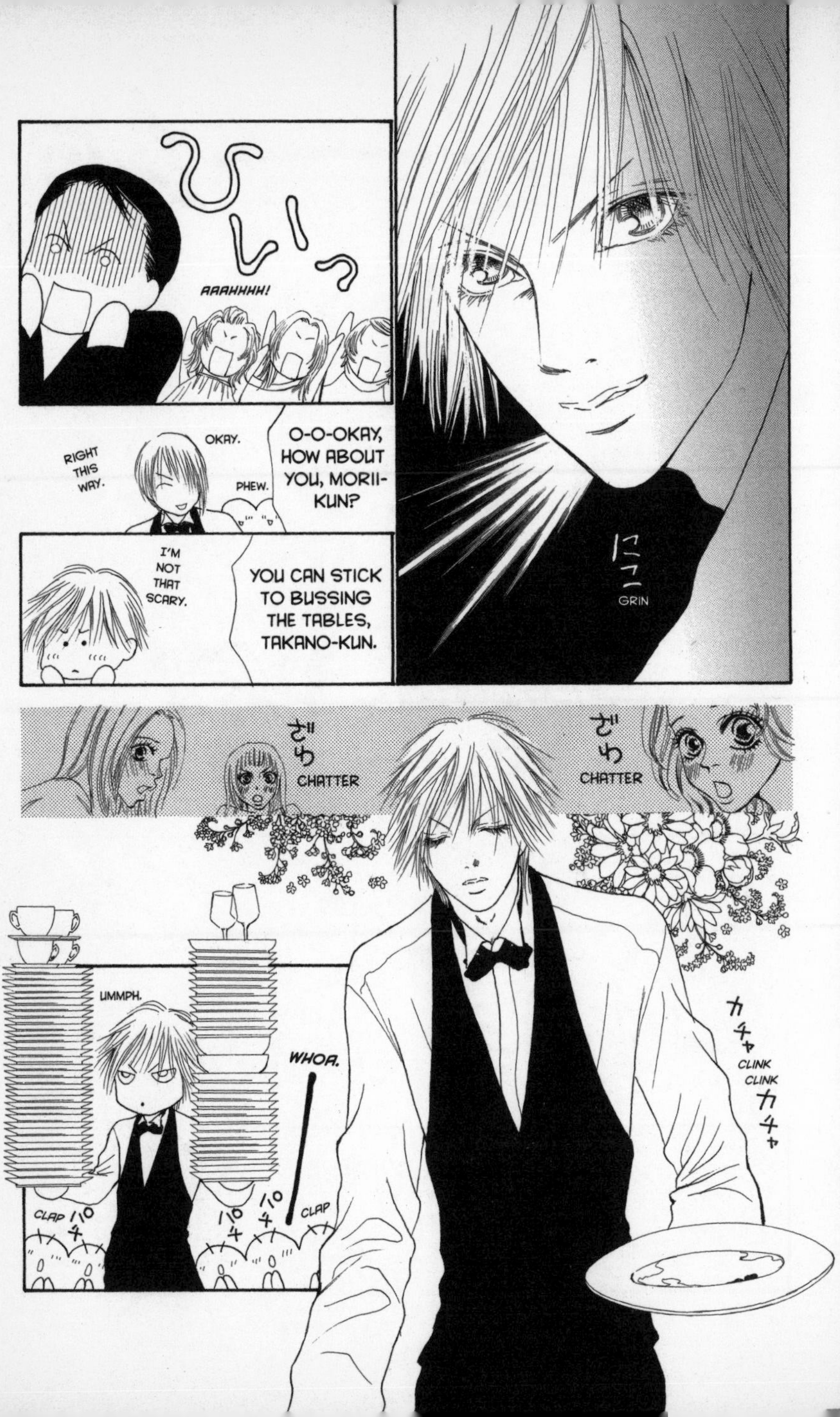
にこ
GRIN
ひぃーっ
AAAHHHH!
O-O-OKAY, HOW ABOUT YOU, MORII-KUN?
OKAY.
PHEW.
RIGHT THIS WAY.
YOU CAN STICK TO BUSSING THE TABLES, TAKANO-KUN.
I'M NOT THAT SCARY.
ざわ
CHATTER
ざわ
CHATTER
カチャ
CLINK
CLINK
カチャ
WHOA.
UMMPH.
パチ
CLAP
パチ
CLAP

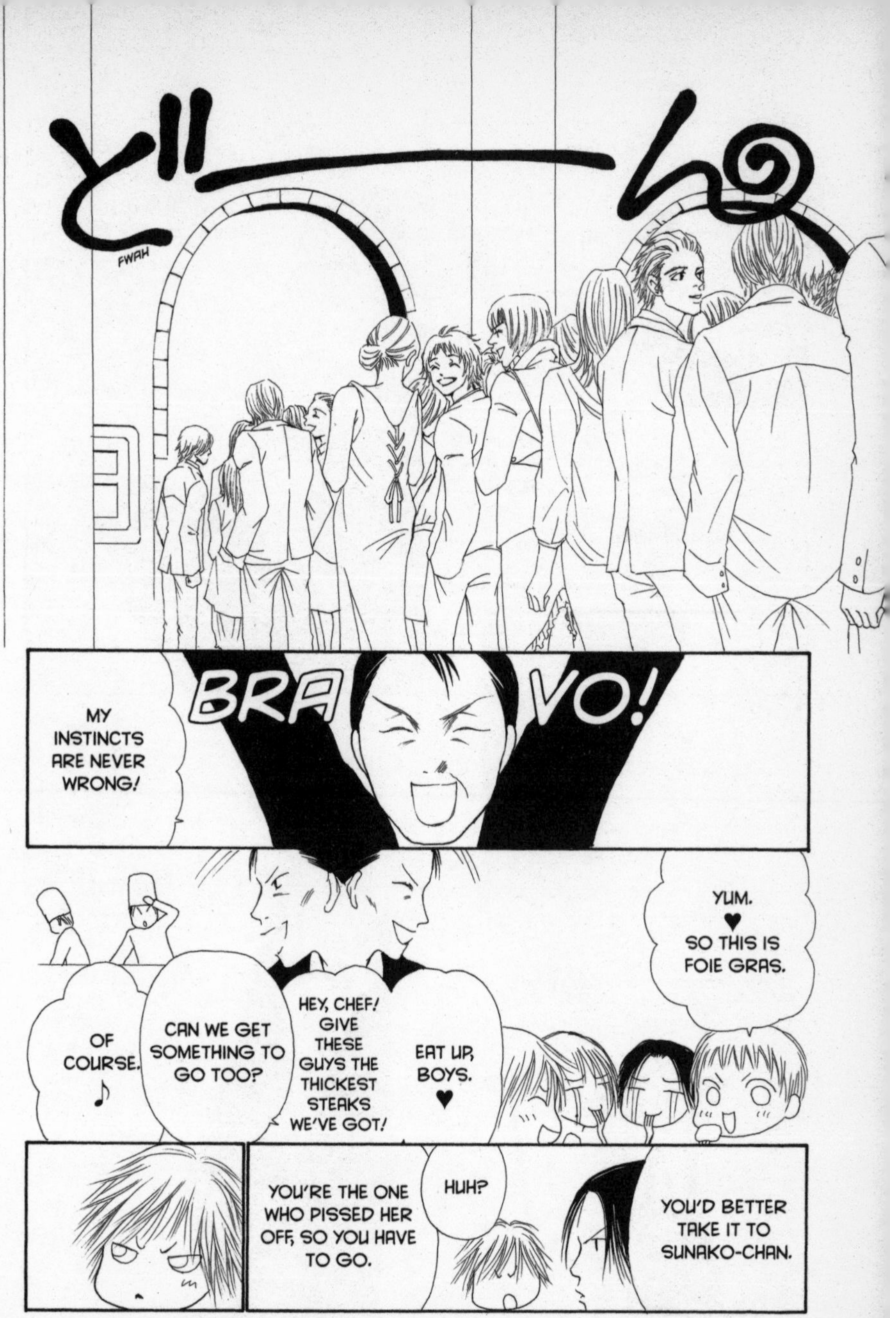
とーーん
FWAH
BRAVO!
MY INSTINCTS ARE NEVER WRONG!
YUM. ♥ SO THIS IS FOIE GRAS.
EAT UP, BOYS. ♥
HEY, CHEF! GIVE THESE GUYS THE THICKEST STEAKS WE'VE GOT!
CAN WE GET SOMETHING TO GO TOO?
OF COURSE. ♪
YOU'D BETTER TAKE IT TO SUNAKO-CHAN.
HUH?
YOU'RE THE ONE WHO PISSED HER OFF, SO YOU HAVE TO GO.

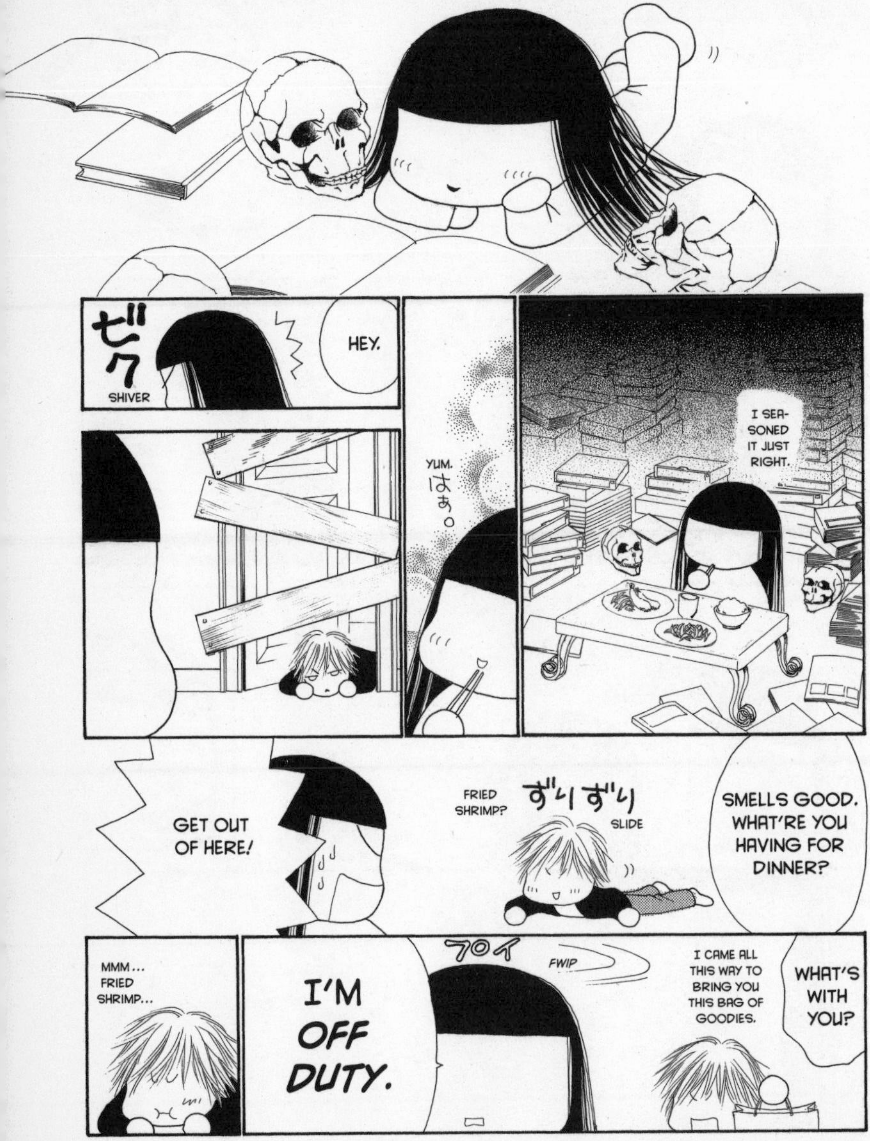
I SEA-
SONED
IT JUST
RIGHT.
YUM.
はぁ。
HEY.
ビク
SHIVER
SMELLS GOOD. WHAT'RE YOU HAVING FOR DINNER?
FRIED SHRIMP?
ずりずり
SLIDE
GET OUT OF HERE!
WHAT'S WITH YOU?
I CAME ALL THIS WAY TO BRING YOU THIS BAG OF GOODIES.
プイ
FWIP
I'M OFF DUTY.
MMM... FRIED SHRIMP...

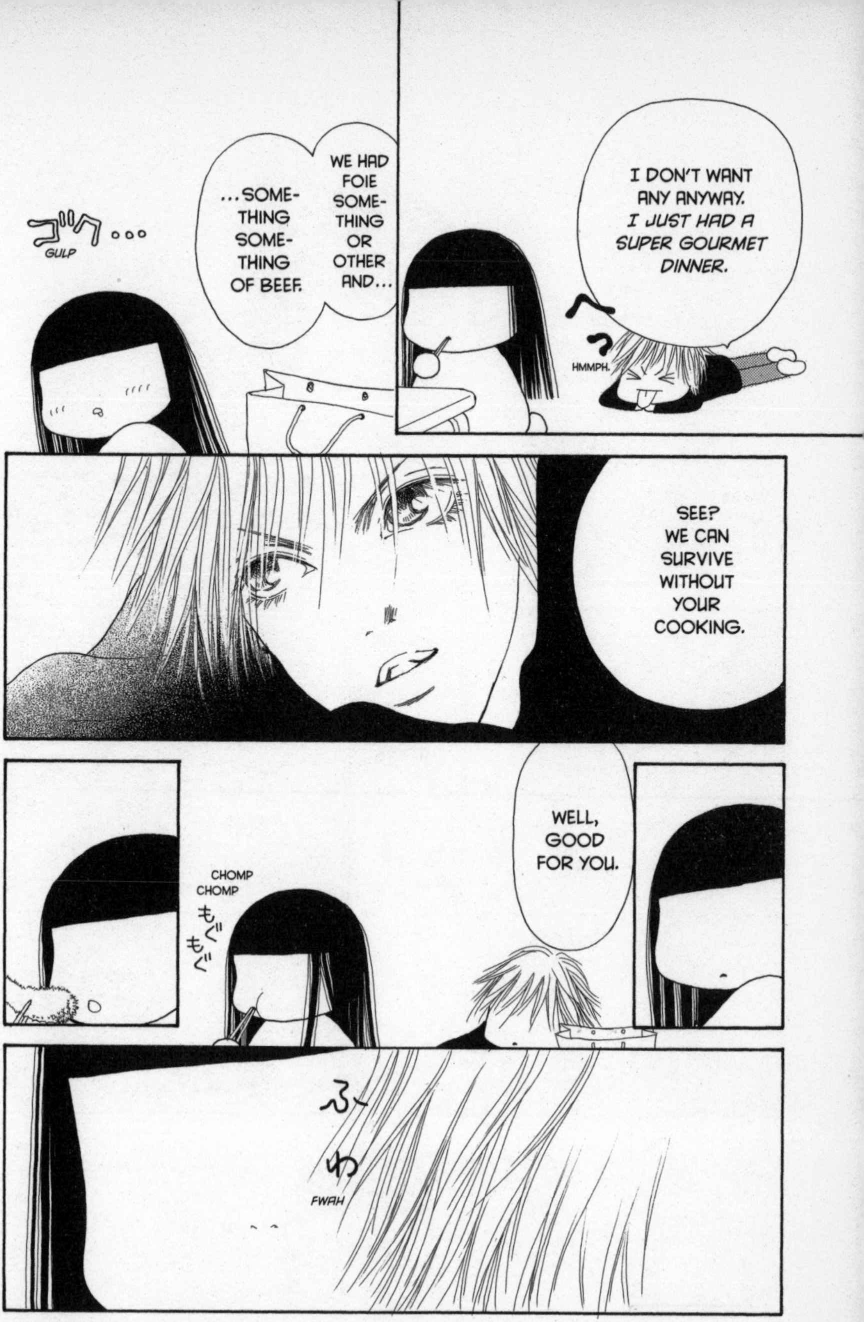
I DON'T WANT ANY ANYWAY. I JUST HAD A SUPER GOURMET DINNER.
HMMPH.
WE HAD FOIE SOME-THING OR OTHER AND...
...SOME-THING SOME-THING OF BEEF.
ゴク...
GULP
SEE? WE CAN SURVIVE WITHOUT YOUR COOKING.
WELL, GOOD FOR YOU.
もぐもぐ
CHOMP CHOMP
ふ〜わ
FWAH

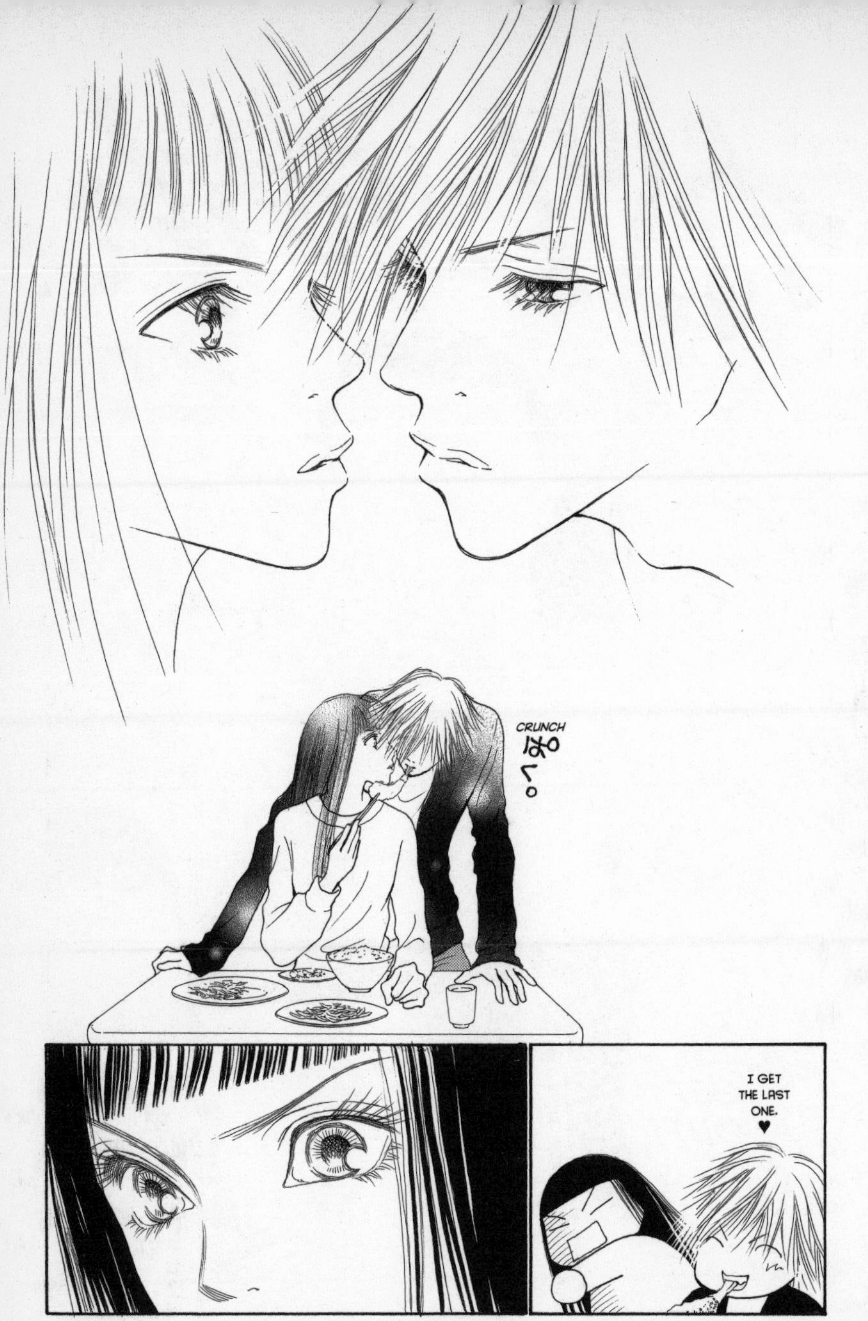
CRUNCH
ぱく。
I GET THE LAST ONE. ♥

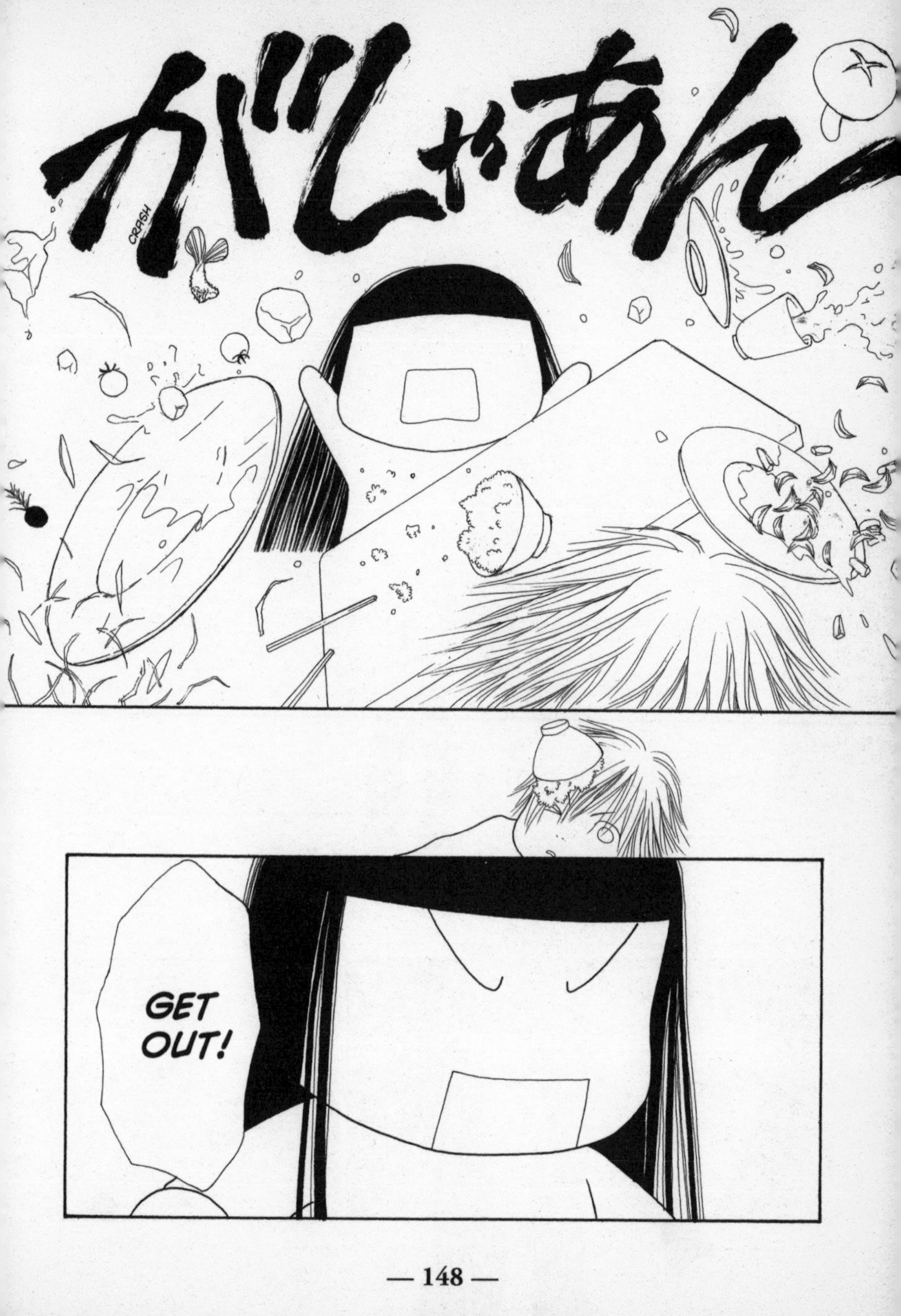
がしゃあん
CRASH
GET OUT!

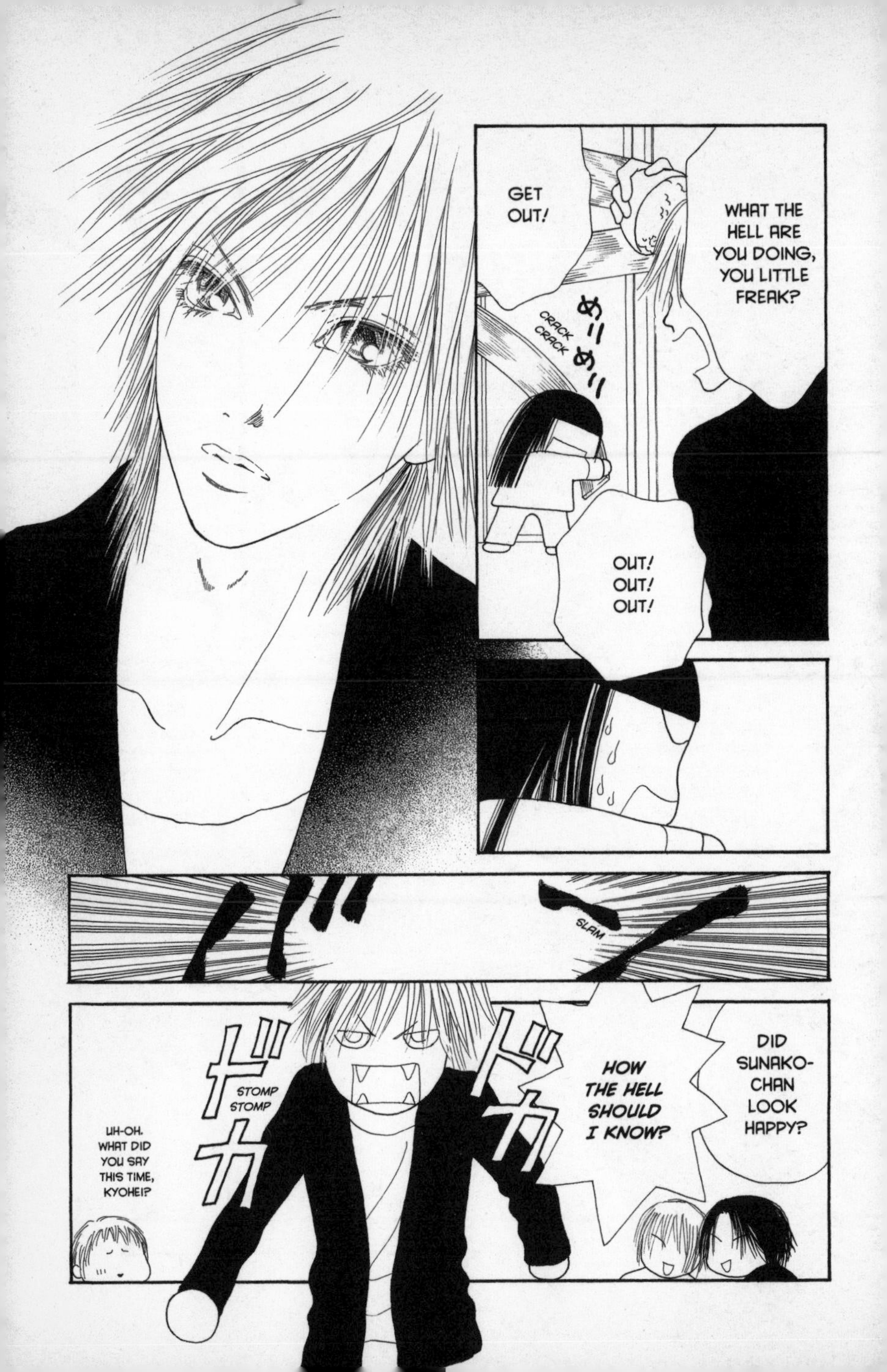
WHAT THE HELL ARE YOU DOING, YOU LITTLE FREAK?
GET OUT!
CRACK CRACK
OUT! OUT! OUT!
SLAM
DID SUNAKO-CHAN LOOK HAPPY?
HOW THE HELL SHOULD I KNOW?
STOMP STOMP
UH-OH. WHAT DID YOU SAY THIS TIME, KYOHEI?

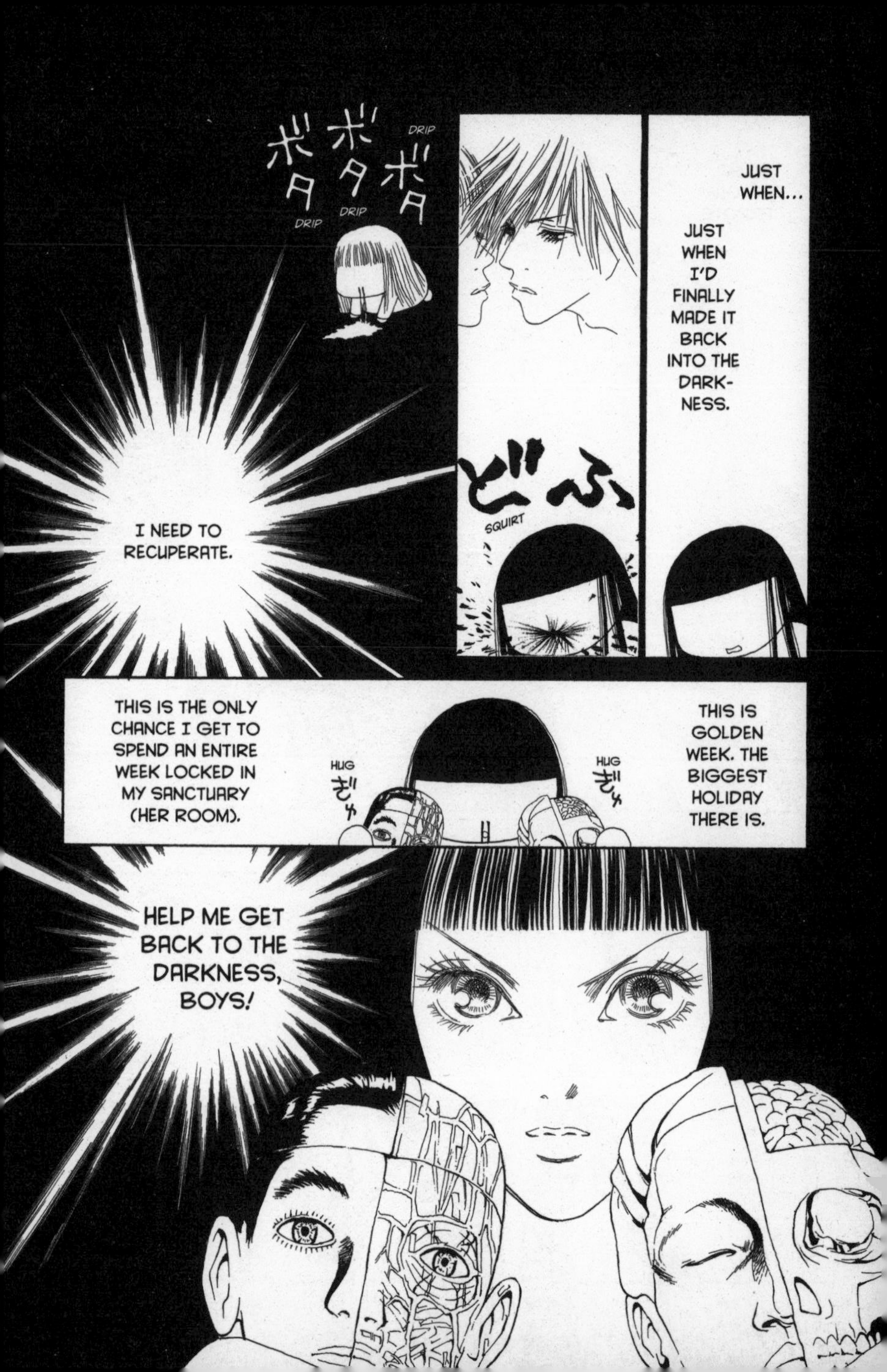
JUST WHEN...
JUST WHEN I'D FINALLY MADE IT BACK INTO THE DARKNESS.
SQUIRT
DRIP
DRIP
DRIP
I NEED TO RECUPERATE.
THIS IS GOLDEN WEEK. THE BIGGEST HOLIDAY THERE IS.
HUG
HUG
THIS IS THE ONLY CHANCE I GET TO SPEND AN ENTIRE WEEK LOCKED IN MY SANCTUARY (HER ROOM).
HELP ME GET BACK TO THE DARKNESS, BOYS!

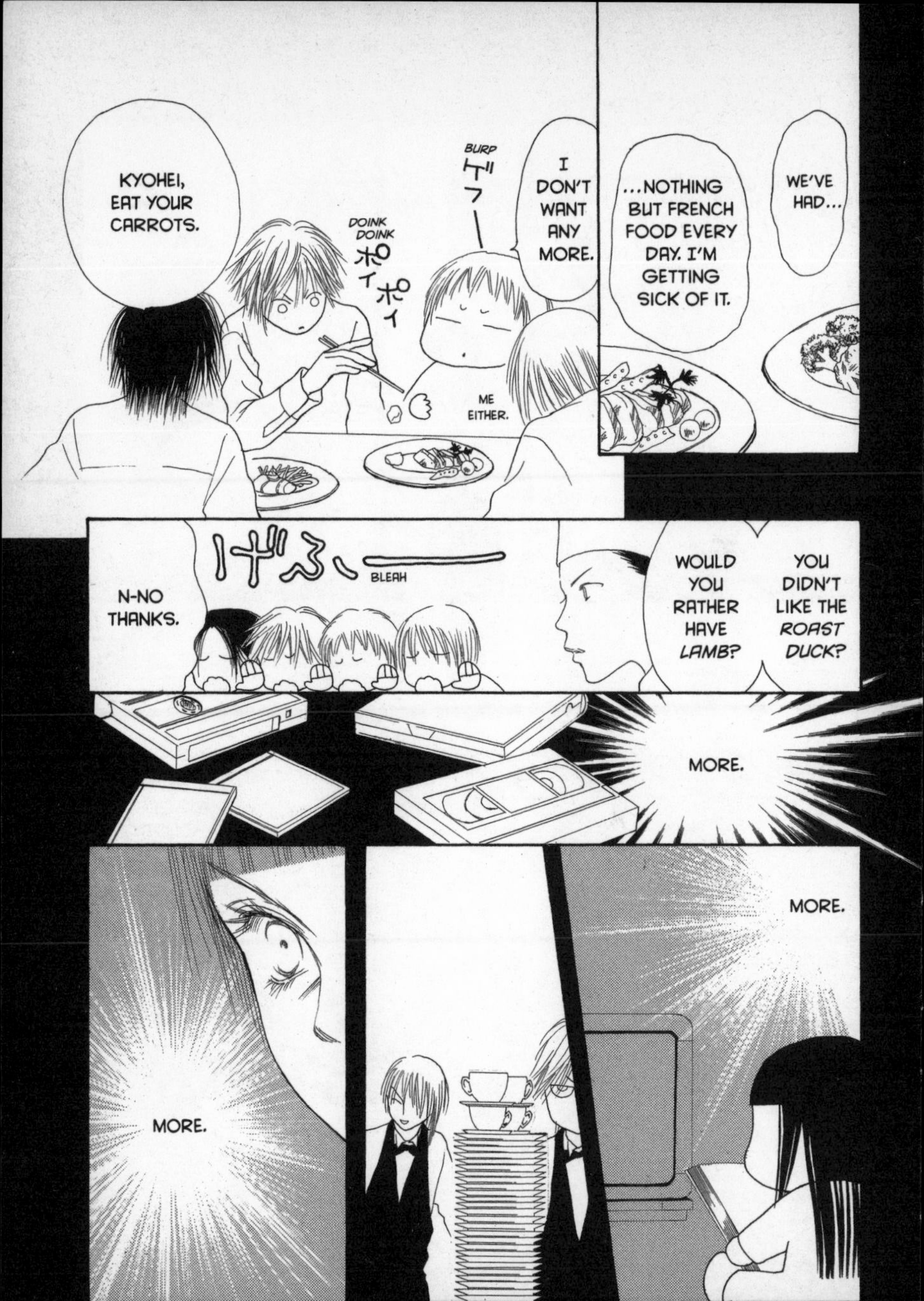
WE'VE HAD...
...NOTHING BUT FRENCH FOOD EVERY DAY. I'M GETTING SICK OF IT.
I DON'T WANT ANY MORE.
BURP
ゲフー
DOINK DOINK
ポイポイ
KYOHEI, EAT YOUR CARROTS.
ME EITHER.
YOU DIDN'T LIKE THE *ROAST DUCK*?
WOULD YOU RATHER HAVE *LAMB*?
げふー
BLEAH
N-NO THANKS.
MORE.
MORE.
MORE.

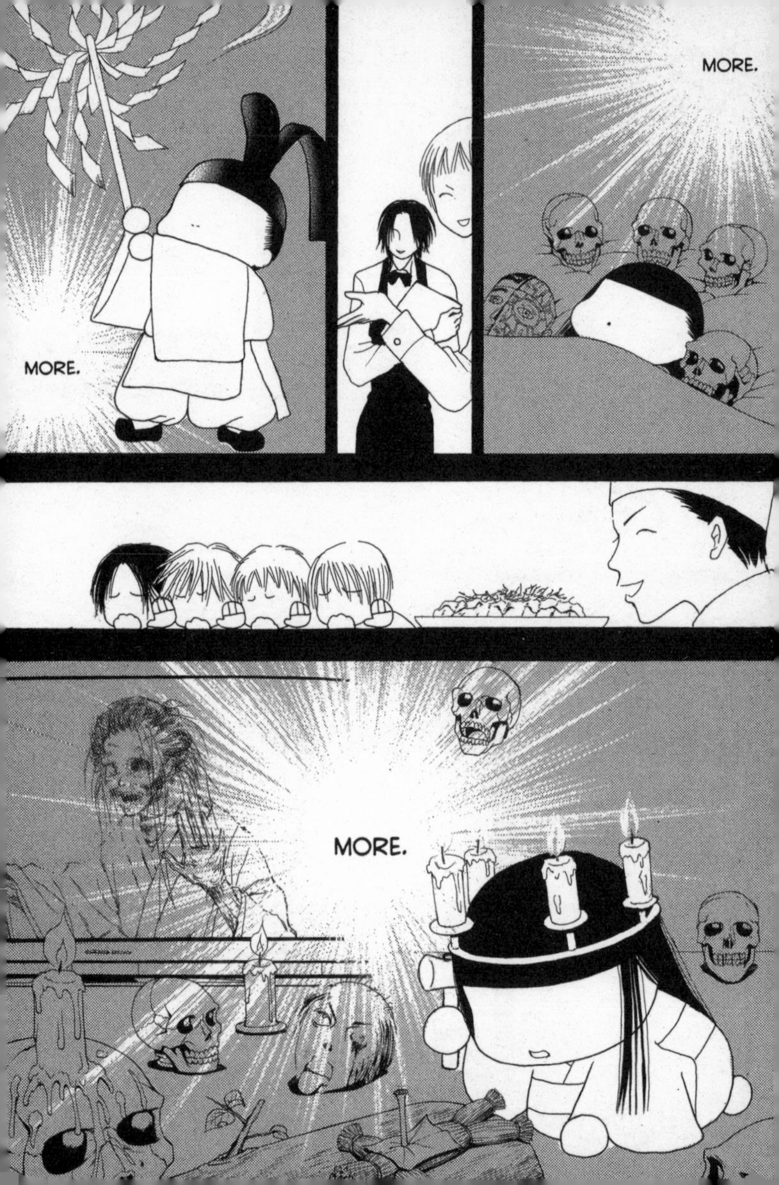
MORE.
MORE.
MORE.

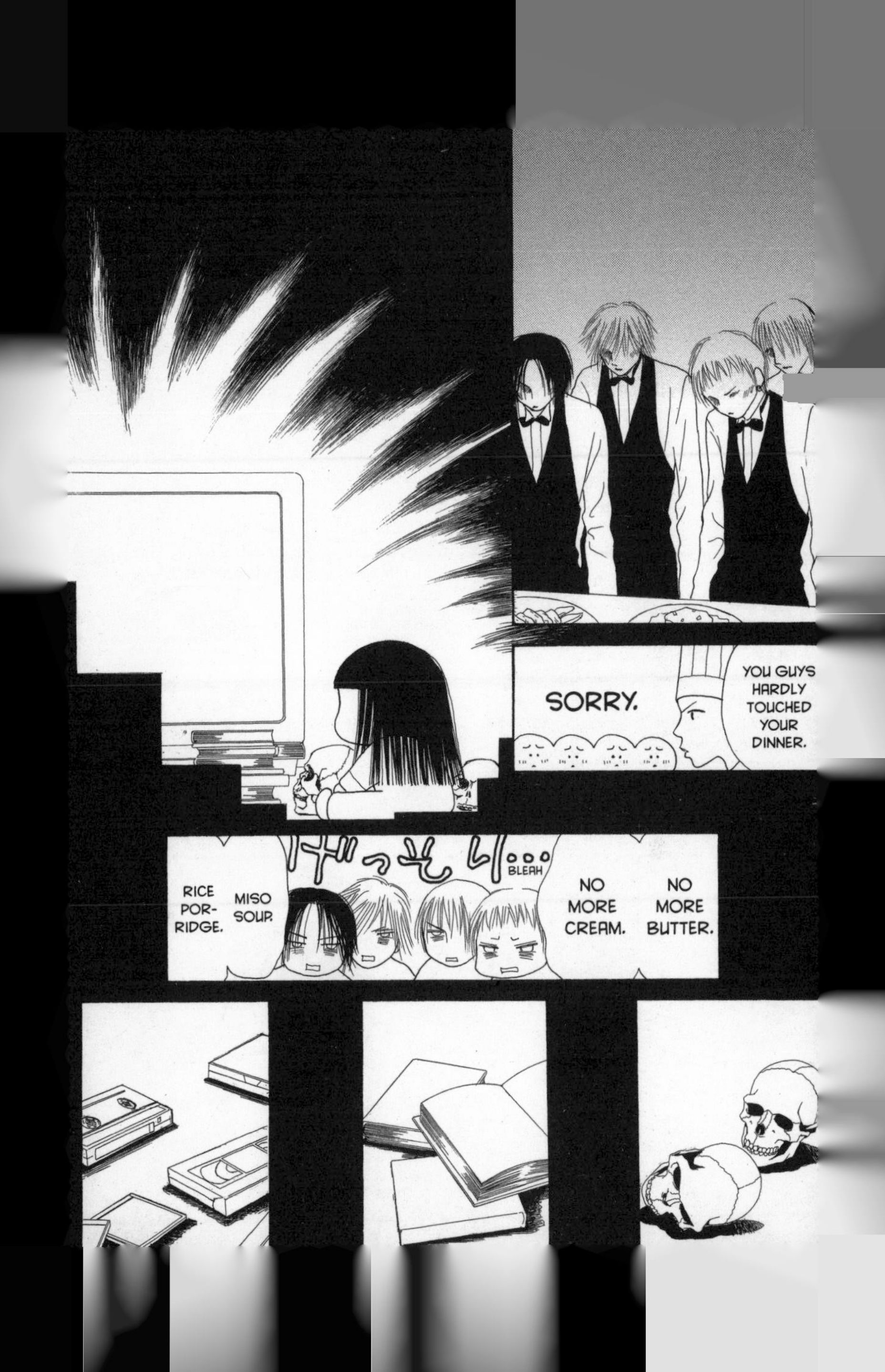
YOU GUYS HARDLY TOUCHED YOUR DINNER.
SORRY.
NO MORE BUTTER.
NO MORE CREAM.
げっそり…
BLEAH
MISO SOUP.
RICE POR-RIDGE.

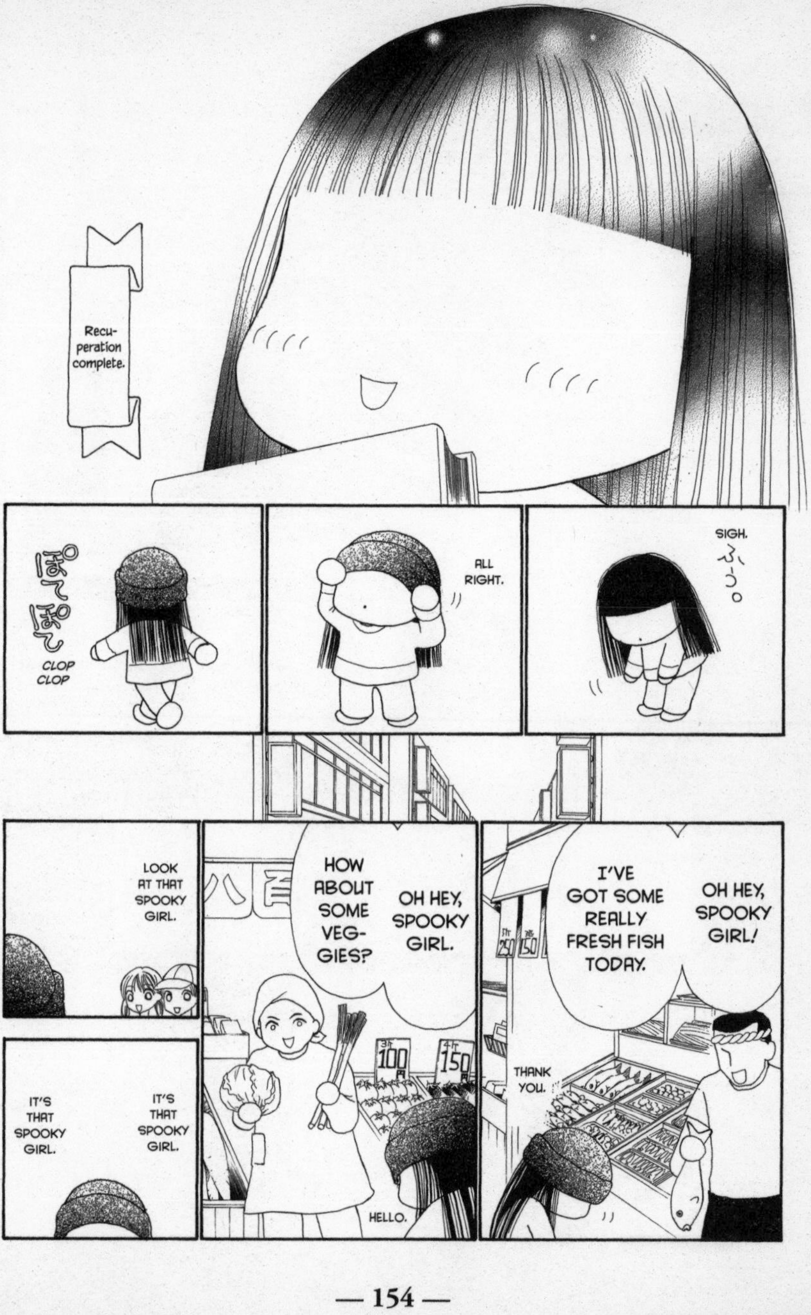
Recu-
peration
complete.
SIGH.
ふー。
ALL
RIGHT.
ぽてぽて
CLOP
CLOP
OH HEY,
SPOOKY
GIRL!
I'VE
GOT SOME
REALLY
FRESH FISH
TODAY.
THANK
YOU.
OH HEY,
SPOOKY
GIRL.
HOW
ABOUT
SOME
VEG-
GIES?
HELLO.
LOOK
AT THAT
SPOOKY
GIRL.
IT'S
THAT
SPOOKY
GIRL.
IT'S
THAT
SPOOKY
GIRL.

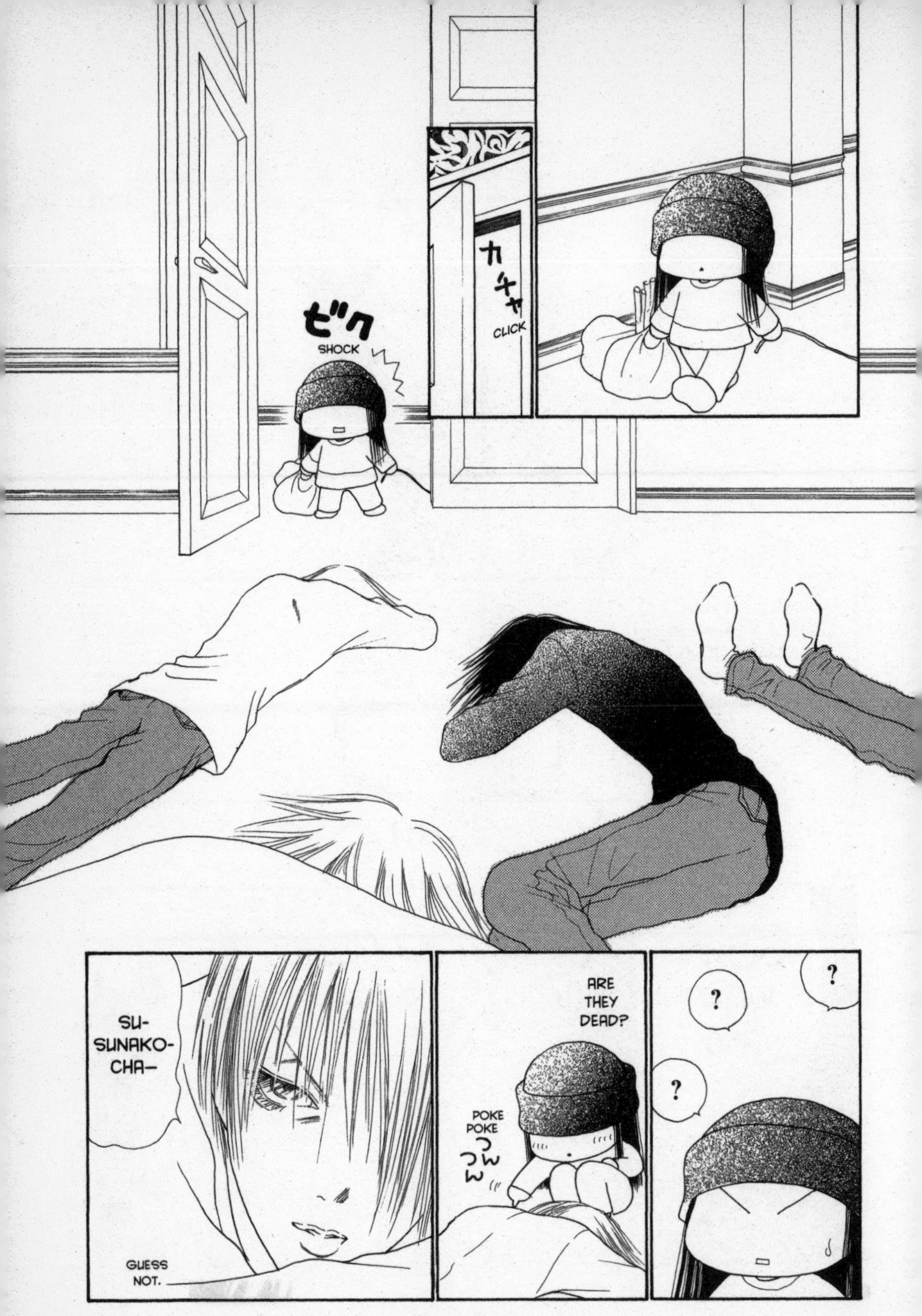

カチャ
CLICK
ビク
SHOCK
?
?
?
ARE THEY DEAD?
POKE POKE
つんつん
SU-SUNAKO-CHA-
GUESS NOT.

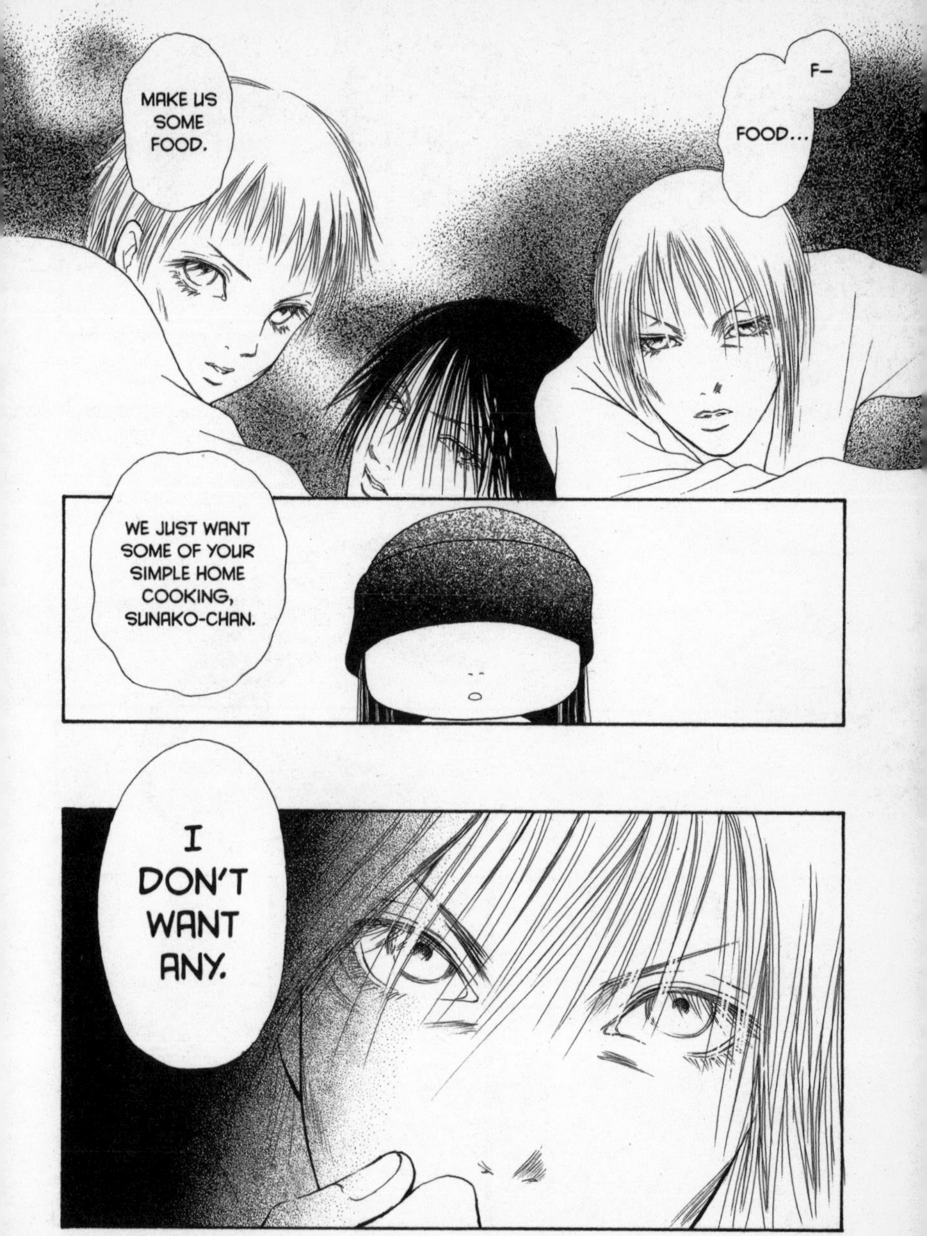
F— FOOD...
MAKE US SOME FOOD.
WE JUST WANT SOME OF YOUR SIMPLE HOME COOKING, SUNAKO-CHAN.
I DON'T WANT ANY.

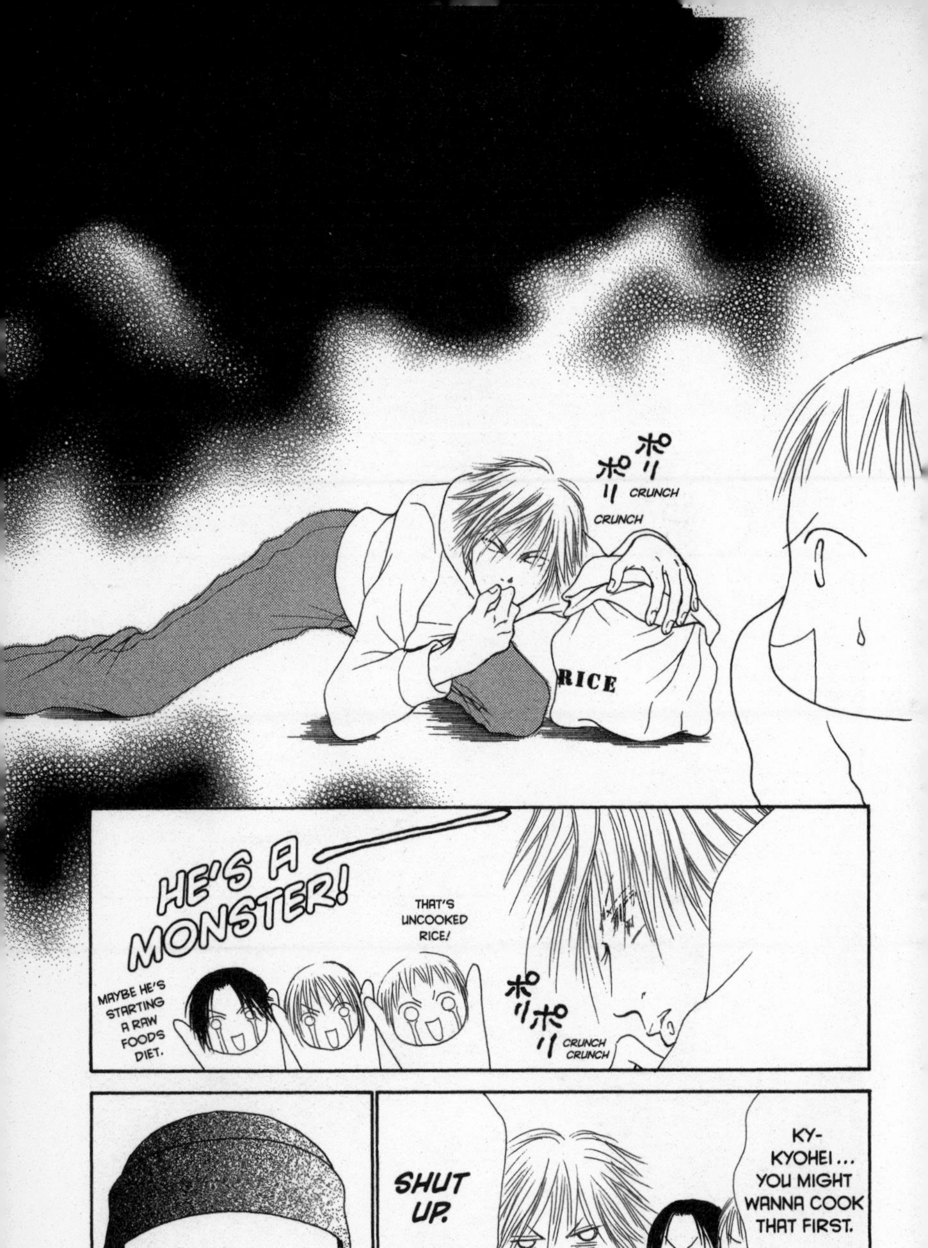
ポリ
ポリ
CRUNCH
CRUNCH
RICE
ポリポリ
CRUNCH CRUNCH
THAT'S UNCOOKED RICE!
HE'S A MONSTER!
MAYBE HE'S STARTING A RAW FOODS DIET.
KY-KYOHEI... YOU MIGHT WANNA COOK THAT FIRST.
SHUT UP.
I WANT RICE, AND I WANT IT NOW.

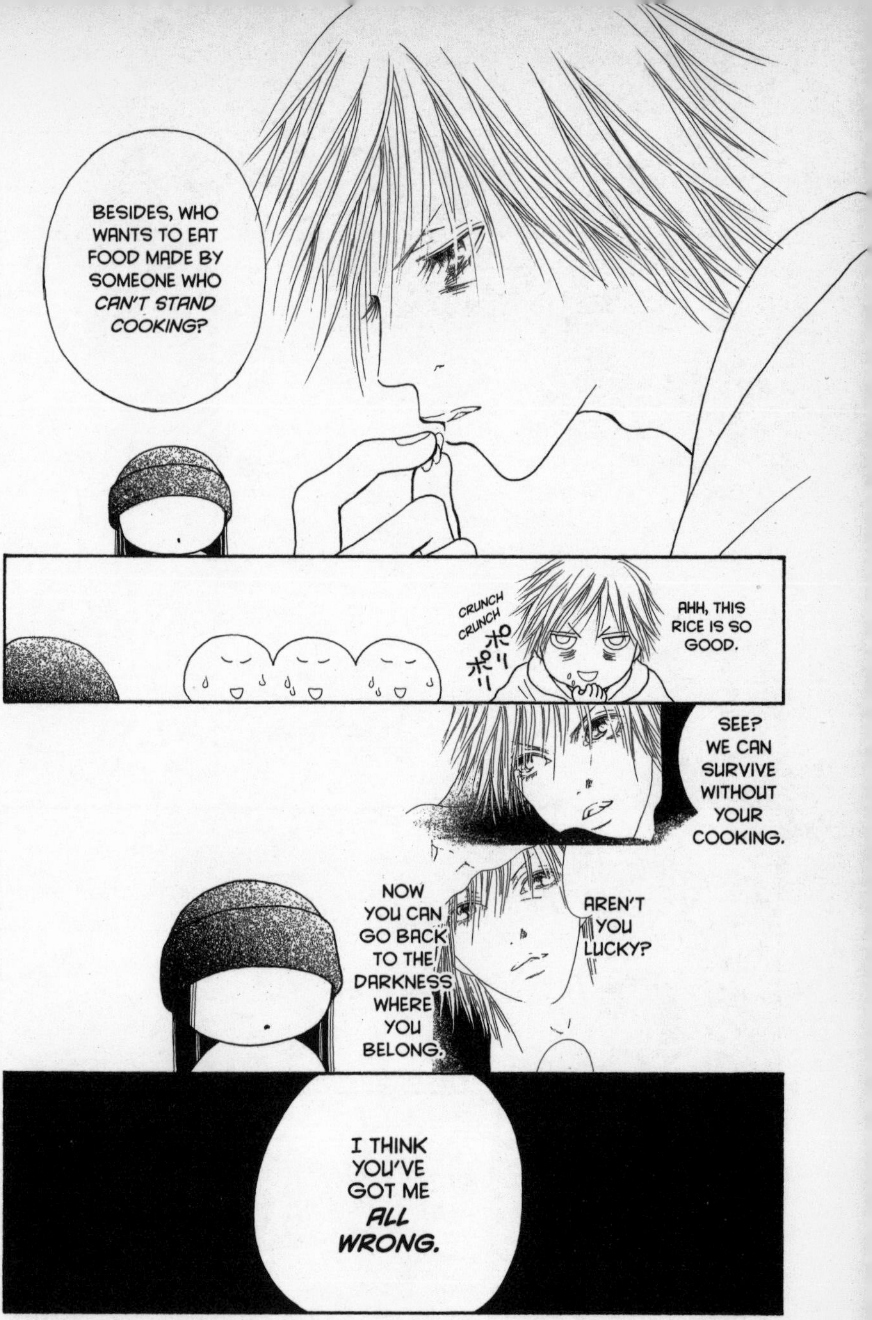
BESIDES, WHO WANTS TO EAT FOOD MADE BY SOMEONE WHO *CAN'T STAND* COOKING?
AHH, THIS RICE IS SO GOOD.
CRUNCH CRUNCH
ポリポリ
SEE? WE CAN SURVIVE WITHOUT YOUR COOKING.
AREN'T YOU LUCKY?
NOW YOU CAN GO BACK TO THE DARKNESS WHERE YOU BELONG.
I THINK YOU'VE GOT ME ***ALL WRONG.***

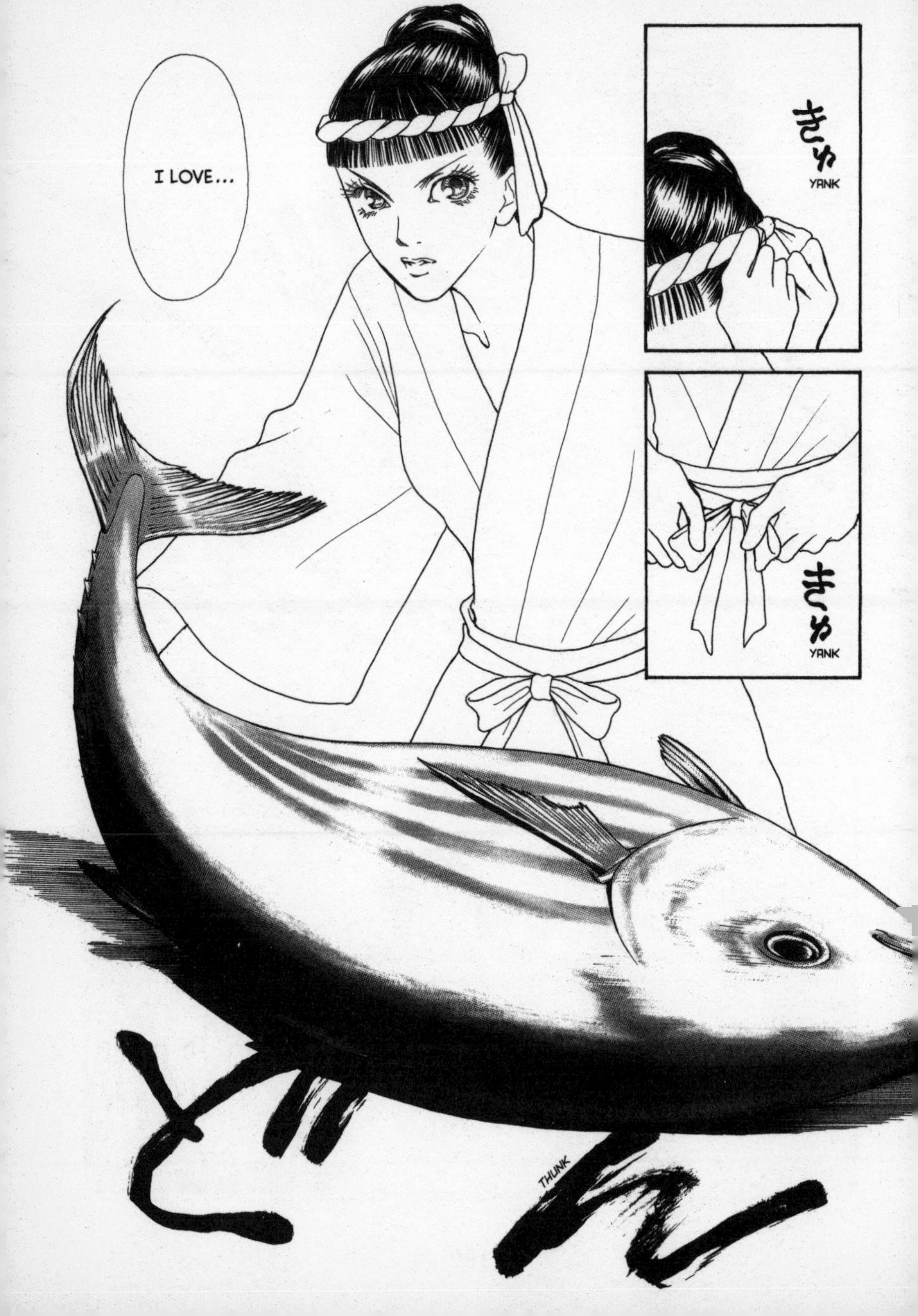
きゅ
YANK
きゅ
YANK
I LOVE...
どん
THUNK

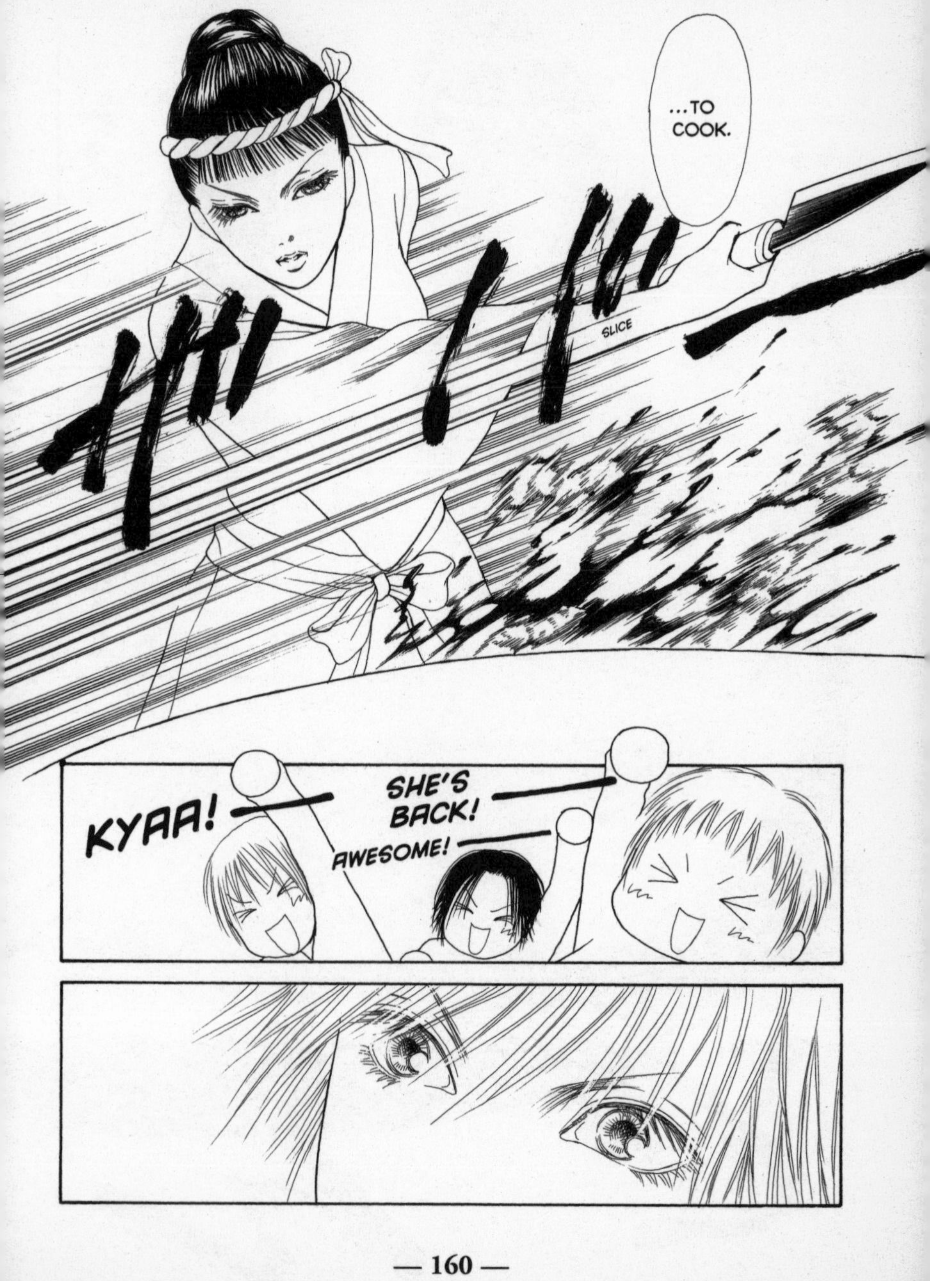
...TO COOK.
SLICE
SHE'S BACK!
AWESOME!
KYAA!

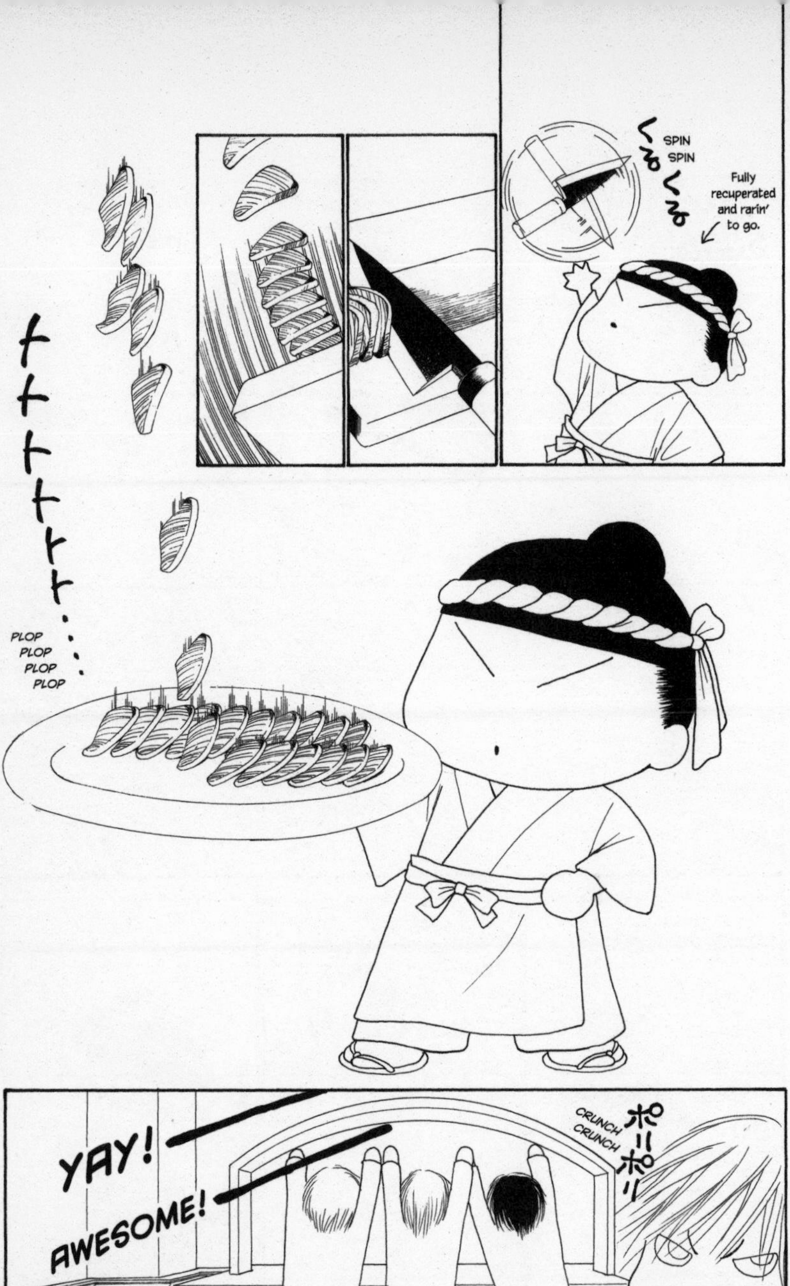
SPIN SPIN
くるくる
Fully recuperated and rarin' to go.
トトトトトト…
PLOP PLOP PLOP PLOP
CRUNCH CRUNCH
ポリポリ
YAY!
AWESOME!

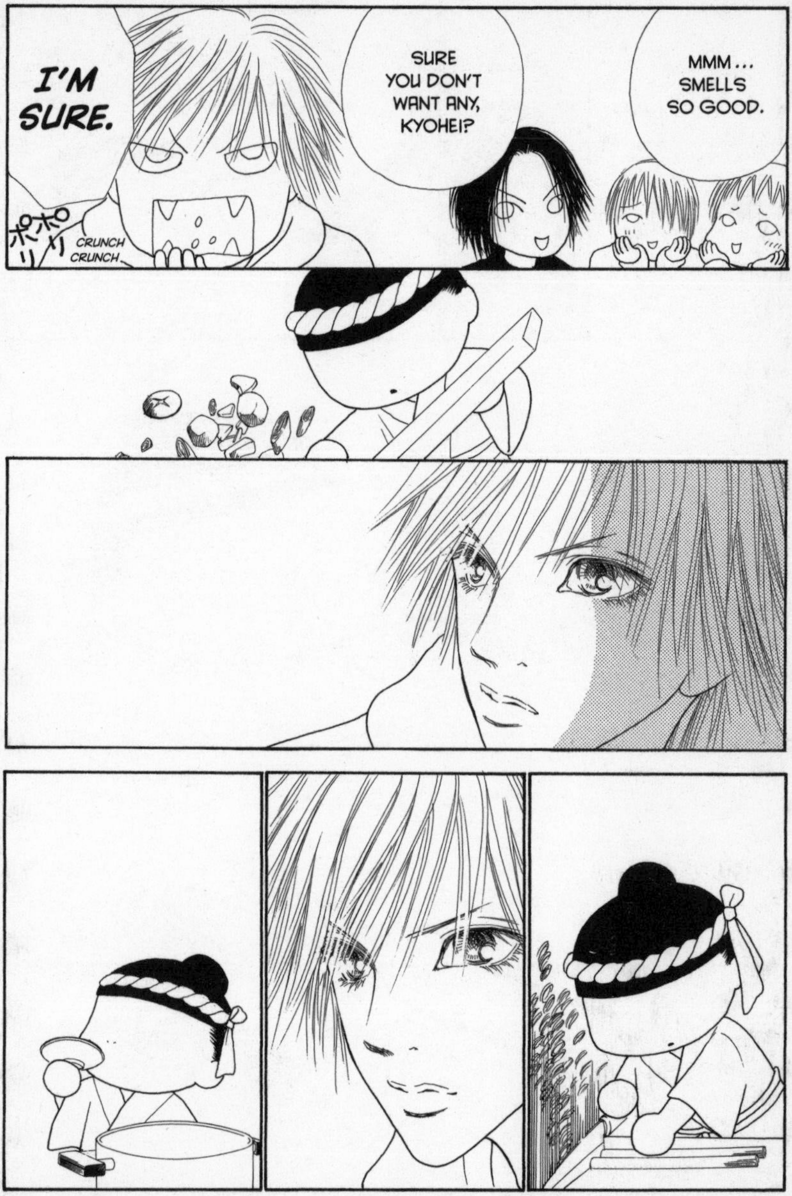
MMM... SMELLS SO GOOD.
SURE YOU DON'T WANT ANY, KYOHEI?
I'M SURE.
ポリポリ
CRUNCH CRUNCH

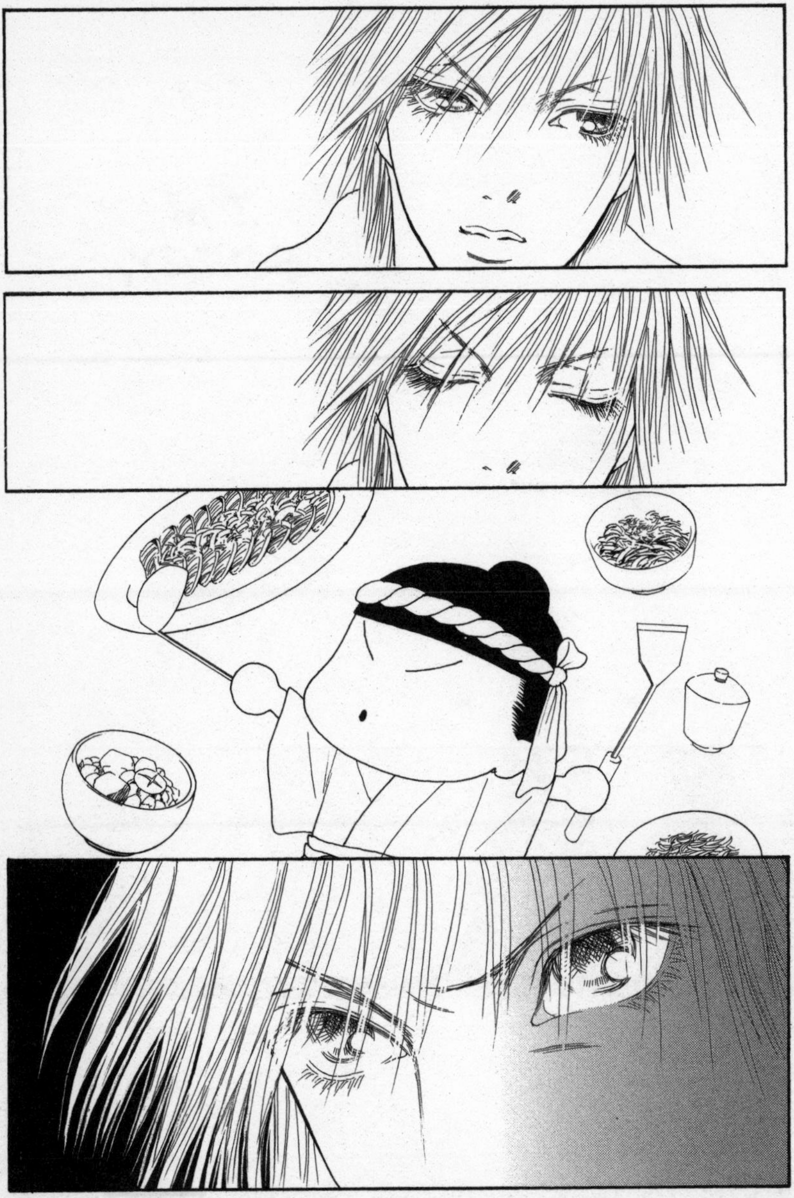

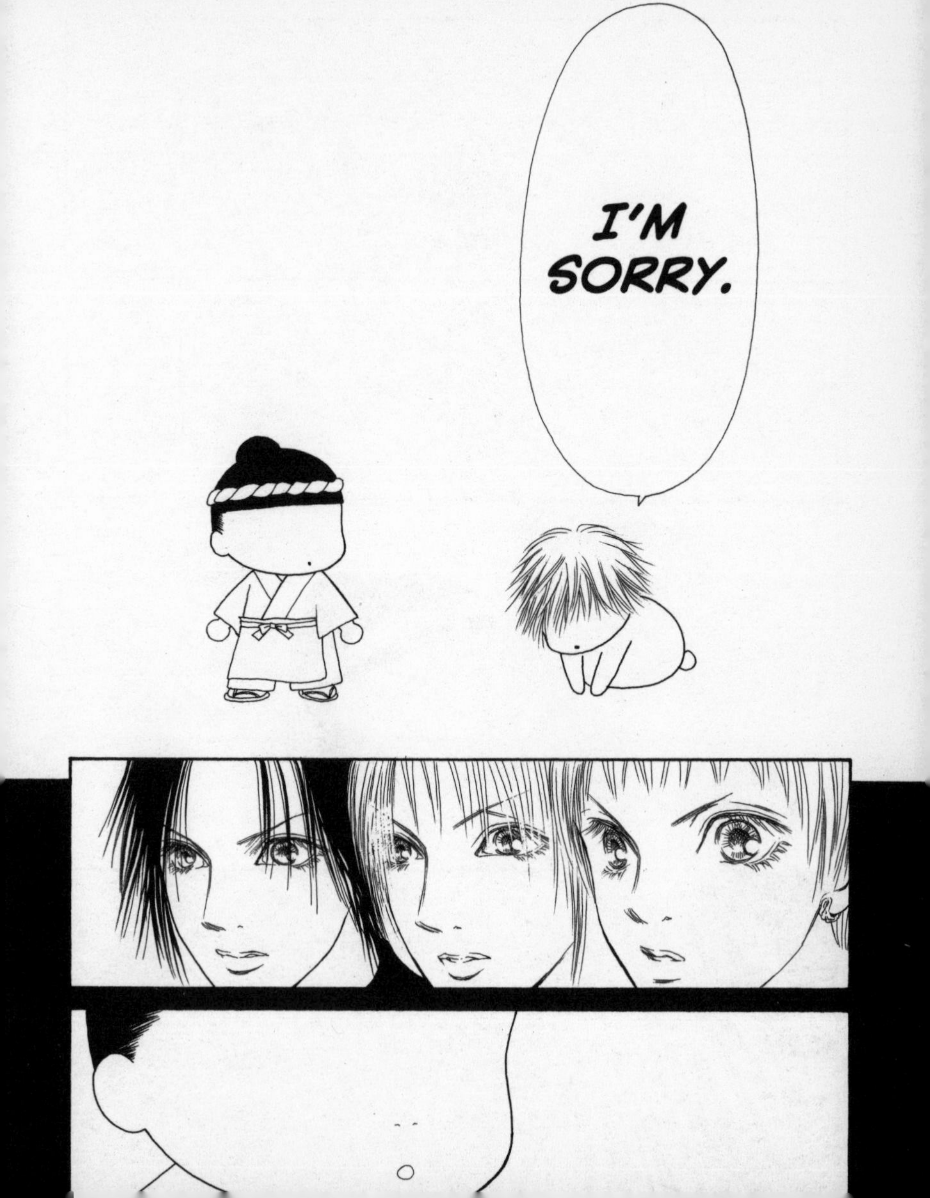
I'M SORRY.

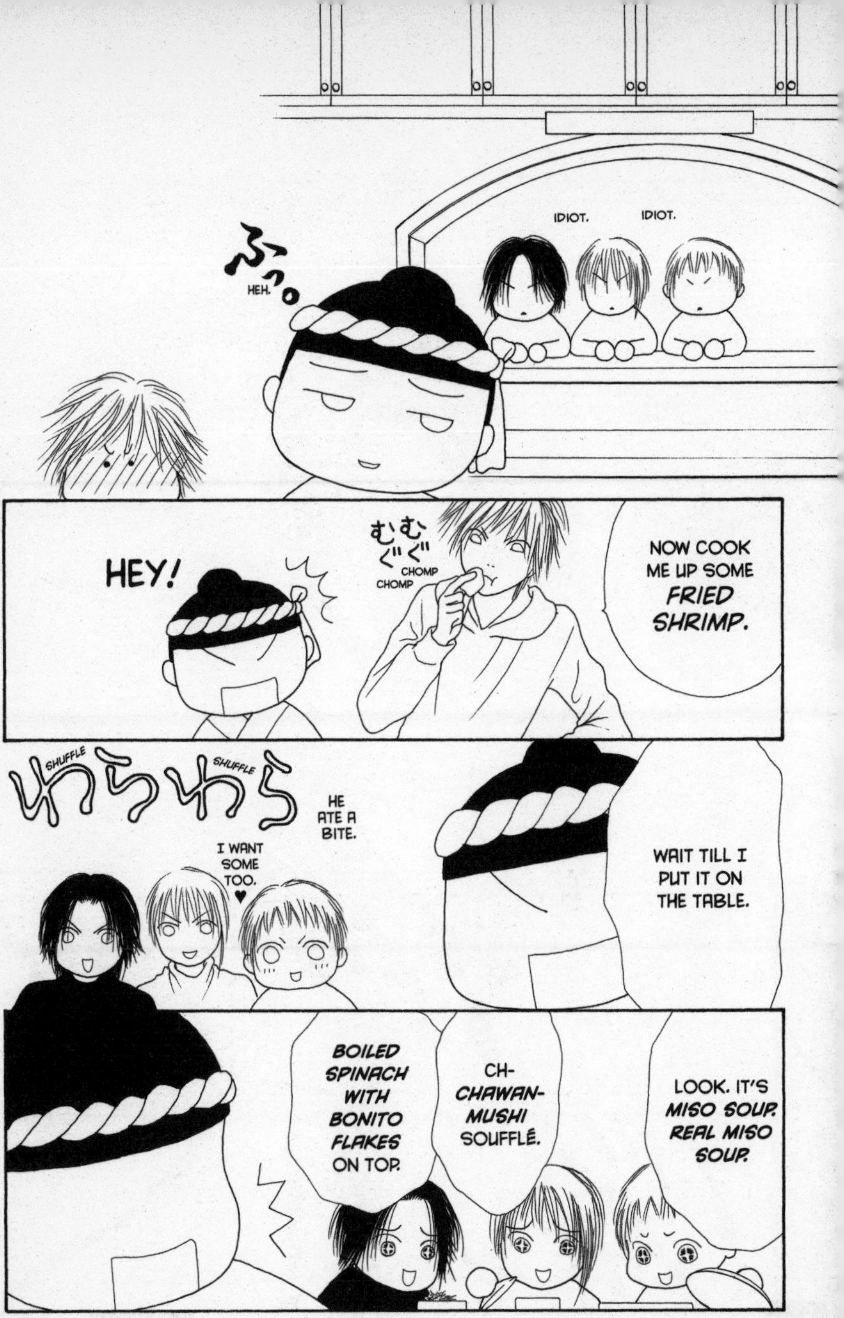
IDIOT.
IDIOT.
ふっ
HEH.
NOW COOK ME UP SOME FRIED SHRIMP.
むむぐぐ
CHOMP CHOMP
HEY!
WAIT TILL I PUT IT ON THE TABLE.
HE ATE A BITE.
I WANT SOME TOO. ♥
わらわら
SHUFFLE SHUFFLE
LOOK. IT'S MISO SOUP. REAL MISO SOUP.
CH-CHAWAN-MUSHI SOUFFLÉ.
BOILED SPINACH WITH BONITO FLAKES ON TOP.

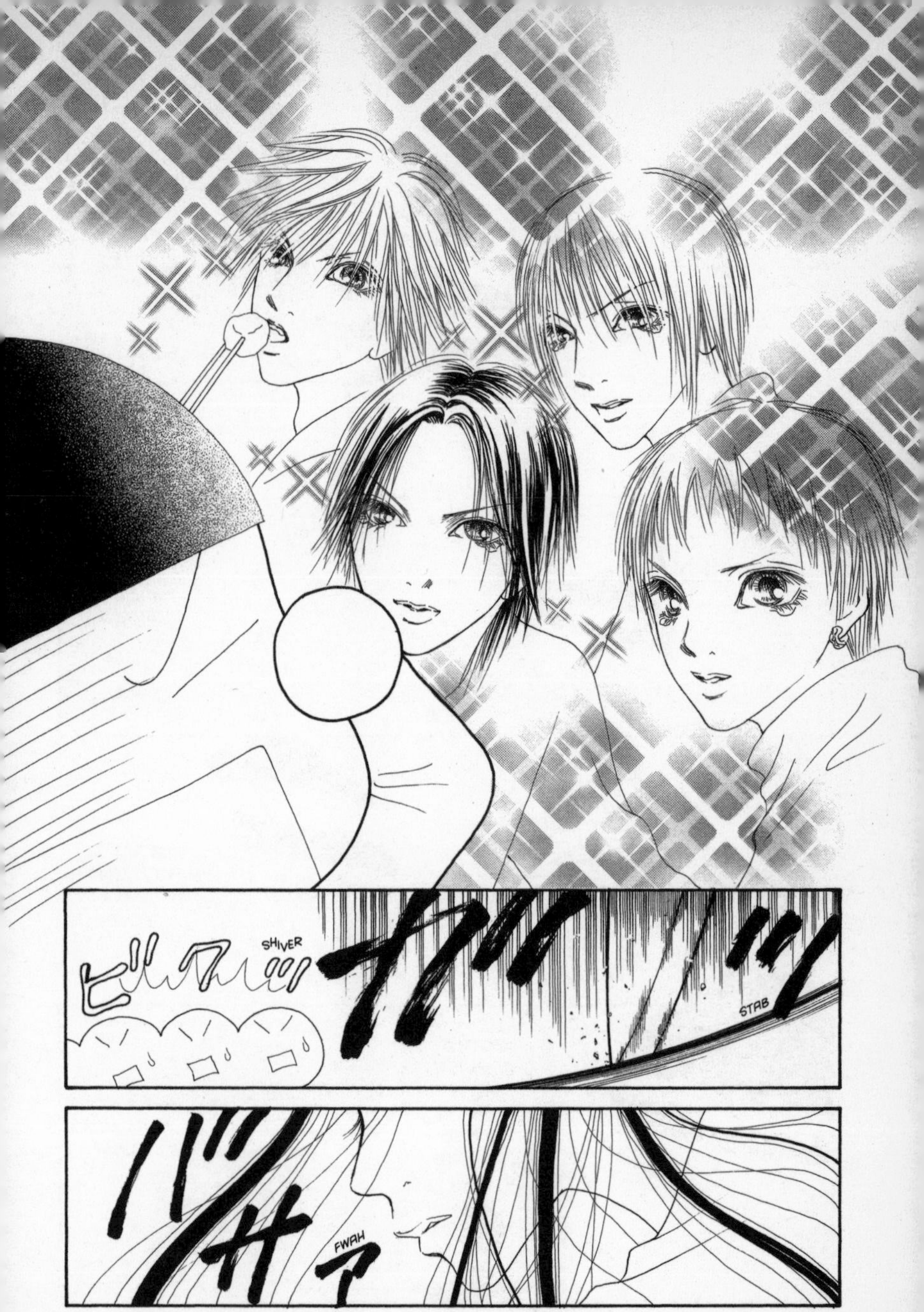
SHIVER
STAB
FWAH

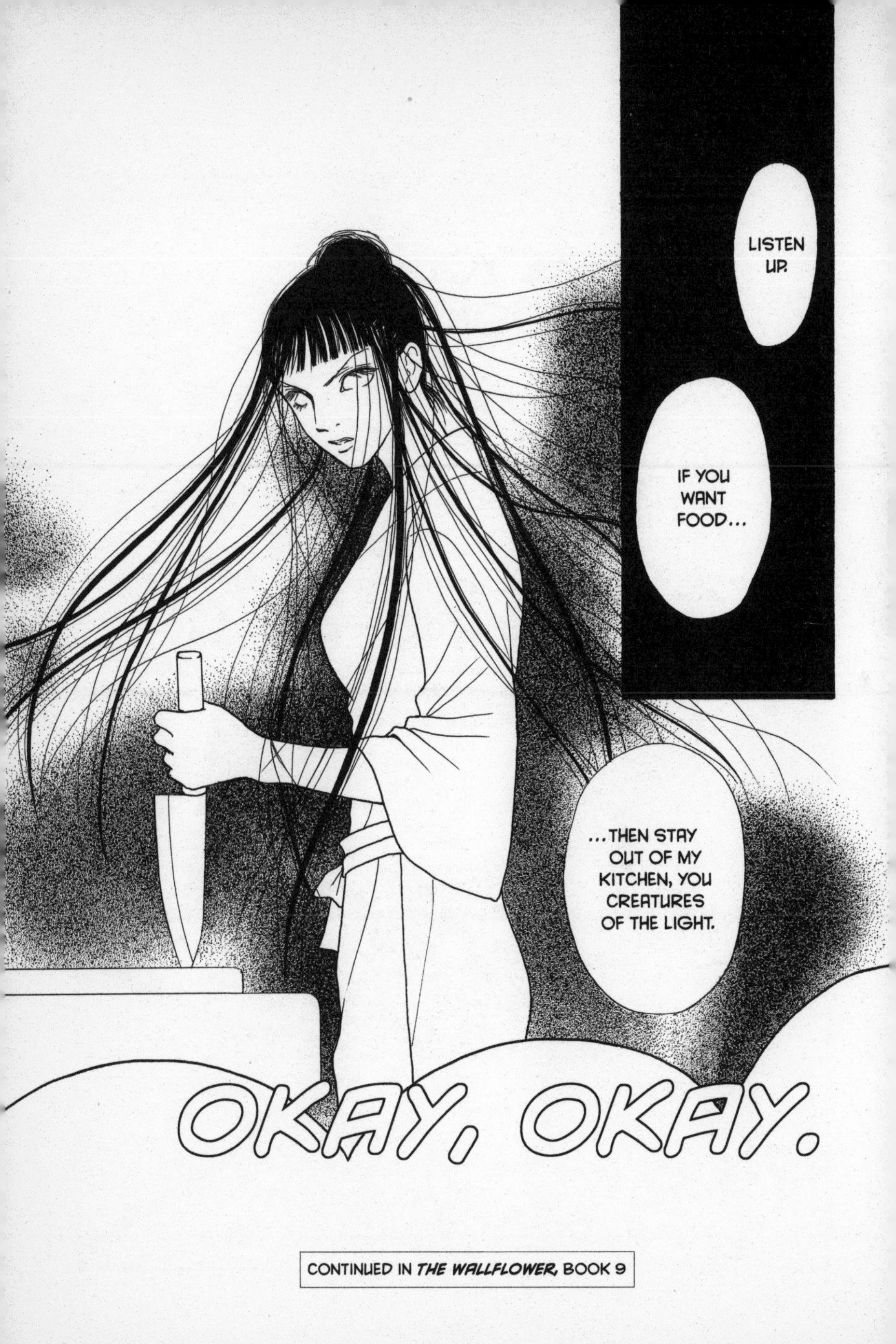
LISTEN UP.
IF YOU WANT FOOD...
...THEN STAY OUT OF MY KITCHEN, YOU CREATURES OF THE LIGHT.
OKAY, OKAY.

CONTINUED IN *THE WALLFLOWER,* BOOK 9

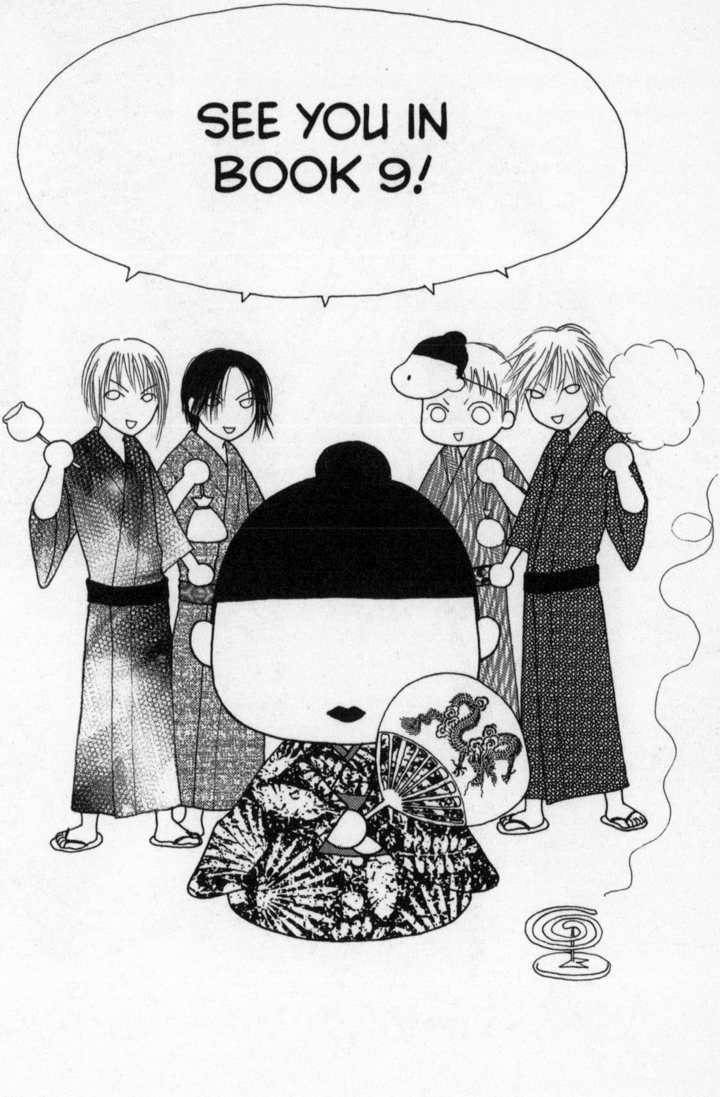
SEE YOU IN BOOK 9!

ALL ABOUT BOOK 7

I DISCOVERED THAT THERE WAS A MISTAKE IN THE FIRST PRINTING.

AND A DRAWING WAS CHANGED WITHOUT MY PERMISSION.

I WAS TOTALLY SHOCKED.

I WAS SO SHOCKED THAT I ALMOST WANTED TO QUIT MANGA FOREVER. YOU MIGHT THINK I'M EXAGGERATING, BUT I'M SERIOUS. I WAS IN TOTAL SHOCK.

I COULDN'T FOCUS ON MY WORK FOR QUITE A WHILE.

FIRST, CHECK OUT PAGE 121. YOU PROBABLY COULDN'T TELL WHY SUNAKO WAS CRYING IN THAT SCENE BECAUSE OF THE MISTAKE. NO WONDER...

IT WAS SUPPOSED TO LOOK LIKE...

拷問部屋……
鉄の処女と鉄の鳥籠だけでもほしかったのに……
はじめて実物見れたのに……
ガチャ
スナコちゃん

...THIS.

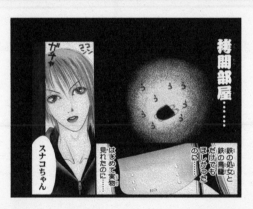

I NEVER IMAGINED THAT ANYBODY WOULD CHANGE MY DRAWING WITHOUT MY PERMISSION, SO I ENDED UP BITCHING ABOUT IT IN MY "BEHIND THE SCENES" PAGE.

I NEVER WANT TO EXPERIENCE ANYTHING LIKE THIS EVER AGAIN. SO THIS IS THE LAST TIME I'LL EVER TALK ABOUT IT.

LOOK AT THE BOOK SIDEWAYS.

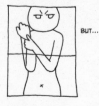

IT WAS SUPPOSED TO LOOK LIKE THIS.

BUT...

I THINK IT CAME OUT LIKE THIS... PROBABLY....

IF YOU GO TO THE NEXT PAGE, YOU'LL FIND THE DRAWING I AM REFERRING TO.

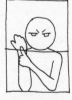

I DON'T HAVE A COPY OF THE FIRST EDITION OF BOOK 7. THAT'S BECAUSE I RIPPED IT INTO PIECES AND THREW IT AWAY.

IT WAS KIND OF SAD TO SEE YUKI'S FACE ON THE COVER GET RIPPED APART.

BUT MORE IMPORTANT...

I REALLY DON'T KNOW WHAT TO SAY TO THE READERS WHO BOUGHT THE FIRST EDITION OF BOOK 7.

I REALLY WISH THE WHOLE THING HAD NEVER HAPPENED. I HAD NO CONTROL OVER IT. I GOT SO UPSET.

THEY DID FIX IT FOR THE SECOND EDITION, BUT IT'S TOO LATE, DAMN IT! I'M SO PISSED OFF.

I WANT TO THANK EVERYBODY WHO BOUGHT THE FIRST EDITION.

I WAS SO UPSET, BUT IT'S NOT LIKE I COULD DO ANYTHING ABOUT IT EITHER...I'M NOT TRYING TO BLAME MY EDITOR OR ANYTHING. REALLY! HONESTLY, I DON'T KNOW WHO I SHOULD BE MAD AT, DAMN IT!

THANKS TO ALL THE LETTERS YOU GUYS SENT IN, I FEEL MUCH BETTER NOW. THANK YOU SO MUCH.

THANKS TO EVERYONE WHO HELPED ME OUT. I REALLY WANT TO SAY THANK YOU TO ALL MY FRIENDS.

SPECIAL THANKS

HANA-CHAN,
YOSHII,
ARAKI-KUN,
SHO HIROSE-SAMA,
AYA WATANABE-SAMA,
ATSUKO NANBA-SAMA,
YUKIO IKEDA-SAMA,
MINE-SAMA,
SHIOZAWA-SAMA,
INO-SAMA,
EVERYBODY IN THE EDITORIAL DEPARTMENT.

EVERYBODY WHO'S READING THIS RIGHT NOW.

THANK YOU SO MUCH.

About the Creator

Tomoko Hayakawa was born on March 4.

Since her debut as a manga creator, Tomoko Hayakawa has worked on many shojo titles with the theme of romantic love—only to realize that she could write about other subjects as well. She decided to pack her newest story with the things she likes most, which led to her current, enormously popular series, *The Wallflower*.

Her favorite things are: Tim Burton's *The Nightmare Before Christmas*, Jean-Paul Gaultier, and samurai dramas on TV. Her hobbies are collecting items with skull designs and watching *bishonen* (beautiful boys). Her dream is to build a mansion like the one that the Addams family lives in. Her favorite pastime is to lie around at home with her cat, Ten (whose full name is Tennosuke).

Her zodiac sign is Pisces, and her blood group is AB.

Translation Notes

Japanese is a tricky language for most Westerners, and translation is often more art than science. For your edification and reading pleasure, here are notes on some of the places where we could have gone in a different direction in our translation of the work, or where a Japanese cultural reference is used.

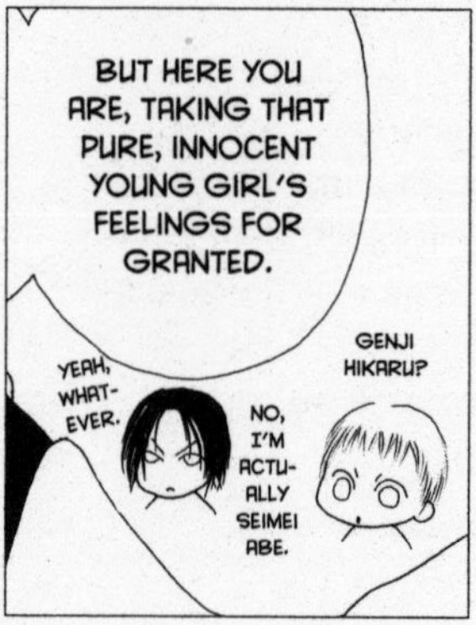
BUT HERE YOU ARE, TAKING THAT PURE, INNOCENT YOUNG GIRL'S FEELINGS FOR GRANTED.
GENJI HIKARU?
NO, I'M ACTU-ALLY SEIMEI ABE.
YEAH, WHAT-EVER.

Hikaru Genji and Abe Seimei (page 18)

Hikaru Genji is the main character in the classical Japanese literary work *The Tale of Genji*. Genji was a real ladies' man, sort of a Japanese version of Don Juan. Abe Seimei is another ancient historical figure. He was said to have been a great astrologer and fortune-teller.

Odaiba (page 20)

Odaiba is a section of Tokyo that's known as a popular date spot.

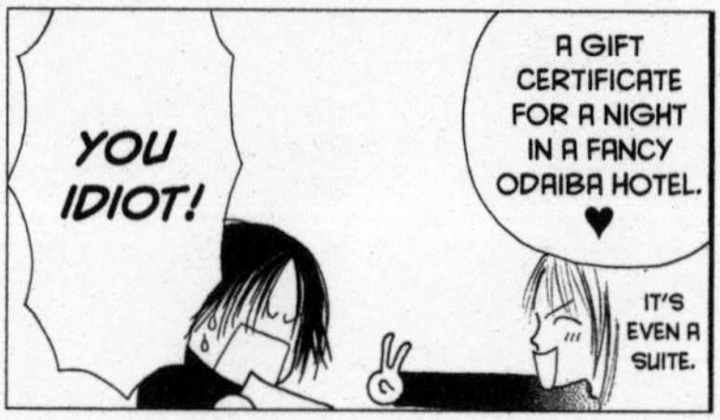
A GIFT CERTIFICATE FOR A NIGHT IN A FANCY ODAIBA HOTEL. ♥
IT'S EVEN A SUITE.
YOU IDIOT!

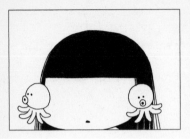

Those octopi (page 46)

The narration next to Sunako is actually making a pun out of the phrase *mimi ni tako*, which literally means "calluses on the ears." However, the word for calluses, *tako*, also means "octopus," hence the octopi clinging to Sunako's ears.

Thumbs up (page 54)

The thumbs-up sign that granny is making means "boyfriend." A pinky finger held up in similar fashion would mean "girlfriend."

HEE HEE
WHICH ONE IS YOUR BOYFRIEND?
NONE OF THEM.

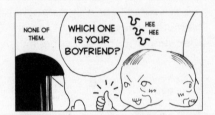

Gou Katou, Takuya Kimura, and Kiyoshi Hikawa (page 63)

Gou Katou is a famous actor. Takuya Kimura, also known as Kimutaku, is an actor and boy-band star. Kiyoshi Hikawa is a young folk musician.

I'D SURE LIKE TO SEE KIYOSHI HIKAWA IN CONCERT.
JUST ONCE I'D LIKE TO MEET TAKUYA KIMURA IN PERSON.
I'VE ALWAYS WANTED GOU KATOU-SAMA'S AUTO-GRAPH.

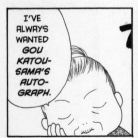

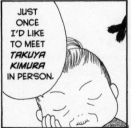

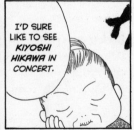

What a catch (page 70)

The coelacanth is an extremely rare fish that is found in tropical waters. The species is said to be around 410 million years old.

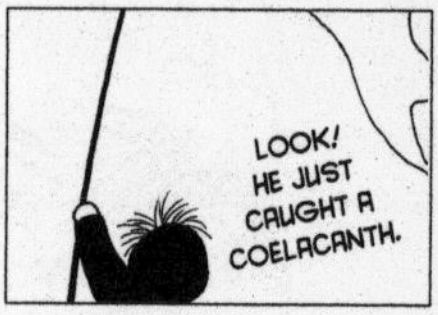
LOOK! HE JUST CAUGHT A COELACANTH.

Armbands (page 83)

These guys are members of a Japanese motorcycle gang. The character on the guy's mask means "bad luck." The characters on his sleeve mean "world domination" and his friend's sleeve says something like "soldier of speed." The joke here is that somehow, at one time or another, Kyohei must've been a gang leader.

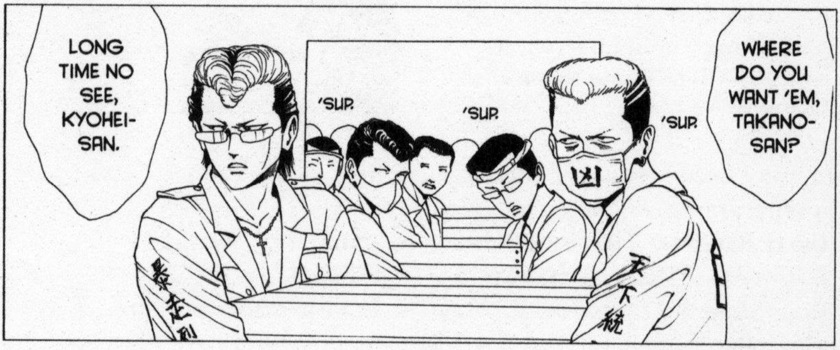
WHERE DO YOU WANT 'EM, TAKANO-SAN?
'SUP.
'SUP.
'SUP.
LONG TIME NO SEE, KYOHEI-SAN.

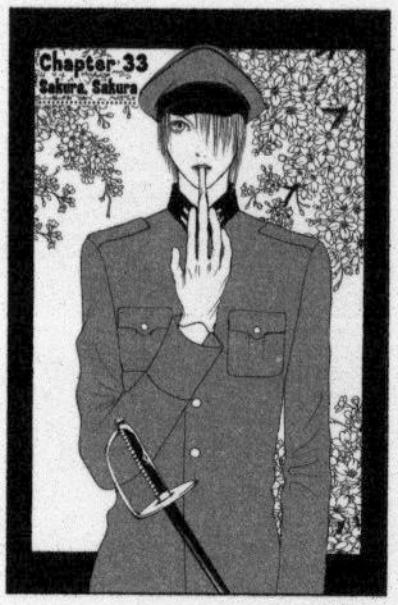
Chapter 33
Sakura, Sakura

Sakura (page 89)

Sakura, Sakura literally means "cherry blossom, cherry blossom." It's the title of a famous traditional folk song.

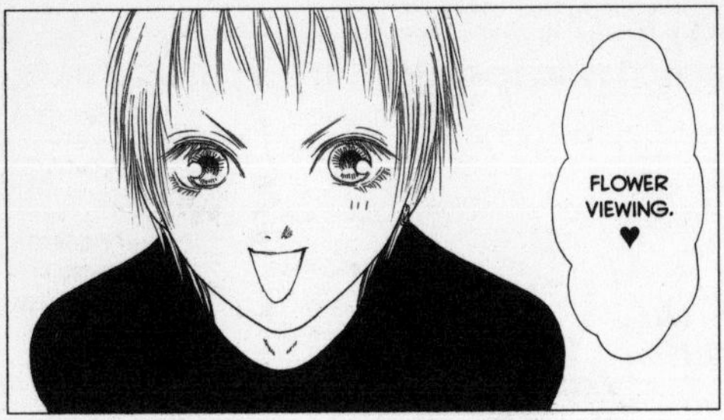
FLOWER VIEWING. ♥

Flower viewing (page 91)

Hanami, or flower viewing, is a popular springtime tradition in Japan. People gather in parks to enjoy the sight of the blooming plum and cherry trees, often while downing large amounts of sake.

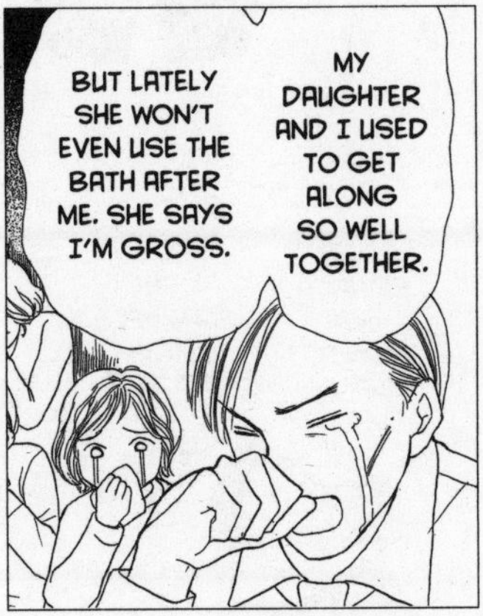
MY DAUGHTER AND I USED TO GET ALONG SO WELL TOGETHER.
BUT LATELY SHE WON'T EVEN USE THE BATH AFTER ME. SHE SAYS I'M GROSS.

Take a bath (page 99)

In Japanese households, the entire family generally uses the same bath water. People wash and shampoo in a separate shower, and then soak in the bath.

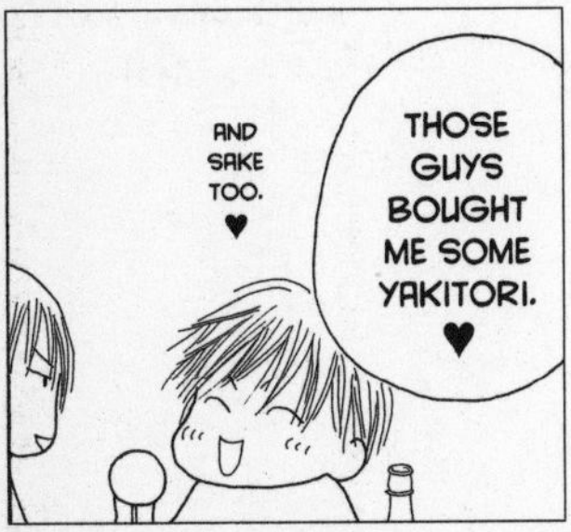
THOSE GUYS BOUGHT ME SOME YAKITORI. ♥
AND SAKE TOO. ♥

Yakitori (page 115)

Yakitori is skewered grilled chicken.

Golden Week (page 132)

Golden Week is a weeklong holiday in early May. It's a popular time for travel in Japan.

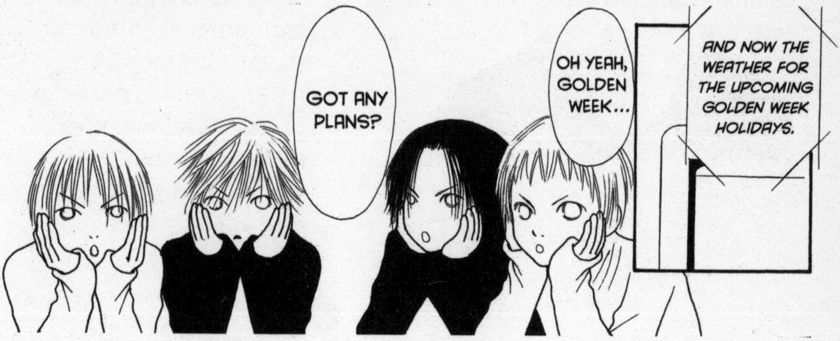
AND NOW THE WEATHER FOR THE UPCOMING GOLDEN WEEK HOLIDAYS.
OH YEAH, GOLDEN WEEK...
GOT ANY PLANS?

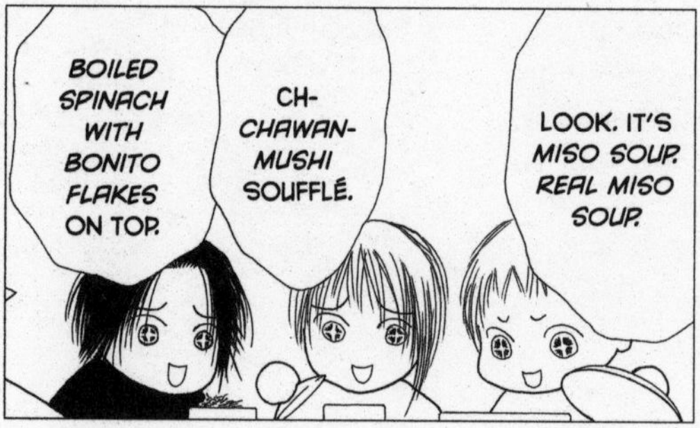
LOOK. IT'S MISO SOUP. REAL MISO SOUP.
CH-CHAWAN-MUSHI SOUFFLÉ.
BOILED SPINACH WITH BONITO FLAKES ON TOP.

Chawanmushi (page 165)

Chawanmushi is a sort of steamed custard filled with seafood or vegetables.

Preview of Volume 9

We're pleased to present you with a preview from Volume 9. This volume will be available in English on September 26, 2006, but for now you'll have to make do with Japanese!

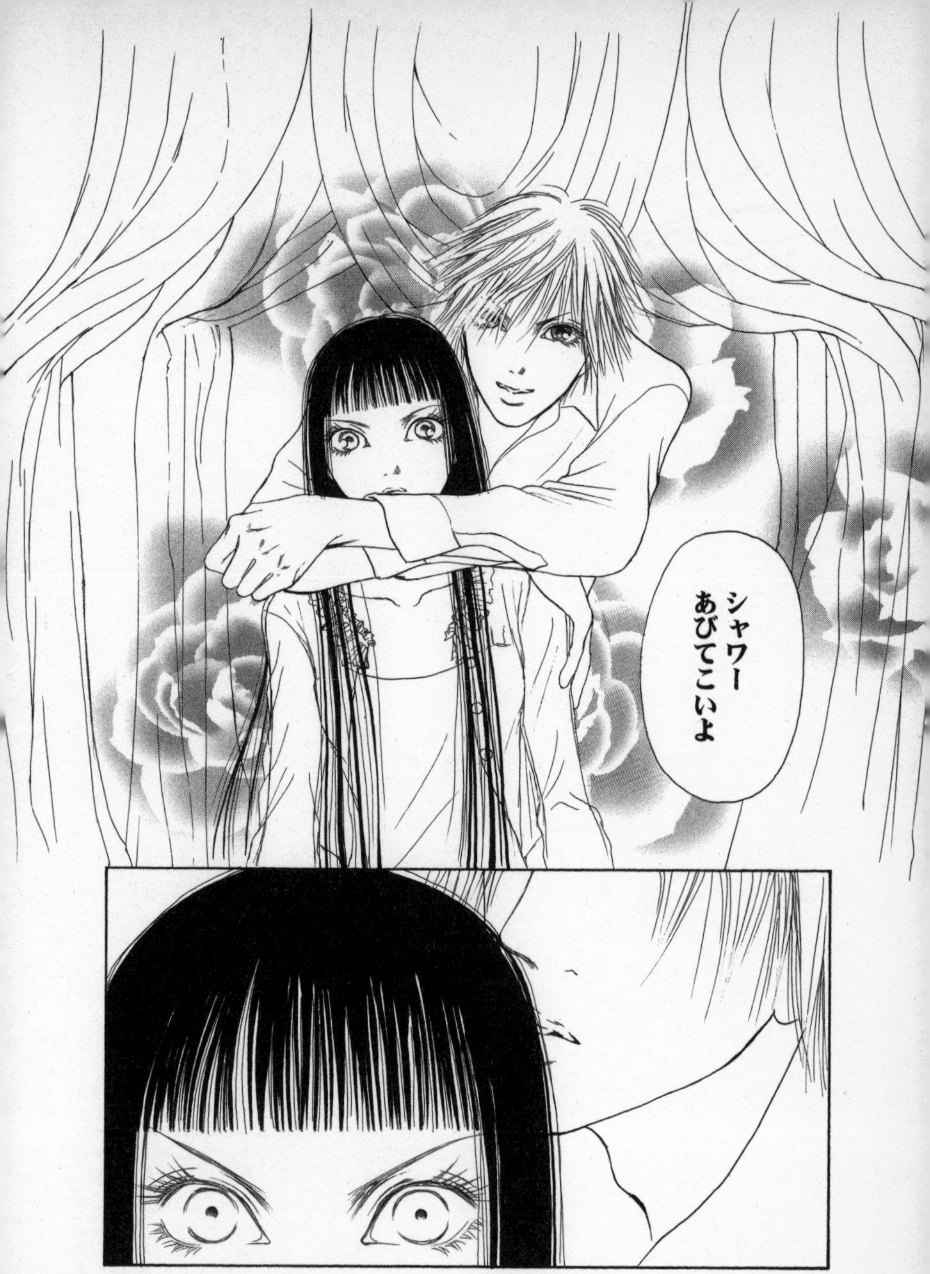
シャワーあびてこいよ

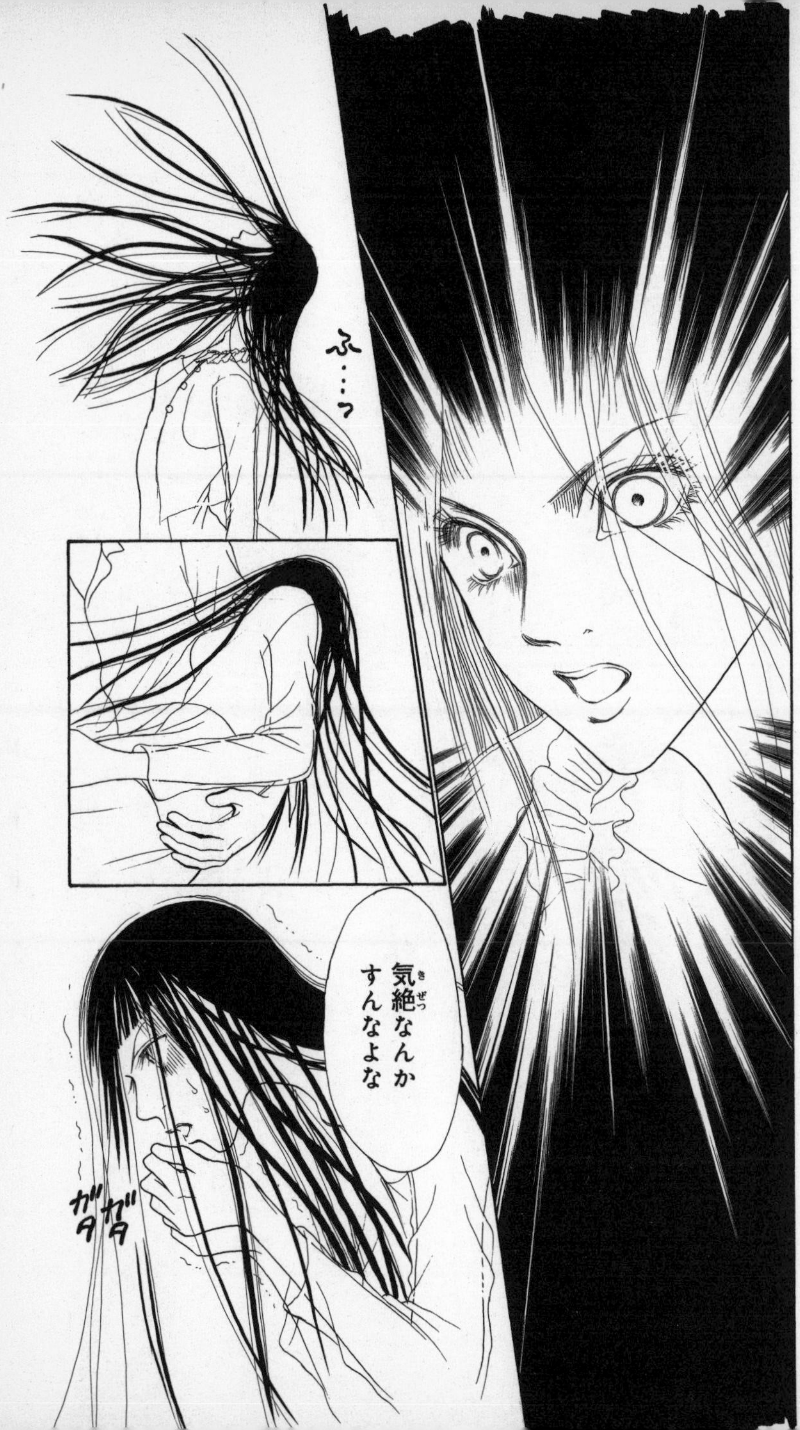
ふ…っ
気絶なんかすんなよな
ガタガタ

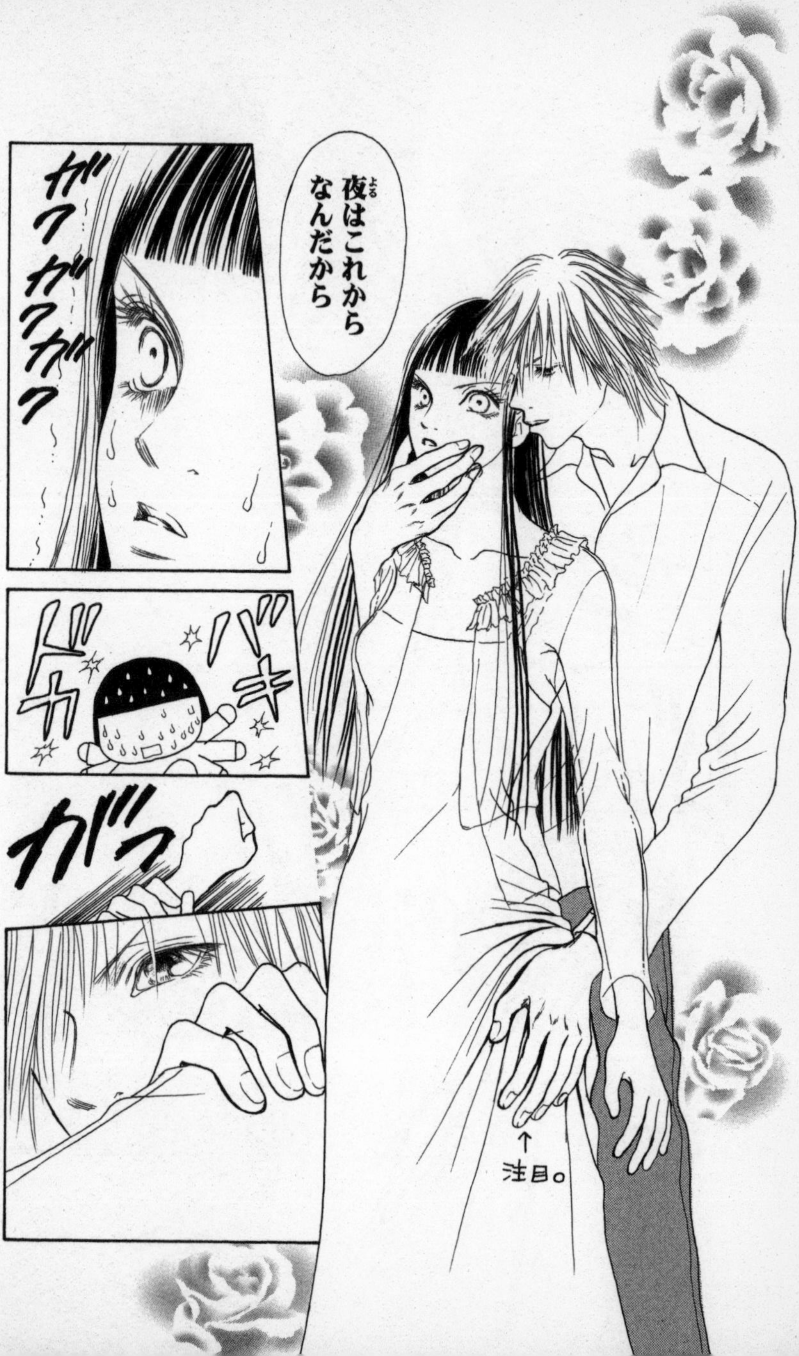
夜はこれからなんだから
↑
注目。
ガクガクガクガク
バキ
ドカ
ガッ

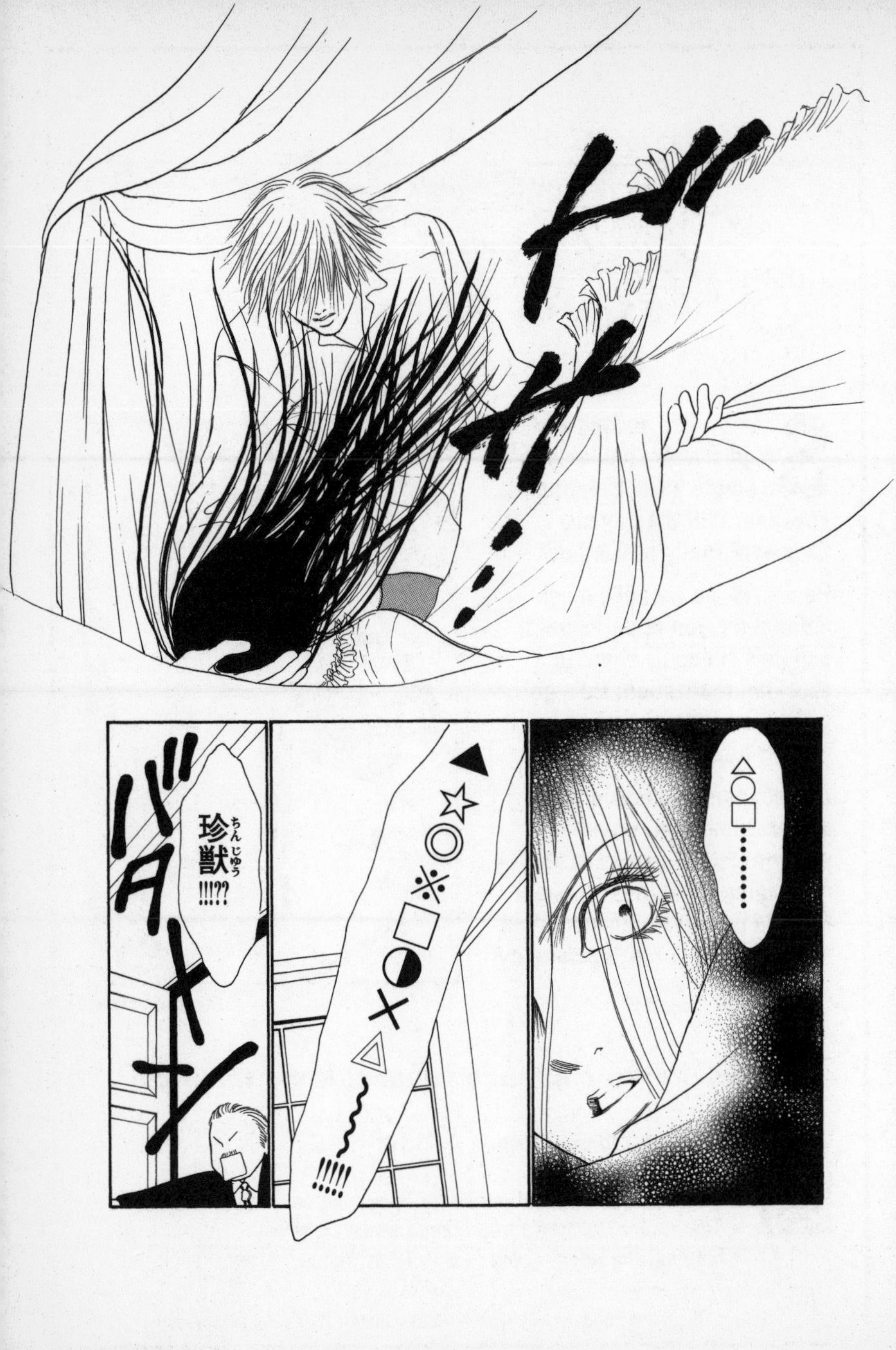
ドサ……
△○□……
▲☆◎※□◐×△〜!!!!!
珍獣!!!??
バタン

School Rumble

BY JIN KOBAYASHI

SUBTLETY IS FOR WIMPS!

She . . . is a second-year high school student with a single all-consuming question: Will the boy she likes ever really notice her?

He . . . is the school's most notorious juvenile delinquent, and he's suddenly come to a shocking realization: He's got a huge crush, and now he must tell her how he feels.

Life-changing obsessions, colossal foul-ups, grand schemes, deep-seated anxieties, and raging hormones—School Rumble portrays high school as it really is: over-the-top comedy!

Ages: 16 +

Special extras in each volume! Read them all!

VISIT WWW.DELREYMANGA.COM TO:
- Read sample pages
- View release date calendars for upcoming volumes
- Sign up for Del Rey's free manga e-newsletter
- Find out the latest about new Del Rey Manga series

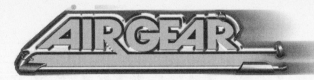

AIR GEAR

BY OH!GREAT

AIR GEAR
1
Oh!great

Itsuki Minami needs no introduction—everybody's heard of the "Babyface" of the Eastside. He's the strongest kid at Higashi Junior High School, easy on the eyes but dangerously tough when he needs to be. Plus, Itsuki lives with the mysterious and sexy Noyamano sisters. Life's never dull, but it becomes downright dangerous when Itsuki leads his school to victory over vindictive Westside punks with gangster connections. Now he stands to lose his school, his friends, and everything he cares about. But in his darkest hour, the Noyamano girls give him an amazing gift, one that just might help him save his school: a pair of Air Trecks. These high-tech skates are more than just supercool. They'll enable Itsuki to execute the wildest, most aggressive moves ever seen—and introduce him to a thrilling and terrifying new world.

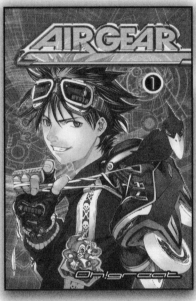

Ages: 16 +

Special extras in each volume! Read them all!

DEL REY

VISIT WWW.DELREYMANGA.COM TO:

- Read sample pages
- View release date calendars for upcoming volumes
- Sign up for Del Rey's free manga e-newsletter
- Find out the latest about new Del Rey Manga series

Eternal Sabbath Vol. 1

BY FUYUMI SORYO

WHO WANTS TO LIVE FOREVER?

Ryousuke Akiba calls himself ES, a code name taken from a mysterious scientific experiment. Ryousuke will live to be at least two centuries old and possesses strange mental powers—he can enter people's minds and learn their darkest secrets; he can rearrange their memories so that complete strangers treat him like family. He doesn't do it out of malice, but for survival. Now he wanders Tokyo for reasons known only to him. No one recognizes him for what he is . . . except Dr. Mine Kujyou, a researcher at Touhou Medical University. Dr. Kujyou lives for her work, but she's about to meet someone who challenges everything she knows about science: ES, possessor of the Eternal Sabbath gene. But is he the only one?

Ages: 16+

Special extras in each volume! Read them all!

VISIT WWW.DELREYMANGA.COM/ES TO:
- Read sample pages
- View release date calendars for upcoming volumes
- Sign up for Del Rey's free manga e-newsletter
- Find out the latest about new Del Rey Manga series

TOMARE!

止まれ

[STOP!]

You're going the wrong way!

Manga is a completely different type of reading experience.

To start at the *beginning*, go to the *end*!

That's right! Authentic manga is read the traditional Japanese way—from right to left. Exactly the *opposite* of how American books are read. It's easy to follow: Just go to the other end of the book, and read each page—and each panel—from right side to left side, starting at the top right. Now you're experiencing manga as it was meant to be!